YOU DO YOU

Edited by Jen Mann

SEVERAL SASSY SCRIBES

Throat Punch Media, LLC

OTHER BOOKS AVAILABLE

People I Want to Punch in the Throat: Competitive Crafters, Drop Off Despots, and Other Suburban Scourges

Spending the Holidays with People I Want to Punch in the Throat: Yuletide Yahoos, Ho-Ho-Humblebraggers, and Other Seasonal Scourges

Working with People I Want to Punch in the Throat: Cantankerous Clients, Micromanaging Minions, and Other Supercilious Scourges

My Lame Life: Queen of the Misfits

OTHER ANTHOLOGIES AVAILABLE

I Just Want to Pee Alone

I STILL Just Want to Pee Alone

I Just Want to Be Alone

I Just Want to Be Perfect

But Did You Die?

OTHER SINGLES AVAILABLE

Just a Few People I Want to Punch in the Throat (Vol. 1)
Just a Few People I Want to Punch in the Throat (Vol. 2)
Just a Few People I Want to Punch in the Throat (Vol. 3)
Just a Few People I Want to Punch in the Throat (Vol. 4)
Just a Few People I Want to Punch in the Throat (Vol. 5)
Just a Few People I Want to Punch in the Throat (Vol. 6)

CONTENTS

Here's to strong women.
May we know them.
May we be them.
May we raise them.

— UNKNOWN

INTRODUCTION

This book came about because a few years ago I was sitting in a parent teacher conference with my daughter's grade school teacher. His report was essentially: she's bright, but she goofs off and doesn't work up to her potential. I nodded automatically, because this was basically the same report I'd heard over the years. All of a sudden I realized he'd said something new. "Excuse me?" I asked.

"I was saying when we have group projects, she can be a bit bossy."

I stopped nodding. "What?"

"She takes over. She tends to order everyone around, rather than letting the group work as a whole, she takes on..."

"A leadership role?" I demanded.

He looked uncomfortable. (As he should.)

My son also takes charge of group projects and never once has a teacher called him bossy or packaged this trait as a negative. I sat there willing myself not to cry. Not because I was sad, but because I was furious. I am mad-crier. And when I mad-cry, men see that as a sign of weakness, when really they should be protecting their man bits with everything they have, because I'm looking for something to hit.

I was so angry that this man was an influential part of my daughter's life. He was going to be her teacher for the next year and he'd already made up his mind that she was bossy, and in his mind, that was a problem. He wasn't going to embrace her quirky nature and encourage her dark sense of humor. He wasn't going to nurture her abilities to be a natural leader, instead he was going tamp them down and remind her that girls are meant to be quiet and docile.

I took a deep breath and calmed my rage-shakes. "She's bossy, because she wants the project to be done the right way," I said. "You said she's bright and she's not working up to her potential and yet, when she tries to work up to her potential—to take charge and make sure a group project is getting done properly—you call her bossy. Got it. I think we're done here." I got up and left before I flipped a table.

Here's the thing, Mr. Teacher, I didn't raise my daughter to be a sheep. I didn't raise her to sit quietly on the sidelines and not advocate for herself. She'll be in middle school in a few years and we both know that middle school chews up little girls and spits them out. I am preparing her for war. I am building her self-confidence every day so that when life chips away at it she has reserves. If the worst thing you can say about her is she's bossy, then I see nothing wrong with her attitude.

You can call her "bossy," or "bitchy," or "shrill," or "opinionated," or whatever insult you want to hurl, but I will teach her that each one of those words aren't insults. They're powerful words when you own them. And she'll own every single one of them. She will also own "girly," and "beautiful," and "delicate," and when she wants to, "quiet." She will be her own person who will be confident in every situation she is thrown into, because she will know deep down in the core of her being who she is. She is all of these things, because she is a fierce and feisty girl who will grow up to be a fierce and feisty woman.

This book is for anyone who needs a little extra armor before a battle.

Jen Mann

TEN SIMPLE RULES FOR GIRLS TO FOLLOW

BY JULIE VICK

Being a girl is easy! You just have to follow a few simple rules:

10. Smiling: Don't smile too much – you'll send the wrong message. But do smile a little – not smiling makes you seem unapproachable and you want to be approached, just not by the wrong kind of people. Make sure your smile is genuine and not fake – somewhere between a creepy clown and a cheerleader.

9. Aggression: Don't be too aggressive – no one likes a pusher and once you start pushing it's probably only a matter of time before you are pushing meth. But stop being such a pushover. Any pushing you do should be moderate – like the amount of pressure you would apply to a vacuum.

8. Kids: Don't have kids, they will ruin your chance at a good career. Of course, if you don't have kids, you will be asked to justify the choice constantly, so it's best to have one kid. Except that one kid will grow up lonely without siblings, so have two; except two will make your life much more difficult and kill your chance at becoming the next Hillary Clinton. The perfect amount of kids is 1.75. Unfortunately, no one has yet figured out how to achieve it.

7. Clothing: Don't dress too revealing – you will invite unwanted attention. But don't be too frumpy – you don't want to avoid *all* attention. Aim for something between sexy and schoolmarm – like an extremely hip librarian.

6. Talking: Don't speak too loudly – you will come off as a bitch. Don't speak too softly – you will come off as too quiet. Speak at exactly 60 decibels so that people can hear you suggest valuable ideas in meetings, but someone can always talk over you.

5. Money: You will probably make less money than most men. But you should try to make more money than some men, just make sure one of them is not your husband.

4. Food: Don't eat too little – you need to get some meat on those bones! Don't eat too much – it's unladylike. Just constantly ask yourself one question: "Are you sure I should be eating that?"

3. Words: Stop adding qualifiers and words like "sorry" to your speech. Speak more like a man who barks orders at people, even if no one really likes being spoken to that way.

2. Brains: It's good to be smart – but not too smart. Only answer about one third of the questions you know correctly.

1. Rules: It's impossible to follow them all. So, it's best to start breaking them now.

JULIE VICK is a writer and mom who lives in Colorado. Her work has appeared in New Yorker Daily Shouts, *Real Simple, Parents,* and *McSweeney's Internet Tendency. You can read more of her work at julievick.com and follow her on Twitter @vickjulie.*

GIRL STUFF

BY ABIGAIL CLARK

Inspired by Eve Ensler's "Embrace Your Inner Girl"

TO BE AN EMOTIONAL CREATURE IS TO FEEL EVERYTHING AS IF FOR the first time. To let it all overwhelm you with enthusiasm, accepting it as you would a gift. Or a handshake. Like looking at the floor of a glass-bottomed boat, seeing everything. Maybe not clearly, but at least seeing it all. You understand a little bit more, the uncertainty in the teenage boy's stance, why that little girl cried so hard when her sister flicked her nose. You sense the things that people rather wouldn't. On the Metro, that uncomfortable woman over there. She would rather not be talking to that man who speaks a lot and doesn't listen. Or the weariness that plagues the other woman's bones, how her colors seemed to fade just a little bit more.

You will be ostracized for caring when no one else does. The world will look at all your feeling and find something weak, worthless. Feminine.

I'm proud to be an emotional creature. I'm moved to tears often— in government class, at a concert, when my mom wakes me up too early. I like it. It's like my superpower, seeming to make everything that much brighter. I like the way the world seems to course through my veins, offer up these little gifts, allow me to feel something so sure that something gets left behind.

People would rather not be that way. Many of my teachers have lectured on the value of restraint, moderation, toning it down. I don't see the point. Why make yourself smaller? Why allow yourself to shrink for the sake of other people's comfort? Why give away your ability to live with unadulterated feeling?

Is there no power in deciding with your heart? Your conscience? Is there no logic in seeing and feeling the situation of another, and taking that into consideration? And isn't intuition knowing, in one way or another?

I don't know. I'm just 16. I think I like being 16. I liked being 13. Fourteen was bearable. Fifteen better. But 16... what an age! There's a kind of roundness to it. Eight times two is 16, eight divided by two is four, four times four is 16. There's a brightness to it, deeming it important in some way.

But 16 also feels like an in-between place. A little bit lonely, a little bit not. Sixteen feels like a precipice over something that could be wonderful.

I wish I had relished being a little girl more. Being 16 is fun; being a little girl more so. You're able to see things that aren't really there – things that make reality a little more fantastic, a little more bewitching. When I was around four, I decided to only wear dresses. I felt beautiful every day. The world belonged to me. It consisted of my mom, my dad, my two brothers, and my best friend that lived next door. It consisted of my dog, still skinny then, the solidness of my grandmother's bones, smelling faintly of detergent and cigarettes. It was the afternoon sun filtering through leaves. Everything feels bigger when you're four. Everything feels more, and there's a little bit of magic in all that feeling.

When does that leave us? When do we decide to give away our intensity? When do we become indifferent?

Maybe when people decide we should. Our capacity for compassion is a muscle we stop working once it becomes hard to do so. When it starts to become inconvenient, as we grow bigger, different values are infused into us: logic, power, strength. Compassion is illogical. Empathy is weakness. Be reasonable. Man up.

One time my mom was worried about one of her students, and wanted to check on her. We drove to their temporary house, and it was apparent that she and her family had been evicted. All I can remember is the sight of her toys lined up by the mailbox as it rained, as if they were waiting. All I could imagine was the little girl who had to leave all of her toys behind. Who cared that she was gone, other than her family and her school teacher?

I've recently read about shootings in the United States. I don't think I cried when I read the names of the people that were killed. I have to wonder, who did? Is there anyone left who hasn't been desensitized? Who thinks about the shootings that don't make news headlines? Who really feels the horror of those deaths, other than the lives they directly affect?

I don't think about it as much as I used to.

I worry about little girls a lot. I worry about how I ended up where I am, about what happened to the little girl I used to be. I never used to temper myself. I felt no shame. Now I worry about my friends. I ask them to text me when they get home, just in case something happens. I teach the younger girls to hold their phone to their ear when they feel unsafe walking alone. My driving education teacher told the girls in our class that if we were ever being followed by a police cruiser, we should call the police, just to make sure it's not someone else entirely, someone who wants to hurt you. You learn to hold your keys between your fingers. You learn to tell yourself that it doesn't really matter; your fear isn't real. It doesn't matter. You're overreacting. Don't trust that feeling. Ignore your intuition. Stop exaggerating. We're girls. It's what we do.

Women have this magic drained out of them through the years. Their compassion, their wonder, their girl stuff becomes a pale, shriveled thing. It slows you down. Why keep it?

But that's the thing. Keeping it locked away is how we got to now. It's how boys are bled of their humanity and girls are punished because of it. It's how we have allowed ourselves to forget the suffering of the world and take it as a given. It's how we justify our failings and blame others.

But imagine with me for a moment. What would happen if we used that magic instead of keeping it hidden? What would happen if we prided ourselves on our ability to empathize, to feel unapologetically? If in doing that, what if we created a culture of empathy that everyone could be part of?

What would happen if our politicians accepted a culture of empathy? Would there still be massacres? Would politics and policy change? Would there still be laws incarcerating groups by the thousands? Would people use GoFundMe.com to pay for their cancer treatment? Would there still be as few women and minorities in government as there are now? Would people be paid a livable wage? Would there still be casual racism and sexism at work? Would people lobby for justice and compassion?

What would happen if *we all* embraced our girl stuff? Would we read the news more? Would it affect us? Would we argue as much as we do? Would we understand each other more? Would we try to change the things we cannot accept?

I like to imagine this world sometimes. I like to picture what would happen if we stopped killing the girl stuff in us: the stuff that still cries at suffering. The stuff that looks at the wonder of the world with wide eyes and an open heart.

When we embrace our girl stuff, we become so much more. We become vibrant, beautiful creatures to behold. We're all so different. We're all intelligent, passionate, soft, strong, hilarious, hardened, bold, independent, young, old, brighter than colors themselves. The world needs us. The world needs that part of us. When we stop being ashamed of it, the girl stuff, that's when things start to happen.

I have a friend who cussed out the boys that said gross things to the girls in gym class. I have a friend who speaks with a soft, lilting tone, like a kind of music, when she talks about her art. I have a friend who wears huge hoop earrings and has a grin in her voice. I have a friend that wants to do good things, and works hard at her abilities to spread goodness. They laugh like girls, guarded yet open, shy yet unflinching, delighting in it all.

I like to think we're all connected by a single thin thread, constantly pulling and releasing pressure. Maybe the whole world is connected by these threads, linking our minds and hearts, but only for moments. Seconds. We forget about the threads, but briefly, we remember. And we're overcome by it all, how clear and complicated it can all be, all the hurt and love there can be. Call it a new String Theory.

ABIGAIL CLARK IS 16 YEARS OLD AND HAS WRITTEN MANY WORDS. At least 12. She aspires to write many more. She hails from northern Virginia, where she likes to dance, especially contemporary and modern. She also plays the string bass (the big, wood one). She's a well-rounded gal. When she's not engaging in these various activities, she exists in a vague state of outrage, as a result of womanhood. This is her first publication.

3

BE YOUR OWN DAMN ROCK

BY JULIA ARNOLD

Despite women all over the media demanding equal rights and equal pay for the last year, it was also a year of women declaring all over social media how grateful they were for the "rock" in their lives. At least it felt that way to me. While on the surface, I suppose, it's a nice compliment: telling someone you are grateful for their support. But scratch—or merely dust—the surface of that statement, and I had to suppress extreme, indulgent eye rolls every time I read it. I was increasingly confused and annoyed every time I read it.

I swear after I read about one woman's beloved rock, I couldn't turn on my phone without another rock being hailed on Facebook or Instagram. In one sitting, I kid you not, I read an adult daughter profusely thanking her father for being her rock, and then I saw another one where a woman declared her husband to be her rock on his birthday. I'm sure there were plenty of other examples across the web that I never even saw. *Why were so many women giving so much credit to so many men?* I was ready to throw up and throw out my computer.

Why did it bother me so much? I asked myself that same question, and it didn't take me long to flesh it out.

I looked over at my own daughter, age five and totally fearless, wearing one of her self-styled outfits where every color in the rainbow and every pattern possible must be visible. She is blissfully unaware of truly difficult struggles; her biggest concerns are usually along the lines of a scratch on her knee, bickering with her big brother, or how mean her mom is for saying it's time to leave the park and head home. She's tough and funny and full of life and, frankly, everything you'd want in a child. I have no fear about the woman she will become and the wonderful things she will accomplish—all on her own.

All these rock statements also made me think about my own life. I realized I've never had anyone I would call my rock – and that's not a sad, selfish, or negative thing. I appreciate anyone who gives me encouragement and support, but I own my hard work and any success I've had. I think that's a good thing, and it's something I want my children to feel as well. I am my own rock, and I want my daughter to be her own damn rock, too.

Part of what especially bugs me when women attribute someone to be their "rock" is that someone is usually male. How can we call ourselves independent, strong women and demand to be treated equally to men, and then in the very same breath, give someone else— a man—the credit for our getting us to, or keeping us in, a good place in our lives? Because that's what it sounds like. It sounds something like: "I've been through a lot in life and couldn't have done it—any of it —without my ROCK." *Is it bugging you yet?*

I don't remember a rock—male or female—surviving the brutal middle or high school years for me, or attending my college classes for me (especially the 8 a.m. Friday ones). I don't remember some personified rock getting my first (or subsequent jobs) for me. I did the interview. I had the experience. There was no one holding my hand in the interviews or drafting my resume a million times. And I sure as hell don't remember any rock carrying my babies for me for over the course of nine months and then enduring having them surgically removed. I'm exhausted just thinking about all of it.

Life is full of challenges, and the old adage is true: what doesn't kill us makes us stronger. Each one of us who gets up every morning and hauls ass is living proof of it. We live by the choices we make and we deserve to own our successes and triumphs.

No one does these tough, challenging things for us, especially some rock we're giving the credit to. Let's take ownership of our struggles and our accomplishments and be proud of them. *That's* what I want my daughter to be spouting off online if social media is still such a constant in 10 years (and I pray it isn't). I never want to hear her say "Thank you for being my rock" unless she's thanking herself.

The good news is that I think I might be on the right track. A few months ago, my five-year-old daughter was shooting rubber bands with a young boy on the floor of a waiting room while my son was in a piano lesson. I warned my spunky little girl not to let a rubber band fly into her new friend's face. The boy's father immediately stepped in and said, "Oh don't worry, he's tough. He's a boy." My daughter stopped what she was doing, furrowed her brow and thought deeply. I opened my mouth to stick up for her and girls everywhere. But before the words came out, my kid looked up at the man and clearly and confidently explained the facts: "I can be tough, too, you know." I closed my mouth and smiled, feeling beyond proud. I was not her rock. She was her own rock.

At the end of the day, I feel at my core that we should be able to make it through the hard times ourselves. We don't need someone to do it for us. Yes, we all need steady support and a nice, hard hug now and then, but we can be our own rocks. Our daughters are listening to us *all the time*. Let's let them hear how their mothers stand on their own remarkable feet.

JULIA ARNOLD IS A WRITER LIVING IN MINNESOTA WITH HER husband, two children, and rapidly growing collection of animals. She writes about parenting, equestrian pursuits, animal welfare, and more. Her work has appeared in publications such as Horse Illustrated, Young Rider, Dressage Today, The Morgan Horse, Mother.ly, *and* Mamalode. *She blogs with humor and honesty at FranticMama.com. Her author site is JuliaStarrArnold.com. Julia has loved writing for as long as she can remember and thinks it is entirely possible she was born with a pencil in her hand.*

4

VOICE

BY MADDIE BELDEN

I may not be strong
I may not be tall
And I may not be loud
But I have an opinion
And I have a right
A right to be heard
A right to stand for myself
So we all must stand for ourselves
If we hope to make a difference
In this world of darkness
We can be the light
Because our differences
Give us a voice
A voice that is our own
A voice that shines a light
A light in the darkness
And sometimes we just need the light
To guide us on our way

MADDIE BELDEN is a middle schooler with a love of books, mismatched socks, and her crazy cocker spaniel, Macy. She has written many poems and short stories, but this is her first published piece. When she isn't reading or writing, she can be found sewing, daydreaming at her desk, or plotting to take over the world.

❧ 5 ❧

UNAPOLOGETICALLY ME

BY SHYA GIBBONS

I have spent the past 30 years of my life apologizing. I apologized profusely for things I didn't even have to apologize for. I was not the child who rebelled and had to constantly see the principal or be put in time out; I was the opposite. I didn't even toe the line. I set up camp far past the line on the safe side, which led me to become overly polite and apologize profusely for everything. Every single thing. I apologized when I did nothing wrong. I apologized for being my strange, quirky self. I spent so long apologizing and thinking I was to blame for everything that at some point along the years I forgot I was my own person with my own feelings. I was not responsible for every other soul on this earth.

Let me back up some. Way back to kindergarten which seems like yesterday, but it was really 25 years ago. Our teacher gave us a simple writing prompt: A horse escapes into the woods, what happens next? The other children said that the farmer went looking for the horse. Some said the horse made its way back to the farm on its own eventually. Not me. No, I wrote that the woods were actually magical and once the horse broke free it turned into what it had always felt like it was destined to be – a unicorn. As soon as it escaped its pen, the horse, now turned unicorn, was free to be the magical, amazing beast it was always meant to be. My teacher told my mother I was adamant the scenario could happen. This story has always been one of my mother's favorite stories to tell people when I talk about how much writing means to me.

Alas, my brush with pushing authority by arguing about turning horses into unicorns started and ended with that assignment. From then on, I was the odd girl who kept to herself, which I was and totally own up to. I marched to the beat to my own drum. I desperately wanted to find my way into a clique; I spent countless hours crying because I could never quite find my group of kindred spirits. I wasn't pretty enough to be popular, I wasn't athletic enough to participate in sports. I was the girl who doodled the name of my crush all over my books. I was the girl who had so many pictures of her favorite celebrity taped up in her locker that it was essentially a shrine. I wrote during free periods at school, went home to complete my homework, and spend the rest of the time writing.

While computers and televisions weren't common for teenagers that age to have in their room (yikes, I am old!) my parents trusted me enough to have both, as long as my grades didn't suffer. I'm eternally grateful they did because I lived and breathed through Word documents. As the weird girl I definitely caught some heat at school for it and on days where it overwhelmed me and consumed my every thought, I would simply leave this world and write a new one.

It was through writing that I made a stunning surprise: I had the ability to become my own heroine.

I became the lead of any story that I wanted or needed at that time. If I needed something serious, I would write a serious book. If I needed emotional support, I would write a story where a man professed his love over and over again. I went from feeling like a puppet with everyone pulling the strings to the master. The page was the one place I let myself be truly myself.

If I wasn't writing then I was daydreaming. I always wanted to have a career where I made a difference in people's lives. There is the saying that you can't save everyone, but I didn't care. I was going to try my hardest to help every person I could. And I like to think I did to the best of my ability.

I helped people through abusive relationships, problems in college, problems at work. I loved it. It became emotionally draining eventually, but I knew by depleting the levels in my tank I was replenishing someone else's. People came and went in my life, usually after I was used as their emotional dumpster and they moved on. Where it would make other people angry, I didn't care. My thought was God gave me the chance to change someone's life for a moment and that's all I saw it as. I was happy to be given opportunities to see a side of people not many were privileged enough to have seen. I loved seeing them move past their hurdles and continue on to flourish. But eventually a car running on fumes quits; it gives its absolute best until it physically can't any more. My fumes ran out recently, which led me to realize a lot of things about myself, both good and bad.

Having had bouts and depression and anxiety off and on from a young age I was guilty of sometimes shutting myself off from friends. I would go radio silence and throw myself into writing. The same escape as always, the same soothing and safe place I have had for decades.

My 11-year-old niece has recently started writing and I keep encouraging her and offering ideas for her to expand upon. I remind her she is amazing and has endless potential with her future. I tell her about things that happened to me at school and how I used writing as an outlet. I told her that if she keeps searching she can find something that makes her heart soar the way mine does with writing, even if her heart is stuck at the bottom of a canyon. She is our future and I keep encouraging her with whatever project she is working on, whether it is writing or designing clothes.

While I have other negative things that I realized about myself lately, I forced myself into a very difficult challenge: find good in yourself. I'm a firm believer that people are intrinsically good and I give people the benefit of the doubt more often than I should. The only person I never afforded that same luxury to was myself. No one could be harder on me or knock me down lower than I did. I have been mentally beating myself up for as long as I can remember. Nothing was ever good enough in my eyes and I always told myself that.

It's hard to break that habit. A habit of 20-some years of overly harsh, critical thinking is hard to stop. It was amusing in a sardonic way that the girl who could find good in everyone else couldn't find any redeemable attributes in herself. I'm still struggling with it, to be honest.

Not too long ago I realized that I apologize for everything, including things I do that are harmless and are simply part of who I am. I would apologize for being emotional and crying when I was happy, or cry when I was sad. I cry constantly. I'm an empath and I'm done apologizing for crying when I'm overwhelmed with emotion. Some people pride themselves on the fact that they can't remember the last time they cried, and while I think that's fine, I know that will never be who I am. It finally sunk in when I was shopping at a big-name store. I had my cart tucked against the shelves, out of the way while I looked at a selection of toys. A woman comes down the aisle and slams into my cart, which there was no need for because I had made sure when I positioned my cart that it wouldn't clog up the aisles for other shoppers. I instantly felt horrible and started to apologize. She ignored me and continued on her way without a single word spoken back to me. My first thought was: How rude the woman was for not extending any words back like, "These things happen" or "No big deal." My second thought was: Wait a minute. She hit me. She didn't say "excuse me" to indicate she needed to pass on the slim chance I was blocking her path. Nothing. What exactly had I been profusely apologizing for? Getting hit? Being ignored as I tried to exchange pleasantries? I had not one, single reason for why I felt that situation deemed an apology from me.

I realized that I apologized about a lot, but more than anything I apologized for who I was. When someone points out that I have a fictional character on the screen of my phone I say, "I know. It's weird. I'm sorry." When my OCD is really bad and someone sees me washing my hands three times in a row I repeat the same as above: "I know. It's weird. I'm sorry."

No.

Nope.

Not anymore. I am done apologizing about everything. I do not need to defend my quirks to anyone. They are what makes me me, after all. It has been a long journey to finally reach this peak where I don't care what others think about me or the things they deem "weird" or "odd." Every person has one thing they do that others would find strange and I think it's time to stop judging people for their choices. Unlocking my phone and seeing that character makes me happy, and I will never again apologize for something that makes me smile when the world is full of frowns.

My best advice to every person, no matter the age, is: You do you. You do what makes you happy. Do what soothes your soul (within reason, of course!). Don't worry about what others might say or think. Worry about yourself and your own happiness. Keep a fire burning inside of you for something whether it is writing, knitting, chopping wood, or playing video games. Every person needs one thing that makes them come alive, and I know that I am incredibly lucky to have figured out at a young age that that thing for me is writing.

Go show the world who you are—the REAL you. Don't put limitations on yourself for fear of being ridiculed or judged. Chances are if people make fun of you for something that makes you happy, they probably aren't the kind of people you want to be friends with anyway. From here on out I plan to be unapologetically me. I hope you find the power inside yourself to be the same way. It is quite freeing.

SHYA GIBBONS IS THE FOUNDER OF THE FACEBOOK COMMUNITY Vintage Dreams With A Modern Twist and a contributor to I Just Want To Be Perfect. *Her work has appeared on* Sammiches & Psych Meds *and* McSweeney's. *She is happily married to an incredible man who doubles as her best friend. They have a five-year-old boy who lights up their life. Check out her work on Facebook and tell her "Hi" when you stop by, she loves meeting new people.*

❧ 6 ❧

WISHES FOR A TWEEN GIRL

BY GALIT BREEN

My girls' birthdays are only four days (and two years) apart. For the past few years, we've celebrated on or around their March birth dates. But this year, our family traded in our usual one-weekend-after-another separate celebrations for a last-day-of-school, hot summer night, everyone-piled-into-the-yard-and-by-the-fire-pit-and-into-our-basement kind of celebration. And it was glorious.

I watched and listened to and heard an absolute gaggle of girls—some of whom I've known since their chubby fingers wrapped around thick crayons as they learned to write their names and thank-you notes and stories, tongues sticking through pursed lips, brows furrowed, smile and eyes lit at success. And others I'm just getting to know, learning what that laugh or this look means. And in that watching and listening and hearing, I was overwhelmed. With their noise and their movement and their talking, yes. But also by their goodness.

And if it wouldn't have been a horrid interruption of their night, here's what I would've said to them by the light of the fire or the stars or the movie.

To the ones with the loudest laugh, the first joke, the cleverest of responses—keep using your voice and your humor. A laugh that can be picked out in a crowd is a gift.

To the athletes, the enviable ball spikers and the perfect hand-spring executors and the swift runners, keep at it. Strength comes in many forms, and this is one of them. Own it.

To the joiners, you're absolutely right—why *not* you? Confidence makes the world go 'round, and you've got it. Hold on tight. It belongs to you.

To the storytellers, keep talking and telling and weaving. It's your story, so tell it. You're the only one who can.

To the quiet ones in the back, I see you. You are understated, and you are important. These things can, and do, go hand in hand.

To the whip-smart ones with all of the answers, you keep flexing those muscles. A smart woman can make the world go round.

To the caretakers, you have it just right. We are meant to take care of each other.

To the ones with the dirty feet and the abandoned shoes, who needs shoes anyway? Don't be afraid to get dirty, to be you, to get the most out of every moment. It's true what your mom and I say – it does all go by so fast. Grasp the moment, the dandelion, the grass, and skip the shoes.

To the leaders, the ones who ran the show and organized the games and kept everyone moving along: That's called leadership, and it's a coveted skill. Anyone who calls it anything different (and negative) is wrong.

To the ones who led by example, followed the unwritten rules, made sure that everyone got their fair share, this, too, is leadership. It's quiet, but powerful and just as coveted.

In so much of life, women demand *different* and *change* of ourselves and of each other. *Not enoughs* and *shoulds* and *shouldn'ts* slip between our lips all too easily and quickly. *Not pretty enough, not smart enough, not popular enough. Too pretty, too smart, too popular.*

But what I learned from watching a group of just-out-of-school tweens on a hot summer night is that right here and right now, they have the exact right idea. So the thread in my wishes for tween girls—

the understated ones and the caretakers and the athletes and the joke-sters—is this:

Trust yourselves and your instincts and your goodness.

Allow input from the world to do nothing but build on what is already pretty amazing – you.

And see how each of your shines doesn't dim the others.

My wish for you is to keep being exactly who you are.

GALIT BREEN IS THE BESTSELLING AUTHOR OF KINDNESS WINS, A guide to teaching your child to be kind online; the TEDx Talk, "Raising a Digital Kid Without Having Been One;" and the Facebook group The Savvy Parents Club. Her writing has been featured on The Huffington Post, The Washington Post, Buzzfeed, TIME, *and more. She lives in Minnesota with her husband, three children, and ridiculously spoiled mini goldendoodle. Find her at TheseLittleWaves.net.*

JUST CALL HER MADAME

BY MAI WEN

"Life's not fair."

This was what I was told. No, I wasn't whining about my friend's newer and bigger house, or the neighbor's brand new car. I was asking why there was only a mother-son dodgeball tournament at my nine-year-old daughter's school, and none for girls. There was a father-daughter dance, was the first counter. But my daughter went to that the year before and found it "so soooo *boring,* Mom. I want to play dodgeball. Why can't I?"

They question hung on me like a wet towel. I felt ashamed that I hadn't really questioned the sexism of these Parent Teacher Organization (PTO) sponsored events before she pointed it out. I knew that it was sexist, but it was an accepted form of sexism that I didn't always bother to see. But once she put the question on me, I couldn't shake it off. I'm a feminist, after all – a strong female who has survived a lot and fought for what I wanted out of life. Growing up with a Chinese, strongly patriarchal family I remember early on resenting the suggestion that in any way I was inferior to boys. When I'd go out to help carry in the groceries and my aunts would chide me, telling me it was men's work, I'd double my load. It's a stubbornness that is only triggered in me when I'm told what I can't do, and in many ways, it has served me well. Perhaps it was the hypocrisy of my family's patriarchal beliefs that gave me the courage to fight against it. They told me that men were the heads of the household, and yet it was my mother and aunts who worked as computer programmers and supported their families. My mother was a single mom, my aunt was as well briefly before she remarried, and my other aunt took care of my uncle and grandma. They showed me a very different version of women than what they told me. As with most children, I believed what I saw more than what I was told.

And so, I was triggered. That *can't* word ringing in my ears and firming my resolve. I turned my daughter's question "Why can't I?" into what I thought was an innocent email to the PTO president.

Years before, our family had moved to Franklin, Tennessee, from Raleigh, North Carolina. Although both are considered the South, Research Triangle Park and the multiple colleges in Raleigh made it a hub for transplants and diversity. Moving to Franklin, I was worried about the lack of diversity, but immediately found the people the friendliest I'd ever met. My hopes rose and then promptly fell when my daughter started kindergarten. The first offense: after school club forms came home. My daughter, ever the creative mind and active hands, loved Legos. I found the Lego club listed and directly under the title were the horrifying words: *boys only*. Something like bile rose in my throat, but it was far worse than bile. It was a mixture of shock, disbelief, and absolute terror. Being raised in liberal Minnesota, this sort of thing never happened growing up. Boys were required to take Home Economics just as girls were required to take shop class. The fear of raising my children in this culture sent me reeling and I fought the people-pleaser inside of me and emailed the organizers, politely asking why the Lego club was "boys only." The response was even worse than I expected: The sons of the moms who volunteered to run the club wanted the club to be boys only, so to please their sons, the moms requested to exclude girls.

Insert open-mouthed emoji here.

Not only are they excluding girls at a school PTO-sponsored activity, but they are also teaching boys as young as five that their every whim will be honored, even if it excludes a whole group of people.

Needless to say, my mama-bear claws came out and I may have thrown an analogy at the PTO saying that since I'm Asian, would it be okay if I started an after school club and only allowed Asians to be a part of it? I never received a response to my last email, but they never had "boys only" or "girls only" clubs again. Mommy win even if the PTO hated me.

Fast forward to the dodgeball email. I received a couple of truncated and unsatisfactory responses telling me they'd discuss it and then suggesting that my daughter join a dodgeball after school club. The PTO President even advertised that there were no gender limitations on the clubs, obviously unaware that it was thanks to me. My daughter couldn't do the club because of other obligations, I told her, and asked her to keep me informed on their discussions.

Meanwhile, my daughter, tall and lanky like her father – dark, silky hair always pulled back in a low ponytail, came home from school every day and asked me if I'd heard about dodgeball yet. After a week of no updates, mama-bear claws started to itch at my fingertips again. I acquiesced and emailed. I listed all the people being excluded from the event the way it currently was set up: mothers without sons, sons without mothers, same-sex couples will either have no moms to go, or will have to pick which mom, and, of course, girls. I suggested some possible solutions. Could we have two different nights of dodgeball and scrap the kind of creepy father-daughter dance? Could we say parent-child dodgeball tournament? I even offered to be in charge of planning it next year. I thought it was a pretty convincing email.

Boom.

I got no response. I started to get frustrated. Finally, I hear from a friend that my email has been sent up to the principal to send to legal and is now an officially documented complaint. And the whole PTO board hates me. Again.

I don't like being hated. It causes my anxiety to go through the roof. I wish I didn't care, but I do. But even more, I don't like my daughter being told at the age of nine that you can't do something purely because you're a girl.

This is where I'm told to tell my daughter life's not fair. Twice by two different people.

The first was my friend who is on the PTO board and who told me about the ruckus my email caused. She told me that her daughter would rather play dodgeball than go to the father-daughter dance as well, but that she just told her daughter "life's not fair."

Next, the PTO President called me. She's a very sweet person and we talked out how everything went down. I didn't mean for things to get all "legal" and she admitted she should have just called me to talk things out with me from the beginning rather than putting me off. It was a good conversation until she told me about how her two boys always want the same video games that their friends have and she tells them, "life's not fair." She compared my daughter not getting to do an activity because she's a girl to her sons not getting spoiled by getting whatever video game they want. And what is my friend's message to her daughter? That "life's not fair" because girls don't get to do all the things boys can, and instead of fighting and pushing against it you just need to shut up and accept it?

Everything in me reels against these messages. I refuse to teach my daughter to shut up and accept sexism, even if that means I must be hated. It's a small price to pay to empower my daughter. My daughter who can run and play sports with the boys and then the next day play animals with the girls; who doesn't feel the need to play to any gender stereotype and instead rests in her own unique spot in the middle. My daughter who loves Harry Potter and Star Wars. Once while playing a game of Family Feud and the question was, "What should grooms be taught to say to their future wives?" instead of the popular responses of "You're right" and "Yes," she wrote down "Madame." When we were confused by this answer, she affected a haughty butler face and stiffly waved her hand in front of her and said in a very British accent, "*Ma-dom.*" Apparently that's how my daughter expects to be addressed by her future spouse if she so chooses to get married.

I can't change the whole world and there are some like-minded friends who live in Franklin who talk about moving away because they can't stand the conservative, old-fashioned views here. But I actually love Franklin. I love the small-town feel and the friendly people (even if we vastly differ in life views). I love all the kid-friendly activities and weather. And what happens if I do move my family away to someplace more liberal? What opportunities would I have to teach my daughter to fight against sexism and other bigotry? What positive changes can I make in communities that already adhere to my beliefs? Here, as frustrating, difficult and sometimes horrifying it is, I can make a difference. I can teach my children that just because something is a certain way, it doesn't mean it's right. And better yet, that *they* can do something to affect change.

So call her Madame. Let her play dodgeball. Let her build Legos. Many argue that no one is stopping her. She can, and does, do these things at home. But it's the message that could stop her if we let it. The message that while you can do these things in the privacy of your home, there's no place for girls doing these things in the world.

And as we all know, kids learn more by what we do than what we say.

MAI WEN IS A FORMER SOCIAL WORKER AND CURRENT CHAUFFEUR TO three lovely children. She is also an aspiring novelist with two completed young adult science fiction manuscripts and working on an adult fantasy. Her novels contain strong social, women's and mental health issues but with a dose of time travel or magic (pick your poison, she's got both). If interested in learning more about her work you can find her on social media at @maiwenwriter.

LOOKING FOR LAUGHS IN ALL THE WRONG PLACES

BY SHERRY STANFA-STANLEY

Slumped over a table in the basement of St. Patrick's of Heatherdowns Grade School, I grew bored with yet another evening of my Brownie troop's lame crafts.

As our leader demonstrated how to make tacky holiday wreaths—by tying colored tissue paper around wire clothes hangers bent into circles—I nudged the second-grade girls on either side of me.

"Who would hang that on their door? It looks like something that belongs wrapped around a toilet seat," I faux-whispered, "where everyone can crap on it."

My Brownie buddies roared.

Spurred on by their laughter, I managed to spout out another joke. And then another. By the end of the evening, potty humor proved to be a far bigger hit than lavatory decorations among the age seven crowd.

I leaned back and glanced around the table. I knew right then that, for me, making people laugh was far more rewarding than any condoned activity. I grinned in self-satisfaction.

By the fifth grade, I had already acquired the reputation of class clown. It also was right about this time that the head leader of my Scout troop, who *oddly* did not appreciate my humor, decided I was an unwelcome distraction. Not only did I not fly up to Cadets, I was booted from the troop.

Regardless, I could get used to entertaining an audience, even if I was looking for laughs in all the wrong places.

I continued to entertain my classmates in other unsanctioned and irreverent ways, like initiating games of truth or dare during our Catholic grade school masses and later using the Resusci Annie dummy as a dance partner—rather than an intended CPR tool—during high school health class.

Along the way, I also found another, more authority-acceptable venue for my humor. I began honing my writing skills.

I wrote poetry and short stories, specializing even then in humor and satire. On one of my sixth-grade papers, my teacher wrote, "If you don't do something with all of your talent, I'm going to come back and haunt you some day." (Side note: She didn't need to haunt me. We have become Facebook friends, and I acknowledged her early encouragement in my first book.)

Being named editor of my high school newspaper cemented the idea of a writing career. But what proved just as rewarding that same year was having my senior class vote me as "Best Sense of Humor." That accolade—sadly—didn't win me a single college scholarship, yet it did reaffirm that I was funny.

Sure, I could make people laugh. I had that going for me. But what I didn't gain until much, *much* later was the ability to laugh at myself.

A few years after my Brownies experience, I sat cross-legged on that same basement floor with my seventh-grade class, watching a holiday school program. Whether it was due to something I ate for lunch, or else just ill-fated timing, my gastric system chose that moment to make its distressed voice heard.

It's often difficult within a crowd to pinpoint the culprit of even the *loudest* intestinal explosion. I can only assume my mortified expression gave me away. When my "friends" seated closest to me promptly figured it out, they showed me no mercy. They elbowed me and simultaneously shouted, "Sherry!" This was followed by multiple animated exclamations of how gross and disgusting I was.

Everyone in the room, including the popular blond-haired boy I was secretly crushing on, turned and laughed at me. I did not laugh. In fact, if it hadn't required scrambling over a hundred classmates, I would have crawled right into a corner and died.

It wasn't until I tossed in bed that night, still horrified by my public farting fiasco, that I realized I should have reacted that afternoon by making a joke. It was a missed opportunity to salvage my self-esteem and win over the crowd with humor, instead of feeling defeated by the all-too-common awfulness of adolescent embarrassment.

But self-deprecating humor is lost on the average 12-year-old. In truth, most of us *never* really learn to laugh at ourselves.

I continued, as all of us do, to humiliate myself on countless occasions through adolescence and adulthood.

While rappelling down a cliff during a high school trip, I discovered the safety harness had somehow become entangled in my shirt. My shirt was already hiked above my belly button.

I contemplated this lose-lose situation: I could attempt to unhook the harness and crash to my death, or I could continue descending and allow the cable and my shirt to keep rolling up toward my shoulders. I finally choose the latter, providing the group below with an unplanned peep show. Not only was I mortified, but the crowd appeared less than impressed with what they viewed.

I avoided eye contact, during the remainder of the trip, with everyone.

Years later, as a young adult, I worked up the courage to try out for a community play. I hoped the entertainer within me might lead to a powerful stage presence. But when the director unexpectedly asked me to sing and dance, my mouth dropped—along with all my self-confidence. I'd never even sung in a school choir, and my old friend Resusci Annie was probably a better dancer than I was.

I had no other option, other than refusing and running from the room, which didn't seem likely to save my pride either. So, I bellowed a Christmas carol and danced—or rather *tripped*—across the stage. Looking out, I observed the director and her colleague nudge each other and grin. It was my first—and my very last—audition.

And, I experienced perhaps the most mortifying moment of all as a presumably grown-up and established business professional. While intending to email a few friends, I inadvertently sent an off-color joke to my company's *entire board of trustees.*

As I realized my mistake, I stared at my computer screen, paralyzed. And then my head dropped. "Good Lord," I prayed, with my hands covering my bowed head, "please let them all have good humor."

Although some mortification hits harder than others, none of us is immune to just-kill-me moments. We all make mistakes and endure personal mishaps. We all find ourselves cringing and cowering in embarrassing situations. We all prove to be—and far too often while in *public*—imperfect.

Yet it's how we react to our displays of humiliating inadequacies or blunders that makes the difference.

A few years ago, I concluded I was tired of living with a suffocating sense of self-consciousness and fear of judgment. I'd grown tired of desperately trying to live my life in the safe zone.

So, I embarked on a year of weekly experiences that each fell far outside my comfort zone. While I hoped these 52 ventures might enlighten me in some way, I knew they also would test me, frighten me, and humiliate me. Holy Hell! What was I thinking?

I went through with them anyway.

I performed in public as a mime, even though my own lack of fondness for mimes was mirrored that day by many passersby. If mimes weren't sworn to silence, I would have screamed "Wait, come back!" to all those who rolled their eyes and scurried away.

I bared it all at a nude beach, with my (clothed) 75-year-old mother in tow. Even *she* refused to sit near me. "I saw you naked as a baby, and I don't really care to anymore," she told me. I finally "ripped off the Band-Aid," and closed my eyes to pretend—like a two year old—that if I couldn't see anyone, then no one could see me. As I heard a helicopter flying overhead, I prayed no one was taking aerial photographs.

I auditioned for *Survivor*, went on a raid with a SWAT team and vice squad, and crashed both a wedding and a fraternity party. I endured fearful, awkward, and embarrassing moments in nearly all of my fifty-two ventures.

As I shared these escapades—and heard from readers living vicariously yet far more safely through them—I learned most of us have very *narrow* comfort zones. Those comfort zones get even tighter as we grow older.

This is especially true for women: since we've been taught from a very young age to not take risks. This includes avoiding situations that not only could physically harm us but that also might frighten or embarrass us. I mean, why would we do anything that might prove awkward or humiliating—which might lead to people laughing at us —*on purpose?*

Yet each time I survived another new and sometimes excruciating experience, I felt less nervous and more self-assured. Because going outside our safety zone ultimately *empowers* us. We learn how to live with humility. We gain confidence. And, even if we seem to fail at some attempt, we succeed just by putting ourselves out there.

At some point, we may even discover the most rewarding experiences in life are those we've been sidestepping all along.

By taking on this "unbucket list," I changed my life. I learned a great deal about the world around me and about myself. Above all, I *finally* learned to laugh at myself.

I discovered that finding humor in difficult situations is perhaps the *best* reaction of all.

I seldom worry anymore about facing new challenges or potentially embarrassing circumstances. Few experiences turn out as we expect anyway. So, why spend our time or energy worrying? You experience a huge rush of freedom the first time you let something roll off your shoulders.

If an experience does happen to go *way* downhill—let's say, if you manage to destroy the lobby of a Segway rental shop during your inaugural ride? Or, if you find yourself unable to face your perfectionist salon technician during your first Brazilian wax? The ability to laugh at yourself in the *worst* imaginable of predicaments manages to help ease the pain—or at least the emotional sting.

My year of crazy new experiences proved to be fear-fueled, fun, and unbelievably self-satisfying. And it didn't result in just 52 weeks of crazy challenges. It changed me—and my life—forever.

I still find great joy in making others laugh. It's forever rewarding to discover people laughing *with* me.

Yet the new me now faces awkward situations with far less concern about how others will react to my success or my failure. Damn if I won't find a way to laugh at the outcome, even if people are actually laughing *at* me. And *that* happens pretty frequently.

By exposing ourselves to uncomfortable situations, we grow a bit stronger and more confident. We find a way to laugh at nearly anything —even if we happen to be the butt of the joke.

If I could travel back in time to that junior high program in my school basement, I'd probably still feel mortified as I tooted louder than the brass section in an orchestra.

But this time, I'd laugh, stand up in the middle of the heckling crowd, and shout, "Thank you! Thank you very much! I'm still mastering the trumpet. But give me a drumroll, and I'll toot even louder!"

Yes, learning to laugh at yourself is one helluva survival tactic.

If you gain the self-assurance to laugh at yourself, you may discover that the crowd will laugh along with you.

Life is funny that way.

SHERRY STANFA-STANLEY IS AN AWARD-WINNING WRITER, humorist, and squeamish adventurer. Her memoir, Finding My Badass Self: A Year of Truths and Dares, *chronicles her insane and enlightening year of misadventures. Sherry's work appears in* The Rumpus, Healthy Aging, First for Women, *and* The Huffington Post, *and in the anthologies* Fifty Shades of Funny *and* Laugh Out Loud. *An empty-nester, she now indulges a menagerie of badly behaved pets.*

RISE UP

BY KATELYN SULLIVAN

Rise up
When you're living on your knees you
Rise up
Tell your brother that he's gotta
Rise up
Tell your sister that she's gotta
Rise up

— HAMILTON

HAMILTON HAS ALWAYS BEEN A STEADY BEAT IN THE BACKGROUND OF my life. I can rap along with Angelica and Hamilton, beatbox and sing with Eliza, and have learned a bit of French from Lafayette. Lin-Manuel Miranda has recreated Alexander Hamilton's life to a backdrop of pop music. Most people listen to *Hamilton* because it's catchy and entertaining, but the meanings behind the words can really teach people amazing life lessons.

In *My Shot,* Alexander tells of how he's dreamed of America, and his ambitions about the new country. Later, his newfound friend John Laurens raps about how, no matter what happens, you have to fight back, rise up, and get back in the game with even more insistence. People all around me my entire life have been telling me the same life lesson. No matter what happens, fight back. Stand up for yourself, and stand up for your peers.

My sisters and mother have been telling me the same thing. I've gone to a D.C. Women's March, and been educated about the importance of equality, equal pay, ending stereotyping, and treating others the same as you want to be treated. Growing up in a wonderful family, I've almost never felt unsafe, insecure, or distressed. And I wish I could make it so everyone felt the same way as I do. Although, at a time, I did understand what some people go through —bullying.

I'm female, unusually tall, and white, with chestnut hair I wear loose around my neck. A braided hair tie is almost always around my right wrist, and dusty blue glasses are pushed up against the bridge of my nose, hiding aqua eyes and long lashes. Nearly 13, but I always look older, shoulders slightly slumped so I look an inch shorter—not that it makes any difference to my towering figure.

When I first transferred to my current school in third grade, I was elated. Both my sisters had gone to this school, and met all their best friends there. I was familiar with the teachers, and I knew the layout of the school better than my old one. I didn't realize that sometimes it isn't all fun and games.

When I first met him, I immediately noticed he was sporty and popular. First impressions aren't always the end product though. He was intimidated by me, most likely because I was at least a head taller than him. Being a third-grader, feelings were hurt easily. He'd just have to glare over his shoulder, make a snarky comment to one of my friends, or not talk to someone for a day, and *WHAM*—half the class was in tears.

I'd come home everyday, eyes livid with the pain of his new, sharp insults. I'd ignore my family's worried glances and go up to my room, burying myself in a book until bedtime. One day, when my mother came in to drop off my instrument, the bully had delivered an especially rude insult. All I'd tried to do was explain that I used to own a snake while he and his friends were talking about reptiles.

"Aaron! Aaron!" I'd excitedly burst in. "You used to have a snake? Me too! Her name was Nagini, after Voldemort's in Harry Potter, and—"

"You're just as much a snake as the one you used to own!" He'd hissed with the likeness of a serpent, then lifting his chin in the air and whirling back around.

I've always prided myself on being able to handle tough situations, but this was a bit too much for nine-year-old me to handle. I burst into tears. And to make it worse, I cried in front of my mother and my entire class. I was rushed to the counselor's office for an entire hour.

It continued on like this for a year, until, thank goodness, fourth grade arrived. This boy wasn't put into my class, which lifted a weight off my shoulders. That lasted for about five minutes. His tormenting was the worst that year. At any given time he'd find me and my friends and verbally attack us.

But that wasn't even the worst part—sometimes Aaron would be nice, and would talk to me like we were old pals. He'd play with my friends at recess, sit with us at lunch. It would be a peaceful, blissful few days for the entire class when he was kind. But once Monday came back around, he was back to his old insults.

The next year—fifth grade—was also different, though. I had the best teacher anyone could ask for, and she didn't tolerate this bully's nonsense. The teacher encouraged my friends and I stand up for ourselves, and by the end of the year the bully had moved to a different school district. Sort of surprisingly, the bully did start being a bit kinder to everyone just before he left.

I haven't really experienced intense bullying, just a somewhat childish type. Aaron never physically hurt me, or threatened me, he just made my life miserable every chance he got for almost three years. Bullying is still bullying, no matter who does it, how old you are, and where it happens. I'll never forget this boy. If I saw him in public, I'd just ignore him and move on with my day. But I will never, *ever* forget that if I hadn't risen up, I might still be unhappy and under his reign.

I've moved past the bully and his antics, and forward into the wonderful new life I lead. I continue to enjoy listening to *Hamilton*, and following more of Lin-Manuel's amazing advice, rapped through the Founding Fathers. I write, read, and draw, with only normal worries on my mind—homework, tests, and sports—instead of the old worries of what would come with tomorrow.

ALOHA! I'M KATELYN SULLIVAN, AND I WROTE THIS PIECE WHEN I was in the sixth grade. I live outside of Washington, D.C., with my family and a suspicious cat and a sweet dog. I'm a Cadette Girl Scout, and I enjoy horseback riding (although I don't get to do it as often as I'd like!), writing, reading, drawing, and listening to Hamilton, *among other things. I'm a very adventurous person, and competed in the Odyssey of the Mind World Finals in Ames, Iowa, in fourth grade, as Aristotle the Eagle. I feel so lucky to have this writing opportunity, and would like to thank everyone who helped make this book possible!*

❦ 10 ❦

BE YOU!

BY TRACY HARGEN

G rowing up as girl in the '70s I was always the peacemaker—which meant that at times I changed myself to make others comfortable or to fit it. As an adult, I became an advocate for girls—and it's my mission to spread the word to all girls that they should be themselves. Don't change for anyone and be proud of who you are!

Although I don't have a daughter, I am one and know what it's like to be a young woman in this world. I'm raising two sons and one of my main goals in raising them was I wanted them to become men who aren't intimidated by strong women and who are good men and good partners. Their father set a great example by the way he treats me—their mom. Once you know what is important to you, you need to be sure that whomever you choose to share your life with embodies these things. For me it is thoughtful gestures big and small, respect and most importantly—unconditional love. Think about what it is for you. The single most important thing is for you to be YOU—once you commit to that, everything will fall into place.

In my lifetime of experiences, this is what I've learned about being a woman in the world today—and what I wish I knew when I was growing up:

1. Don't dim your light for anyone. Not your family, not your friends, and certainly not for a guy. Anyone who finds someone else attractive who "plays dumb" or downplays their accomplishments and gifts is competing with you, not loving you. When someone loves you, they want you to excel and they love you for who you are. They do not feel threatened by you—they feel inspired—they want to do better and be better.

You don't need to be "somebody else's something." You don't need to be treated as princess or strive only to be "Daddy's girl" or someone's girlfriend. You will go much further in life (and be infinitely happier) when you own your power and stand in your own light. You don't need anyone else—you can choose someone else if you want to, but stand on your own first and foremost before you invite someone else in. My Mom drilled it into me that you must be able to support yourself before you can get married. You don't want to be stuck in a relationship because you have no alternative. "Stay because you want to, not because you have to." Find someone who supports your dreams and wants you to support theirs—don't become someone you're not so that others feel more comfortable. There are plenty of men who love strong women—and strong women can stand on their own. So go out there and be your best, do your best, because you are more than enough just the way you are!

2. Jealousy does not equal love! When he is jealous, tells you how to dress, and constantly finds fault with you then says, "No one will ever love you the way I do." Believe him—he means it, but not in the way you think. I promise you this, you don't want to be "loved" this way. He may come across as attentive and caring at first but when you're not allowed to think for yourself or be yourself, you are entering dangerous territory.

This controlling behavior will escalate slowly over time until you find yourself conforming for someone else. And when you get fed up and try to stop it, this change will not be welcome. In fact, someone may try to enforce their ways to keep you the way they want. Run! Run fast and far. He won't shove or hit you the first time but he'll make it clear that you need to "get in line." If you've found yourself in this situation, ask for help and take seriously any threats he makes. You've just stood your ground, and that will seem threatening. When a guy really loves you, he loves you for who you are, not how you look standing next to him or how he thinks you should be. A real guy is confident in himself and is not threatened by you talking to the people you choose to talk to, wearing what you want, speaking your mind, and standing on your own. A real man doesn't want to control you or compete with you—he wants you to shine!

3. It's okay not to be okay. If you'd asked me to describe myself growing up I would have said "positive, upbeat, and happy." I'm a "glass half full" kind of gal and see the good in most situations so being happy was easy for me. I was kind to others and empathetic—in how I spoke to them and how I treated them.

I was not always so kind to myself. I held myself to standards that no one could achieve. I was determined and persistent and saw my ambition and striving as some of my stronger qualities—and they were —when they were in check. But I also saw every flaw and every mistake, and those terrified me. I saw them as weaknesses to be conquered. In my mind, I was never smart enough, thin enough, pretty enough, accomplished enough—I could and should always try harder. The kindness I showed others I didn't necessarily show myself. And when all of this striving for perfection and clearly unattainable goals exhausted me and crippled me with fear and anxiety, I had no clue how to ask for help. So I just kept pushing through it—never learning coping mechanisms until I was an adult who was terrified to fly in a plane and was paralyzed with a fear of making a bad decision, certain it would ruin me. Ugh—it was a terrible way to live (all while acting like I was sailing through life without a care in the world.)

So, please, know that it is okay not to be okay. It's okay to make honest mistakes. It's okay not to be perfect—in fact, it's impossible to be perfect so don't do that to yourself. Once you talk to yourself in the caring way to talk to others, you'll be so much happier. Tell that negative voice in your head that you won't allow it to rule your life. Tell it that it can be very cruel, and that is not okay with you anymore. Then talk to yourself the way you would to your best friend when they are struggling. People can't relate to someone who is "perfect"—they relate to someone is human who makes mistakes and forgives themselves. If you're feeling down, or fearful and can't brush it off, ask for help and listen to those who love you—accept their kindness and their love. You'll be amazed how much people are willing to help you when you just ask.

4. Always follow your heart. You know what it feels like—that "gut instinct," that feeling that something feels right or wrong. When you're in a situation and you know instinctively the right thing to do, do it. If you've been taught to doubt yourself—by a parent, sibling, teacher, friend—if you've been taught that your opinion doesn't matter (or worse, that your opinion is "stupid"), you must stop listening to those outside voices. I've made decisions in my life that people responded to with, "You're crazy!" You know what, it might have been a crazy decision for them, but not for me. I'm not a risk-taker but eloped with my husband of 29 years after knowing him for only six months. I know that does seem crazy but I was 23 years old, had a career, could support myself, and was deeply in love. We both knew it was right for us—and we were right! I'm not advocating marrying someone so quickly, but I'm saying that in my heart, I knew it was absolutely right.

I've taken leaps of faith in my life not with my eyes closed, blind to the risks, but with eyes wide open after evaluating the options—and then following my heart. I've hired people, helped people, taken jobs, left jobs, taken chances throughout my life by relying on my instincts. I distinctly remember walking the city streets when my sons were a baby and a toddler. A man passed us who gave me the creeps the way he looked at us. My older son, while holding my hand tightly, moved in closer to me without saying a word and then looked up to me as if to say, "I feel like something is wrong." Once we were safely in the store, I looked at him and said, "That weird feeling in your stomach—it told you something was wrong and made you move closer to me for protection – that's your gut instinct – always listen to it. It will always tell you the right thing to do." If you've ever felt like, "Hmm, something doesn't feel right in this situation," or, "That explanation just doesn't make sense to me," that is your gut or your heart telling you the truth. We all have it, we just have to listen to it—don't try to squelch it or blow it off as "just a feeling"—it's real and it's there for you. Trust it—it's the best guide you have!

5. Being kind beats being pretty any day of the week. I know, what girl doesn't want to be called beautiful? Yes, it's superficial but somehow we've been ingrained to strive for this in a way that guys just don't. It's "the ultimate compliment." Or is it? When I was young I entered a teen beauty pageant. (Hey, it was the '80s in the South— what can I say?!) I wanted that crown and the ginormous trophy that went with it—and if I'm honest, I also wanted proof that I was pretty. What I got was "Miss Congeniality." (I didn't even know it was a thing.)

Don't get me wrong, these were nice girls, but this was a beauty pageant after all and for some of these girls and their moms it was a way of life. After all, we were asking people to look at us as we paraded around and to judge us for how pretty we presented ourselves on the outside. When I saw the other girls had stylists, makeup artists and hairdressers, I should have realized I didn't stand a chance. I'll admit the competition for Miss Congeniality wasn't that tough—I was the only girl there who would rather make new friends then steal someone's makeup. (Yes, that happened.) It took me years to understand that the tiny trophy I received was not the "consolation prize"—it was The Real Prize. A prize that my husband found about 25 years ago in a box of my things. He's proudly displayed it on a shelf in our room ever since. I love that! Being pretty is not sustainable – being kind is who you are at the core. Being pretty serves no purpose - being kind not only feels good to you, it also feels good to all those you come in contact with. So please, choose being kind over being pretty any day of the week. As my dad used to say, "Beauty is only skin deep but ugly is down to the bone." Cruelness, spitefulness, jealousy—those are all ugly, and ugly is hard to change so don't let it ever take root. Be kind—the world needs more kindness.

Now go out there and shine! If they don't accept you, take your light and your power and go shine somewhere else. I promise you this —there are good things ahead for you as long as you are true to yourself and stand in your power. *You are amazing just the way you are so be YOU!*

TRACY HARGEN IS A SOUTHERN GIRL BORN AND BRED WHO DID A stint in the North after meeting her Yankee husband! With their sons out of the house, they're empty-nesters with two beloved pups.

Tracy has worked in Corporate America for over 30 years, but her passions are writing and removing the shame and stigma around mental health issues. Her family's deeply personal journey with depression was featured on CBS This Morning. *Look for her work on GrownandFlown.com and LoveWhat-Matters.com.*

I KNOW YOU ARE, BUT WHAT AM I: CONFESSIONS FROM A CHILDHOOD BULLY

BY HARPER KINCAID

O kay, let me start by stating the obvious: I couldn't have picked a more unsympathetic topic if I tried. I mean, seriously, if my goal was to have you like me, confessing I used to be a bully is a ridiculous strategy.

If it's any consolation, my bullying tenure was short: it was only for a month during sleep-away camp. By the way, that was also the first and last time I could ever count myself as one of the "cool kids."

Anyway, it was the summer of 1982, when almost everything clicked.

I had a cute boyfriend, an avid tennis player who matched his sweat bands with the colored rubber bands on his braces. Trust me, in the early '80s, that was smoking hot, especially if he sported a Members Only jacket to complete the ensemble.

Also, by some miracle, I made the cheerleading squad, which, considering I couldn't even do a cartwheel, should illuminate all you need to know about the competition. Watching us during try-outs was like witnessing a group of freshly clubbed Nancy Kerrigans return to the ice.

It was painful and *so*-not-pretty.

The girls in Bunk Nine ranged in age from 11 to 13, which meant we were all getting our periods around the same time (many for the first time) while having to listen to The J. Geils Band and a newly sober Elton John. In short, we were living through a level of Hell not ever imagined in Dante's Inferno. We got stuck inside more often than not because it rained almost every day—and there's only so many rounds of jacks to play, or letters on your favorite unicorn and rainbows stationary you can write home with, until people start to crack.

Her name was Susan. In a cabin filled with knobby-kneed awkwardness, she had more than the rest of us, but that's not what made her a target. She was a whiner—about everything—and would speak in a baby voice while tattling on us to the counselors. She also hated anything athletic. None of us were going to be recruited for the all-star team of any sport, but enthusiasm counted. So did grit—two things she had none of.

All that was bad, but what was worse was her affection for her Cabbage Patch doll: Miss McSnuggleMuffins. I swear, I wish I was making this up. That was her name. It was even on that Cabbage Patch birth certificate that came in the box, which was a shame because that creepy doll would be the only one I'd ever want to deport. Keep the immigrants—send back all the dolls.

None of us could believe that, at almost 13 years old, she still had one of those things, saying she couldn't sleep without it. But she didn't just sleep with it; she brought the doll to activities outside the cabin too, at least until the counselors put their foot down.

Looking back, Susan Holly was probably just holding on to childhood a bit longer and harder than the rest of us, but in the late '70s, early '80s, there was no room for such macro-lensed sensitivities. Her eccentricities made her a target. Most teased her, but soon, even that grew dull.

So, one night, when she was out of the cabin, my friend and I stole her Cabbage Patch doll, tied a shoelace around her neck, and hung her off the shower curtain rod with a note attached, saying, "I'd rather die than be with you a minute more. You smell and you're weird."

The next morning, when she returned and found her doll, we all woke up to her screams. She screamed like a SAG actor on a *Law &*

Order show. Everyone laughed, including the counselors. I thought it was hysterical, until she ran by and I saw she was actually crying.

I bet you're hoping this is the part of the story when I finally grow a conscience and rectify my bad behavior, right? Sorry, pookie—at this point, I'm still a little asshole. In fact, I enjoyed a swell of mean girl popularity that made me higher than snorting Pixie Stick sugar off a hooker's ass.

By the way, my friend and I endured a scolding that only lasted a minute and a half, and there was no follow-up punishment. How's that for negative reinforcement?

I know I am telling this story with attempted humor. It's my favorite coping mechanism, but trust me, I look back and cringe at my behavior. Actually, I do more than cringe: I experience a profound sense of shame, horrified I was the architect of someone else's suffering and trauma. It would have been bad enough if I had followed along some other mean girl's nefarious agenda. But the McSnuggle-Muffins *coup d'etat* was my Damian-incarnated brainchild. Even though what happened was my sole improv stint as a Heathers-incarnate, I have to live with the knowledge I was capable of such callousness. But that's not the end of the story.

Ironically, before—and after—the Cabbage Patch Incident—I would deal with my own share of mean girls. Not enough to scar me, but enough to show me how awful it was to be on the other end. I thought that was enough to balance the karmic scales. I was wrong.

Flash forward 20-odd years later. My older daughter is enrolled in preschool and, because she's my first, I'm there all the time, volunteering for a million jobs instead of working one for pay, much to the chagrin of my husband. Since we were living in Miami Beach at the time, my husband and I were near where we grew up, which meant we were constantly bumping into people from various stages of our lives. So, in my daughter's preschool class, it was not unusual that I would've recognized many faces: some from elementary school, others from summer jobs. But there's this one mom who looks familiar, but I can never quite place how I know her.

After six months, I finally figured it out: it's it was Susan. She looked almost the same as she did when she was a 12-year-old camper, which means meant she was one of those kids with an older face early on, so you get the mental picture, but moving on. I don't know why it took me so long to put it together, but it did. Anyway, she's now a hot-shot lawyer surgeon married to another hot-shot lawyer surgeon and has one son—who's adorable, by the way. I can tell she has had no idea who I am, but it's not like I can blame her. Back in our camp days, I was rocking a mouthful of braces, an over-processed perm, circa 1982—complete with Sun-In "highlights" which added a lovely greenish hue in the right light, thanks to the ammonium thioglycolate.

But she does not recognize me. In short, she didn't have a clue who I was. We were all grown up, we were friendly, always smiling at one another and doing the small talk thing during drop-off.

If I wanted, I could be home free. I could keep my newly unearthed knowledge all to myself, with her none the wiser. And hey, she was obviously happy and successful now, maybe what happened wasn't a big deal after all.

I didn't want to bring it up. I wanted to forget all about it, which of course meant I couldn't.

So, I worked up the courage one day, pulled her aside and told her who I was and that I had been the one to hang her doll. The face of the confident woman in front of me fell. She was back to being that almost 13-year-old girl. I felt terrible and so did she.

And so, I did what I should have done years ago. I gave her an earnest, contrite apology. I told her I was sorry for causing her any pain, especially in such an insensitive and graphic way.

Then she asked me why I did it—why did I pick on her? The truth was, she was an easy target. She was out of step with the rest of the groupthink, holding onto regressive behaviors not socially acceptable. But there was no way I was going to say all that. For one thing, I didn't want to blame the victim, even if there may have been kernels of truth to my analysis.

And more importantly, she wasn't looking for truth—she was looking for validation and it was my job to give her what she needed to heal. So, I offered a half-truth—that by picking on her, I avoided getting picked on myself.

After that, she was civil, but basically avoided me if she could help it. I deserved that. Actually, I deserved a lot worse. I had gotten a little bit of power and I abused it, because someone was different and out-of-step—or as hella-hipster-musician, hella-hipster-cool, Beck, would have said: "In a world of chimpanzees, she was the monkey," meaning she was flagging behind on the perceived, socio-evolutionary scale. But the point wasn't to make me feel better, it was to make her feel better. And, like many other things in my life, I failed at that goal as well. I still think people should apologize when they do wrong, own up to their crap, but I'm also of the belief the apology is more for the sinner than the victim.

Ironically, a few years later, I had the opportunity to be someone else's Susan. My former high school nemesis-slash-perpetrator of mean girl nastiness tracked me down to apologize for all of her therapy-worthy torment. She is actually a good friend of mine today, but back during The Many Apologies (which I swear she did, like the first 10 times we saw one another socially) she was tormented by how she had treated me. I decided to ask her the same thing Susan Holly had asked me: "Why me?" She said she didn't know. Maybe she remembered, but didn't want to hurt my feelings. I remember me back then and I was a hot mess. I gossiped. I lied. I was like a walking *ABC Afterschool Special* of everything not to do.

Today, I have two daughters and I have shared my stories of being bullied and being the mean girl. They were horrified, as they should have been. I have taught them to not take crap from anyone and to stand up to such injustices when they witness them. I tell them being kind means more to us than being the top of the class or popular.

When I worked as a school social worker intern during grad school, most of the anti-bullying efforts focused on mediation between bullies, perpetrators, and victims. I'll give you the short version: They didn't work. It was my job to bring together two kids who despised one another and to somehow conjure a sort of social-scientific Kumbaya miracle between recess and lunch. I'll cut to the punchline: It never worked.

The methodology and vernacular may have changed, but bad behavior rarely does. So I did what every grad student does: I scoured the latest research on bullying prevention, because us nerd-girl goobers get off on charts and longitudinal studies.

But who was I deluding? Professional curiosity was not the only motivator: the Susans were. Except now some of the Susans may feel more like Stephens inside. And maybe some of the Susans and Stephens want to be accepted for being Sams, something fluid and uniquely in between. I graduated with a masters in Gender History in the early 2000s and most of today's gender identifiers didn't even exist back then. So, maybe our collective, myopic lenses are widening.

However, while being able to identify with one's tribe is a critical component towards self-hood, such actualizations do not eliminate the problem. While researching for effective anti-bullying initiatives, I am happy to share that there are programs that have proven effective. In Finland, they have something called the KiVa program. It is a pre-K through twelfth grade, anti-bullying curricula which alters entire school cultures against intimidating behavior. Apparently, without a supportive audience, it seems bullying conduct fizzles out before it ignites. The KiVa program is not fool-proof, but studies over the last several years have shown statistically significant results in lowered aggressive behaviors.

Imagine if such a curriculum had existed at my summer camp, that the minute someone realized I had grabbed Susan's doll and wrote that note, the entire cabin would have turned on me. Maybe someone would have come up and said, "This is not who we are or what we do." Imagine that.

I still insist on the importance of self-awareness and personal responsibility. But having one's community set us right is also appealing. And although this alternate scenario sounds like an unrealistic dream to me, it is a reality in Finland. Of course, last I heard, Finland also has the highest suicide rates in the world, but I think that's due more to living in perpetual winter with lots of vodka, but what do I know?

In all seriousness, such programs and studies give me hope, especially in our country's divided socio-political environment, with bullying behavior on both sides of the aisle. For a country so passionate about God, we are all in serious need of a come-to-Jesus moment. We have to try something different to go beyond our standard modus operandi, of only working with victims and perpetrators.

Because it doesn't work. It has *never* worked.

Maybe it's too late for us aging and jaded Gen Xers (I don't believe that), but it isn't for the next generation. What I do believe, with everything I am, is in the power of grace and redemption. Personal responsibility, accountability, and collective kindness are the values which can truly save us. I know this to be true because they saved me.

Born in California and raised in South Florida, HARPER KINCAID moved around like a gypsy with a bounty on her head. She's been a community organizer and a professional matchmaker. Ms. Kincaid is a published author, known mostly for her romantic comedies, such as The Wonder of You *and her new release,* Love in Real Life. *She also writes creative nonfiction, poetry, and, most recently, cozy mysteries and suspense.*

She is a self-admitted change junkie, but is now happily settled in the cutest 'lil town of Vienna, Virginia, with her wife-whisperer husband, and their two girls.

SOME DAYS

BY KATY FARBER

Some days
I show up in the world
like an open wound
ready to bleed
for whoever wants me to
apologizing for whatever it is
I haven't said yet
whatever you need
whatever you did
or didn't do
I'll take the blame
fill in the blank
for not enough...
mothering
listening
care-taking
being quiet silence
being compliant compliance

I'll bleed apology

before you even open
your mouth.

Other days
I show up so angry
my blood boils
at every indignity
of the female kind
at every glossy representation
of who I will never be
at every subtle way
the world tells me to be
pretty
friendly
happy
smart but not too smart
enjoying the male gaze
having it all!
while making less than men
again and again
while being interrupted
questioned
silenced
again and again
until I remind myself
to breathe
and turn away.

Other days
I'm so gaslit
I'm so confused
by the world
by the news
by the reality
that I think
I must be

what's wrong
it must be me
losing my mind
slow but surely
unraveling like
a ball of tightly
wound string.

Other days
I feel the power
of one woman
who tells her story
and she is heard
and how it helps
another woman
tell her story
and bit by bit
they share the truth
the often messy
complicated
imperfect truth
of female lives
and I feel that we
just might be
making progress
and in the very least
I am not alone.

Some days
as a woman
in America, 2018.

KATY FARBER is an educator, researcher and author who lives in Vermont with her husband and daughters. She has books published across genres including education and middle grade fiction. Her most recent book is a picture book called *Salamander Sky,* which was a finalist for the New England Book Award. She regularly writes about education, the environment, parenting, and current issues for various websites, journals, and blogs. Learn more and connect at katyfarber.com or on Twitter at @Non_Toxic_Kids.

DEAR DAUGHTER, YOU ARE ENOUGH

BY DEVA DALPORTO

Dear Daughter,
You are enough.

You are enough just as you are. You don't have to be prettier or faster or smarter or sparklier or cooler or quieter or smaller or perkier or smilier or stronger or anything other than what you are. Because you are enough.

I see you comparing yourself. To me. To your friends. To your brother. To random people you'll never know.

I see you putting yourself down. Telling yourself you aren't good enough. Staring at your reflection in the mirror with critical eyes as you brush your hair and wish it were silkier. Putting yourself down for running the fastest mile in your P.E. class, but not the fastest mile in your school. Ripping up your art because it's not quite as good, in your eyes, as one your friend drew.

I see you deflecting credit for great accomplishments and beating yourself up for perceived failures. I see you expecting yourself to be perfect. And I want to scream,

DO NOT DO THIS TO YOURSELF.

Because let me tell you, baby girl, there will be so many people in this life that will try to rip you down. So many others who will judge you and try to make you feel small so they can feel big.

DO NOT DO IT TO YOURSELF.

Do not buy into the script the world serves us girls at birth. That we are not enough. Not pretty enough. Or thin enough. Or strong enough. Or quiet enough. Or worth enough to make the same amount of money as a man who does the same exact job as we do.

It's time for that script to be rewritten.

You don't have to be perfect to be enough. There's no such thing as perfect. Perfect is BS. We are all flawed, every one of us, and that's what makes us interesting. If it existed, perfect would be boring.

But what you do have to be is accepting. Of yourself. Of your flaws. Of your strengths. Of your "You-ness." You have to be your own greatest champion. You have to take credit for your greatness. You have to believe in your awesomeness. You have to be as strong and brave and loud and big as you really are. Do not dull yourself for anyone.

Shine.

I want you to see yourself for the glorious, magnificent, kick-ass creature you truly are.

And I want you to always remember,

YOU ARE ENOUGH.

Just as you are.

Love,
Mom

DEVA DALPORTO OF MYLIFESUCKERS IS THE CREATOR OF DOZENS OF viral videos. She is known primarily for her funny music parody videos for which NBC dubbed her the "Weird Al of YouTube Moms." Her videos have garnered more than 300 million views and have been on Good Morning America, The Today Show, People, CNN, NBC, ABC, Good House-keeping, *and many more. Deva is a three-time BlogHer Voice of the Year*

Award winner for video, an Iris Award winner for Best Parenting Videos, and was selected by ABC News as "Best Fan Cover Artist" in their Billboard Music Awards Special. *She has essays in two Jen Mann anthologies* I Just Want to Be Alone *and* I Just Want to Be Perfect. *Deva blogs at MyLife-Suckers.com and you can find her on YouTube, Instagram, and Facebook.*

❧ 14 ❧

DEAR MOM, YOU ARE ENOUGH

BY A.M. DALPORTO

Dear Mom,
  You are enough.
  You don't have to be the perfect mom. You don't have to be stronger or softer or kinder or craftier or make more organic meals.

I see you beat yourself up whenever you raise your voice. You don't have to be perfectly calm all the time.

I see you disappointed when you don't have everything under control. You don't have to do it all alone.

I see you calling yourself out of shape and criticizing your body. But your "muffin top" just shows that you created two children. And that's pretty cool.

I see you saying you're getting old and staring at your wrinkles in the mirror. And that's true. Everyone is getting older. But the older you get, the wiser you are and the more beautiful you become. Because your marks and lines are memories of your life.

I see you worrying that everybody is better than you, but if you really think about it, nobody is better than anyone else. We're all special in our own way.

You think everything you do for us has to be a masterpiece. But that's not true. If everything was perfect nothing would be special.

You think you have to do it all—the cooking, the cleaning, the cuddling, the planning, the packing, the picking up, the dropping off, the helping with homework—and actually, you do have to do it all. Without you, we wouldn't survive a week. So give yourself some credit.

Even though you're a mom, it's okay to be human. And have flaws. You don't have to be perfect.

YOU ARE ENOUGH.

Just as you are.

Love,
Your Daughter

A.M. DALPORTO IS 12 YEARS OLD. SHE'S ALWAYS HAD A LOVE FOR writing and dreams of becoming an author. She creates humorous videos with her family on their channel MyLifeSuckers and has written a few of her own parodies. She is currently working on her first children's book and is very excited to be included in this anthology.

AUDITION SHIRT

BY JANEL MILLS

I found my audition shirt on one of my many shopping trips to Salvation Army during high school. It was a blue gingham, button-up blouse with short sleeves, a Peter Pan collar trimmed with eyelet lace, and bright red cherries hand-embroidered along and in between the top buttons. It was an anomaly in my closet, hanging next to my faded second-hand t-shirts and oversized flannels, this ultra-feminine, slim-fitting blouse. It was my secret weapon, my red herring, my invisible sucker punch straight to the gut.

❧

DRUMLINE IS A BOY'S CLUB. I'VE BEEN IN MANY DIFFERENT drumlines over the years, in a few different organizations, and in each line I can count on one hand the number of female members. I guess there could be a lot of reasons for that. For starters, the whole point of drums is to bang on something very hard and make very loud noises, and if you've ever once spent an hour with a two-year-old boy, you know that this in and of itself is like a siren song for testosterone. In addition, you don't generally see girls being steered towards percussion in beginning band classes. Also, real talk: The equipment is *heavy*. The lightest piece of equipment starts at about 30 pounds, and it just goes up from there. So yeah, it's a tough sell for most girls physically, and keep in mind, you're trying to sell the idea of carrying something extremely heavy not to athletes, but to girls like me who may or may not have signed up for multiple music classes specifically to avoid taking gym class.

Despite the heavy drum and being suckered into playing the oboe in junior high (arguably the most obnoxious instrument of all), I decided that I needed to join the marching band, and my route to do that was going to be the drumline. Several of my good friends were already members, and served as my ambassadors to the existing drum tech when early winter practices and tryouts began. The tech soon discovered that my friends were right about me: I was tough, I wasn't a complainer, and I could read and learn music pretty damn well. I picked up the smallest bass drum on the first night, and after five minutes, I was sold. Drumming became my passion: it was my thing, and I loved everything about it.

After about a year and a half, three of my friends in the line and I decided we wanted to try out for a winter drumline. Winter drumline is when drumlines compete against each other during the off-season, playing music and marching around gymnasiums. While the bigger, richer high school across town had a winter line, our school, which was less than flush with cash, didn't have one. Somehow, one of us (to this day, I have no idea how we did this, as it was before the dawn of the Internet) figured out that there was a newly formed winter drumline in a rich suburb about an hour away that was holding open auditions. We jumped in the car after school and drove there, ready to kill this audition.

What I failed to realize, however, was that the reason I had never been bothered by being one of the only girls in my high school's drumline was because I had basically grown up with nearly every single member of our tiny line. They knew me already, so my gender wasn't an issue. I quickly realized that outside of my little comfort zone of familiarity, these new drummer dudes were going to assume certain qualities about me, including:

- Can't read music very well
- Only joined the drumline because they ran out of percussionists
- Will constantly ask to set down her drum because she can't handle the weight
- Has no chops (i.e., hand/arm muscle strength, which enables you to play well and play longer)
- Doesn't possess a penis (this one was true)

I remember feeling more and more annoyed as I got the sense that the person running the bass drum auditions fully believed most, if not all, of these things about me. He gave a shitty, condescending nod when I said I was typically used to playing bass one. This instructor made the fatal mistake of assuming that because I was a girl and only weighed 100 pounds soaking wet, I played that drum because it was the lightest. In fact, I continued playing that drum because it's one of the more technically challenging bass drums in the line; I was playing college-level rudiments and doubling some of the snare drum music.

Big mistake. Huge.

He thought he would be funny and put me on bass two, which is actually the toughest drum to play in a bass line, because your notes constantly fall on the upbeat. I'd never played bass two before, but you know what? Sure. I was working myself up to being pissed, and was more than ready to prove how sorely mistaken this guy was for under-estimating me. We started playing the audition music, and it became very clear, very quickly that I was the strongest player in the line. I was catching all of the oddly timed notes the first time through the audition exercise, and the instructor noticed. His attitude changed dramatically after we finished running through that piece. As I straightened back up after setting down my drum for a 10-minute break, I realized I was wearing my silly new gingham shirt with the little red cherries and the eyelet lace. It dawned on me that I had worn the most saccharine-sweet, feminine shirt that I owned to compete against a horde of Y chromosomes.

After that night, I wore my audition shirt any time I had to try out for a new drumline. When I moved on to college and wanted to try out for the drumline at the Big Ten school I was attending, I knew it was a long shot. I knew I was going to deal with the same bullshit I dealt with in other lines – having to prove myself beyond their expectations of female players. However, I still had my secret weapon. It was probably 100 degrees at that first weekend tryout camp, but I still wore that cotton button-up shirt with the Peter Pan collar and the eyelet lace.

Because I had an impression to make.

Because I had false expectations to grab and suddenly shove back into the face of those holding on to them.

۞

I'D LOVE TO TELL YOU THAT I STILL HAVE MY AUDITION SHIRT, THAT I eventually retired it, hanging it from the rafters of my attic in a place of honor like a retired NHL jersey. Sadly, however, I'm not quite sure where it is. It could be in my basement with my other clothes that I can't bear to part with, or I could have returned it from whence it came, tossing it into one of my Goodwill donation boxes once I finally admitted to myself that it doesn't fit, and will never fit me ever again. Either way, it's all good. Even without the shirt, I've held on to the thrill of annihilating people's false expectations of me because of my gender. Was I wearing my cherry shirt the day that pompous judge tried explaining to me, a librarian, how law libraries and legal research works? Nope. I wasn't, but I still smiled while I blasted him with my knowledge of how *modern* legal libraries were set up and managed, including the one that I currently ran. My years of drumline taught me that I'm a bad bitch, to have confidence in the face of doubt, and that even if the men around me don't realize it right away, they will very, very soon.

JANEL MILLS IS THE LIBRARIAN/THUG BEHIND THE BLOG 649.133: Girls, the Care and Maintenance Of, where she writes about raising a princess, a wild child, and the sassiest redhead on Earth using as many curse words as

possible. Janel was a contributor to several super successful anthologies includ-
ing the I Just Want to Pee Alone *series. When not blogging or librarian-ing,*
she keeps busy raising three beautiful little girls in the wilds of metro Detroit.

❧ 16 ❧

MY PENIS MAKE MILK

BY MONICA GOKEY

I was a two-kid kind of person until I had two sons.

By the time my second was six months old, the #MeToo movement had been unfolding in the news for weeks. Personal #MeToo disclosures blossomed across my Facebook feed, making an at-large movement suddenly feel very much at home. It made my heart hurt.

All the men in my life were under fresh scrutiny. I wondered which were the ones I perceived them to be, versus the ones with transgressions under their belts (pun intended). When I did a mental line-up of the men I felt the most positive about, a single trait ran through them like a ribbon: They all had strong women in their lives—awesome moms, stubborn sisters, or kick-ass girlfriends and wives.

Family planning is a pretty shit casino game. You get 50/50 odds the female body of a slot machine deposits you a boy or a girl. But in the wake of #MeToo, I readied myself to run the gauntlet. I signed up for a third pregnancy like it was an Oprah sweepstakes (although the odds of winning were definitely higher). Fifty-fifty isn't too shabby... and every gambler knows the house can't always win.

Ahead of our third baby's arrival, I did my best to brainwash my sons into wishing for a sister. I hyped the girl-wishing to them like we were on the cusp of winning a trip to Disneyland. We're gender-surprise people, so we didn't have a 'big reveal' until the baby made its earthly entry. Everyone in our family had been thoroughly inoculated with "we want a girl" fever.

(For the record, I would've been over the moon with a child of either gender. Babies make you soft that way.)

After 42 weeks of pregnancy (yep, you read that right), an unpleasant day at the hospital, and a flood of mushy-gushy emotions—we *did* end up having a girl. The moment felt huge. I'd been entrenched in boy world for three years, and the arrival of a girl left me feeling like balance had been restored to the proverbial Force.

Behold, household! There are two of us now!

When my sons finally met their sister at the hospital, it was immediately clear to me something was amiss.

"Where's her penis?" the oldest, age three, asked.

"She doesn't have a penis," I explained. "She's a *girl*."

"Why she no have a penis?" he said.

I realized I'd been operating under the blind assumption he *knew* the difference between a boy and a girl. He knew Mama was "a girl," but the details of that label had clearly escaped him.

"Girls don't have penises. They have vaginas... and boobies," I patiently explained.

My three-year-old nodded knowingly.

His little brother, one-and-a-half, just screamed "PENIS!... NOOOOO!" at the decibel level he's used to communicating at.

Both knew about boobies. But "vagina" was new to them. "Gi-nuh? ... GI-NUH... VAHHHH-GI-NUH!!" They tried out the new word with alacrity.

Progress.

I was somewhat blindsided by the fact that they didn't know the mechanics of the boy/girl distinction. We live on a cattle ranch in central Idaho. Ever since their eyes have been open they've seen roosters having their way with chickens, bulls mounting cows, and countless other iterations of "the birds and the bees."

Our daughter's first few weeks were marked by this total lack of gender awareness—which was its own kind of awesome.

The boys didn't understand why our families had gifted us a mountain of severely pink clothing. (I didn't understand either, to be fair.)

Too young to know any foolish adages like "girls don't poop" – they ooh'd and ahh'd at the ferocity of their sister's buttery yellow discharges.

"Wow, dat one so big!" my oldest would cheer.

"Yeah, like a fire hose," I would add as I frantically tried to contain any escaping squirts.

And they didn't hesitate to call her the kind of names they called each other. For the first week they called her Dirt. We put the kibosh on that after worrying family outsiders would think we were living some kind of twisted Cinderella story.

During my daughter's first few weeks, I saw their tiny mental light bulbs flicker with more vigor on the whole boy-girl front.

One morning my 18-month-old was reading in bed with me when the baby needed to nurse. I stopped our book to get her latched on. I clenched my teeth and curled my toes while she chomped on to a sore nipple. My younger son put his chubby hand on my arm in a gesture of comfort.

"Hurt?" he said.

"Yeah, hurt," I replied before resuming our book as the latch-on pain faded.

When the baby was crying, my oldest would offer her the kind of comfort he liked.

"She want a cookie?"

"No, thanks. She just drinks milk," I'd tell him. But mentally I logged his comment as a win for budding empathy skills.

We've always tried to stress the importance of character traits like empathy and kindness to our sons. But it wasn't until having a girl that I started to see those teachings bear fruit. Maybe it has nothing to do with having a girl. Maybe it's just the presence of a mewling, helpless, adorable newborn that encourages our best selves shine forth. Either way, there was a change in our family—more helping, more teamwork, and more understanding between everyone, big and small. Although I'm hardly one to live by the old adage "mother knows best," I can't help but feel like the added feminine presence had something to do with our family synergy.

The she-power soon escalated beyond my wildest dreams.

Monday is the only day I swing an entire shift of stay-at-home mom life. We drive an hour each way to preschool (because it's the kind of thing rural parents do to socialize their kids). On the way to our favorite "apres-pre" burger joint, some heavy conversation rocked the minivan.

My three-year-old told me sadly that Ducky (his stuffed bestie) can't drink milk from a cup. He sighed heavily.

"Can Ducky drink milk from a straw?" I asked.

"No."

Long pause.

"Ducky drink milk from me," he said, perking up.

"Oh, like how Mama feeds Virginia? From your chest?"

OMG this is so cool... he's having boob envy!

"No. Ducky drink milk from my penis."

Oh shit... what the—

"Yeah... my penis make milk."

I internally facepalmed. Three is too young to understand that it's not cool to conjure up the visual of anything sucking from your pecker, not even a stuffed toy duck.

We dropped the conversation and stuffed our faces with burgers and fries when we got to the restaurant. (Restaurants: also a big novelty when you live out in the wop-wops.)

That night when my husband got home from work I told him about our three-year-old's milk-making penis. He laughed, and then gently prodded me to read between the proverbial lines.

"Vern wishes he was like you," my husband said.

"Like me?"

"Yes. Like you," he insisted. "Think about how amazing it is to a kid his age that you can make milk to feed a baby. And all the other things you do."

I internally blushed at the thought... but this line of thought felt right.

In the coming weeks my oldest son would sometimes sigh wistfully and say, "I want to be a girl." Those words made me feel warm and fuzzy inside. The female body is an amazing thing... so much more than a baby-making slot machine. Even a three-year-old gets it.

And the female psyche is pretty amazing, too. I can't speak for all women, but being emotional has always been a pillar of my life. As far as I can tell, it's normal. I may be short-tempered, impatient, and hot-headed—but I'm also deeply loving, committed to my family, and perceptive of other people's emotions. Those traits aren't exclusively female, but I know a lot of kickass, amazing women with similar temperaments. I want my sons to know that all of it is normal. The whole package isn't anything like looks in magazines. (It's way more explosive.)

It probably shouldn't have taken a third kid to ensure my sons grew up acclimated to all-that-is-female. But I like having back-up.

MONICA GOKEY IS A PRINT AND RADIO JOURNALIST IN WEST-central Idaho, where three kids, a cattle ranch, and low-speed internet interfere with her persistent attempts to be a real writer (whatever that means). Her work has aired on public radio stations in the West and Alaska.

HOW TO BE SHRILL LIKE A PRO

BY SARAH COTTRELL

In 1989, I was in the fifth grade. My teacher, Mr. Brown, was a very stiff British sort of man. He always wore ill-fitting gray wool suits. Every day he would lift up a rogue mitten or scarf and hold it out like it was the most revolting thing he'd ever seen while asking, "To whom does this belong?" He would always drawl out the 'whom' and purse his already puckered up face into a scowl. The top of his head was balding while the sides and back were long and gray—and not a nice gray either, it was more of an elderly mothball gray. He would comb his hair up into a long sausage curl on top of his head.

That curl held a peculiar amount of curiosity with me and my classmates. So, it wasn't much of a surprise when Tom, the annoying kid who sat perpendicular to me, dared me to stick my finger through Mr. Brown's curl. I did. Mr. Brown was not amused and made a rather loud example of how disrespectful I was. As he pointed at his head—that was now shiny bald since my finger snagged the curl and it all fell down—he stammered out a quick comparison between my inexcusable insolence and Michelle, a very polite and quiet girl who always did what she was told. Michelle and I both blushed in embarrassment.

Mr. Brown was boring, for sure, and he may have disliked kids what with the way he spoke to us. But that man, whether he intended to or not, would give me the most potent introduction to feminism that I ever could have asked for. He showed me that being shrill, which apparently meant vocal if you're female, is a gift, not a curse—and to this day it is still my superpower.

One day, Mr. Brown announced that we would break up into four debate teams. He stood in front of the class and held two newspapers, one was national and one was local. He talked about the current events that the general public was debating. Most of it was political but some of it was cultural.

He asked the class to read through each newspaper and identify several topics that we could debate in a friendly classroom competition. By the end of the hour, we had several topics written up on the chalkboard in perfectly illegible fifth-grade writing.

Mr. Brown wrote all the topics on pieces of paper and then added them to a hat. He broke the class into four groups.

I was stuck with the three most irritating boys, Tom, Jason, and Eric. I couldn't stand them and I was dreading this activity. These were the boys who ran up to me during recess and poked me in my back then ran away screaming. They pulled my hair. They teased me incessantly. And no matter how many times my mother told me, "It just means they like you," I was never left with an overwhelming feeling of being respected by them. They were basically jerks.

"And now, each of your groups will choose a team captain," Mr. Brown said while holding back his imaginary British accent.

Of course, I was not chosen. Jason said that he would be the captain. He looked right at me as he explained loudly that boys are natural leaders. I was bored to tears with the classroom exercise that was obviously not meant for me. My three teammates were distracted by talk of wall ball and Jason's new sneakers. I imagined that this was how the boys must have felt during Home Economics class when every activity was clearly invented for girls in order to learn how to run a home. Teachers must have thought that girls weren't capable of ambition beyond learning to sew a button by hand. Middle school was turning out to be hard.

Mr. Brown walked over to our table and offered the hat toward the center of the table. Jason reached in and pulled out a long marigold-yellow piece of paper.

"Ah, I see you'll be debating a classic today. Should women be allowed to play professional basketball?" Mr. Brown was talking to Jason but glanced sideways at me. I couldn't tell, but it felt like he was sending me some kind of message. What, I had no idea.

The boys started talking about basketball. This is a sport that I knew nothing about and to this day I have less than no desire to ever watch a game. But while the boys sat there chewing on details of Michael Jordan and Charles Barkley, I was looking at the clock and realizing that time was running out.

I took out a piece of notebook paper and drew a line down the middle. "Hey, guys, we should really come up with all the reasons why girls can play basketball and reasons why they can't that way we can be ready for whatever the other debate team will throw at us."

Tom rolled his eyes and asked me if I could even spell basketball.

"Um, duh...can you even think of a reason why girls can't play?" I shot back.

The three boys stared at me as I did something that to this day still disturbs me. I listed off all the reasons girls are told that they—that we—aren't capable of playing the same sports as boys. We have periods that make us unstable and crazy. We might bleed to death. We wear distracting clothes and makeup and shoes. We can't run fast because we run like girls. Our long nails will break off if we try to dribble a ball. We are offensively distracting to boys, which is inexplicably unfair to boys. We cat fight. We're dumb. We're weak. We're girls.

Notably, some of those same reasons were given by the public for why couldn't or shouldn't be able to play any sport professionally.

The looks on the boys' faces were incredulous. They didn't seem to think that I should know these reasons. Eric accused me of stealing his ideas, never mind that I was the only one doing any work.

Mr. Brown was quietly watching our group from his oak desk at the front of the classroom. He stood up and smoothed out his necktie before walking over to our cluster of desks that we had pushed together. He perched behind Tom, who was sitting in front of me, crossed his arms and peered down at our group list of pros and cons.

Mr. Brown looked at me and asked how it felt, as the only female in our group, to see and hear all of the negative things listed about girls and women. But before I could answer, Tom said, "Sarah came up with all of the cons and she told us to come up with the pros but we're stuck."

"And you don't think that's odd, Tom?" replied Mr. Brown.

"Why? She was being bossy and took over our whole project! Jason was supposed to be the leader but she started doing all the work," Tom complained.

Mr. Brown looked at me and repeated his original question.

"I feel frustrated and angry that boys are so stupid about fairness when it comes to sports, Mr. Brown," I started. "I'm the third fastest runner in our whole grade and I'm a girl but that doesn't count because I'm a girl. It's a lazy and stupid argument."

My hands shook a little and I remember being quite taken by surprise by how strongly I felt about girls being allowed to play sports. But it was more just that. I was angry about boys feeling like they could speak for me, that they could take over anything from an opportunity to play in sports to a classroom group exercise. I wanted to cry but I knew I my point be lost on these boys if they saw tears.

So, I sucked it up and I looked Mr. Brown right in the eye and I said, "I took over the assignment because no one was working and this needed to get done."

Mr. Brown smiled at me for the first time really ever. It was a warm smile and I felt like something important had just transpired. A sense of power that I had never felt was mine settled into me and I sat a little taller.

I can't say for sure if those boys learned anything that afternoon. And I don't fully recall the eventual debate that we had against an opposing team of classmates, although I do recall the laughter and jeering at my delivering a list of reasons for why girls shouldn't play basketball.

What I do recall, with laser-sharp clarity, is that I felt empowered to use my voice and speak up about an issue that felt squarely unfair. Girls and women may be different than boys and men but they ought to be given equal access to opportunities, power, and influence.

As a woman, I have a voice and I am obliged to use it to question authority and speak out against inequality even if that means upsetting people. As I raise my daughter and two sons, I am hopeful that they will carry this lesson close to their hearts.

SARAH COTTRELL IS A FREELANCE WRITER LIVING IN MID-COAST Maine with her husband and three children. Her work has been widely published online and has been included in six other anthologies including the New York Times *bestselling series* I Still Just Want to Pee Alone. *You can follow Sarah on Facebook under her moniker @housewifeplus.*

❧ 18 ❧

DO AS GRANDMA SAYS: RECYCLED ADVICE FOR MY TEENAGE DAUGHTER

BY SUSANNE KERNS

S ince no teenage girl wants to listen to her mom's advice, I've decided to give you someone else's advice instead: Grandma's. She gave me this advice when I was your age, and after decades of testing it out, it ends up she actually knew what she was talking about.

GRANDMA'S GOLDEN RULE: GET A GOOD JOB SO YOU CAN support yourself, and never have to rely on anyone else.

If you want some serious, no-nonsense life advice, talk to a single mom who raised two kids in rural Idaho in the '80s without a college degree. Somehow, she managed to make this advice sound empowering and not all, "*Geez, Mom, I'm only 13, I'm not planning my divorce proceedings quite yet.*" It's still the best advice I've ever received. Over the years, I've seen friends triumph over horrible situations by heeding this advice and I've seen friends' lives crumble due to seemingly minor issues by ignoring it. I may look like "just a stay-at-home mom," but I was able to make that choice because I bought my own house and saved up a nest egg before I even got married. I also always keep one toe in the water so that I could go back to work tomorrow if there was an emergency.

Golden Rule Part B: Work hard in school so you can go to a good college in order to get that good job.

This one is a subcategory of the Golden Rule, but I would like to clarify something: A "good" college education depends on what you put into it. You can learn a lot at a $40,000-a-year university or at a $4,000-a-year university. You can also waste a lot of time and money at the same universities. Your time is even more valuable than money—don't squander it. Never again in your life will you have the dedicated time and freedom to immerse yourself in things that interest you or things that bore you and learn the difference between the two.

Take it from me, after spending over a decade in a career that wasn't a great fit for me, it's easy to see classes as a means to an end, (graduate and get on with my *real* life!) and try to cram your schedule with mandatory classes while skipping electives. But college is *the* time to take some "I wonder" classes: *I wonder what architecture is all about. I wonder if I would like journalism. I wonder if I would be any good at archery.* It may mean it takes you an extra semester to graduate, but you'll be a much more interesting person when you do, and you'll be in a better position to tell the difference between a good job and a job that's good for *you*.

Travel and do all the things you want to do before you start a family (that is, *if* you want to start a family).

I know you think that the only reason we keep telling you to consider a semester of college abroad is because your dad and I want fun places to visit, which is true, but the world is a big, wonderful place and there's so much to learn from other cultures. Travel builds your sense of empathy and respect for others, especially when you visit a place where you feel like the "other" for once. And yes, you can certainly still do this after you have a family, but remember how we used to have to feed your brother an entire box of Ritz crackers to make him sit still on the plane? You don't have to do that if you're flying alone.

ALWAYS PAY WITH CASH OR CHECK, AND ONLY USE CREDITS cards to buy airplane tickets.

Okay, this one made more sense back in the '80s, when people actually knew what checkbooks were, and you didn't face the angry glares of a long line of grocery shoppers if you had the audacity to whip out a checkbook at the register. But the rationale behind it is still sound: Only buy things you can pay for *now*. That being said, even with a tight budget, grandma knew that travel was a good investment, especially travel to visit and build memories with long-distance family and friends.

DATE LOTS OF DIFFERENT BOYS.

This advice was always perplexing to me because Grandma started throwing it at me way before I was allowed to date boys. Plus, even at 13 years old, I knew that this advice had the potential to earn me a pretty nasty reputation at school, so I revised it a bit to "be *friends* with a lot of different boys." Learning to relate to boys in ways that have nothing to do with dating or a physical relationship is a real gift—many of my best friendships were with boys. This was especially easy for me because I had a mullet, Coke-bottle glasses, and headgear – so being friends was a much more realistic goal than dating anyway.

THERE ARE LOTS OF FISH IN THE SEA.

This one is for when you do start dating and some cute boy breaks your heart. Not only are there a lot of fish in the sea, there are also lakes and rivers all over the country and all over the world. Your heart will be broken by a lot of fish-sticks and farm-raised tilapia, but you deserve Copper River salmon. Sure, they may be harder to come by, but they are worth the wait. Except, since you're a vegetarian, hmmm...There are a lot of carrots in the field.

FISH IN THE SEA, PART B: NEVER CHASE DOWN A BOY OR BEG him to be with you.

Okay, Grandma didn't tell me this one, Oprah Winfrey did (and don't you dare ask, "Who is Oprah Winfrey?"). She once shared a story of some fool who treated her horribly, but as he drove away, she practically jumped on the hood of his car so that he wouldn't leave her. No, I've never literally jumped on a car, but I have metaphorically jumped on some cars by changing the ways I acted or dressed, or by overlooking a boyfriend being disrespectful when I should have used that as the opportunity to kick him to the curb. Refer back to the "fish in the sea" advice. It's cliché because it's true. Plus, there's only room for one fish on your hook so throw the junk fish back in the pond—he's taking up valuable space.

BE CAREFUL WHAT YOU SAY AND DO—THE ONE PERSON YOU don't want to find out always will. (AKA my first boss's version: Don't do or say anything you wouldn't want the world to see on the front page of the *New York Times*.)

Friends will be jerks, teachers will be annoying, and parents will be sooooooo lame, but be very careful what and who you confide in. Back in the '80s it took forever for a jilted friend to humiliate you by passing an embarrassing note you wrote around the school. These days it only takes a screenshot and a tweet to instantly broadcast something you did or said to your entire universe of friends (and strangers.). Will you survive the humiliation? Yes, and it will likely be a hilarious story someday. But spare yourself the drama in the meantime – only say stuff about people that you would be willing to say to their face, or to have your principal read over the intercom at school.

DON'T TAKE SIDES (UNLESS IT'S *YOUR* SIDE).

There's a 99 percent chance that your friend who is pissed off at her boyfriend who is a "lying, stupid, jerk-face who she never ever wants to see again as long as she lives" will be back to holding hands with him by tomorrow. Do not show your support for her by agreeing with all of her angry insults because when she's back with him tomorrow, *you're* the one she'll be mad at. However, if that same boyfriend's behavior goes beyond "jerk" to "dangerous," that is a side that you should take and share with me or another parent or teacher you trust.

LISTEN TO YOUR GUT AND SPEAK UP FOR YOURSELF.

There will be a million instances in your life when you're going to have to make hard decisions without anyone around to help: whether to accept alcohol or drugs, to do more than just kiss some cute boy, to get in a car with someone who has been drinking, to do more than your share on a group project, or accept a job that doesn't sound like a great fit. If you're questioning and doubting what to do, the answer is usually no, and you shouldn't be afraid to listen to your gut and say it. Don't worry about being rude. Don't worry about hurting feelings. Don't worry about needing to come up with an excuse. "No" can be a full sentence by itself. You've only got one you to worry about, and she's my favorite "you" in the world.

YOU'RE PERFECT AND BEAUTIFUL AND I WILL ALWAYS LOVE YOU, no matter what.

It did not take long for me to discover that Grandma was lying when she told me that *"everybody has those little bumps on their arms, you just can't see them."* (They're keratosis pilaris, by the way, and no, not everybody has them.) However, I think her bigger point was that everybody has something about themselves that they think isn't perfect, but it's all of our combined imperfections that make us who we are. Who you are is amazing and there will never, ever be another one of you in the world. That makes you the most perfect you that there is.

The "no matter what" part usually came up when I was crying in Grandma's arms after getting in trouble for doing something stupid, oh, like the time I went and bought a (mint-condition, cherry-red

Honda Elite Deluxe with digital readout) motor scooter without permission while she was at work and drove it 20 miles home with no helmet on.

Which brings me to the most important, universal parenting rule:

DO AS I SAY, NOT AS I DO. (BETTER YET—DO AS GRANDMA says.)

SUSANNE KERNS IS A WRITER LIVING IN AUSTIN, TEXAS, WITH HER husband and two children. She's currently writing her first book, which she'll finish as soon as her kids stop asking her to "come look at this." Her stories have been featured in several parenting anthologies as well as a variety of websites, including her blogs, SusanneKerns.com and The DustyParachute.com. Susanne was also the co-producer of the 2017 Listen to Your Mother show in Austin. Follow her on Facebook to see why she's frequently featured on Today Parents' "Funniest Parents on Facebook" round-up. You can also find her on Instagram, and sometimes on Twitter when she accidentally hits the wrong button on her phone.

RUN

BY ALICE GOMSTYN

We need women on the ballot.
We need women on the trail.
We need smart and kind and brazen—brazen!—
Women to prevail.

Calling future heroines and mavens:
We need you to train and run.
We need you to prove the critics wrong,
Who say it can't be done.
We will stand behind you proudly.
We will stomp and chant and cheer.
We will insist, persist, and argue
Until everybody hears:

We need women on the ballot.
We need women on the trail.
We need smart and kind and brazen—brazen!—
Women to prevail.

ALICE GOMSTYN IS A WRITER AND JOURNALIST WHOSE WORK has been published by *The Washington Post*, ABCNews.com, NBCNews.com, Yahoo.com, *Business Insider*, *The Boston Globe*, *The Providence Journal*, and *Babble*, among others. She has also contributed to two parenting humor anthologies. As a senior editor at a content marketing firm, Ms. Gomstyn specializes in business, technology and health articles. When she's not writing and editing, she's promoting important causes as co-founder of the northern New Jersey grassroots group, Glen Rock After the March.

20

EVERYDAY ACTS OF GIRLHOOD REBELLION

BY DANA ARITONOVICH

"A girl should be two things: who and what she wants."

— COCO CHANEL

OHIO, 1980. MY IMMIGRANT GRANDPARENTS' UNFENCED SUBURBAN backyard. I was seven years old and wearing a sensible yet fabulously green ensemble of shorts, a checkered button-down top, and some toe-killers, which was what my family called flip-flops. It was a lovely summer afternoon, a light breeze in the air but the sun approaching scorching hot. I have always loved to marinate in the sun.

Since they lived around the corner, I visited my grandparents often. My middle sister—at this point, my only sister—and I slept over at their house on Fridays and every New Year's Eve. On this day I was visiting *sans* sister, and at this moment I was outside by myself, sitting on the brief concrete patio, my butt resting on an adult-sized lawn chair. I was really living the life that day, taking swigs from a sixteen-ounce glass bottle of Pepsi, emulating the way the men in my family enjoyed their beer.

As sweat began to form on the small of my back, my thoughts turned to watching my father do yardwork topless. I noticed that my mother was never topless in the backyard, and I was curious about it. What was so different about her body? I knew she had boobs, but why couldn't she show them outside like my father showed his? Surely my mom also wanted to keep cool while she worked outside. It didn't make any sense.

In the distant future, I would go out of my way to study the civil rights movement and feminism, always identifying with those who utilized direct action rather than those who preferred patient waiting and assimilation. My first act of public—well, outside my own bedroom walls, anyway—civil disobedience took the shape of unbuttoning my button-down and letting the summer wind flow over my bare skin, Pepsi bottle in hand, feeling completely free and equal in every way. Nobody was around to see my rebellion, but that didn't matter. I chose to live as I pleased, whatever the consequences.

WHEN I WAS A KID, I ALWAYS SAID I WANTED TO BE THE ONE TO GO OUT to work so my husband could stay at home and take care of the house and kids and have dinner ready when I got home. My family knew I was serious.

AT AGE SEVEN, I WAS ACUTELY AWARE THAT MEN AND WOMEN, BOYS and girls, were treated differently in the world. My parents had only girls, so my poor father was the only male in our house. It was very clear to me that my mother and father were equals. I never heard my dad speak down to my mom, he didn't call her names or say anything sexist to her. My mother never asked my father permission to do anything (as if!), and she never told him he was right when he was wrong.

Because of my parents, I never internalized what I saw in society that said I had to look and think and feel a certain way because I was a girl. Before I was even five years old, my dad would take me fishing on Saturday mornings; that was our time. I loved getting in the dirt like boys did. I played with toy cars and pretended I was in the Army (thanks to *Stripes* and *Private Benjamin*) and Marines (I salute you, Gomer Pyle!). I pulled the legs off spiders and cut up worms, fascinated that they kept moving for so long. I'd race my yellow plastic Zoomcycle down the driveway into the empty garage, pretending I was doing dangerous, daredevil stunts like Evel Knievel. I taped random wires to my little red wagon, put one of my dad's dirty red rags in my back pocket, and slid myself under that wagon to "fix" it.

My sister and I each had a Barbie townhouse with an elevator in it. We were pretty excited that our Barbies and their families—our main Barbies were first cousins—had such cool, modern homes. They also had sweet Corvettes; mine was a metallic dark blue. We played dress-up with our mom's and grandma's old clothes, competing to see who could create the tackiest outfits; we cleverly called this game Tacky. With two of our human cousins, we pretended we were genies; we even made our own *I Dream of Jeannie* costumes—mine was blue, of course, because I refused to wear anything pink. I have never liked pink, and neither has my mother.

I wasn't told that I shouldn't like what I liked or play how I played. Not by my parents, anyway. Some girls thought they should only like light colors and be polite and quiet and not get themselves dirty. But that was never natural to me. Sometimes I thought I was a bad kid because my grades weren't perfect and I talked too much. I liked being in charge and saying what I wanted to say and standing up to bullies who bothered my sisters. I didn't know how else to be!

When she was a kid, my grandfather taught my mother to do basic plumbing and change a car battery. He wanted her to go to college because he knew that she was really smart and college helped you succeed in America. He encouraged my sisters and me to be competitive, directing us to race each other to the hill at the end of his backyard and back. We were girls and his only grandchildren, and he was so proud. He taught us how to play *tablić*, a popular Serbian card game. He gave us scraps of wood to build things with. He took us around the backyard on the riding mower and let us steer.

We watched our grandmother make soups and special breads for the holidays; sometimes we got to help. She made Serbian doughnuts and crepes for us on the weekends, and always let us drink coffee out of these kitschy plastic green cups with matching saucers. She was a crocheting and knitting phenomenon, and though she was super patient as she tried to teach me, I just never had the knack for it. I was better at making elaborate structures with my Lincoln Logs.

One afternoon we were at a church picnic. My middle sister and I were on the playground with our cousins and kids from Sunday school. In the 1980s, playground equipment wasn't particularly safe. Everything was wood and metal and chain, and though it was sturdy it still broke and had horrible jagged pieces that would definitely give you tetanus.

Two of my cousins were on one end of the ancient, wooden seesaw and I was on the other. Every 30 seconds, they thought it was hilarious to stop so I was stuck up in the air. I was never fond of being practically airborne, so about the fifth time it happened I jumped ship. As I fell the approximately five feet down onto the dirt, my right arm decided to grab a long, sharp splinter sticking out of the seesaw. That daring escape left me with a pretty cool wound that was sure to provide a gruesome scar I could brag about to the kids at school on Monday. My sister ran to tell our mom, who then stomped over to see if I was okay. I didn't cry or complain that it hurt, but I'm sure I blamed my cousins because I've always been a tattletale. After my near-disfiguring injury was cleaned and bandaged, I resumed my regularly scheduled program with the other kids. Nevertheless, I persisted.

In Sunday school as we lined up to go to church, the boys went first because of "tradition." I always heard "ladies first" was how we do it in America, but that certainly wasn't the Serbian way. I was conflicted.

I was at my friend Rori's house during summer break. We were nine years old. Her backyard was pretty big—not really bigger than mine, but it bordered the woods so it seemed bigger. One of her boy neighbors was playing with us. I had met him before, and he was kind of a jerk, actually. He asked me about the music I liked, and when I mentioned The Beach Boys, he laughed. I was annoyed.

"They're old!" he declared. "You listen to that stuff?" This was a dumb question, because obviously The Beach Boys were awesome and I only listened to awesome music.

I explained to him how important The Beach Boys were to the history of rock and roll, how they were influenced by Chuck Berry, and how they made surf music popular. Despite my expertise, he was not swayed. He was even lamer than I thought.

The Beach Boys have been in heavy rotation on my record player since my parents bought me my first one when I turned five and The Beach Boys' music turned seventeen. I listened to my mom's old records all the time, so The Beach Boys, Elvis, Chuck Berry, The Beatles, and Jerry Lee Lewis didn't seem old to me. I produced a radio show on WDRS 113.2 FM in our basement and played their songs for my audience, which consisted of my two sisters (one of whom was a toddler) sitting in the next room.

None of my friends were really interested in this kind of music. Michael Jackson was just about to release *Thriller*—and I was about to become a superfan—but I was still just listening to my parents' music at the time. Whenever I was at Rori's house and that stupid boy was over, he would make fun of me for listening to The Beach Boys. But that didn't matter, because I knew I had good taste in music and could talk to grownups about it and he couldn't.

I took pride in learning about things my schoolmates didn't care about. I obsessively studied everything that interested me: rock and roll, archaeology, stamp collecting, dentistry, Shakespeare. Being an authority was important. If I was ever questioned by some kid who was trying to be a smartass, I wanted to be able to shut them down with my mad knowledge right away.

۞

My parents used to tell me I was strong enough to beat up all the boys. I took that as a compliment. They knew that too many males were intimidated by strong females, and that I wouldn't put up with anyone's crap.

BOYS LOVED MY FRIEND LESLIE. SOME OF THEM SEEMED TO LIKE ME as a friend, but none of them wanted to be my boyfriend in fourth grade. One time I asked Leslie if she could teach me how to get boys to like me, since I really liked boys and wanted to go with somebody already. Her first piece of advice was that I should wear a skirt at least once a week like she did, because all I ever wore were jeans. *Girls who wear pants never get a second glance.*

I was not excited about this suggestion. Skirts and dresses were definitely not my thing, but I still had to wear them to church and weddings and other fancy places. Wearing that stuff to school seemed like a bad idea for many reasons, especially on Fridays because they were Flip-Up Days, meaning the boys were expected to flip up your skirt whenever they could so everyone would see your underwear and laugh at you. Having my personal space violated like that didn't interest me, and I was ready to fight anybody who tried it.

Leslie and I agreed to wear skirts this one day. It was February, but I forced myself to deal with the frigid temperature so I could learn this first of the many important boy-catching secrets Leslie had to share. My mom knew I hated skirts and suspiciously asked why I was dressed like that for school, especially when it was so cold. I told her that I just felt like wearing one that day, and there's no way she believed me.

Ready to fiercely conquer all the ten-year-old boys, I showed up to school in my cute-but-uncomfortable skirt and watched Leslie walk down the hallway. She was wearing pants! I felt betrayed. I asked her right away why she wasn't wearing a skirt since it was her idea that we both do it that day, and she claimed she forgot. I knew she was lying and probably did it because she wanted to make fun of me for being so desperate for attention from the boys. I spent the whole day feeling mad and awkward and freezing in that skirt, just waiting for some stupid boy to try me. And wearing a skirt didn't make even one of them like me.

The next time I decided to wear something other than jeans to school was in warmer weather a year or two later, and I wore it because I felt like it, not because I wanted anyone's attention. It was a button-up denim dress, much more my style since jeans were my life. I still had to be on alert for Friday Flip-Up Day, but was otherwise satisfied with my choice of outfit. In seventh grade, I cut off half that dress and turned it into a denim jacket. That was even better! I drew a big peace symbol on the back of it and put some cool pins on the front. I made myself a set of groovy love beads and wore them to school most days. *Yes*, I told myself, *this is my look now: a hippy born thirty years too late.* Other kids called me a hippy as an insult and constantly asked what I was protesting, but I didn't care. I knew who I was and their opinions didn't affect me.

❦

WHEN I REALIZED THAT ALL I EVER NEEDED TO DO IN LIFE WAS BE myself, that made everything so much better—not always easier, but I was much happier. I don't apologize for who I am, because who else can I be?

DANA ARITONOVICH GOT OVER HER HATRED OF DRESSES AS A grownup, until she hit 40 and started living in yoga pants. She wore assorted yoga pants while writing essays for Red State Blues: Stories from Midwestern Life on the Left *(2018) and* A Race Anthology: Dispatches and Artifacts from a Segregated City *(2016). Since 2009, Dana has run several blogs including What I Like Is Sounds and Food is the New Sex.*

SPIRAL PERMS AND OTHER GIANT PILES OF STIFF REGRET

BY KIM FORDE

S piral perms. They were a thing—a very big thing, literally and figuratively—in New Jersey in the '80s. Bigger. Higher. Taller. Fuller. Pair that chemically altered hair with a can of Aqua Net and a comb, and the sky really was the limit. I have the eleventh-grade school photos to prove it. My girlfriends and I spent considerable time and money on this look, and it required dedication. I can remember getting up for high school before dawn and listening to my favorite cassettes and CDs while I undertook the daily task of readying my hair. My mom tried to tell me, sometimes more subtly than others, that perhaps there would be a day when I looked back on this style with, well, some pause.

What the hell did she know, my 16-year-old self wondered, exasperated by the mere suggestion with my signature audible eye roll.

Turns out she knew a lot. That hair forever remains a giant pile of stiff regret, and also an inescapable time capsule fixture of humiliation in my family.

There's probably some decent analysis out there somewhere about why so many of us teenage girls felt this was a good look, and why we went to such lengths to achieve it. Were we hiding under a shield in those fragile years? Or perhaps we were dressing a part to protect ourselves from the social pitfalls of the high school hallways?

Or—and I'm just spit-balling here—maybe we were just raised in New Jersey in the '80s and we really thought we looked good, as we became self-fulfilling stereotypes that could have put us on a long-term style trajectory with a *Real Housewives* franchise.

That awful and voluminous perm was definitely the most outward sign of what I regretted in my high school years. It's the easiest thing to point to and wish I'd done differently. And, yes, if given the chance, I'd march right into the Department of Life Moment Do-Overs and file a priority application immediately, while frantically waving my 1989 photos. But there were so many other things about those years— choices that shaped who I am—that I'd love another shot at. Because at some point along the way, those years defined me in some binary terms and conditions to which I never should have subscribed, or at least not without some fine print caveats and the representation of a Debate Club captain.

OH, YOU'RE A WRITER. YOU'RE NOT GOOD AT MATH.

GODDAMMIT. TAKE ME BACK TO MRS. DEBLOCK'S ALGEBRA I CLASS, stat, so I can re-do math. Give me all of the math, so I can ignore the ongoing suggestion by teachers and guidance counselors that, because I had a knack for writing, I had found my strong suit—I couldn't also excel at math, and that was okay. You know what? The repeated power of that suggestion had a big impact on me well beyond high school. It guided how little I rounded out my liberal arts classes in college in order to avoid Probability and Statistics. It led me to a corporate life-time of hating workplace finance meetings, thinking I couldn't absorb the nuances, or even have a qualified seat at that table. Because I was the writer girl, not the math girl. It creeps back into my life even now, as I supervise my kids' homework.

Take me back and show me that I'm not committing right here and now to decades of assuming I'm just not good at this. Believe in me the way that the English Department did, by throwing more at me, pushing me, and making me slug through *The Heart is a Lonely Hunter* (the literal worst), *The Odyssey,* and *Ulysses* (alternate title: *Just Kill Me Now, Please, With Irish Whiskey*), even when I thought it was tough and unnecessary. Tell me I will use math in my career because I am going to be accomplished and well-rounded.

You're the funny friend. Not the pretty friend.

Yeah, it turns out that wise-ass girls with a brain make many teenage boys highly uncomfortable. But still, no, you don't get to paint me as The Funny One and not One Of The Pretty Ones just because I am quick-witted. Fun fact: I was both, and shame on me for not knowing it at the time (despite my gravity-defying perm, prominent orthodontia, and acid-washed jeans). Why? Because I was parsed into this role of the sarcastic one who didn't put up with a lot of crap from boys drooling their chewing tobacco into bottles while surrounded by giggling, agreeable girls.

One of my most refined talents from a young age was the accuracy of my bullshit meter, having come from a long genetic line of similarly skeptical people. And although a cherished trait, it did land me oftentimes on the social periphery. I took this Funny/Call It As I See It, But Not One Of The Pretty Ones identity with me to college and possibly beyond, dragged it around and leaned on it far more than I should have. How ridiculous. Where were the Tina Feys and the Amy Poehlers then to show me that the Funny Girls can be so much more? If only my 1989 self could see that funny and snarky were not disqualifiers for being attractive, successful fucking badasses. I know this now, but it's less impactful once you reach an age when you start applying eye cream with a firming solution before bed.

I'm not blaming anyone else for these 1980s dynamics—this is the way things were (if I end this sentence with "back then," please just meet me at Bingo at three in the afternoon, followed by an early buffet dinner). Maybe the perm chemicals seeped into my brain and clouded my judgment, because Lord knows the tanning beds didn't turn out to be harmless. And if I'm being honest, the hair wasn't the only style problem back then. There were also big, elaborate accessories, multiple popped collars, neon, ruffles, and so much more. Even the music—it was loud and offensive and synthetic. It was all so big, so excessive. So assaulting on the senses. And underneath all of it, so much was happening. (Why on Earth did I not major in psychology? Oh, wait, probably because of the math pre-requisites.)

As the height of my hair has settled and even outright flatlined at times over the years, one consistent habit I've had since high school is that my worries, ideas and most plans come about in the dead of night. After I'd untease my 1989 hair and remove my make up, I'd play my cassettes and CDs for hours into the night, wishing I'd understood the math homework and instead writing short stories to fill my brain and my journal, because they came easily. It was then when I wired my life-long body clock to stay up far too late in the quiet to simultaneously accomplish things and worry about every issue over which I have no control (the latter being my specialty). Now, some 30 years later, that has not changed. The things I accomplish and the stories I write and the worries I count have all evolved over time, but their space to breathe and flourish still exist well past an acceptable bedtime. It is a distinct part of who I am and how I operate.

At 16, I worried about math and boys and fashion and being with the right friends, and at 46 I worry about parenting, about my kids being with the right friends and everything else that affects them.

My daughter is nine years old. She is a go-getter who will try anything, anticipate what's next and report back on the nuances of any given situation. Her heart swells with kindness and generosity. Her sense of adventure is boundless, and she does not miss a single thing. Late at night, when I worry and plan and think, I hope she will grow up to surround herself with girls and other influences that won't chip away at her fabulousness, but I wonder how realistic that is.

I want the world for her—all of it, because she will grab it and harness the hell out of it, if given the chance.

If she's not told she has to make choices between things at which she can excel.

If she's not told she can be some things but not others.

She has to know that she can be an All of the Above answer—plus the bonus essay.

KIM FORDE WRITES ABOUT THE ART OF DOMESTIC FAILURE ON HER blog, The Fordeville Diaries. She has appeared in the NYC production of "Listen to Your Mother," and has written for The Huffington Post and Scary Mommy. She was twice named a Humor Voice of the Year by BlogHer and, against all odds of writing full sentences when her three kids are home, this is her seventh humor anthology. When not busy managing her Starbucks addiction and healthy fear of craft stores, she can often be found carbon dating items discovered in the depths of her minivan. She may also spend more time on social media than she is prepared to admit.

⚘ 22 ⚘

WHAT IF YOU FLY?

BY JOY HEDDING

What if you fly? I look down at my wrist and see my bracelet. I'm about to take my first certification exam as a snowboard instructor. My classmates are 15, 17, 19, and 31.

I'm 42 years old and have been snowboarding for considerably less time any of these other riders. All have been riding for more than a decade. I'm in year five and this is my first year teaching on the snow. I'm sweating. A lot. "Fearless" reads my other bracelet. "Never Give Up" is on my watch band.

As I take off my bracelets and watch—wristguards, yo!—I repeat each in my head. Over and over.

I get my teaching task for the exam. To pass we must teach an assigned task to our classmates while being observed by the clinic director. We have to instruct in a particular manner and nail the teaching methods. I almost throw up. "Boxes." I have to teach boxes. Boxes are terrain park features a rider or skier can glide across, jump onto, end tap, or slide perpendicular across. In my case, I've ridden many a box on my bum. I'm fearful of falling face first onto a box and have avoided them like the plague since a bad wipe out two seasons ago. On a snowboard, boxes are not a thing I love.

What if you Fly? Fearless. Never Give Up. What if you Fly? Fearless. Never Give Up. What if you Fly? Fearless. Never Give Up. What if you Fly? Fearless. Never Give Up.

You know what? I nailed it. I did it. I did fly. I passed, got my pin, and more inspiration. Now I'm going after my Level 2 certification. In the past few years something has changed. I've changed. No longer do I let fear stop me. I go after what I want. My resume is long, curvy, and disjointed. Software developer, house cleaner, writer, weapon systems instructor, mathematician, mom... all of these things make up me. But not a single one defines me. I'm a moving target for definition. I define me. I want my children to see that a degree doesn't have to dictate who you are. It can be a part of who you are and lead you to any path you choose. It took me until March of 2018 to find my passion. My real and true passion. I wouldn't have found what lights my fire without the long and often circuitous path I've traveled. Remove any of my past experiences and I may still be on the search.

I've been up and down. I've loved jobs and hated them. Sometimes at the same time. But I pushed through. I knew my happy was out there. There have been months, years even, when things simply didn't make sense. I had these little people watching me get through my days. I noticed they emulated things I did. Little things. I drink water with no ice. Three of my four do this. I loved a cold can of soda first thing in the morning. One of them started to try to do this and I quickly gave up soda and switched to coffee. (They never have picked up the making your bed as soon as you wake thing though – it's still something on their chore list.) I am not capable of sitting and 'just' watching television. I have to keep my hands busy—folding laundry, making dinner, stretching—doing something other than just sitting. Watching my children fidget as I do has taught me to seek my calm and if that means cuddles or counting to ten while I make my mind and body quiet, I do it. I want them to be able to be in the moment.

If my kids were emulating the little things, what else were they picking up on? I decided I didn't want them to see me simply 'getting through' my days. I wanted my children to see me embracing life, going after dreams, picking myself up after a fall, and figuring out what to do after a success. Sometimes succeeding is as difficult as failing. Then it's time for the next step. That step can be terrifying.

My oldest is off to college in a few weeks. His path has yet to reveal itself. We had an argument where he succinctly nailed the issue I was having. "I'm adulting. Just not the way you want me to. I'm making decisions and dealing with stuff. In. My. Way."

What if you fly?

What if he flies? Isn't that how we raised him? We get these children for a few short years if we're lucky. We teach them to be independent, self-sufficient humans that we set loose on this planet. He's simply doing what we've prepared him to do his entire life. What if he flies? My girls are still home for years yet. I need to remind myself to be fearless. I don't even own makeup. My 12-year-old ("nearly 13" I hear as she reads over my shoulder) helps me pick out clothing. My 15-year-old keeps me in on what slang terms to use and which are "so last year." My little 10-year-old is so tech-savvy she figured out how to call me on the computer (I had password protected) when our phone lines were down.

My oldest daughter is in the throes of high school. Learning to drive, navigating changing relationships, trying to care for her friends, and already—ALREADY—forgetting that she, too, needs care. I strive to make her understand that taking care of herself is not being selfish. If I can instill in her the drive, the fearlessness to go after her dreams —whatever they may be—I will have done part of my job. She's already on her way, carving a beautiful path. Her journey already has twists and turns, even a few circles, but it belongs to *her*. We talk frequently about the future and yet I remind her to enjoy *today*. Live in the moment so you don't lose today's happy wishing for tomorrow. We are forging that relationship that one day will be a deep friendship. She's a pretty amazing human.

My littles. They aren't so little anymore. Each is nearly as tall as me. Although we all look alike in some ways, we are drastically different. Physically, emotionally, and personality-wise. Feisty in their unique ways, they will own their worlds. One is ready to take on each day, balls the wall, bull by the horns, and full of more energy than a classroom of kindies. Her happiness is infectious and even when she's down, she'll flash that megawatt smile, giggle, and find her path back to happy. She's my mini-me and while I see epic battles in our future, I also see the beginnings of the closeness we will share.

The other greets the day in her quiet, calm, self-assured manner. She observes and puts a plan into action that others simply follow. This one a natural leader although I don't think she yet realizes it. She doesn't say as much as the others, yet the words she chooses to share create a spark in those around her. I never want her to lose herself in the ever changing landscape of middle school and the challenges she will encounter. As she gains confidence, she will soar. One day she and I will be confidants.

How? How did I get so lucky?

Teaching each of these children to fly while learning myself has been a challenge. If you've ever flown, the crew always reminds you to put on your mask before assisting others if there's an emergency. I needed to take time, teach myself to fly and be fearless, before I could teach them. And they watched. They saw me take a beating during falls on my snowboard, get rejection after rejection writing, dismiss toxic friends, and stagger through challenging work days. I got up each time. Sometimes more slowly than others, but I always got up. They also watched as I chased after and caught a few of my dreams. At times I feel guilty for leaving them for an extra week in the winter to be in the mountains. Then I remember. I remember I'm taking care of me, setting a good example, and will come home refreshed. My cup will be full and I'll be ready to face another day—whatever that day may be.

My kids see me navigating life a with a smile. Because life is too short to not get after it. Go for it. If you don't ask, if you don't try, if you don't seek... let's flip that around. Why not ask? Why not try? Why not seek? If my children try, I consider what they did a success. Sometimes that first step is the hardest and taking it needs to be celebrated. Played a ball game that didn't go well? Did you have fun? WINNER WINNER CHICKEN DINNER. Tried a new trick on the snowboard and ate snow? Are you ready to go again? Yes? GAME ON. Life is about seeking your happy. And enjoying the path to find it.

If you're always waiting on the next step, you're wasting what's right in front of you. If you're not happy, change your path. Be empowered. You don't have to be stuck. Take the challenge of where you are right now, map a route forward towards what you want and take that first step. No. *Leap* for that first step. You can do it. If you find that path has led you to the wrong location, try, try again. Keep on trying because *what if you fly?*

My happy is out there waiting for me. I've got to go now. It's time to take another step. My kids are watching.

JOY HEDDING IS A SNOWBOARDING FANATIC AND LOVES TO SHARE her exploits – snowboarding and otherwise – on Instagram. Frequently funny, always honest, and occasionally serious, Joy blogs about everything from dealing with teenagers to navigating life after PTSD. Joy has been published in Surviving Mental Illness Through Humor *and* Only Trollops Shave Above the Knee *and been featured on RealityMoms.rocks and UrbanMommies.com. Her blog is Evil Joy Speaks and you can find her on Facebook, Twitter, Instagram, and Pinterest.*

BETTER THAN A BOYFRIEND

BY DORRIT CORWIN

The summer of 2013 was my second of five summers spent at all girls sleep-away camp in rural New Hampshire. I was ecstatic to be back with the friends I had made the year before in an environment that fosters creativity, collaboration, and personal growth. To this day, there is no place where I feel as safe and as genuine as I do at camp.

Upon my arrival, I was greeted by familiar smiles from far and wide, as well as many new faces. By the end of day one, I knew almost everyone in my bunk by name, except for one girl who hadn't said a single word to anyone. She sat in the corner with her rainbow loom, vigorously folding rubber bands over plastic pegs to create bracelets that symbolize friendship, though she didn't yet have any friends, herself.

I asked if she would make me one—not because I thought she was cool and wanted to actually be her friend, but because her bracelets were cool and I wanted to wear one. At twelve years old I was already fixated on my relationships and how others perceived them. A necessary break from our fabricated Instagram lives for a month meant popularity was determined by how much skin was showing between your wrist and your elbow. The more friendship bracelets you wore, the more friends you had.

The girl finished my bracelet later that evening. She tightened it around my wrist and looked at me through doughy aqua eyes. "I'm Sophie," she said, "I'm from Connecticut." She already knew exactly who I was and where I was from because I was so excited to be back at camp that I hadn't shut up all day. I was fairly certain she thought I was insane and that she had absolutely no interest in the bracelet she made me acquiring any kind of deeper meaning of friendship. "It's nice to meet you!" I said, "You're really good at making bracelets."

It wasn't a "and the rest was history" moment, but it was certainly a start. Due to the close proximity of everyone during camp, bonds build quickly. Each day that passes feels like a week, and each week feels like a month. On our walks to and from the waterfront, Sophie and I talked music, politics, and family life. By our third or fourth trip back from water skiing, Sophie was so captivated by the stories I had told her about my grandmother that she decided to write her a letter. Soon, they were exchanging notes weekly, and my grandma was booking a plane ticket for Sophie to come meet her the following February.

It was like talking to a mirror. Sophie and I would sit on my top bunk during rest hour, my iPod on shuffle, flipping through home magazines and designing our very own beach house. I'd skip a song with the assumption that no one but me would actually listen to it, and Sophie would ask me to go back because she knew by the sound of the first three cords that it was one of her favorites.

It didn't take long for us to become recognized as a dynamic duo of sorts. We harassed the camp photographer to take photos of us for our parents. We showered together (in side by side showers), brushed our teeth together, and stayed up late together, ranting about our disappointment in certain bunkmates' limited knowledge of current events and the American government. Together we neglected to complete our chores, took ourselves on impromptu adventures, and made our counselors' jobs extremely difficult. Yet, some of these counselors have remained our dearest friends and supporters as they have watched our relationship grow and blossom into something incredibly special.

Over the next three summers and two years, Sophie and I would grow so close that by our final summer at camp, we'd shed a tear not out of the fear of never seeing each other again but because we both knew that the second we crossed the border into Massachusetts, we were losing a vital part of our childhoods. We'd never again be enveloped by greenery and surrounded by our best friends without the distraction of technology. Every time I'd see her after our final campfire, my iPhone would be in my back pocket. It wouldn't necessarily be a bad thing, but it would never be the same.

Two years have passed since our final campfire, but our friendship has only grown stronger in each other's absence. I talk to Sophie every day – multiple times per day. Since she is always three hours ahead of me, she wakes up to texts that contain random thoughts I have between 9 p.m. Western Time and 6 a.m. Eastern Time, and I wake up to a good morning text from her. We send each other memes, sometimes the same ones without even meaning to. We pick out each other's outfits. We wish each other good luck on every test we take. We know each other's weekend plans. We wish each other's parents happy birthdays and happy anniversaries. We track each other's locations, and when the blue dots on the map meet together, it's like the stars have aligned.

Even our friends at home know that while our bonds with them might be strong, the bond we have with each other is on a completely different level. When I went to visit Sophie in Westport this September, she took me to a party at her friend's house. As I walked downstairs into the furnished basement, a setting I don't normally encounter in Los Angeles, everyone stopped what they were doing and sprinted in my direction. "Dorrit!" they shouted in unison, "We have heard SO much about you!" Since this was true, it was like I'd known them all for years.

The same has been true when Sophie has visited me. She crashed my Thanksgiving dinner this year, and it was as if I simply gained a twin at the table. My parents treat her like their fourth child and my grandparents like their sixth grandchild. We are so frighteningly similar that we've had the exact same feelings towards every college we've each visited on separate occasions, so her mom eventually figured that rather than waste time and money touring a bunch of schools, they'd just use my list!

Sophie is the only friend I've ever had who I've never had a legitimate fight with. We never argue, and we never disagree because we are simply the same exact person. It's not like the cliché of a best friend who is more of a sister because I fight with my sister all the time about trivial matters. Sophie falls somewhere between a best friend and a lover—like a boyfriend, but better.

Whenever we're together, our lives miraculously seem to change for the better. The weekend adventures we've planned to New York City and Boston have worked out so seamlessly that being with her truly feels like a dream. We've decided that since we are quite literally each other's lucky charm, we'll be living together after college in an apartment in New York City. We'll both hit our strides at the exact same time because living together will be the ultimate dream. We'll be each other's maids of honor, have our kids at the same time, raise them together, and vacation together... Our husbands will be there, too, I guess.

Most teenage girls fantasize about weddings, college, and tropical vacations, but I fantasize about my truly wonderful and irreplaceable best friend. It's almost like we're dating. People have asked me if we are. And honestly, if we weren't straight, we would make the long distance relationship thing work and be everyone's favorite power couple.

Yes, the friendships I made and life skills I learned at camp changed my life. But the five summers I spent at camp were the only time periods during which I had no access to my phone and the Internet, which is something I took entirely for granted. Since my final summer in 2016 when I went without my phone for a month, the longest I've spent without it is a few hours. And I hate it.

Yet at the same time, my friendship with Sophie would most likely not still exist if it weren't for technology and social media. While my relationship with my phone might be love/hate, my relationship with Sophie is absolutely nothing but love. I am so blessed to be her best friend, and I cannot imagine my adolescence without her as my rock, keeping me grounded and loved from 3,500 miles away.

DORRIT CORWIN, A SENIOR AT MARLBOROUGH SCHOOL IN LOS Angeles, serves as editor in chief of the art and literature magazine and writes a music column for the school newspaper. "Peaches & Mangoes," a short story she wrote at the Kenyon Review Young Writers' Workshop, won a Scholastic Gold Key and was published in Smith College's Voices and Visions Journal. The Rising Voices Fellowship combined Dorrit's passions for writing, Judaism, feminism, and social justice, and she serves on the Teen Editorial Board for Fresh Ink for Teens.

❦ 24 ❦

GO-GO GIRL

BY JENN BELDEN

When I was in seventh grade, I was a very awkward 12-year-old. It was the early '80s, when perms were all the rage, and my mother who disliked her straight, limp hair also despaired of *my* straight, limp hair, so off to the beauty salon she dragged me to rectify the situation with smelly chemical wave solution and colorful plastic curlers and mortification.

As the mentality at that time was a tight curl would last longer than a loose curl, a tight curly perm it was. I was more Jan Brady (with the bad wig) awkward than Marsha, sleek and popular. Combine that with glasses, horsey braced teeth, and hand-me-downs from an older cousin with a penchant for buying a shirt or pair of chinos in *all* the colors if she liked the style, and I was a sight to behold. Stir in a bucket of self-consciousness and a cup or two of self-criticism, and mix with a complete lack of athleticism and a massive love of books, and you have the hot mess that was me.

I was (as I still am) very introverted except when around my closest friends. It was helpful that both my seventh and eighth grade classes were composed of 14 people—seven boys and seven girls. Helpful, that is, until someone decided *you* would be the center of negative attention (for whatever reason they came up with).

Then as now, standing out was not a goal. Attention is one thing; it's safe to say most people enjoy positive attention, but being the *center* of attention created dread in the pit of my stomach.

Enter the period of the Go-Go Girl.

Thinking about it all these years later, I still cringe.

It was an ordinary day when I walked onto the playground for lunch recess, only to be greeted by the shout of "Hey, Go-Go Girl!" It took a few more shouts and laughs to realize the hoots and calls were directed at me.

Go-Go Girl? Being 12 or so, I possessed a vague idea of what a go-go dancer was, and believe me, that description couldn't be further from reality. We're talking about a plain schoolgirl in a Catholic elementary, complete with nuns, planted in a small town in the Midwest—and far from any dance club, with the closest thing to spur even the image of go-go boots being the *Soul Train* reruns after school. My dependable footwear at that age was either polished penny loafers (complete with a shiny penny in the little pocket), no-name deck shoes, or inexpensive tennis shoes purchased at Value City, and the closest thing to risqué might have been my purloined, forbidden copy of Judy Blume's *Are You There God? It's Me, Margaret.*

Soon, more boys in the seventh and eighth grades caught on and joined in to the catcalls when I entered a classroom or the cafeteria, or even during PE class when I was up for bat, or knocked out in the hated dodgeball matches. They may as well have been lobbing rotten tomatoes at my head for how mortifying it felt. In reality, it likely lasted only a few weeks, but it felt like forever and the humiliation was complete. I felt one step away from getting a bucket of pig blood dumped on me at prom, only without Carrie's supernatural ability and a really uninspired, dorky nickname.

It shouldn't have hurt so badly, hearing those words, but they cut deep. In hindsight, I think pain and distress from words like that come from the want for understanding. It's just a three-letter, one word question, "Why?" but it takes on gargantuan weight when seeking reason. If you're thin-skinned, it's simply excruciating.

Hindsight and experience revealed that there was likely no reason for it other than one (a) obnoxious or (b) equally awkward and trying-to-fit-in pre-pubescent boy overheard the phrase somewhere and decided it was as good a time as any to use it. Some adults even offered the suggestion that one of the boys might have had a crush on me, to which I responded in horror: "Why would they think that would make me LIKE them?"

It wasn't the first time that a stupid phrase lobbed my way utterly stopped me in my tracks. In high school, it was members of the football team who would hoot the nickname of the boy I was dating any time I walked into the cafeteria. (I broke up with him because it was easier than sinking into the metal folding chairs.) It happened later, in college, when the instructor of my two-dimensional design class mocked me with taunts of "middle class and mediocre"—because in his world, middle-class kids didn't suffer and one needed to suffer to create good art, and absolutely nothing I did met with his approval. At the end of the semester, I ended up changing my major instead of enduring the other requisite design courses he taught, my confidence crushed.

That I could allow the words of another to cut so easily baffled and frustrated me. My skin was tanned, smooth—and paper thin—and I might have sold my former altar girl soul to make it thicker. I loved words—but the perfect comeback struck later, when I was alone in my room replaying the day's latest mortification in my head.

Years later, I found myself blessed with a fearless, spunky and outgoing little girl. That side of her personality clearly came from her father; from me, she inherited anxiety and imagination.

Lucky kid.

But here's the rub—no matter how confident a face a person puts on, no matter how outgoing they might be, kids can still be hurtful and cruel and words still sting. And here I was, tasked with teaching her how to stand up for herself and not be cowed by the words of others, when I had failed so badly myself.

I would teach my girl to stand up for herself. She would develop her self-worth. She would learn to stand up for herself, and *never* accept "Oh, that's just how he shows you he likes you" as justification for any bad boy behavior. She would demand more.

She would be everything I wasn't, my heart sang as my fist punched the sky.

Which all sounds well and good in theory. It's easy to give advice when you are standing on the outside, but true learning and growth really comes from personal experience, and the ability of kids to be cruel or to box you out from the rest of your group is timeless. So we talk, a lot: about different ways to handle a situation, about when to get an adult involved, about when it's best to stick up for yourself.

We talk about how the best way to defuse a bully is to take away his or her power, which is really both your attention and your fear, and we practice responses because words *are* a weapon if used wisely to protect and not to stab back. Politely but dryly responding, "Wow, that took a lot of thought, thanks for sharing" and sealing it with a big smile before walking away confuses the pants off of most bullies. When a boy is mean to a girl, calling him on it with a surprised, "Is that comment supposed to impress me? It's not working!" takes the steam out of their approach.

She may also have punched a boy when he and his group of friends repeatedly followed her and a friend home from school, taunting and being cruel with words she would not even repeat to me, and refusing to leave them alone. I can't say it is something I would have done myself, but I suppose if you say "Stop, or else," you follow up with the "or else." She stood her ground and they never tried it again.

The biggest lesson to be imparted was the hardest learned by me, and that is that you should never, ever value your worth through the eyes of others. Be true to yourself and hold your head high, because you are wonderfully made; people that try to bring you down to lift themselves up should be pitied, and cut from your life (or pushed to the side until they come to appreciate you and all your bad jokes and quirks.) There's really no avoiding hurt, not if you want to live a full life that is true to yourself, so you allow yourself that cry and then you walk out tall and as confident as you can muster.

Find your people. Surround yourself with people who have your back, and who are just as goofy or awkward or curious or interesting as you are.

My daughter is petite and quirky and mismatched socks and one hundred percent her own person. She feels deeply, for herself and for others, and that makes her an easy target.

But now she can ask herself of the bully *"Would I choose to be friends with them if I were to pick first?"* and realize that the often answer is likely *"no,"* regardless of how popular that person is. She can hear the words thrown at her, and she can take a step back and figure out where they come from. (Is it jealousy? Is it hurt? Is it a badly worded demand for attention?) And she knows that is absolutely okay to cry when her heart or her ego or her confidence is wounded, because that is a perfectly normal response. Crying doesn't make you weak, but when you're done, you have to dry your tears and put on your game face and let them see that they can't beat you down.

And she knows she can throw a clean right hook, thanks to her mixed martial arts classes, although I pray that never becomes necessary. (The boys are a little afraid of her anyway.) Fierce balances well with unicorn tees and iridescent Converse high tops.

She still has the rest of middle school and high school to navigate, but the 12-year-old Go-Go Girl I was admires her and thinks she'll do just fine.

JENN BELDEN IS A WRITER AND MOTHER TO A TEEN, A TWEEN, AND one slightly mad spaniel. She is the voice behind the blog Momma on the Rocks, where she writes to avoid folding laundry or ever finishing her book. Her life goal is to finish a cup of coffee before she loses it somewhere in her house. Jenn's writing been featured on Mamalode and HumorWriters.org. You can find her at mommaontherocks.com and on Twitter @jenncaffeinated.

❦ 25 ❦

HERE BE DRAGONS . . . AND THEIR CUPCAKES

BY E. R. CATALANO

Y ou could say I went out of my comfort zone when I had my daughter.

First, with the whole pregnancy and childbirth thing. Of course, both of those are probably outside the comfort zone for most women. Unless their zones include nausea and heartburn. And they can chillax while having labor induced which doesn't work and so after 36 hours with no progress they end up having a C-section, which was my experience.

So pregnancy and childbirth were outside of my zone, which, if I'm being honest, is fairly limited. Its borders actually begin and end at my couch, where I like to sit reading a book and drinking chai, an old sweater stretched over my knees.

So why did I do it? Why does anyone do what they're afraid to do? Why did Magellan, who saw the map with "here be dragons" written in the margins, still say, "I'm going to circumnavigate this mofo,"—"circum" being the part of the word on which he'd hung his hopes? Because Magellan wagered the reward was greater than the risk.

I was just like an intrepid sixteenth-century explorer, except I was a twenty-first-century woman who'd reached her late-thirties with not a lot of desire but a lot of fear surrounding having a child yet still thought, "Well, Dwindling Egg Supply, it's now or never." Okay, so maybe Magellan had more ambition.

After pregnancy and childbirth, the child itself will require you to leave your comfort zone. A lot. The discomfort I've experienced since my daughter was born has ranged from physical discomfort—holding a crying sleepless child all night, being vomited on, frequenting unsavory bathrooms due to avoidable "emergencies"—to the emotional discomfort of socializing with strangers at kids' birthday parties, arranging play dates, and realizing you have become your mother.

Love for a child can take you way off the map. I'd also been afraid when I learned I was having a girl that I'd fail her somehow.

I'd long struggled with the question of what it meant to be a woman and if that was the same as being feminine. I've always felt uncomfortable with femininity, both because the rigid roles that went with it rankled me as a feminist—nurturing mother, demure and passive wife or girlfriend—and also because I felt myself a failure at achieving them—I didn't like wearing dresses, hated manicures and pedicures, etc.

Sure, these were clichés, but I was still afraid that if my daughter loved princesses or other girly things, my disapproval might show through and, at best, I'd ruin her fun, and at worst, damage her sense of self. How could I balance being myself with letting her be *herself*, especially if that meant hiding my opinion of what she liked? Turns out all my agonizing was for nothing since children have a way of thwarting our expectations, good and bad.

Here, after all, be dragons.

And by "here" I mean, in my own home.

I'm not being metaphorical. I think my daughter is a dragon. She certainly wishes she was. She LOVES dragons and anything dragon related. We have all the dragon Lego sets, tons of dragon books, toys, and figurines. She draws pictures of dragons. Her name, she told me the other day, is Drago the Destroyer. The next day it was Dragon Girl 19. Why 19? I asked. Because one and nine are her favorite numbers, silly.

Number confusion aside, dragons are way cooler than princesses, so I supported her in her love, bought all the dragon things, oohed and aahed over all the dragon stories she told me. Then came her birthday, for which she wanted a dragon theme, naturally. And here's where my whole "you be you and I'll be me" personal practice turned into "I'll be someone else so my daughter can be a dragon." All because I decided to make Dragon Fire Cupcakes from a recipe I'd seen on Pinterest.

Note: As you can guess from what I previously said regarding all things feminine, I am not a Pinteresty/arts-and-crafty/cake-from-scratchy kind of mom/person. But, god help me, I wanted to make my dragon daughter happy. Magellan faced sea monsters; surely, I could face decorative baking. Plus, you only live once, so you might as well torture yourself to please a seven-year-old who hasn't learned empathy yet.

This would be my first time using a pastry bag to apply icing. Previously I'd only ever used the tried-and-true dull-knife method. *And* I needed to apply three different colors of icing: red, orange, and yellow, the main three colors comprising "dragon fire."

On, now, to the tragic display of humanity that was me loading a pastry bag with three separate colors and trying to keep them separate and then trying to pump them through the icing-delivery-system nozzle thing that was supposed to create swirls of yummy-tasting, amazing-looking, verisimilitudinous dragon fire.

DRAGON FIRE CUPCAKES (AS MADE BY ME)

Step 1: Buy cake mix from the store and make the damn cupcakes.

(I used Devil's Food because that's the alias chocolate uses when it wants to seem "street.")

Step 2: Buy pre-made buttercream frosting, icing-delivery nozzles, pastry bags, food dye in red, orange, and yellow.

Step 3: Go back to store because you mistakenly bought two oranges and zero yellow.

Step 4: Watch online tutorials on how to add color to your buttercream frosting.

Then do that part, after washing your cereal bowl from breakfast because you only had two clean bowls and you'll need three (which later turns out to be four).

Step 5: Watch online tutorials for how to load a pastry bag in general and how to load a pastry bag with three different colors.

Try doing that. Get frosting all over your hands. Clean hands and watch another tutorial. Try again. Same result. Sigh. Press on. Literally. (By the way, do you know how much hand strength it takes to squeeze buttercream frosting through those icing nozzles? I wouldn't want to make a pastry chef angry is all I'm saying. They could probably crush your throat with one hand. While icing your funeral cupcake with the other.)

Step 6: Keep trying, Mother of Dragons!

Try a different nozzle. Try different wrist movements. Visualize the word "finesse."

Scoop frosting off cupcakes and get another bowl and then load that mixed-color frosting into a new pastry bag. Despair of ever getting the three colors to feed evenly. Have a vision of the future in which the pastry bag explodes, shooting frosting everywhere.

Your vision is half right.

The pastry bag does indeed explode, but the frosting shoots out in only one direction, onto your shirt, your dirty, tasty shirt. You probably should've put your antipathy toward feminine clichés aside and worn the apron you'd received as a gift from someone who doesn't know you.

Also, you should've noticed that you'd been losing bag integrity, but you'd been so focused on the icing struggle itself. Varying pressure, placement, and wrist flicks be damned, you cannot make the cupcakes look like they had on Pinterest. Orangey-red schmush is not dragon fire.

Step 7: Remember, perfect is the enemy of good, and decide that perfect cupcakes are as mythical as dragons.

AKA, you're done.

All told, I watched eight damn YouTube tutorials on icing cupcakes. How did they make it look so easy? Why didn't they warn me it was harder than it looked? How did that one lady with perfect makeup ice cupcakes while wearing trumpet sleeves? Trumpet. Sleeves.

Still, one thing I had learned, albeit too late to avoid the day's drama, was to have faith in myself. And by that I mean faith in *my estimation* of myself, and my skills, including where they fall short. As my inner motivational speaker often says, "Liz, you *can't* do this. But, sweetie, that's okay. You're good at reading. And drinking chai. I guess." She is supportive but pragmatic.

So my Dragon Fire Cupcakes were not what I'd hoped, and it took me so long I was unable to finish before my daughter dragon came back from an outing with the Husband.

When she came in, she saw the sugary crime scene, and looked at me like, *Explain.*

I told her I was making Dragon Fire Cupcakes for her birthday and she looked at the cupcakes for a few moments before turning back to me, and patting my frosting-covered hand, she said, "At least you tried. That's what's important."

Empathy, after all.

E. R. CATALANO IS THE MOTHER OF ONE EVIL MASTERMIND LIVING IN Brooklyn, New York, and writes a humor blog at zoevstheuniverse.com. She is a contributor to But Did You Die? *and* I Just Want to Be Perfect, *the previous two books in the* Pee Alone *series;* The Bigger Book of Parenting Tweets; *and* Lose the Cape: Never Will I Ever (and Then I Had Kids); *and her humorous essays have appeared on* McSweeney's, RAZED, The Huffington Post, Little Old Lady Comedy, MockMom, *and* Scary Mommy, *among others.* Today Parents *has also named her one of the "Funniest Parents on Facebook." Though some may say she exaggerates when it comes to the antics of her seven-year-old offspring, her actual fiction can be found online and in literary magazines. She's currently working on a novel about Nancy Drew called* Becoming the Girl Detective *as well as a collection of short stories called* Prove You're Not a Robot. *Please follow her on Twitter at @zoevsuniverse and on Facebook. She needs all the validation she can get!*

❧ 26 ❧

THIS ONE IS FOR THE GHOST
GIRLS

BY KIM BONGIORNO

I was born a ghost girl.

Colorless and silent, I floated into my family and settled in place at the end of the line. It didn't take long for me to understand that my invisibility was a gift.

Our home was pungent with a potpourri of order held in rough dishes of fear that would appear in every room with no notice. The floors were patterned with uncrossable lines drawn years before I arrived, color-coded by gender. I had many more lines I could not step over than my brothers. Girls cooked, baked, set the table. Girls swept, washed, hung the laundry. Girls were to be barely seen and never heard. If they were heard, it was when called upon and only a recording of what they had been told girls were allowed to say or think or report.

When I was little, none of this made me angry. Logic told me it was wrong, but I was too busy learning and following the rules to bother with feelings. Emotions, opinions, and words were things I kept pressed inside in my belly. Those were bright, colorful adornments too risky to release: they'd draw attention. Luckily, I wasn't particularly striking at the time. Beauty and pigment weren't interested in phantoms.

It was exactly as it was supposed to be. I remained, if anyone bothered to glance my way, benign. Men didn't bother hiding their disinterest in my presence. They never asked why I had come.

Eventually, I became old enough to go to school. In a habit of watching and reading people rather than engaging with them, I got to know my classmates and teachers well before they knew me at all. I was the peaceful apparition in the schoolyard, one they became so used to they'd forget it was there. But my name was still on the class list, so sometimes I was invited to social gatherings. I used them to collect more data. One thing was clear: Whether at a home, restaurant, or roller rink, the men were in charge and the boys were in training to be in charge. Not all of them took advantage of their positioning in hurtful ways, but they didn't seem too bothered by having an advantage that hurt the beloved girls and women in their lives. They weren't offering to give it up. Girls craftily achieved power within their gender by means of small cruelties played out by withholding friendship bracelets or sleepovers in front of an audience.

I got older.

I stayed silent.

I kept watching.

Other adults took my silence and restraint as a sign of maturity, and at an age far too young to be in charge of other human beings I was asked to babysit. The family consisted of an exhausted woman in frumpy, ill-fitting clothes and a sharp-dressed husband who barely looked at her unless they were making yet another child to put in my care for far below minimum wage. Over time I understood that the father and sons were of highest importance under that roof, watching the mother turn away time and time again, biting her lip instead of offering a correction, opinion, or need to a disinterested audience. At times when we were alone, she'd get lost in telling me stories over tea. Her light would slip through the cracks, dazzling me, but then her husband would come home wondering why dinner wasn't ready, spackling over what I just witnessed until I questioned whether I ever saw it at all.

I started feeling angry.

I stayed silent.

I kept watching.

It was this babysitting job that earned me the money to treat myself to something I never thought I'd wear: stripes. Slim black and white ones dashed horizontally across a skirt passable for trendy. Thrilled with my purchase and hoping I'd be seen that day at school, I walked into our kitchen to eat breakfast with my head held high. One brief scan of my outfit from his throne at the kitchen table and I wasn't allowed out of the house, for only a whore would wear a skirt like that. Sure, I hadn't yet so much as kissed a boy, but my hemline grazed the top of my kneecap and, really, what was the difference between me and a woman who allowed men to masturbate inside her for cash? Clearly nothing anymore, for this was a truth as declared by the man of the house. I faded from his presence like mist, pulled off the whole outfit, shoved it to the back of my closet, and changed back into something that felt like shadows again.

The skirt debacle piqued my curiosity, so I quietly paid more attention to what people wore, what people thought about what other people wore. The message was clear: I was not the only whore around. Men made the rules and it was so easy for us females to break them: a neckline that dipped, a hem that rode up, a heel higher than on grandma's church shoes and it was determined that the girl was easy. How could she possibly complain about a guy getting handsy if she dressed in a way that showed her appealing curves? She was asking for it.

I got angrier.

I stayed silent.

I kept watching.

Soon I had curves of my own and the hands started reaching for me. Boys in school halls, grown men at the movies, strangers passing me by as I trailed behind my mother during errands—they'd squeeze my butt or brush my breast or try to slide their hand up my thigh without permission, without warning, without even introducing themselves first. I was confused because I followed their dress code. I fought away the hands, but did not tell on them. Who would I tell? The people in power were on the same team as the people I wanted ejected from the game. There was no way they'd do it, that's not how you win.

When I was twelve someone saw me at the mall. As much as I

tried to fade from view, a professional scout recognized that the planes of my face formed angles that the light liked and my bones stretched up, up, up against my preference for shrinking away. It made them see dollar signs. They took a Polaroid and handed me a business card. They kept the Polaroid and I gave my parents the business card. When my father saw dollar signs, too, I suddenly had value. A fluke of genetics gave me value. Not my heart or mind or ability to make my brothers laugh so hard they spewed milk from their noses. It was what it was, and at least it was a safety net instead of a cage. I tolerated being inspected like a cow at auction, judged for what appealed to men over anything else. It wasn't different than any other day, really. I couldn't complain.

I got angrier.

I stayed silent.

I kept watching.

Despite my penchant for hiding behind walls of my own construction, I made a group of female friends. We climbed out of childhood into womanhood together. We forgave one another our missteps. We respected one another's boundaries. We traded lipsticks and laughs. When I was with them I felt safe enough to share my emotions, opinions, and words. I felt like a real person.

My friends began dating, so I dipped my toe in, too. I was hard to catch, often disappearing right when someone was ready to talk. If he stood very still, I'd eventually float his way, appear before him with a smile. But just because a boy genuinely liked me didn't mean he would stop putting his wants first. I backed off. I knew I deserved better than that. I'd try again and have to physically fight a date off of me after saying, "I said no" far too many times. I saw my friends get hurt over and over again, get physical with boys before they wanted to over and over again. Romance shouldn't be so sad. Love shouldn't feel like you've relented. None of it sat well with me.

I got angrier.

I stayed silent.

I kept watching.

It was a typical Thanksgiving dinner. Various male family members sat around the table as the girls and women set food before them, discarded aprons, ensured there was salt and pepper within reach of both ends of the party, as was expected of them. My mother went to grab one last thing as I sat with a straight back, hands on my lap, as was expected of me. Nobody touched their food until the last person sat. That last person was always Mom. As she rattled around in the kitchen—always a servant, never the served—my father made a derogatory joke about "broads," the term he regularly used when referring to women.

In that moment, the anger that had been building in me for years finally pushed me into full form. My flesh flushed pink with rage, my eyes steel with determination. My hands were blotched like bruises in white-knuckled fists, raspberry crescent moons forming on my palms beneath my nails. I was possessed with too much understanding of my failure to be nothing but a bystander and how that only helped the misogyny thrive around me. The disrespect of women had gone on too long. I had a choice to make: Take my anger at the unfairness I had experienced out on others in order to get my own power, or use it to fuel myself to help correct the balance of power for everyone. It was an easy choice. I slammed my fist on the table, silencing the room.

"You are never to use that word to refer to my mother or any other woman again."

I turned and looked him in the eye. "Never."

Everyone froze. My gut told me I would pay for the scene, but I did not care. Let there be witnesses.

I simmered, fists clenched, prepared. He did not get up. He did not yell. He looked at me as if a stranger had taken his youngest child's seat and he was contemplating what to do about it. He chose to tell my sister to pass the turkey. Everyone sprang into motion, flicking napkins onto laps, scooping vegetables onto plates. I slid my arm back under the table, unfurled my hands, and released the breath I had been holding, exhilarated.

The silence I wore for 16 years was peeled off by pure rage. Maybe I couldn't end misogyny altogether, but I had to start trying. My first step was taken while seated, but there was no question that I was moving in a new direction.

From that point on, I stubbornly became part of the solution.

I drew my own uncrossable lines. I stroked the hair of girls who needed to be told their true value. I made eye contact with boys and was clear about how girls are to be treated. I publicly and privately questioned authority. I donated time when I had that and money when I got enough. I continued being angry, watching and listening, picking and choosing when and how I could make a difference. They didn't all have to be big changes. Little ones add up. Hope grows. I did it imperfectly, but I tried. I got better at it over time.

I often thought of the sound of my fist hitting that table, announcing that I was present and to be accounted for.

The ghost girl still lives inside of me, though our form is more that of a vengeful revenant now. Able to hide in plain sight when needed, I relentlessly haunt the patriarchy to take misogynistic men down, strip them of the power they stole from women by force, coercion, or negligence. They think they can run, they think they can hide, but I find them. When I do, I reveal myself. I rattle my chains in their ears. I whisper with a grin, "I came for you."

KIM BONGIORNO IS THE AUTHOR AND FREELANCE WRITER BEHIND the blog Let Me Start By Saying. A crafter of everything from funny parenting tweets to fantastical fiction, her work has received praise from the likes of Buzzfeed, The Today Show, The Huffington Post, *and The Erma Bombeck Writers' Workshop. Kim lives in New Jersey with her family, who are wonderfully tolerant of her book hoarding tendencies. Learn more at kimbongiornowrites.com.*

27

OF STARBUCKS AND SHIN-KICKING—MY FRAUGHT CHILDHOOD ATTEMPTS AT FEMINISM

BY MEGAN SULLIVAN

Since I was old enough to understand the word, I've proudly called myself a feminist. I just wasn't always very good at it.

Oh, sure, I tried—my heart was in it, but that didn't mean I knew what I was doing. My parents encouraged me to read and play in the mud and do anything a boy could do, which are great lessons unless your kid is a loose cannon with a penchant for starting drama in the good name of Women's Rights.

Case in point: When I was seven, I had a friend named Nate who I was sometimes taller than, but usually not. (The one good part of hitting puberty a few years later was the delight of no longer being just the tallest girl, but the tallest student overall in the class.) Nate was into *sports*, like *football* and *wrestling*, and I was not, but I also was not about to be outdone in anything, at all, ever. This string of facts and personality—mixed with several strong opinions on how I could absolutely take Nate any and every day—and the echo of my mother's voice saying I was just as good as boys, led to me standing in his nice suburban front yard under the climbing tree, arms resolutely crossed, calmly telling him he had to hit me. There was no particular impetus beyond my fiery blood and need to prove myself, but whatever the reason, I was raring for a fight.

He refused. His mother said he couldn't hit girls, he told me. Obviously, I was a girl.

DOUBLE STANDARD, lit up the neon lights in my head, minus the exact wording because I didn't have the vocabulary for that yet. Still, I knew unfairness when I saw it, and I was out for blood and/or justice. Girls can do anything that boys can! I was *just* as hittable as him!

"You *have* to *hit* me," I implored/protested/yelled, stressing every other word like the worst Shakespearean actor imaginable. "I *told* you to. You *have* to!"

"My mom *said* I can't hit girls," he repeated, which is generally solid advice, but not to a quick-to-anger seven-year-old's ears.

"That's sexist. Your mom is sexist." Before he could get in a retort, I swiftly kicked him in the shins, my light-up Skechers scuffing up his skin.

And that's when he hit me. Tackled me, rather, which was what I had been going for, plus it circumvented his mother's directive. This was one of the unfortunate times when Nate was taller than me, so I did not win the wrestling match, but in my heart, I won the fight.

That was my elementary school contribution to women's rights—a literal fight for equality with misplaced motive but true passion. But I didn't stop there—I continued to be just terrible at being a feminist through middle school, too.

In middle school I was Not Like Other Girls. I was Not Like Other Girls because I read *books* and participated in *fandoms* and absolutely did *not*, God forbid, wear *makeup*. And, unlike Other Girls, I also had a nemesis, though I'm not even sure she knew it. Her name was Sophie (or actually it wasn't, but it's a good enough pseudonym), and I *hated* her.

Our conversations usually played out something like this:

INT: YEARBOOK ROOM, DAY.

EARLY IN THE SCHOOL YEAR. THE ROOM IS FILLED WITH fluorescent lights, motivational posters, and preteens who don't want to be there. MEGAN, budding emo, is seated at a computer, intently pretending that she knows what she's doing with the yearbook software, when she is approached by SOPHIE, popular and trendy.

                    SOPHIE
        (holding a vanilla Starbucks frappuccino)

Oh my God, are you wearing mascara?

                    MEGAN
   (voice quaking with the wrath of a thousand gods)

    NO.

                    SOPHIE
   (confused as to why MEGAN sounds as if she has
   just watched SOPHIE light her homework on fire
               and steal her lunch money)

Oh, it's just your lashes look really nice.
MEGAN, who refuses to ever look nice or understand how to accept a compliment she deems unworthy, stalks away with a glare to complain about SOPHIE'S stupid new iPhone 4 or listen to Evanescence, this cool indie band no one else has heard of that just really gets her.

TRAUMATIZING, I KNOW.
    I was convinced that I was special, that I was the exception, fighting alone against the impenetrable bastion of teenage girls' egos. But that was *my* ego speaking, my own arrogance convincing myself that I was better because I was different, even if I was neither better nor different. All those other girls read books and complained about

teachers and did everything else I could do; things as superficial as whether I wore makeup or talked about boys never really mattered. By trying to defeat the vague but formidable enemy of teenage girls as a group, I'd fallen into the trap of fighting myself.

Years later, I realized that purchases from Starbucks are not an indicator of someone's moral character (plus their cake pops are over-priced but really good), that Sophie was making an effort to be nice while I was making an effort to be an asshole, and that I should prob-ably stop insulting people for being stereotypical white girls when I, too, am a white girl. I realized that it's probably a good idea to teach your sons not to hit girls, though one can make an exception for a battle-ready one who is quite literally asking for a fight.

Now, at 17, I still don't think I'm a good feminist, but I'm trying. (I can see myself 10 years from now, laughing like "Wow, I really thought [insert common value that will abruptly become outdated in the near future here]?! What an idiot!") I'm learning, and I'm not hating on people for the way society paints them, and I'm not asking Nate (who is now several inches taller than me and a football player) to beat me up. I'm thinking before I act, and I'm trying to be a good feminist and a good person.

And I still do *not* wear mascara, thank you very much, Sophie, but I can take a compliment on my eyelashes now.

MEGAN SULLIVAN, 17, LIVES IN THE WASHINGTON, D.C., AREA with her parents, her two sisters, her dog, and a terrible cat. When she was 13, she decided she intended to be a writer, and a few thousand handwritten, painstaking notebook pages later, here she is, published! Megan spends her free time having strong opinions on everything, avoiding math homework, and talking people's ears off about Ancient Rome.

THE WOMAN SHE WAS MEANT TO BE

BY MARY KAY JORDAN FLEMING

"My head is *not* red!" my two-year-old declared from her stroller, eyes wide and back straightened. Not a typical reaction to a stranger's innocent compliment about my beautiful redheaded girl, but then my daughter was not a typical toddler.

Julia sported two tiny clenched fists in her newborn photo, one in the left-jab position. That was our first indication that she would take her place in a long line of strong women in our family, eventually earning the same force-of-nature reputation as the grandmother she never met. I loved seeing the similarities, including their unbridled displays of affection.

Each night at bedtime, Julia offered kisses and declared that her love was as boundless as the universe. "I love you more than a thousand universities!" She asked her dad to kneel by her big-girl bed and give "pats" to help her fall asleep. If his actions became too vigorous, she corrected his technique: "Just light, not hard." If he dozed off, she woke him to resume his post. It was important to follow protocol.

Julia was equally eager to express other desires and opinions. When our large energetic dog dragged her across the soccer field by the leash, she decided that she needed her own, smaller, dog to train. At dinner, she requested a "picky bowl" for dispatching wayward celery or cabbage or other non-approved ingredients. She hand-selected her clothing ensembles each day, including a pink tutu she wore almost constantly for two years. On tutu days, the major fashion decision came down to complementary footwear—everything from flip-flops to gym shoes to cowboy boots, regardless of weather.

My husband, Don, was sometimes exasperated by Julia's appetite for spirited debates. Would there be no opportunities for him to have the last word? I advised him to pick his battles. In the preschool world of green vs. purple pants, and I-open-the-package-in-five-seconds vs. Julia-opens-it-herself-in-five-minutes, there is much more at stake than time and technique.

Toddlers and preschoolers are curious and eager to learn about their world and abilities. We parents find it more expedient to make all the decisions, zip all the zippers, and buckle all the carseats, but children's developmental needs are better served by taking a longer view. What qualities and experiences will prepare an adult woman to solve her own dilemmas, defend her convictions, and advocate on behalf of herself and others? The skills needed to make informed decisions and resist bullying and peer pressure do not emerge overnight; they must be learned and practiced, starting early in life.

Julia's strong feelings and opinions came as a surprise to Don, who claims he was an easy-going and compliant firstborn. That left me— the youngest of five in a family where the choices were to speak up or be overrun by wisecracking older siblings—as the presumed cause of Julia's assertiveness. It didn't help that my brothers egged on my husband in this attribution. Even I recognized our similarities when Julia and her older brother were horsing around in the backseat of the car and Julia piped up in her best sing-song voice, "Helloooo, does anyone care that Stephen is punching me?" Shades of my own childhood.

Any remaining skepticism about our similarities was dispelled in a Mother's Day poem my daughter wrote years later.

People sometimes tell me
They see a resemblance between my mom and me.
If only they could see inside my soul,

There would be no doubt.

Julia's unique sense of style continued even after her two-year love affair with the pink tutu waned. She and her best friend dragged me to the fabric store to recreate the colorful, ruffly-sleeved costumes in Mary-Kate and Ashley Olsen's "Miami" video. The girls performed this song in their satin-and-leotard get-ups so often that they hatched a plan to record a music CD and sell it at our local drug store.

When the time came to choose a dress for First Communion, Julia preferred her own creative imagination to any of the poufy numbers at local department stores. She asked the seamstress across the street to fashion one according to her specifications: white lace top and shimmery skirt connected at a V-waist with an illusion neckline (foreshadowing her wedding dress) adorned by hanging teardrop pearls. Julia was the only girl in second grade to design her own dress and wear a flowered headband instead of a veil.

After the soccer-field incident, Julia succeeded in talking us into getting a second dog. With Meghan, the world's most headstrong bichon, Julia became the youngest handler in her Puppy Kindergarten class. She enjoyed the challenge so much that her first career aspiration was to become a dog trainer. Against some odds, she managed to teach enough obedience for Meghan to earn a Canine Good Citizen Award, complete an agility class, compete in a 4-H dog show, and become a popular therapy dog at a local nursing home.

After mastering dog training, Julia considered careers in pharmacy or law. I advised her to ask her cousin about her career as a paralegal. When I explained the difference between a lawyer and a paralegal, Julia quickly clarified her goal. "Oh, I wanna be the boss of whatever I be."

Julia's peers recognized her leadership and elected her to school president in grade school and senior-class president in high school. Her coaches selected her as captain of the track team because she practiced hard and cheered even harder for her teammates. Together, they went on to earn state titles and school records. She received the Most Distinguished Graduate award at her high-school commencement where the valedictorian later sought out our family for congratulations.

"Whenever I face a hard decision, I just ask myself what Julia would do."

I have long admired my daughter's ability to cultivate friendships, which was never more evident than at a bridal shower hosted by her fiancé's mom. Extended family and friends swarmed me at the door of the church hall. "Please come in, come in. We've been waiting so long to meet you. We love Julia!" My daughter's second family included a mother, two grandmothers, a sister, and dozens of cousins, aunts, friends, and neighbors. Without my even realizing it, she had done what we all hope our children do: She created a supportive network to sustain her marriage and adult life.

Today, Julia is a 27-year-old neuropsychologist-in-training who has earned grants, awards, and a coveted fellowship at a top pediatric hospital. In a recently completed internship, she submitted reports that were so thorough and scholarly her supervisors couldn't believe they were written by an intern. One particularly demanding mentor came to her office to ask, with some skepticism, "Who *are* you?"

That is the question that each of us must answer throughout life in a constant cycle of self-discovery and definition. As she has done all her life, Julia will speak her own truth to provide the answer.

Meanwhile, in this mother's heart, the memories are clear. Julia is the newborn who came out swinging. She is the toddler who corrected a well-meaning elderly woman in the middle of a department store by declaring that red hair did not give her a red head. She is the girl who traded her tutu for soccer and track uniforms. She is the confident college student who navigated foreign countries to study abroad, and the graduate student who ventured out on clinical internship a year early because she was ready to build a career.

Julia is every girl who is lifted up rather than shut down, celebrated rather than stifled, and encouraged to forge her own path with clarity and purpose. She is every woman who is given the chance to be her best self—the strong and capable woman she was always meant to be.

MARY KAY FLEMING IS A PROFESSOR OF PSYCHOLOGY AND WINNER of the 2016 Erma Bombeck Writing Competition for humor. She publishes online at HumorWriters.org, McSweeney's Internet Tendency, Boomer Café, Sammiches & Psych Meds, *and* Pulse: More Voices from the Heart of Medicine, *and contributed to anthologies about loss of a parent* These Summer Months: Stories from the Late Orphan Project, *and sisterhood* In Celebration of Sisters.

29

GIRL POWER SOMETIMES STILL REQUIRED DAD'S ADVICE

BY MANDY WAYSMAN

"If you take him back again, I will beat you and then I will find him and kick his ass."

Words of wisdom from my father. Oh, you didn't read it as advice? You read it as a threat? I guess I can see why, but I intend to convince you that it's not only advice but the best advice I have ever received.

First, I should tell you my father would never beat me. I mean, don't tell him that I know that. He's worked pretty hard at his rough exterior. I hate to be the one responsible for unearthing his sensitive side. He is the best kind of dad. The kind that knows how to do the manly things and will help in a heartbeat with car or house repairs. He cares a lot about his baby girl (me). He doesn't always know the right words to use to portray it, as evidenced above by the crap that spilled out of his mouth when I was bawling. To be fair, my dad's language he thought he was saying, "I love you and don't know why you are allowing this to hurt you. I would beat up anything that hurts you. This is a goshdarn pickle." This isn't an exact translation, but pretty solid if I say so myself. It's probably best now to explore why this advice was required in the first place.

My boyfriend had broken up with me. The boyfriend would be the "him" that was going to get his ass kicked if I took him back. He was my first boyfriend. My first "real" kiss. My first love. My first everything. I must not be saying that right because it meant everything to me at the time, yet as I reread that sentence it's not making me feel the urgency and heartbreak that was palpable for so long. I'm not getting that flutter in my gut with the spicy heat of heartache that travels up the throat into my face. The feelings that I thought I wouldn't ever get on the other side of.

When I was 16, I got a job at Sears. I went in with my friend, Tina. We didn't expect interviews that day. We were simply filling out applications. I may have been trying to put on a good show at attempting to get a job and crossing my fingers it would not pan out. Joke was on us (the standard for life experience) because we filled out the applications and then they wanted to interview us right on the spot. I would like to think that it was because we were so poised and presented ourselves very well. I'm not delusional though, so I'll be straight with you. We were dressed in cutoff jean shorts and tank tops. Classy. We got the jobs. I don't want to belabor this point or brag, but our personalities had a lot to overcome in the interview—and we did. My friend Tina got a job in the shoe department and I was placed in the children's department.

There was a handsome guy in the shoe department with Tina. He was super friendly to everyone. I was shy and reserved, so seeing him so completely at ease chatting with people was both confusing and kind of magical. I needed to get closer to the subject so I could discover what this magic was. I didn't say anything to anyone because I wasn't quite ready to play Peg Bundy to his Al. Important notes include: I had no plan on how to get closer to him, nor did I have any game whatsoever when it came to attracting boys.

Everything changed one night when I got a call at work from Tina. It might even have been at work. (We dialed each other to plan breaks.) It seems like something she would do during that time.

"There is a male specimen that is interested in you," Tina said. She really had a way of making things romantic, huh? Everyone needs a friend like that.

I think that I might have instantly blushed from head to toe. It must have been a slow time at work because I don't remember anyone attempting to pull me back together. No slap across the face with a "Pull yourself together, girl." After that didn't happen I tried not to sound too anxious to know who it was and failed. I said: "Tell me now."

Obviously, the specimen was my very own Al Bundy. I'm not here to rewrite how high school romance goes. So, that was the start of it. Tina had a party at her house where Al and I shared our first kiss on her deck. Her parents still live in that house and I'm sure they think about my first kiss every day. Unless they never knew about the party —in which case, never mind.

After the kiss, Tina asked me how it was. I said, "Lots of tongue." She told him to back off. Because that is what friends who find you male specimens do. They take charge and fix it, especially when you're uncomfortable.

We proceeded to date for three years. It was through my prom, my graduation, and him growing into a man. He graduated a year or two ahead of me. He was in the real world and renting an apartment and house. I did half days through my senior year and spent a lot of time with Al missing out on school things. All kind of cliché. To abandon high school friends, etc...to hang with the older man. I was okay with it at the time. I knew high school wasn't going to be the best time of my life. I "knew" it with all the confidence that a 18-year-old knows everything.

The boyfriend was someone who always had a plan. His plans changed a few times and reversed and then went back to the beginning. There was always a plan, though. I found that was very appealing. My plan was to just get through high school. When that was checked off my list, I had quite the opening in my calendar. Looking back, I don't remember a lot of plans being made together. He seemed to have a lot of his things figured out, but neither of us interjected with what *I* was going to do while he followed his. I would just marry him and move where ever he was and I guess have kids. It was so beautiful because I was so anxious about my future and having to decide. Staying with him was like not having to think or care about myself ever. How refreshing. No dreams to have to fulfill on my end. What a relief. I mean who wants to have the pressure? Just selfish, really...

Now sure, at this age I see that was probably red flags and sirens and smoke telling me that it's not great. At the time though, I wanted to support him. I wanted to support him so I could ignore me. Figuring me out gave me stress. Nodding my head to support him was very easy and perfect.

He broke up with me. Oh, were you blindsided by that coming in right here? Yeah, I was too. It was, I think, a little bit after Christmas, but I'm not sure. I was heartbroken.

Worse than that: I was pathetic.

Truth be told, for Christmas he had gotten me a necklace and there was a minute where I was afraid it was a ring. On some level I knew he wasn't for me. There were nights I told my mom that I didn't think he was supposed to be with me. I just never could break up because I never wanted to hurt him. Turns out not as big a blow to him as I would have thought.

Knowing that I didn't think we were totally meant to be, I still never thought he would leave me. I was completely co-dependent. I didn't want to figure out my life. I called him a lot. I cried a lot. I am so embarrassed. I'm so glad texting and social media weren't things. I can't imagine what kind of shame I would have brought upon myself with that.

Here's the thing. He eventually decided to take me back. That's a weird way to put it because it makes it seem like I did something and needed to make amends to receive forgiveness. No wonder my father wanted to beat me. The boyfriend wanted to break up with me before because he just didn't love me anymore. Just 'cause. The boyfriend's feelings changed. Now a few months later he loved me again. I'm fairly certain I should have seen right through that bullshit. Yet I remember feeling like it was an accomplishment to have won him back.

We dated another few months or year. I never felt at ease again. I always questioned if I was lovable enough now. If he was going to change his mind again. He got a job out of state. About an hour and a half drive from me. I traveled to see and stay with him occasionally. I had a little feeling that he might be cheating or looking. You ever hear someone say the name of someone and just know that there is feeling attached? I had that experience.

He broke up with me again. I carried on again like I had before. It was a learned reaction – and it worked before. I would take my phone to go in my walk-in closet and beg and cry and beg and pathetically try to find ways to talk to him.

He got a new girlfriend (pretty quickly). It was that name I heard him mention before that I had wondered about. He put her on the phone with me once. It stung in a way that I hadn't ever felt before. I was so embarrassed and humiliated. He wasn't doing the humiliation. Truth be told, I was relentless in calling him and looking back it was probably a Hail Mary attempt to be left alone. At the time it was the cruelest thing a person that used to love me could have done.

It was after one of these closet call cry sessions my father saw me and he said the wise words, "If you take him back again I will beat you and kick his ass."

I wish I could say in that moment it clicked. So often though the wisest words have to bounce around before they land. Weeks later I put it together. I was tying myself to someone who didn't care about me. Trying to make their fate intertwine with mine. Making the pain all mine. Loving someone means taking their lumps with them. I was willing to do that. He was definitely not. How is that ever going to work? How would that ever amount to anything? He didn't even care what lumps I was taking in my life (willing to be beat up.) I was a foolish fool that did fool-y things.

So my father was telling me not to be a fool. That this goshdarn pickle was over and I needed to not do things that I would regret. For example, like... hmm... let's say beating someone up. Do I believe that profound lesson was what he was selling in that moment? Yeah. My dad's been pretty solid when he steps in with advice.

The boyfriend married that girl, had kids and then divorced. He contacted me after the divorce and said he regretted our breakup. He would have wanted me back. I was with my husband and happily in love. He went on after that to marry and have more kids. I believe we are both happy now. Neither in danger of getting a can of whoop-ass opened on us.

No matter how good I get at Girl Power, it would never have happened without my Dad's advice. Ladies, don't take a beating (emotionally) for anyone that won't for you. Don't allow yourself the "easy" route of going along for the ride to someone else's plan. It's scary to make your own plan, but it's pretty amazing to feel it when you "make it."

MANDY WAYSMAN IS A FREELANCE WRITER FROM SOUTH DAKOTA. She is the mother of two daughters. She once watched all the episodes of the reality TV show Whisker Wars *and still doesn't know why. She has appeared in* Working Mother *magazine,* Lose the Cape: Never Will I Ever (then I had Kids)*, and* The Narcissist's Playbook. *Her work can be found on* Today's Parent, Sammiches and Psych Meds, Scary Mommy, The Week, Parent Map*, and many more parenting websites.*

THE SUM ALL FIGURED OUT

BY HARPER KINCAID

I am not your plot twist
Or your manic-pixie-dream-girl,
Solely existing
To make you better.
Nor am I your salvation
In a swishy skirt.
Like some cornflake cinnamon girl who
Walks around campus
Without shoes. You milk fed boys so high.
Greedy even.
Suckling on a fairy tale and a smile.
You boys can't get enough
But sorry, I'm fresh out.

I'm not the woman who brings home the bacon,
All fried up in a pan, served hot, bent over the counter.
Like the porn you sneak at work.
When you think no one's watching.
Is that why you like me in pigtails and Mary Jane shoes?

Man, you must be ten kinds of stupid, and yet,
I'm the one who's not enough?

I'm still not good at math,
But that doesn't mean I don't have the sum all figured out.
That the heart of a soul
Should never be measured by
A number on a tag
Or a grade
Or a ranking on a list.

My worth is not determined by
An algorithm
Or the number of followers
on Instagram.
Although, if I'm going to be really honest,
I wish there were more.
I wish I was more. Or at least enough.

Someday, the brain will convince
What the heart knows to be true.
But until then,
Underneath all my bravado
Is a big bucket of bullshit,
Protecting a heart made raw
By everyone's unmet expectations,
Especially my own.

BORN IN CALIFORNIA AND RAISED IN SOUTH FLORIDA, HARPER KINCAID moved around like a gypsy with a bounty on her head. She been a community organizer and a professional matchmaker. Ms. Kincaid is a published author, known mostly for her romantic comedies, such as The Wonder of You and her new release, Love in Real

Life. She also writes creative nonfiction, poetry, and, most recently, cozy mysteries and suspense.

She is a self-admitted change junkie, but is now happily settled in the cutest 'lil town of Vienna, Virginia, with her wife-whisperer husband, and their two girls.

❦ 31 ❦

GUIDEPOSTS FOR MY DAUGHTER
AT THE CROSSROADS

BY LESLIE GAAR

Dear Daughter,

You are nine now, fully halfway through the time it is supposed to take me to "raise" you. Your first nine years were dirty diapers and potty training, wobbly first steps and equally-wobbly first dance classes. And while we don't yet know exactly what this next half will bring, we do know that the end of it will see you setting out to face the world on your own. So while I still have you here with me, close by my side, at the crossroads of child and young woman, there are some things I want you to know.

People will judge you by impossible beauty standards. They will tell you you aren't tall enough, or you're too tall. You're not thin enough, or you're too thin. You need makeup, or you look like a clown. Soon, too soon, you will start to question your beauty, and I don't just mean your looks. At this point in your short life the only change you would make to your body would be the addition of a mermaid tail, but soon you will be tempted to pick yourself apart, piece by piece.

But they don't know that "Beauty" was the name of the melody drummed out into the world the second your heartbeat thumped through that ultrasound machine and into my waiting ears. The beauty of that sound, of that incredible gift slowly growing inside me, was lovelier than anything that could be found in the pages of a magazine, no matter how glossy the cover. That wonderfully wild, untamed song belongs to you alone, and its radiance can't be squeezed out of a tube or plucked off a shelf in a store.

People will make you believe your body's sole function is to be a dispenser of pleasure. In time, your body will be constantly evaluated, commented on, degraded, legislated, and maybe even violated by those who inexplicably think they have the right to do so. They will at once praise you for its appearance and crucify you for it based on nothing but their own selfish whims. They will try to make you forget that your body is a palace more wondrous than any built by human hands, and that it is ruled by one, and one alone.

But they weren't with you in the NICU during those small, anxious hours of a Texas morning nine years ago as your body, brand new and marble pink, fought and rested and then fought some more. They can't fathom the strength your body possessed, even when it consisted of fewer than six pounds. To be sure, your body is capable of pleasure in all its forms, but leaving it at that would be laughable. Creation and destruction, work and play, joy and pain, struggle and ease- these are only a few of the abilities already coursing through your veins.

People will demand that you keep quiet in countless ways, some more subtle than others. They will say you're not smart enough, that you're using the wrong words, the wrong tone of voice, the wrong moment, that you hold the wrong viewpoint. They will put words into your mouth and laugh your admonitions off. They will belittle the things you do say, wondering at your insistence on having an opinion at all. They will reward others who play their game, making you question your own voice.

But they don't know that you come from a long line of noisy women who refused to be silenced, and that you took your place in that line as soon as you came screaming into existence. Those women passed on to you a crown of outspokenness, encrusted with jewels of bravery and stubbornness and tenacity. The price of this crown is high, I must tell you. There will be times when you want nothing more than to take it off and just fit in. Don't. There will be times when you think you have lost it completely. You haven't. There will be times when it seems too snug or too loose. It isn't. It is as much a part of you as your wild, curly hair.

People will define your worth by what you can do for others. They will teach you an equation that places your womanhood in direct proportion to your ability to maintain a clean house, wash clothes, prepare meals, and produce and care for children. They will tell you these things are in your nature so many times that you will think something is wrong with you if the scent of fabric softener doesn't set you on fire. They will guilt you into this role of servant, making it seem far more important than any secret desire your heart whispers.

But they don't know that your hands, once chubby and small, now slender and elongated, have bigger aspirations than to fold endless piles of laundry. The books you curl up with on rainy days detail adventures of fairies and witches, not shiny kitchen sinks and perfectly vacuumed floors. You dream of becoming a vet, a ballerina, a chef, and a mommy, all in one spectacularly jumbled-up fantasy. Your worth is wrapped up in these dreams and in your "youness." Don't let anyone tell you differently.

I know these words mean little to you now, dear Daughter, but someday they will. And so, for now, my wish is that they seep into your skin and filter into your bones. Let them stay there, dormant, until you have need of them. Remember them when life becomes more complicated than it is just now, when your soul is crying out with a dissonance you don't understand. And just in case these words leave you, in case you forget, I'll be here to remind you of them, now, then, and always.

Love, Mommy

LESLIE GAAR IS A WRITER, EDUCATOR, AND PERFORMER WHOSE WORK has appeared in The Washington Post, Scary Mommy, Babble, and TODAY Parents' "Funniest Parents on Facebook." She is currently *writing her first book because, honestly, life as a mother of three, (twins and a singleton), just felt way too easy, and she wanted to kick things up a notch. Leslie blogs at lesliegaar.com, and can be found on Facebook, Twitter, and Instagram, particularly if she's avoiding work. She lives in Austin, Texas, with her family in a house that will never, ever be free of clutter.*

32

BETWEEN BREATHS

BY MIRANDA RAYE

One...

"Will you help deliver my baby?" The question was asked casually over coffee. A bystander might have thought my best friend was asking to borrow a cute top.

I nearly spit out my coffee. "What?"

"You know Randy is still out West for work. I'm confident he'll be back in time, but you know me. I like to be prepared." She flashed me her winning smile. "Will you be my back-up plan?"

Our adult friendship of ten years had begun at work. We were rookie high school teachers, fresh out of college, struggling to stay a day ahead of our students. I was going through some personal issues, willingly isolating myself from others. I remember watching Kathy in the staff lounge during lunch, mesmerized by her eternal optimism, laughing with fellow teachers as I silently munched on my PB&J.

I decided to send her an email which amounted to, "My life sucks right now. I could use a positive person in my life. Will you be my friend?"

She kept a copy and, four years later, read it at my wedding.

We have been through a lot. Bad breakups. Divorce. Diagnoses.

Premature birth. Death. We were roommates. Maids of honor. We were each other's cheerleaders through every event, both joyful and sad.

I was ready to be a part of another joyful moment.

"Of course I will!" I gave her a hug and then we went back to laughing and gossip.

Two...

"KATHY SAID THE CONTRACTIONS AREN'T TOO BAD. SHE'S GOING TO drive herself to the hospital."

"Like hell she is!" My husband proceeded to do an abrupt one-eighty in our Jeep Patriot and floor it to Kathy's house.

We were headed home from a Spartan football game, sleepy from sun and tailgating when Kathy called to say I "shouldn't be alarmed" but she was having some "really close contractions."

She was three weeks early and her husband, Randy, was still in North Dakota with no flight home. We were in Michigan.

It was go time.

Within minutes, my husband was dropping me off at Kathy's condo.

"I'll keep you updated," I told him, "but I have no idea how long I'll be gone. Give the boys a hug and kiss goodnight for me."

"I will." He squeezed my hand. "Take care of Kathy."

Kathy greeted me at the door, her face one of calm serenity in typical Kathy fashion. "I just need to take care of a few things..."

I pulled gently on her arm. "Let's go."

Three...

THE 30-MINUTE DRIVE TO THE HOSPITAL FELT OKAY. WHILE SHE WAS having strong contractions, she managed to keep her spirits up. In fact, we had a great laugh when I wheeled her in to the hospital and a sweet old lady looked over at us and said, "You look like such a happy couple."

In spite of the shared laugh, the absence of Randy hovered over us, leaving a flicker of fear in Kathy's eyes. As soon as we were in the hospital room, the first thing she said was, "My husband isn't here. How long can we wait?"

Kathy got her wish. We waited. And waited.

After a few hours, it was determined she was not yet ready to have the baby. When? They couldn't say, but when Kathy asked if we could go back home, they agreed. Fantastic! We had just found out Randy had secured a flight that would have him back in Michigan late the next morning. It was only seven in the evening now. He would make it.

Capitalizing on our good fortune, we decided to relive our lives as former roommates and order our two staples—B-Dubs and Cold Stone. Why we thought spicy wings and dairy was a good idea when she was having pre-labor contractions, I'll never know. With our take-out strewn across her condo coffee table, we ate, laughed, and enjoyed a trashy romantic comedy. It felt like old times.

As the night wore on, the conversation veered towards the more serious. Kathy asked to hear more about the story of my first son's birth. She had heard most of it before, but then I shared something more intimate.

"I'll never forget looking at Connor, then looking at my parents and thinking, Wow. *This* is how much you love me? I had no idea." I smiled at the memory. It was such a simple revelation, yet it had changed everything for me.

Four...

WE DECIDED I SHOULD DEFINITELY STAY THE NIGHT AT HER PLACE. We didn't want her to be alone until Randy got there. Her parents lived a couple of hours north and were on their way down as well. Soon, Kathy would be surrounded by her family.

It was almost midnight when I rested my head on the spare bedroom pillow. Two minutes later, I heard my phone ringing. It was Kathy, calling me from her room.

I had never heard her voice sound so strained before. "We have to go...now."

I don't remember getting her into the car. What I do remember is driving 90 mph on the dark, empty highway, adrenaline and the after-effects of spicy wings coursing through my body. Kathy was moaning beside me, eyes closed, her hand clutching the door handle for dear life.

Five...

No cute comments about what a happy-looking couple we were this time. It felt like a lifetime ago we had been in the hospital, even though it had only been about five hours. We were greeted immediately, and Kathy was quickly put through the rigmarole of hospital gown, IV, and cervical check.

Waiting was no longer an option.

Kathy and I are modest women. When given the choice between a form-flattering top or an oversized hoodie, the hoodie reigns supreme. Like most women, we have a love-hate relationship with our bodies.

Delivering a baby together changed everything. All of those predisposed fears about our bodies simply didn't matter anymore. Kathy was about to give birth, to literally bring life to the world through her body. And I was going to bear witness.

Stretch marks and dimpled skin can't hold a candle to that.

At first, we were awkward with each other. I felt clumsy, but my hands quickly took over and created their own kind of choreography. Squeeze Kathy's hand. Feed her ice chips. Rub her back. Repeat.

I acquired a newfound respect for my own husband in that room. Being Kathy's birthing coach was by no means as strenuous as giving birth (I had already given birth two times myself and knew there was no comparison), but still, I was struck by the sheer exhaustion of watching her strain and struggle, the feel of her hand grasping mine with a strength I never knew she had until that moment. She chose no epidural. That alone impressed me (I had taken it the first chance I could).

Time lost meaning that night. It comes in flashes.

Frantic texts from friends demanding updates.

Sweat.

Chatting with her parents in the waiting room. "No worries! She's doing great!"

The metallic smell of blood.

Her mother wearing a cheery yellow blouse.

Their faces, bearing excitement and fear and anxiousness, the faces of soon-to-be grandparents.

Stained sheets.

On the phone with Randy. "You need to be here! How much longer?"

Kathy hyperventilating, both in pain and exhaustion.

"Just breathe. Slowly, in through your nose, then out through your mouth."

Thankful she doesn't scratch out my eyes or shout obscenities for such feeble advice.

Dizzy exhaustion.

I lost track of how many hours we had been awake.

She tried every position possible. On her back. Standing. Crouched. Walking.

At first, she didn't seem to mind the delay. After all, she was still holding out for that small hope that Randy would make it.

Time was an ironic tyrant. We longed for his tyranny to end, yet were desperate to hold out a little longer.

After nearly eight hours of laboring, Kathy was finally told she had to have a C-section, and it would have to happen immediately. Devastated, tears ran down Kathy's face. Her pushing had been in vain.

Randy would not make it in time to see the birth of his first child.

Six...

I LEFT THE ROOM TO INFORM HER PARENTS AND JUST BROKE DOWN. It was unintentionally cruel as they immediately thought something was wrong.

"No, no, she's okay, she's fine. I'm just so disappointed for her! It's not fair!" As I cried, her father held me.

"It'll be okay," he told me. "She's strong."

"Yes, yes she is."

As I made my way back to the room, I became acutely aware of how ill-prepared I was to help Kathy with this phase of her delivery. Both of my children had come naturally; getting a C-section was a whole new realm.

They took her away to prep her. I remember sitting in that empty room, silent, mentally preparing myself for what was to come. After what felt like hours, but was only minutes, the nurse came to retrieve me and walked me back to the surgical room.

Seven...

IT WAS COLD. KATHY WAS LYING FLAT ON HER BACK WITH HER ARMS extended, the metal table looking harsh against her hospital gown and bare skin. A sheet hung vertically from the ceiling, shielding the lower half of her body. I was thankful for the face mask covering my look of fear.

"Where do I stand?" I asked awkwardly.

"Sit here on this stool and hold her hand. Don't look behind the sheet."

"Okay."

I held Kathy's hand, still strong. She had Randy on speakerphone. His plane was just touching down. He would be arriving soon. So close, yet too late.

Eight...

THEN THE SHAKING BEGAN. IT SCARED ME, BUT IT SCARED KATHY more. Her whole body started convulsing.

"Normal," we were told, but there was nothing normal about it for us. I remember her grip becoming firmer.

It was shocking how quickly the baby came after the hours she had endured.

"Here he is! A healthy baby boy!" the doctor exclaimed as she held him up for us to see.

"I can't stop shaking." Kathy's eyes were wide with fear. "I don't want to drop him. You hold him."

"Me?" I was aghast. What right did I have to hold her child first? "No, I can't."

"Please." Her eyes met mine. She smiled. "It's okay."

The nurse handed him to me gently. I remember his cone-shaped head, wrinkled red face, and delicate hands. He was perfect.

"Welcome, Bradley."

It was not long before Kathy's shaking subsided and she was able to hold him. I felt a surge of relief as I passed him over to her. This was her moment, not mine. Yet, here we were, sharing this joyful moment together.

Nine...

BACK IN THE HOSPITAL ROOM, I STOOD BESIDE HER AS SHE LEARNED to nurse him. Her parents joined us, their faces in awe as they gazed upon their first grandchild. It was a quiet, beautiful moment—a mother looking down at her daughter as her daughter looks down at her son.

Kathy let out a little gasp, then met my eye. "You were right," she said, her eyes glistening. "I had no idea." She grasped her mother's hand, gazing up at her adoringly.

I quietly left, both as participant and witness to the miracle that is being a woman.

Ten.

MIRANDA RAYE IS A HIGH SCHOOL ENGLISH AND THEATER TEACHER in Southeastern Michigan where she lives with her husband and two young boys. Her blog, Mommy Catharsis, is about raising a child with autism. She has also written for Scary Mommy, Sammiches and Psych Meds, Mamalode, The Mighty, *and* Finding Cooper's Voice. *Connect with her on Facebook, Instagram, and Goodreads.*

❧ 33 ❧

WONDER WOMEN—THE NEXT GENERATION

BY WHITNEY DINEEN

R aising girls is a journey. Much like climbing Mt. Kilimanjaro
stark naked, with one leg, no food, covered in only honey
and optimism is a journey. In other words, it's treacherous,
wonderful, exhilarating, and possibly deadly—the jury's still out on the
last one.

Being a girl myself, I know how important it is to guide my daughters and instill confidence in them. In a world that's going to try to tear
them down, I need them to know they are the only ones who can do
that. No other person has that power, unless they give it to them.

So, I tell them, "Believe in yourself, believe in other people, believe
in magic. The world is a miraculous, undiscovered mass of possibility
and potential, and it's your job to help unleash that splendor. Go forth
and kick some bootay!"

What I don't tell them, and only because they're so young, is that a
large chunk of the planet feeds on the misery and insecurity of others
—everyone from mean girls to future bosses, politicians, and Holly-
wood will tell them they aren't smart enough, talented enough, thin
enough, pretty enough...the list goes on. Sadly, they'll learn that on
their own and it's my job to be there to tell them not to trust the nay-
sayers.

So far, my daughters are so full of "Girl Power" and confidence in their gender, they've started to actually pity boys. My youngest, Hope, is seven. She's oft heard opining, "I feel sorry for so-and-so (insert boy's name here)."

Inevitably, I ask, "Why?"

She responds, "Because of the fashion! He doesn't get to wear great clothes and earrings. He'll never have boobs or a closet full of high heels. Plus, he eats his boogers on the playground. A girl would never do that."

So, I ask her about her two particular male friends, and why she's friends with them. To which she answers, "They're sweet little boys. They can't help being gross."

My older daughter, Margery, while still vigorously in love with being a girl, is a little more tolerant of the opposite sex. She's nine and beginning to see that boys have their place in the world. Although she often complains about the stupidity of men *back in the day*. "Can you believe there was a time when women weren't allowed to vote? Can you believe we haven't had a woman president? I hope they're not waiting for me. I haven't decided if I want the job, yet." Never has it occurred to her that she won't be the president if she chooses to be.

When the male-bashing starts to get out of hand, I ask them about their Daddy and Poppy, reminding them, "You know, Daddy and Poppy are boys."

"But they're not stupid boys. They were smart enough to marry you and Moses." Moses is the name my daughters call my mom.

Hope inserts, "I've never seen Daddy eat his boogers. Plus, he lets me read to him every night and he teaches me about history. *And* he's a great basketball player!"

I'm trying to raise my daughters to be comfortable with themselves, proud in their abilities, and tolerant of the world around them. I want them to grow up feeling sure they can do or be anything they want and to know they have my full support in their endeavors.

Will they encounter people who try to make them feel less-than? Will they work for people who don't see their worth? Will they ever feel insecure? The answers are all the same. Hell yeah, cause that's just life, folks. That's part of everyone's journey, man or woman. It's how they process those experiences that will dictate their success.

Our girls are learning the world is often perplexing. Fairness and kindness do not always win out. So, we're teaching them that when they notice something that makes them mad or upset, it's up to them to step forward and make a difference. Complaining is never the answer, action is.

Margery is ruled by compassion and a desire to make the world a better place. At nine, she's already succeeded. Three years ago, she spearheaded a campaign to collect fifty purses and backpacks for the homeless. With the help of our friends, we filled them with food, hats, gloves, scarves, toiletries, and a small amount of money. Margery drew a picture of an angel and wrote a beautiful letter of encouragement that we enclosed in each.

Hope will defend the downtrodden to the death, although her actions are a little more aggressive than Margery's. For instance, if you're unkind to someone in her presence or treat them unfairly, you had better protect your kneecaps. She probably won't ask you nicely to change your ways. But for your own safety, you should.

Both girls were behind me writing a children's book called *The Friendship Bench* that they, along with their classmates, illustrated. One hundred percent of the proceeds are donated to our PTC to be used for acts of kindness.

I know my daughters will have their hearts broken and be the recipients of unfair treatment, but that isn't because they're girls. It's a human condition. My job is to make sure they know that standing up for themselves is the answer. They may not always get the job they deserve. They may not always get paid what they should. But they should always know their worth.

I'm not looking forward to wiping their tears as they learn some of the ugly truths about the world. But I'll tell you this, I'm not going to let them wallow in self pity. Things change when people demand change. I'm teaching my girls that they have a voice and an obligation to be part of the change. I'm teaching them to be kind and courageous. Other than that, it's a crap shoot.

Since their births, I've been cobbling together a list of things that I think is mandatory for my future Wonder Women to learn. It evolves on almost a daily basis, but the current rendition reads as follows:

- You are no better than any other person on this planet.
- The Karmic wheel is real! Seriously, only put out there what you want to come back to you because it will, tenfold, like a hurricane in the shape of a fist or a kiss, your choice.
- You *can* wear white before Memorial Day.
- Underwear is not optional. You can recover from the embarrassment of torn pants if you're wearing undies, but there's no coming back from commando.
- Things are only placeholders for the important stuff, like kindness and love.
- Whining is never productive.
- French fries can solve most problems.
- Marry a person who makes you laugh.
- Your mistakes don't define you. They're no more than a stairway to growth.
- Be loyal.
- Don't take any crap.
- Don't be an a-hole.
- Swiss buttercream is often a better choice than American buttercream as it won't overwhelm the palate with sweetness.
- Be the kind of friend you want to have.
- Don't be afraid to be vulnerable.
- Always sing at the top of your lungs to Queen, even if you sound awful. It's good for the soul.

Now that my daughters are on the planet, and not just imaginary, I feel the weight of responsibility like an elephant standing on my neck. I want to do right by them and make sure I equip them with everything they need to succeed. It's terrifying and invigorating at the same time, and I can't wait to continue my journey with them.

WHEN NOT ACTIVELY RAISING HER GIRLS, WHITNEY DINEEN CAN often be found organizing their drawers, chasing chickens around the backyard, or hiding in a closet to swear. Dineen is an award-winning author of nonfiction humor, romantic comedies, and middle grade fiction. Her memoir, Motherhood, Martyrdom & Costco Runs, won a gold medal at the International Readers' Favorite Awards in Non-fiction/Humor and was a finalist at the Book Excellence Awards. Whitney loves to connect with her readers. You can find her at whitneydineen.com, Facebook, or Twitter.

34

RAISING A STRONG DAUGHTER WHO IS COMPLETELY HERSELF IS MY ULTIMATE GOAL

BY KATIE BINGHAM SMITH

I grew up in the '80s hearing things like "You can never be too skinny or too rich," and "Nothing tastes as good as skinny feels." Perhaps people think they are just words, but try telling that to an 11-year-old girl who has developed earlier than all of her friends, is wearing almost a C cup, and has hips that could bear children. I took that shit to heart. I believed it. I felt it in my soul, and so did all my friends, by the way. I'm pretty sure those phrases affected many females the same way – in a negative one.

To be skinny and rich was to matter; it meant you'd made it. And if you weren't thin you weren't strong; you had zero willpower and, well, you didn't deserve to be validated. You pretty much sucked.

We've made some progress since then, but a few months ago as I was shopping with my daughter, she held up a tank that said, "Strong is the new sexy," as she asked if she could buy it, I was cringing.

Not because I don't think strong can be sexy—I do. But being strong has this physical and mental connotation associated with it. I'm not talking about muscles either.

"What do you think being strong means?" I asked her. As she thought for a moment she said she thought it meant being able to stand up for yourself and not care what other people thought about you.

While I agree, I've learned a few things about being strong since my divorce happened a year ago—our horrible circumstances are always teaching us something if we choose to accept the lesson. I've cried almost every day since my ex-husband and I decided to split. Does that make me look strong to my kids? I don't know, I've never asked them. But I'm thinking instead of asking them I need to tell them that being vulnerable, crying, and asking for help is what makes you a strong person, too.

At first, I tried to hide my blubbering self by only allowing myself to cry in the bathroom while I had the door shut and the shower running, then I got my water bill.

I'd cry in the car after dropping them off at their father's house, but if I had a date that night, had plans to meet up with friends, or was taking myself out for a Diet Coke and a shopping spree, I'd look like a hot mess, so that wasn't working either.

I didn't want my crying to be another reason to add to the list of all the other things I felt I was doing to screw up my kids' lives, so I was hiding it, which is the opposite of what I should've been doing.

Before I knew it, I had no control when they tears would come and I was getting really tired of trying to hold it in to appear "strong" for my kids all the time. I just needed to be myself. I am an oversensitive over-thinker who talks too much. I grew up constantly feeling like I had to censor myself or overcompensate to make other people comfortable. I'd shut my mouth when I wanted to disagree, hold in emotions – and now as a woman in her 40s, I realize this has benefited no one.

That part of me is slowing being peeled away layer by layer because I'll be damned if I am going to teach my daughter you make other people feel good about themselves by compromising your needs, stuffing your emotions, and censoring yourself. How can I raise my daughter to be a fierce, strong independent female if I'm afraid to shed a tear for fear it will make me look like I can't handle life and I don't know what I'm doing?

The truth is, I have no fucking clue what I'm doing. This single life of mine is new, and scary, and I've never done this before. But I show up every day for her and her brothers. I am not going to fall on my face *every day*, but I can promise there *will* be days all I can manage is a face plant in a bag of chips with a squishy sofa supporting me. It's okay not to know what's next, or to not appear strong and in control—it's more than okay, it called being human.

Being brave and strong and all these things that are deemed as the "new pretty" don't mean your aren't ever afraid. They mean you are afraid, but you are willing to put yourself in an uncomfortable spot because you know that's what is right. And you keep doing it because despite how hard it is, you know it's the best way for your to show up for those you love, and more importantly, it's about showing up for yourself.

I will never tell my daughter to cheer up if she's really freaking pissed. I will never make her feel like she needs to smile if she doesn't feel like it; it's her body. If she doesn't feel like smiling, she shouldn't any more than if she should hold hands with someone she doesn't want to touch. If she needs to cry every day for a year, then so be it. That's what she should do.

While these messages about being brave and strong and all are much better than letting our girls know they are only worthy if they are rich and thin, I want my daughter to know being herself is the new pretty, or sexy, or beautiful—or whatever. And there are going to be days when she doesn't give a damn about being pretty, and she doesn't need to stuff that emotion, either.

I want her to be herself at all costs, even if it is hard and makes those around her uncomfortable. Because what will happen if I don't teach her that all the things which make her unique will slowly be stripped away because she's trying to live up to someone else's defini-tion of how a woman should be. And from a woman who has been there—she, and all the other young girls walking this earth, deserve so much more.

KATIE BINGHAM-SMITH HAD THREE KIDS IN THREE YEARS AND crafts her ass off in order to stay sane. You can often find her wearing faux leather pants, drinking Diet Coke, and paying her kids to play with her hair and rub her feet. She is a staff writer for Scary Mommy *and regular contributor to* Babble, SheKnows, Grown and Flown, *and* Mom.me. *Feel free to harass her on Instagram @katiebinghamsmith and Facebook @Katiebinghamsmithwriter.*

35

FREE BLEEDING: AN EXPERIENCE

BY MOLLY SANDLER

I have this theory that if every woman on earth refused to wear any products when they were on their periods—what would be called "free bleeding"—then tampons, pads, and all other period-related products would be untaxed within, like, two hours. Honestly, I think they'd probably be free, since many men (including my father) seem to have a major problem with anything involving a period, especially the blood part (and the cramps part, and the mood swings part...).

During a "situation" in the eighth grade, I found out that if you tell anyone that you're bleeding out of your vagina, even if this bleeding is purely accidental, they will let you do whatever you need to do, just so they can avoid discussing anything remotely near the topic, or the blood you are currently bleeding.

And this story is where I tell you that I was once, in fact, a free bleeder, and have lived to tell the tale. So if it happens to you, you will too. And maybe we'll even get free tampons out of it.

Here's what happened...

It was a typical hot day in June, and I woke up with a visit from Aunt Flo. So naturally, as one does, I go put in a tampon. I don't know if this was a known fact for everyone except me, but apparently a tampon can be kinda diagonal up there and just not catch any blood at all if you put it in slightly wrong, quite possibly leading to free bleeding. But obviously that would never happen to me, right? Wrong.

Very wrong.

It was sixth period, and my chair was feeling... sticky. We all know the struggle of leg sweat on hot days, so that's clearly what I assumed it was. But just to make sure, I looked down to confirm. Instead of cutoffs and slightly sweaty thighs, I saw a literal crime scene going on between my legs.

We're talking at least six murder victims worth of blood. Possibly seven. I cannot explain in words the horror that was happening to me right then. Everyone reading this, take the worst period situation you can possibly imagine, and multiply it times ten. Then another ten. And did I have any sort of product on me? No, no I did not. So me, being the strong independent woman that I am, immediately turned to my friend Laura next to me and simply pointed at my crotch so she could tell me what to do about it.

Her helpful advice was a quick grab of the arm and a hissed, "We need to get you to the bathroom *now*. I'll bring you a pad from my locker on the way."

I come from a school with very strict bathroom rules, like what I imagine the rules must be like in prison. You can't leave the classroom to go to the bathroom if anyone else is out already, you can't go during the first, or last, 15 minutes of class, and you definitely cannot go with a friend. Unfortunately, Laura and I were going to break all three of these rules by leaving.

I asked my teacher Mr. Smith if we could leave. As expected, he basically assumed we were joking by even asking him this and told us to go back to our seats. That's when I was like, "Uh no, we need to go together," adding, "It's an emergency, I swear."

But since that's what everyone who wants to leave class with their friend says, he responded with a strong no. After probably three minutes of me pleading with him and being met with continued unsympathetic looks from Mr. Smith, I decided I was utterly and completely done with his patriarchal nonsense, and did what needed to be done.

I pulled my shirt slightly away from my body so he could see the crimson tide I'd been attempting to conceal up until this point during our prolonged conversation.

His entire attitude completely changed within half a second. Guy couldn't get me out of his classroom fast enough. "Oh. Oh. *Ohhhhh*. Oh no. I wasn't aware it was that type of situation. Of course you two can leave. Do you need anyone else? Should I call a doctor? Here's the hall pass. Here, take two. Take as much time as you need."

As we were about to leave he even yelled out a final helpful suggestion, "Actually, don't even bother coming back, there's only like ten minutes left in this class anyway."

Laura and I took the passes and made a stop at her locker for a pad before continuing to the bathroom.

The first thing Laura said was, "God, Molly, do you even have any blood left in you?"

We concluded I had no choice but to change my shorts ASAP, but of course I didn't have gym clothes with me that day, and making the situation even better, neither did Laura. Then the bell rang (Yay! Super-helpful timing!) and the only rule at my school more strict than the bathroom policy was the not-being-late-to-class policy.

I slowly walked to my next class, desperately hoping I'd run into someone whose clothes I could borrow. Luckily, my sometimes-we-interact, occasionally, maybe, friend Angela was walking practically next to me, and we happened to share our next class.

Without even giving her an explanation, I pulled her towards the lockers and showed her my own personal bloodbath situation. Without me even asking, she immediately insisted I take her gym shorts, since my shorts were clearly unwearable at that point. My only obstacle between me and cleanliness was our next teacher, Ms. Link.

Based on how the last bathroom request I made went, I decided I wasn't going to waste any time reasoning with her. I told her I was having an emergency and needed to go to the bathroom with Angela, and showed her my shorts without waiting for her response to my request. Giving me a disgusted face, Ms. Link told us to hurry up and be back in, like, two minutes, leading me to the realization that female teachers can be assholes about periods, too.

Long story short, I changed, returned to class with Angela, and was saved from the worst and most embarrassing moment of my young life. But all in all, still pretty much one of my worst days ever.

The one small bright spot was that I now knew that Angela, even though she wasn't even close to being my best friend, was absolutely willing and able to take on the BFF role when I really needed her help. And hopefully Angela knew I would do the same for her or anyone else who needed me to share a pad or a pair of shorts because their rogue tampon did not do its only job.

I should also add that when I got home and told my mother the horrific story in all its gory details, she immediately took me out for ice cream, as much as I wanted, with literal whipped cream and a cherry on top.

In conclusion, free bleeding is a very effective way to get things to go your way in school, make new friends, and get a parent to buy you ice cream. I ten out of ten recommend it for everyone considering the idea.

MOLLY SANDLER WAS BORN IN NEW YORK CITY AND IS NOW A HIGH school student living in New Jersey with her family and dog, Daisy.

36

FINDING MYSELF

BY JULIA BOZZA

When high school students complain about their lives, adults always respond with, "Stop complaining. Wait until you are an adult with *real* problems." And, while there is no doubt that the problems of being an adult carry a much different weight, being in high school today is still a challenge. Anyone who has ever been a teenager once understood the social pressure to make friends and be popular. Countless high school students live those four years in envy of the "popular kids" and their epic parties and perfect lives. For a while, it seemed like I was being set up to become one of them. It felt like the high school dream was being handed to me. Freshman year I found myself in the middle of a friend group of kids who were smart, athletic, and actually nice. It was wonderful, I felt like I was in with the in-crowd—and for a freshman, it was an amazing feeling. However, at some point during our freshman year, these friends started to throw parties. They were fun parties, but they often left me uncomfortable. Even though I enjoyed the get-togethers, I hit a point where it felt like instead of being a part of the group, I was looking in from the outside. I found myself becoming unhappy with my life, specifically with my friends.

Was there something wrong with me? I was a part of a group

containing some of the most well-known students in my grade, a group that many students wanted to be a part of. Why was I so unhappy? Trapped, I continued to attend the parties and get-togethers, wanting to stay in the "popular group," but in the back of my mind, I knew that this wasn't where I wanted to be. I hit a point where I was unhappy all the time, spending countless nights stressing over how alone I felt until one day I had a sudden realization. All the advice my parents had given me about friendship had finally sunk in, and a part of me began to listen. I realized that life isn't about having the most friends or being in the most well-known group in school—it's about finding people you are happiest with. In that moment, I realized that I was trapped in a prison, one I had made for myself, by defining myself by the people with whom I hung out.

I wasn't always disappointed in my friend group, I was happy for a long time before high school. In third grade, my family moved, causing me to switch schools, leaving behind a lot of my old friends, and I needed to make new ones. Throughout the rest of elementary school, I had a few friends, but I couldn't help feeling jealous of all the people who had "best friends" that they had known since kindergarten, something I would never have in a new school. Finally, middle school rolled around and my friends from third to fifth grade were scattered into different classes and I was alone once again. Going into middle school, I knew only one girl in my classes. I had taken tennis lessons with her when we were younger so we kind of knew each other, and we clicked immediately. We had most of our classes together, ate lunch together, and she introduced me to all of her friends. By the middle of seventh grade, we had become a part of a new friend group of girls in our math class. We were a tight-knit group. We all stayed friends through the rest of middle school and I was overjoyed that I had finally found a friend group, true friends who wouldn't disappear on me. This was everything I had dreamed of socially. But every good thing must come to an end, and my social life began to unravel with the dawn of high school.

My group and I stayed close throughout freshman year, and our tiny group of girls had expanded into one large group of people from all different middle schools. One of my friends began to throw parties during the holiday season for the group. The parties weren't huge, but they were always posted all over social media afterward and people would talk about them for the rest of the week. People would tell me how they wished they were invited to her parties and how they wanted to be in the friend group with us. Despite how happy I had been through middle school I remained socially insecure, so, I admit that I somewhat enjoyed the feeling of having people look up to me and my friends. I was well-liked and it seemed as though my friends and I were gradually becoming more and more popular.

Then came my sophomore year and everything changed. The parties continued, but the focus of the conversations changed and I became more uncomfortable and out of my element. While I still had fun with my friends, I felt anxious being there and I'm sure it was evident. I began to feel like an outsider in this group that I had always enjoyed being a part of. Outside of school the girls formed smaller groups within our large one and began to exclude other girls, including myself. Technology certainly played a role as there were a dozen group text chats that were running, and even though everyone was not included in all of them, my friends would mention the other group chats in the larger ones. The feeling was, "not only are we excluding you, but we are also going to make sure you *know* you are being exclud- ed." Being my anxious and "don't want to make waves" self, I continued to stay passive and allowed my emotions get tossed around by the girls I thought were my "good friends." I realized that the amazing social life I thought I had was just a facade and my heart was broken. As most teenagers do, I had identified myself by the friend group I was in. If I wasn't one of them, who was I? My parents could see how unhappy I was and would suggest that I find new friends if these ones were only bringing me sadness and disappointment, but I didn't know how. For years, I had created a tunnel vision view of my social life and when I imagined leaving, I couldn't envision myself actually belonging in any other group. I felt trapped. My sadness grew and, finally, I found myself in the depths of a depression that I was sure I would not be able to crawl out of.

However, I continued to talk to my parents and continued to imagine a different future for myself. And I also began to realize that my friends weren't bad or evil. We simply had different priorities and different ideas about what friendship should be. And little by little, I began to care less about what they thought. When they would all be going to a party that I wasn't invited to, I found that I didn't care quite as much anymore. And sometimes, when I was invited, I would decline. I remembered all of the things that I liked about myself and realized that I wasn't going to spend my life alone if I chose a different group of friends, or even decided to be part of multiple groups of friends. I could still be friends with these people without having them be my everything. I began to be happy again. And once I opened myself up to that happiness, new opportunities for friendship came my way.

In my drawing class, there was only one other sophomore, and at the beginning of the year, we sat together to avoid sitting alone. While I somewhat knew her from theatre and middle school, we were not "good friends." She was also in my history class and she sat with her best friend in the front of the room. They were always smiling and laughing and having a great time together while I sat in the back of the room with a few girls from my friend group who consistently excluded me from the conversation. In mid-January, this girl and her friend approached me before class and invited me to sit with them. I would be lying if I said I wasn't surprised. They barely knew me, yet somehow had sensed my exclusion and actually *wanted* me to join them. I accepted and they happily welcomed me to their table. I was included in every conversation they had and we laughed together often. My least favorite subject in school had become the class that I would find myself looking forward to every day. I felt happier than I had felt in a long time. I finally felt like my life was on the right track. The self-conscious freshman who began high school a year and a half earlier no longer existed and a confident young woman was growing in her place.

As I distanced myself from social life with my old group of friends, an interesting thing began to happen. Other members of the group reached out to tell me that they, too, were unhappy with the way things had progressed within the group. Those who reached out also were struggling to find a new path, and we leaned on each other when we were feeling unsure. The realization that I hadn't been alone in my feelings was liberating and helped to solidify my understanding that I had made the right choice.

While I was becoming closer with my two new friends we were still in the early stages of friendship. Then, one of my old friends from middle school came back into my life. We had met at a summer band camp in fourth grade and again, a year later, when I joined the youth group at my church. We had a rocky relationship during middle school as we were both involved in similar activities and there was a competitive edge to our relationship. However, as we both matured in high school, we reconnected and became close. She became my closest confidante and we spoke constantly. By the end of the summer, the girl who had been my "frenemy" in middle school had become my best friend. She listened to my stories and valued the things I had to say. When I was with her, I felt like I mattered and that through all my hard times there was always someone on my team, rooting for me.

By the end of the summer, it was very clear to me that this was the year I had changed my life. I had learned to stand on my own, and by doing so, had made myself open to new friendships and new opportunities. I learned that, in life, you can't expect others to provide you with your self-worth. You need to claim it and own it and not worry about what anyone thinks. Your happiness is up to you.

As I write this, I am wrapping up my junior year, and it is safe to say that I have never been happier or more confident. I eat lunch with my new friends in the cafeteria every day and we are welcoming to anyone who wishes to join us. Throughout the year, other girls began to sit with us as well and our group expanded. We have a "the more the merrier" mentality and seek to not exclude anyone. My friends continue to fill my life with so much happiness and joy, and I am so grateful to have met each of them, as they were part of a positive change in my life. I don't think that they will ever understand how grateful I am for their friendship and for that one day when they invited me to sit with them in class. That one small act of kindness, which probably didn't hold any significance to them, changed the course of my year, my high school career, and my life.

I am still friendly with the old group of friends. I don't get invited to their parties but it doesn't upset me anymore. I have opened myself up and have made so many new friends who I enjoy spending time with, but I don't rely on them to define who I am. I know who I am, what I enjoy, and what I deserve. I put my time and attention into things I am passionate about, like dance and theater, and I spend no time trying to be popular and fit in.

Needless to say, walking away from my friend group was one of the hardest decisions I have ever made, and I sometimes look back on my life and wonder where I would be if I had stayed in the group. Would I be a different person? I honestly can't answer that question. But without a doubt, I know that I made the right decision. My hope is that the message I've delivered is simply this: be true to yourself. If it doesn't feel right to you, then it's time to walk away. And being different from others doesn't make them or you wrong. But until you value yourself over the acceptance of others, nothing will feel right.

JULIA BOZZA IS A HIGH SCHOOL SENIOR IN NEW JERSEY. SHE LIVES with her two loving parents and three younger brothers in a very noisy house. She wishes to pursue a career in medicine, however, she also loves dancing, musical theatre, and is a member of the mock trial team. This is Julia's first published work and she is very grateful for the opportunity to be able to share her story.

❧ 37 ❧

PHENOMENALITY

BY CATHERINE KREMER

maya angelou once taught me how to be a woman
  phenomenally.
but being a woman in my own body has harbored such a
  complex definition.
i'm a gen z kid, who grew up in the early stages of the internet
  age
impacting my journey of finding self at every turn.
i was taught i was beautiful, my struggle was beautiful,
and it was all totally normal.
true.
i was told i was beautiful without makeup, without pretty
  clothes, without altering my body in any way, even if i
  wanted to.
also true.
but this ideal of beauty created this culture of guilt within
  my mind.
i strove to be this girl that i didn't want to be.
pushed in the direction of not caring about my appearance even
  if i wanted to and turning my nose up at boys even though
  every late night sleepover i would talk about one or more.

it was difficult.
the first time i put on makeup i felt foreign.
caring about clothes felt fake.
my journey became a story of reversing guilt of indulgence
*   within the things i loved.*
a realization that myself, my body, is merely a composition of the
*   best things i found in other people and the best parts of*
*   my past.*
forgetting my appearance, the caked on makeup, the style i strive
*   to perfect, i have to remember what i truly am.*
my tiny body a composition of everything i've ever loved and
*   ever done.*
being a woman in my own body is a complex definition made of
*   simply nothing less than the most important things in my*
*   life. my heart, my love, and the things i yearn to become.*

CATHERINE KREMER, AGE 17, IS A HIGH SCHOOL STUDENT, writer, and spoken word artist. She is a member of the Wordplay Cincy Scribes slam team. She is a Louder Than a Bomb Cincy teen poetry slam finalist. She attended the Denison University Reynolds Young Authors Program and is a winner of numerous Scholastic Keys. She has had work previously published in *FotoFocus, The Poetry of Felix J. Koch,* in partnership with the Cincinnati Museum Center.

❧ 38 ❧

ADVICE FROM MY FUTURE SELF

BY ABBY BYRD

NOTE: TO PROTECT THE IDENTITIES OF MY HIGH SCHOOL FRIENDS, THEIR REAL NAMES HAVE BEEN CHANGED TO THOSE OF WELSH PRINCES.

5-year-old me [knocking on window]: Abby! Abby!

15-year-old me [rising from a restless sleep and stumbling over piles of books, jeans, and flannel shirts to open the window]: Oh my God! Are you me?

35: Yeah. Quick, let me in. I have stuff to tell you about the future.

15 [staring]: Are those wrinkles? [steps back] How much do you weigh?

35: That is a very rude question. Listen, I only have a few minutes. Are you gonna let me in or not?

15 [helping 35 in]: What...How old are you?

35: Thirty-five. And I don't have much time because I was granted only a few minutes between feedings to come see you. So please shut up.

15: Feedings? Do we have a horse?

35: For god's sake, NO! A baby, dipshit!

15: A *BABY*?! At thirty-FIVE?

189

35: Yes, a baby. Now listen. I need to talk to you about being a woman.

15: Oh, I already got my period.

35: Um... not that. More important things.

15: Hey, I'm married, right? Am I married to William?

35: This is what we need to talk about. The first question you ask your future self shouldn't be if you're married. But since you asked, no. And you need to let go of that obsession. Sorry, but William doesn't like you.

15: [crestfallen] He doesn't?

35: No. I mean, he likes you, but he'll never love you. Don't take it personally, though. He's gay.

15: Gay? You mean like, homosexual? [confused] We have those in our school?

35 [rolls eyes] Christ in a handcart. Yes. Incidentally, everyone except you figured this out during the eighth-grade talent show, when he dry-humped the stage to Madonna's "Express Yourself." And don't count on your backup best friend, either. He's also gay.

15: William *and* Harry are gay? [with rising anxiety]

35: [gently] You know how Harry says everything is "fabulous?" And how he's always late coming to hang out with you because he says he "ran out of gas?"

15: Yeah?

35: Well, "I ran out of gas" is code for "I was engaging in sexual exploration with that guy who lives over on Leeds Avenue."

15 [sits]: This is all very overwhelming. [pauses]

35: Okay, I can see that I'm traumatizing you.

15: [ignoring her] This can't be right. Who will I marry, then?

35: You're doing it again. You're too much of a planner. Stop worrying about the future and just let life happen. You're making things harder for yourself by trying to control everything. Look, I get it. Right now, you think the ultimate fulfillment in life lies in being a wife and mother.

15: I don't think that.

35: You do, Abby. You don't even know you do. You've been conditioned to think that way, to believe that you'll marry right out of college and start a family and life will go trippingly along. That's not going to happen. I can promise you you'll eventually get married, okay? But I won't lie to you. The next two decades of dating and relationships are not going to be pretty. They're going to be like...a sickening carnival ride. It will start out fun, but as you age, the carnival will grow more and more sinister, and each revolution less and less tolerable, until you want to vomit and swear off carnivals forever.

15: [stares]

35: [weakly] Try to think of it as an adventure. You'll travel the country. The world, even! And you'll learn about new things, like Tuvan throat singing and Czech military aircraft. And those are both from the same boyfriend! He also plays the bagpipes! [seeing 15 panic] Uh, scuba diving? Breeding wild cats? Making biodiesel from used cooking oil?

15: [whispering] My God.

35: There are going to be quite a few breakups. After every one, you'll feel afraid and alone. And completely adrift. Once, you'll fall sobbing off your desk chair onto the floor, which will prompt your mother to remark, "Remember, honey, you can't solve your problems with alcohol." But you'll get through it! Not exactly unscathed. I mean, there will be some weird post-traumatic tics. Whenever you see a man playing a mandolin, the murderous rage rising inside you will make it difficult for you to refrain from seizing it and bashing him in the head. And then there's the hissing at passing UPS trucks.

15: I have no idea what you are talking about right now.

35: Okay, never mind. I guess that won't make sense until later. Anyway, your entire twenties are going to pass in a blur of urinary tract infections and bad judgment, and by the time you're 30, you'll be looking at women with engagement rings and measuring yourself against them, wondering what you're doing wrong. You'll even stroll by jewelry stores wistfully and peruse wedding magazines at the pharmacy, the whole time feeling like a fraud. Weddings are seductive. The social approval of being a bride is seductive. But being a princess for a day is different from making a commitment to be someone's partner for life. And neither a wedding nor a marriage is an accomplishment. It's like... you know that floating ducks game at the carnival where you pick up a plastic duck, and if the "magic number" is on that duck, you win a prize?

15: Again with the carnival metaphors.

35: Marriage is like that floating duck game. You don't earn it; it's a matter of luck. You can be the prettiest, wittiest, most charming woman in the world, but whether or not you get married is really just a matter of picking up the right duck.

15: How... how do I pick up the right duck? I mean, how will I know if I pick up the right duck?

35: If you have to ask if it's the right duck, it's probably not the right duck. And I don't want you to consider the relationships that end as wrong ducks mistakes. Every relationship is valuable. But just because you pick up a duck doesn't mean you have to keep it. [pauses] And I will go on record as saying that evaluating potential dates by their facility with the semicolon is a really shitty strategy. As is online dating in general.

15: On...line...dating?

35: In the future, you can... use a computer to talk to people. [glances at Brother® word processor on desk] Forget it; it's too hard to explain. Before I go, I have to tell you about the potatoes.

15: Potatoes.

35: Yeah. Biology complicates the search for a mate. As you get older, the desire to have children can...manipulate your behavior. You might find yourself doing strange things. Like at the grocery store, while holding a five-pound bag of potatoes, you'll bounce them and try to comfort them. It's called "dandling." It's perfectly normal. And just so you know, being pregnant commands even more social approval than getting married. You'll also begin to worry that you won't find a suitable partner to have a baby with. When you find yourself in the same room as a pregnant woman, you'll give a vacuous smile and hollow congratulations, but inside you'll feel...worthless. Dead, like a pile of ashes. Like someone could blow you away. Needless to say, during the parade of pregnancy announcements you'll experience in your late twenties, you're going to have to struggle to muster up some anemic cheers.

15: Rah, rah, reproduction?

35: When it gets overwhelming, I highly recommend taking to your bed with Fudgie the Whale. The cake. To eat, I mean. Not to sleep with.

15: Ew.

35: That feeling you will experience at other women's milestones is fear. You're scared to be alone. You don't know how to be alone. I hate to break this to you, but nothing saves you from being alone, Abby. Nothing. Not marriage, not kids.

15: [tears up] Okay.

35: I gotta go. I love you. Just breathe, all right? There's nothing wrong with you. Oh, and in a few years... can you remember this word for me? Zoloft.

15: Zoloft.

35: [climbing out window] Good girl. [turning back] Oh! And save all that flannel. Hipsters are gonna kill for that vintage in 20 years.

ABBY BYRD's WORK HAS APPEARED ON HUFFPOST AND SCARY Mommy, *among other sites, and in several anthologies. She runs the blog Little Miss Perfect—a trove of existential angst, biting humor, and bile. Hundreds of clowns once prayed for her en masse; clearly, they achieved nothing. Connect with Abby on Facebook and Goodreads.*

39

I'M NOT EVERYBODY'S CUP OF TEA. AND THAT'S OKAY.

BY JEN MANN

"What's your little book about?" a man asked.

I looked up from the book I was signing. A youngish, clean cut white guy, with no wedding band, and the name "Dave" embroidered on the breast of his neatly pressed polo shirt stood in front of my table. I recognized him immediately. He'd been in the back of the room sort of frowning during my entire speech. I knew the type. This conversation could go one of two ways:

1. He uses dickish behavior as a way to cover up his insecurities, but deep down he really liked what I had to say and needed to hear it, but he needs a few minutes before he can admit it, or

2. He's an asshole.

"Didn't you listen to my talk?" I chided, because I tend to meet hostile remarks with sarcasm.

He grimaced. "You spoke very fast."

I didn't argue. I had a lot to say and not a lot of time to say it.

"Well, my *little* book is actually my third book in a *New York Times* bestselling series of books." I closed the book, revealing the title: *Working with People I Want to Punch in the Throat.*

"Hmm. Sounds violent," he said.

"It's humor, not how-to," I replied, motioning to the next person in line. I ignored Dave so I could speak to the woman who actually wanted to buy a copy of my book.

"Can I at least look at one before I decide if I want it?" Dave asked.

"Of course," I replied. "Help yourself."

He took a copy off the pile and thumbed through it. I ignored his dramatic sighs and tsking (I assumed over my use of f-bombs like commas). My line died down and there were only about six women left when Dave barged up to the table again, ignoring the women he'd cut in line. He held up the book. "This list," he said, shaking the book at me. "What is this?"

"It's my Punch List," I said. "I make a list for all my books. They give you an idea of the topics I'm going to cover in the essays."

He read aloud, "Mansplainers." He grunted and rolled his eyes.

Oh, great. He's an asshole with absolutely no sense of humor, I thought.

"I don't think you even know what mansplaining is," Dave snapped.

The women gaped at Dave.

I smiled coolly. "The fact that you're telling me that I don't know what the word means is incredible," I said. "I don't think *you* know what it means."

The women giggled.

That was all it took. What is that quote from Margaret Atwood? *"Men are afraid women will laugh at them, women are afraid men will kill them."* I felt like that. I saw the shift in Dave. I watched his eyes go dark and his face go hard. If we'd been sort of ribbing one another before, now it was on like Donkey Kong. Dave wanted to go to war.

Dave glowered. "Oh yeah, well, what do you call a woman who thinks she knows it all?"

The women gasped softly.

"I'm smart, so I'd call her *right*," I said, looking straight into his eyes, refusing to look away or cower.

The women chuckled.

Dave fumed and glared at me. "You're not everybody's cup of tea," he spat, his mouth curled into a mean-spirited sneer.

The women exclaimed and Dave looked triumphant.

Here's the thing, Dave had been trying to get a rise out of me and up until that point, I'd refused to take the bait. But I knew men like Dave. I've dealt with many Dave's over the years. You see, I write a lot of observations on everything from politics to pop culture to parenting. My opinions can be a bit polarizing at times and although the bulk of people who read my work like what I have to say, there is always someone who disagrees. No matter what I write, I tend to receive harsh criticism and backlash on just about any topic. I am known as someone who likes to "stir the pot" and sometimes when I'm at an event like that one, I get someone who decides they'll try and stir my pot. Dave had brought his own spoon.

I considered Dave's words. They were meant to hurt me. They were a jab at me. He was telling me what so many men (and even a few women) had been telling me over the years:

"Pipe down over there!"

"Shut your yap!"

"Do what you do best: make us laugh!"

"No one cares what you think! You are nobody!"

Anytime I've crossed a line where I offended or insulted or even simply irked a man with my opinion, he has been quick to lash out at me. To tell me that I'm just some fat housewife in Middle America who doesn't know shit. I've been called every name in the book, I've been threatened with violence, my family has been threatened, and yet I continue to raise my voice.

"Why?" you ask.

Because many years ago I found my voice and I found my tribe. I found that I could say the things that others couldn't. I could speak for the ones who were unable to speak up or who weren't brave enough. I could speak for the ones who felt like their ideas were meaningless. I could speak for the ones who felt alone and unseen. The one's who apologized for merely existing. I'm not everybody's cup of tea, but I'm *their* cup of tea and that was the part Dave couldn't understand.

I still hadn't responded, so Dave tried again. "What do you have to say to your haters?"

I laughed loudly. (Because so many men like Dave hate that. They hate how much space I take up, how much air I use, how loud I am.) "I say, who cares about them?" I snarled.

Dave was incredulous. "What? You don't care what people think of you?" he demanded.

"That's exactly right, Dave," I replied, taking the wind completely out of his sails.

"But, but," he sputtered. "I can't believe it, but you actually sound like you're okay with that!"

"Here's the thing, Dave. There are only four people in this world whose opinions I care about: my husband, my two kids, and my own. Everyone else can get lost. You are not the first person to ask me this question and you won't be the last, but I am done trying to be everybody's cup of tea. I reach the people who need me and those are the people I write for. I don't care if you hate what I have to say. I don't care if it bruises your ego or hurts your feelings or makes you think or whatever set you off. I have no plans to change who I am and if you don't like what I have to say, I suggest you move on and find someone else to talk to, because you are blocking my table and the people who actually want to speak to me."

I snatched my book out of Dave's hands and his mouth flapped open and closed, but no sound came out. I stared him down, unwavering. Inside I wavered a bit, because while I knew I was right and I was not afraid to poke the bear, one of these days I will get punched in the face by some pissed off dude and I still had another appearance that night and I didn't want a black eye—although it would have looked badass and I'd have a great story to tell, but still.

Dave lurked around my table for the rest of the event. He challenged anyone who approached me. "What do think of this stuff she writes?" he'd demand. Almost everyone ignored him or brushed him off, including me. I never spoke to Dave again and I refused to acknowledge his presence. I would not give that troll any sunlight in which to grow.

When I got back to the hotel that night I called my family and told them to story. My daughter was on the phone. "You have haters?" she asked, sadly.

I shrugged. "Yeah, so?"

"And you don't care?" Her nine-year-old brain couldn't comprehend. In those days she was dealing with her own mean-girl antics at school and she was working overtime to convince those girls to be her friend. She couldn't understand the idea of completely writing off people instead.

"Why should I care what someone thinks of me?" I replied. "That's on them. They are the ones who spend their time worrying about what I'm up to and what I'm doing. They're the ones taking time out of their busy lives to let me know just how much they think I suck. Dave spent an hour today of his life trying to make me feel bad. He's the one who wasted his time. I got work done, I made money, and I met new people. Dave is the loser here," I said.

"But don't you want everyone to like you?" she asked. "If they don't like you, they won't buy your books. That guy didn't buy a book, did he?"

I shook my head. "I don't do this to sell books. Selling books is a nice thing, but that's not why I write what I write. I write because I need to and my audience needs me to. We need each other. They are my people."

"Doesn't it hurt your feelings to know people don't like you?" my daughter said, her voice thick with emotion. I imagined the tears brimming in her eyes.

"It's taken me a long time to get to this point," I said. "That's why I need you to learn faster than me."

"Learn what?"

"No one can make us feel bad about ourselves unless we let them make us feel bad. Yes, my love, I am not everybody's cup of tea. Dave was right about that. But, do not worry about the people who don't like your tea. Find your tea-drinkers. Those are your people."

This is something that took me 25 years to master. Twenty-five very long years. I wish my mother had told me this in kindergarten when I came home in tears because an older girl (probably a first grader, but she seemed very worldly to me in those days) made fun of my awesome striped knee socks and I refused to ever wear them again. I wish my mother had told me this in sixth grade when I developed faster than other girls and the boys were relentless with their teasing and their constant attempts to grope me. I wish my mother had told me this in tenth grade when I moved from New Jersey to Kansas and I had to figure out how to fit my East Coast cynicism and sarcasm in with the pearl-clutching Midwestern kids. It was a hard lesson to learn, but I finally did. I don't care what others think of me. I don't try to keep up with my neighbors anymore or compare myself to my friends. I don't stress over fitting into the right wardrobe or having a magazine-worthy home. I don't allow myself to suffer from mommy guilt or second-guess my parenting. In the, now immortal, words of Elsa, *I let it go*. And I've never been happier.

Once my daughter was born, I vowed I would always try to teach this lesson to her. To show her that you never need to change who you are, rather you need to find the people who like you for you. Embrace your quirks, know your strengths, celebrate your differences, find your happiness inside, rather than seeking it elsewhere. Laugh at yourself, rage against injustice, be loud, be soft, be tough, be girly, get dirty, cry, dream, imagine, work hard, have it all. You do you, my love.

JEN MANN IS BEST KNOWN FOR HER WILDLY POPULAR AND HYSTERICAL blog People I Want to Punch in the Throat. She has been described by many as Erma Bombeck—with f-bombs. Jen is known for her hilarious rants and funny observations. Jen is the author of the New York Times *bestseller* People I Want to Punch in the Throat: Competitive Crafters, Drop-Off Despots, and Other Suburban Scourges *which was a Finalist for a Goodreads Reader's Choice Award. Her latest book is* My Lame Life: Queen of the Misfits, *her first fiction book for young adults. She is also the mastermind behind the* New York Times *bestselling* I Just Want to Pee Alone *series.*

NOTES FROM THE EDITOR

Thank you for reading this collection of essays. I appreciate your support and I hope you enjoyed it. I also hope you will tell a friend—or 30 about this. Please do me a huge favor and leave me a review. Of course I prefer 5-star, but I'll take what I can get. If you hated this book, you can skip the review. *Namaste.*

OTHER BOOKS AVAILABLE

People I Want to Punch in the Throat: Competitive Crafters, Drop Off Despots, and Other Suburban Scourges

Spending the Holidays with People I Want to Punch in the Throat: Yuletide Yahoos, Ho-Ho-Humblebraggers, and Other Seasonal Scourges

Working with People I Want to Punch in the Throat: Cantankerous Clients, Micromanaging Minions, and Other Supercilious Scourges

My Lame Life: Queen of the Misfits

OTHER ANTHOLOGIES AVAILABLE

I Just Want to Pee Alone

I STILL Just Want to Pee Alone

I Just Want to Be Alone

I Just Want to Be Perfect

But Did You Die?

OTHER SINGLES AVAILABLE

Just a Few People I Want to Punch in the Throat (Vol. 1)
Just a Few People I Want to Punch in the Throat (Vol. 2)
Just a Few People I Want to Punch in the Throat (Vol. 3)
Just a Few People I Want to Punch in the Throat (Vol. 4)
Just a Few People I Want to Punch in the Throat (Vol. 5)
Just a Few People I Want to Punch in the Throat (Vol. 6)

CPSIA information can be obtained
at www.ICGtesting.com
Printed in the USA
BVHW03s1923111018
529921BV00001B/92/P

To Dean and Laura

Chapter One

London 1817

"Please, Caroline. Just take someone's name off your dance card and replace it with mine."

"No. How many times do I have to say it?" came the sharp reply.

Julian Palmer, Earl Newhall, stopped in his tracks at the harsh words. He had been hoping to find a quiet spot away from the other guests at the ball in which to finish his brandy, but from the sound of the argument, he was in no such luck.

"I am not taking anyone's name off my dance card. I don't wish to dance with you this evening, Timothy Walters, and that is that."

Julian waited, in two minds as to what he should do. Some men would turn on their heel and head toward the safety of the crowded ballroom, but Julian's protective instincts could not allow him to ignore the edge of panic in Caroline's voice. He stepped forward and turned the corner.

In front of him was a young couple. The man, whom he assumed was Timothy, had his back to Julian and was standing with his head bowed. As Julian approached, he turned. His face was flush with obvious frustration; beads of sweat sat on his temple. In his hand he held a dance card. It was still attached to Caroline's wrist by means of a pale cream ribbon.

Caroline met Julian's gaze. She looked him up and down, showing scant regard for his presence, then looked away.

Julian knew that look only too well. His mother was the supreme mistress of the disdainful glare. Pity the man who fell on the wrong side of her favor.

"What is the problem? Perhaps I may be of assistance," he said.

"Everything is the problem. She is determined to vex me this evening. What is a chap to do when his lady will not save a place for him on her dance card?"

Caroline harrumphed. "Timothy, I have told you, I am not your lady and shall dance with whomever I please.

Julian had dealt with enough negotiations during his time as a diplomat in post-Napoleonic Paris to know when parties were at an impasse.

"Can I do anything to help resolve the situation? Help the two of you to find a happy medium," he bravely offered.

Caroline snatched the dance card from out of Timothy's grasp and marched toward Julian. She stopped in front of him. Her emerald-green eyes glistened with rage. "What you can do sir, is mind your own bloody business."

With a whirl of skirts, she brushed past Julian and disappeared around the corner. Timothy quickly followed.

Julian closed his eyes for an instant as long-buried memories of his childhood resurfaced. How many times had his parents played out that scene? And every time his father would scurry after his wife and do her bidding. All in order to remain in her good graces.

"Don't do it, my good fellow. That path only leads to misery and pain," he muttered.

He downed the last of his brandy and went in search of another drink.

Chapter Two

C aroline Saunders arrived back in the main ballroom ready to commit murder. Timothy Walters was yet again pushing her to the limit.

"Ah, there you are, I was wondering where you had got to. Oh, and you found a friend. Walters, how are you?"

She forced a smile to her face. Her brother Francis did not need to know that the latest in a long line of persistent suitors was in grave danger of being stabbed through the heart with the pencil from her dance card.

"Yes, I was on my way back from the ladies' retiring room when he found me," she replied.

Alongside Francis stood his best friend, Harry Menzies. Harry had often stepped in to save Caroline from her overenthusiastic admirers. She caught the angry glare he shot at Timothy.

"You are not making a nuisance of yourself are you, Walters?" said Harry.

Timothy took a step back. Over his shoulder, Caroline saw several of her other gentleman admirers pointing in her direction. An excited cry rose from them as they hurried over to join the gathering.

"Miss Saunders!"

Francis rolled his eyes. Her regular circle of courtiers had found her.

"Well, I see you are set with your group of gentlemen friends. Harry and I would not wish to get in the way of you selecting your future husband, so we shall take our leave. I will be in the cards room for the next hour. See you at supper, Caroline," said Francis. Her brother bowed low and added a flourish of his hand.

On any other night, Caroline would have simply laughed off his tease, but tonight she felt hot tears sting her eyes. With her older sister, Eve, recently married, suitors were now pressing their case for Caroline's hand.

She turned to face her group of admirers, steeling herself for yet another long evening.

On the other side of the ballroom, Julian stood and watched proceedings. Gentleman after gentleman lined up to pay respects to the young woman who had been so rude to him. It was only when he felt a gentle tap on the arm that he finally looked away.

"Watching the latest batch of doe-eyed dandies throw themselves at the Ice Queen's feet, are you? Fools, every one of them."

He raised an eyebrow and looked at his companion. "The Ice Queen?"

His late father's mistress, Lady Margaret, snapped her evening fan open and held it in front of her face before leaning in. "Caroline Saunders. Father is French-born, hence the exotic looks. Mother, Lady Adelaide, is the sister of the Duke of Strathmore. Very good *ton* family. Miss Saunders is considered to be the most beautiful young lady in all of London society. A top catch in the marriage stakes."

Julian nodded. Caroline did not have the typical look of an English rose; rather, she was more enticing. In the hallway, he had noticed her pale blond hair and green eyes. She was a stunning beauty by any man's standards. It was little wonder she had a court of admirers clustered around her, no doubt hanging on her every word.

She was a rare creature indeed, but bitter experience had closed his heart to that sort of woman. He would bet a sack of pennies that beneath her enchanting looks was a cold, hard heart.

"She might be beautiful, but she has a sharp temper on her. I had the misfortune of encountering her a short while ago. That tongue of hers could cut through leather," he replied.

Lady Margaret snorted. "I don't expect too many of her admirers have even noticed the disdainful way she treats them. They are just happy to be within her circle. Many men would give their right arm to be a member of her select court. And of course, the man who finally manages to secure her hand in marriage shall be the envy of all the others. Rumor is she has already turned down more than a dozen marriage proposals."

One of the Ice Queen's courtiers offered her a glass of champagne. She shook her head and waved him away. Another gentleman stepped forward and presented her with a glass of wine.

She accepted it, took one sip and with a loud huff of indignation promptly handed it back to him. She pointed to the back of the group and both hapless gentlemen retreated from her presence.

Julian and Lady Margaret exchanged a sideways glance.

"You know who she reminds me of . . ." Lady Margaret started.

"Do not mention her name," Julian replied through gritted teeth. In the short time he had been studying her, she had displayed several of the more unpleasant traits of Julian's mother.

Even after she had married his father, the Countess Newhall had continued to reign over her own select court of admirers and lovers. If there was one person in London who did not envy the man who eventually married Caroline, it was Julian Palmer.

"When the time comes for me to start looking for my countess, I shall be particular in the sort of woman I seek. I will not repeat the same miserable mistake my father did," he said.

Lady Margaret nodded. "We all hope for that."

Julian turned and met her gaze. "Rest assured, dearest Maggie, I will never marry Caroline Saunders."

Chapter Three

The following morning, Julian was finishing a plate of eggs and pickled herrings when Lady Margaret arrived in the breakfast room. He took one look at the large navy-blue diary in her hands and his appetite disappeared.

It was never a good sign when Lady Margaret produced her diary and even less when her face displayed the look it currently did. It meant she wanted to announce something big. Julian didn't like unexpected announcements.

"I have some good news and some not so good. Firstly, I have been thinking of our conversation from the ball last night and have come up with a plan," she said.

"And to what particular part of our conversation are you referring?" he replied.

"Why, marriage of course. While the Saunders girl might be dithering about choosing a husband, I decided it was high time that we did something about securing the Newhall line. I have come up with a plan to find you a wife."

Julian puffed out his cheeks, which resulted in him receiving a swift clip over the ear.

"Don't be a cheeky thing. You might be Earl Newhall, but that does not mean that I cannot pull you back into line. Your father gave me express permission to beat you if I felt it necessary," she added.

"As I recall, I was twelve at the time, and even then, I don't think he was actually serious about it," replied Julian, rubbing his offended ear.

Lady Margaret took a seat in the chair next to his and gave him one of her warm smiles. He leaned over and gave her a forgiving kiss on the cheek. She meant more to Julian than his mother ever could.

"Tell me your plans, dearest Maggie. I am eager to hear them," he said.

She opened the diary and Julian caught sight of several pages of detailed lists and notes. His heart sank further. Lady Margaret had been busy.

"A week-long party in the country. Lots of lovely young unwed ladies, with their chaperones in tow. At the end of which, you will fall hopelessly in love with one of them and we shall have ourselves a new countess. What do you think?" she said with a smile.

Julian's brain had frozen as soon as it had registered the word party. The thought of having a house full of guests filled him with dread. Meeting with diplomats in palaces and embassies was one thing, but actually having guests sleeping under his roof was less than ideal.

"I have just had a whole month of dealing with the Prussians over the issue of trade with France; I don't think I could stand a house full of people," he replied.

Lady Margaret waved away his protest and turned the page of the diary. Julian saw that she had already drawn up a long list of guests for the event.

He shuddered. "Are we really going to invite all those people? It does seem a lot."

"Trust me, I know what I am doing. You need a good selection of young ladies from which to choose. Your father has been gone for over two years, and he would no doubt be telling me off if I didn't prod you into doing something about getting married. You are twenty-eight years' old, and you need an heir," she replied.

He gently placed his hand over hers. It still seemed at times like only yesterday that he had received word of his father's untimely death. A short illness which had taken him, a fit and healthy man, within a matter of days.

"Yes, as usual, you are right. But don't you think it is getting a little late in the year for a house party? Those things are best held in summer. Perhaps we could wait until next year," he said.

Lady Margaret patted the top of Julian's hand. "You need to marry. Besides, any girl who does not want to come to Derbyshire at this time of the year would not make a sensible countess. Your wife has to be able to endure the chill of a country winter. If any young woman on my list does not own a heavy wool coat and a pair of strong leather boots, then I shall strike her name off. We will find you someone practical. Pretty, but with an intelligent mind. In time, you may even fall in love."

Julian screwed up his face. There was no use attempting to dissuade Lady Margaret from her plans. Once she had an idea in motion, there was only one outcome. He would have to go through with the house party. With thirty earls of Newhall having gone before him, he had the bloodline to consider and to continue.

"Alright, I shall have a house party. But can we agree to keep it to a small and manageable number? I don't want to find myself having to fight off a horde of unwed ladies and their marriage-minded mamas," he replied.

Lady Margaret chortled. "Say that three times fast. Marriage-minded mamas. Marriage-minded, oh never mind. We shall find you a lovely girl, and you shall both be happy."

Julian ignored the last remark. The lords of Newhall and happy marriages did not go together. His parents had been an outstanding example of a terrible, and ultimately failed, union.

"Well then, now that we have that settled, could you please tell me the good news?" said Julian.

The smile disappeared from Lady Margaret's face. She closed her diary and set it down on the breakfast table. "That was the good news. The bad news is that his highness the Count of Lienz arrived in London last week. And he brought his wife with him."

Julian gritted his teeth. His mother was in England.

Chapter Four

Adelaide Saunders put down the orange wool scarf she had been examining in the woolens section of Mack and Bennet, and brushed her fingers across her daughter's cheek. "You look tired. I didn't think you and Francis came in that late last night. If you needed more sleep you should have cried off our shopping trip."

Caroline shrugged. She picked up a pair of white wool gloves before deciding they were impractical and putting them back down. Sleep had not come to her the previous night.

She had hoped that a morning out shopping in central London would help clear her thoughts, but lack of sleep only made matters worse. A dull headache sat just behind her eyes.

Her half-hearted attempt to summon a smile for her mother failed, and she sighed. "I am tired, but it is not from lack of sleep. I am weary of everything at present. London can be a strain at this time of the year."

The season was over and many families had returned to their estates in the country. Only those with business in the city, or who lived permanently in London, remained. The fewer number of guests at balls and parties did nothing to ease the almost constant sensation of being suffocated by the presence of people all around her.

"Perhaps it is your sister you are missing. I miss her too, but since she and Freddie have decided to stay on in France until next month, there is nothing to be done but await their return," replied Adelaide.

Caroline did miss her newly married sister, Eve. The two had been at loggerheads with one another for several years and had only recently reconciled. While she wished her sister all the happiness in the world with her new husband, she secretly wished that they had been granted more time living as friends under the same roof.

"It will be good to see her again, but to be honest, that is not what troubles me," replied Caroline.

"I can see you are unhappy and I do not like to see any of my children out of sorts. Please darling, tell me what troubles you, perhaps I can help," said Adelaide.

Caroline considered her mother's offer. Sharing her problem would bring relief, but she wondered if it would also open a Pandora's box of troubles. In confiding in her mother, Caroline would need to choose her words carefully. "It's Timothy Walters. He will not leave me be. I cannot attend any function without him trailing behind me like a small puppy. He does not seem to understand that I am not in any way romantically interested in him."

"But for the sake of our families you have kept quiet about this until now. And since you have not been able to figure out a way to let him down without causing a fuss, you have finally decided to confide in me. Do I have the right of it?" replied Adelaide.

Caroline nodded. "Yes. Ever since Eve married, he has stepped up his efforts to woo me. Last night at the ball, we had a most unpleasant encounter which threatened to turn ugly. If another guest had not disturbed us, I fear I might have struck him."

Her mother's face registered first shock, then understanding of Caroline's predicament. Timothy and his father conducted business with Caroline's father, Charles. A public falling out would have ramifications for a number of people, and had to be avoided at all costs.

"You are going to have to tell Francis. As he is the one who regularly chaperones you to social functions, he cannot be allowed to remain in the dark over this issue. You are his sister," replied Adelaide.

And therein lay the heart of the problem. If she was to say anything to her brother, he would chastise her for showing such scant regard for yet another young man's heart.

She was about to tell Adelaide that it was no matter when her mother gave her a look which made her hold her tongue.

"I shall speak to Francis. I will tell him he needs to gently persuade Timothy to look elsewhere for his future bride. I won't mention the incident last night; I will just let him know that the attentions of young Mister Walters would be better directed at someone else." She picked up the scarf again and held it up. The light shone through its fine merino threads, and Caroline nodded her approval. The burnt orange would look perfect against her mother's deep brown hair.

"Thank you. Hopefully both Timothy and Francis understand," replied Caroline.

Francis sat back on the leather bench seat of the Saunders family town carriage and stared at Caroline. He was clearly not happy.

"Mama and I had an awkward and, at times, embarrassing conversation this afternoon. I thought you were more than content to have young men running around at your beck and call. Don't tell me you are beginning to tire of your court of admirers?" he said.

Caroline sighed. Her private concerns as to Francis's response about her behavior were showing themselves to be well-founded.

"I have never encouraged Mister Walters. I am polite and friendly to him, the same as I am with Harry. Harry seems to understand that, which is perhaps because he is your friend. But Timothy does not," she replied.

"Harry does because he is Harry," said Francis.

Neither Francis nor Caroline were prepared to voice the fact that Harry also carried a flame for Caroline. It was an open secret between the siblings that Harry had loved her for forever, but valued his friendship with Francis enough never to openly pursue her. And for that, Caroline was eternally grateful. She saw Harry as a kind and sweet man, but one who could never stir her soul.

Francis met her gaze. "And you have never once given Walters any sign that he had a hope in winning your heart?"

"No. I treat him exactly the same as I do all my gentlemen friends," said Caroline.

"To be honest, Caroline, I don't understand why any man would want to throw himself at you when you treat all your admirers so badly. Sometimes even I believe that you have become the ice queen: with no heart."

Caroline huffed angrily. Francis was no help. If he was going to spend the evening punishing her for voicing her concerns to their mother, Caroline would much prefer to stay home. She leaned forward on the carriage bench and reached for the handle of the door.

The carriage lurched forward, causing her hand to miss the handle. She quickly sat back in her seat and glared at her brother. "If this is what you truly think of me, then why are you bothering to take me with you this evening? If you would rather not accompany me, then just say so and I shall ask the driver to turn the carriage around and take me home."

Francis waved his hand at her. "No. It is just that I would have preferred that you had told me Walters was making a nuisance of himself. It's a tad embarrassing for a chap to have his mother take him aside and give him the news. While Mama didn't go into specifics, I was left in no doubt that his attentions toward you have become somewhat problematic."

"My apologies, Francis, but you were in such a hurry to get to the card tables that I didn't get a chance to talk to you in private. You just abandoned me," she snapped.

She immediately regretted her harsh words. Her wide social circle had of late shrunk to become almost exclusively centered around her group of male admirers. With Eve now gone, there was only Francis left at home to escort her out for evening entertainments. If she fell out of favor with him, she would have to resort to following her mother to social gatherings. She would rather stick pins in her fingers than spend the evening with society matrons. There had to be a solution to the problem of unwelcome suitors. If she could just get away.

An idea popped suddenly into her mind. "Perhaps getting out of London might be what I need. If I ask Uncle Ewan, he might let me travel up to Strathmore Castle. Someone from the family is bound to be making the trip north soon, so I can go with them."

Time and distance from London would do her good. Strathmore Castle, the family seat, was located in the lowlands of Scotland, not far from Falkirk. Everyone within the extended Radley family usually made the trip north to spend Christmas at the huge Norman-era castle. If she went up early to Scotland, she would have time and privacy in which to find her good humor once more.

She loved Scotland. Being so far from London, it afforded her the opportunity to go tramping over the hills and enjoying the fresh mountain air without the worry of having to observe all the social niceties of London society. In Scotland, she could relax. She could be herself.

"That is one possible solution. I shall of course have a quiet word with Walters when I next see him. In return, I ask that you hold your temper when it comes to dealing with him. You may not be in love with him, but that is not to say that he won't be disappointed when he discovers that you do not return his affections," replied Francis.

"Thank you. In the meantime, I shall try to be as tactful as I can if I see him again."

Scotland would not be the panacea for all her ills, but it would give her time and distance to come up with a better approach to the incessant demands of suitors such as Timothy Walters.

Chapter Five

The carriage stopped outside an elegant townhouse in Bird Street, and a footman opened the door.

"I thought we were going to the party at East India House?' said Caroline.

Francis jumped down from the carriage and offered her his hand. "Change of plans. Before I was advised of the delicate situation with Timothy Walters, I made mention to him of our plans for this evening. In light of that, I thought it might be prudent for you and I to attend Viscount Munroe's party instead. I hardly think Walters will try and hunt you down if he discovers you are not at East India House."

Once inside, Caroline fell into her usual routine. A small group of admirers quickly formed around her, but she felt safe with them. One or two of the bolder members of the group asked to place their names on her dance card, but the rest seemed more than content just to be close to her.

"I shall be in the cards room if you need me," said Francis.

Caroline was about to remind her brother that as Harry was not present this evening, he was leaving her unchaperoned, but she thought the better of it. The idea of having an evening without Timothy, Harry, or Francis lurking nearby was suddenly quite liberating.

If pressed, Julian would have confessed to cowardice. Since Lady Margaret's revelation that the former Dowager Countess Newhall was in town, he had steadfastly refused to attend any social functions. At the end of the week, Lady Margaret had finally called him on his behavior and ordered him out of the house.

Stepping into the ballroom of Viscount Munroe's home, Julian held his breath. As a child, he had turned avoiding his mother into an artform. He called upon all those finely-honed skills once more as his gaze slowly scanned the room. He would do all he could to avoid having any contact with her.

You are a grown man, Newhall. When are you going to stop being afraid of your mother?

But the scars from his childhood ran deep, right to his bones.

He quickly sought out a footman and downed two large brandies in rapid succession. With the edge taken off his nerves, he slowly began to circulate, ever conscious of checking and rechecking the people around him. A trickle of sweat worked its way uncomfortably down his back.

A space had been cleared to one side of the main reception room for dancing, and he stopped to watch four couples as they stepped through a quadrille. The smooth motion of feet and swirling skirts moving in time, coupled with the brandy, soon calmed his mind.

He was still swaying gently with the music when the quadrille finally came to an end. To his surprise, the orchestra then quickly changed tempo and he caught the opening strains of a waltz. Other dancers now crowded onto the dance floor. In some quarters the waltz was considered scandalous, but its popularity in London high society continued to rise.

With an impending house party, it occurred to him that he would have to brush up on his footwork. It wouldn't do to go stepping on the toes of any young ladies who may have it in mind to be his future countess. Crushed toes did not win hearts.

Lady Margaret's plans for the house party were moving forward, and he was now reconciled to playing his part in securing the Newhall line. He would do all he could to make the event, and the search for his future countess, a success.

He was still in two minds as to whether to seek out a dance partner to practice his waltz, or indulge in a third brandy, when the decision was taken roughly out of his hands.

From out of nowhere, a hand appeared under his arm and he found himself being dragged toward the dance floor. When he looked down, he was shocked to discover that the owner of the hand was the same blond beauty who had insulted him in the hallway at the recent party. The very same woman who had told him to mind his own bloody business.

"Dance with me," Caroline Saunders commanded.

Julian was the prisoner of the Ice Queen.

Words of protest died on his lips as they neared the edge of the dance floor. Across the ballroom, to the right of the orchestra, he caught sight of his mother. She was standing to the side, so had not yet seen him, but it would only take a small movement of her head for their gazes to meet.

The long years apart were swept away as he beheld the hard face of the Countess of Lienz. Her disapproving frown had now become permanent in the lines around her mouth.

Caroline tugged on his arm and he tore his gaze from his mother. Caught between his lifelong nemesis and the presumptuous beauty who held him captive, he immediately chose to dance. He would choose many other things before he would voluntarily speak to the countess.

He took hold of Caroline and spun her into the waltz. "We meet again," he said.

She looked up at him and when their gazes met, he was certain he heard her curse under her breath. But to her credit, she quickly recovered. Impressive.

"Caroline Saunders, and you are Earl Newhall. Since this is the first time we have made proper introductions, I think we should both forget about our previous encounter. I know I certainly have done my best to put it behind me," she replied.

He raised an eyebrow. She was a feisty creature, beyond just a little rude. He tightened his grip of her hand and was rewarded with a hard stare. "And yet you have chosen me to rescue you from something or someone. I cannot think of any other reason why you would pressgang a chap into dancing with you. Don't tell me you inadvertently misplaced your group of sycophants this evening? How careless of you."

The flash of anger which crossed Caroline's face was deeply satisfying. "How dare you! Why I should . . ."

Her gaze drifted to something behind him, and she immediately fell silent. At the next turn of the dance, he checked to see where she had looked. Across the floor, some ten feet away, stood the same young man she had been arguing with at the party some days earlier. The man who had demanded that Caroline dance with him. *What was his name? Thomas or something?* Whoever he was, his gaze never wavered from Caroline.

"Your fiancé?" he asked.

Caroline grasped his hand tighter. "No. His name is Timothy Walters. He is an admirer. An unwelcome one. I had hoped to avoid him this evening but he has managed to run me to ground," she replied. The earlier haughtiness in her voice disappeared.

"I take it you don't share his sentiments or affections," he said.

"No," she replied.

Julian had heard it all before. His mother's constant lament at having been forced into an arranged marriage with his father. How her ethereal beauty had been squandered on a man who was short and fat. She was a shining light of London society, while the late Earl Newhall had been little more than a boring country squire.

The fact that he worshipped his wife and did everything to make her happy mattered nothing to her.

Her disdain for her husband had then been transferred to her son from the moment of his birth. Julian's mother had never attempted to hide her disgust at his very existence.

"Are you here with someone who can take responsibility for your safety? You cannot hide out all evening on the dance floor," he asked. He had no intention of becoming the man responsible for protecting her.

The sooner he was rid of the tiresome Caroline Saunders, the better. Women like her would never be satisfied with their choice of husbands. Pity the poor fool who did marry her. He, for one, was determined not to be a cuckold the same as his father had been.

Her shoulders dropped. "Yes, my brother, Francis, is in the card room. If you could see your way to accompanying me to locate him, I would be forever in your debt. He is a very tall young gentleman with a shock of white hair, he should be easy to spot in the crowd. While I don't wish to cause a public scene, I fear that if I am forced to speak to Mister Walters, I may not be able to hold my tongue."

Having already been on the receiving end of Caroline's fiery temper, Julian did not wish to witness it a second time. "Of course."

They fell silent, after which Julian was content to let his thoughts wander as he continued to pull Caroline skillfully through the turns of the waltz. When she stepped closer to him, and he was forced to adjust his hold on her waist, he did his best to maintain the distance between them.

At the end of the dance, he quickly ushered Caroline from the dance floor and went in search of Francis. Her brother could deal with his self-centered sister. Francis, however, was not in the card room.

She turned to him, then nodded toward the doors which led outside to the garden terrace. "He may have gone out into the garden to smoke a cigar; he does do that at times. I shall see if I can locate him outside," said Caroline, stepping away from him.

Julian kept his hold on her arm. She was still his responsibility and he was most definitely not going to let her go outside on her own. It was a crowded party, but if her unwelcome suitor had it in mind to find her, he would. Julian was not going to let Caroline go until he delivered her safely into the hands of her brother. "Let me help you. One of the benefits of being as tall as I am is that I can spot people in a crowd."

His mind now occupied on finding Francis Saunders, Julian failed to see his mother when she appeared from a nearby room. By the time he did see her, it was too late. The countess crossed his path and then stopped. She turned and gave both him and Caroline a look that would wither grapes on the vine. "Newhall."

"Your Highness," he replied.

His mother's eyes sparkled at the acknowledgement of her exalted status. Her new husband was of royal Austrian blood.

Caroline dipped into a curtsey, giving his mother the respect to which her title deserved. Julian knew the woman herself did not merit any sort of deferential treatment.

The countess did not acknowledge Caroline's elegant manners. "I see you have put on weight Newhall. I hope you know the name of the tailor the Prince of Wales uses, because from the look of your girth, you shall also require his services shortly," she sneered.

Julian ignored the spiteful and unfounded comment and dipped into a respectful bow. Years of his mother's constant berating of him for his physical appearance had afforded him a degree of thick skin when it came to her barbed insults. "Mother," he replied, loudly enough so that others around may hear.

The downturn in the corner of her lips was payment enough for him. The former Countess Newhall had always been one to lie about her age. Having a fully-grown son was not something she would appreciate being mentioned in public.

When he lifted his head, his gaze fell upon the emerald and diamond choker which the countess wore at her throat. A pair of emerald drop earrings completed the set.

He gritted his teeth. They were part of the Newhall estate collection. She had taken them, along with a number of other priceless pieces of jewelry, when she'd abandoned Julian's father and fled to Austria to be with her royal lover. She had no right to them. None at all.

"Madam, those jewels do not belong to you. I demand that you return them, along with the other estate items you still have in your possession forthwith. I can supply you with a list if you require one, starting with the Crusader Ruby," he said.

The ruby and diamond necklace had been the centerpiece of the Newhall estate jewels for more than seven hundred years. To this day, Julian could not understand why his father had let the symbol of his family's honor be taken out of England. To be stolen by a woman who hated the very sight of him.

"As you have not yet married, that still leaves me as the Countess of Newhall. So, I am fully within my rights to wear them," she tartly replied.

Julian held back the satisfied grin he would have loved to have shown her at that moment. "Actually, madam, since you have remarried and are now the Countess of Lienz, your point is mute. You are no longer the Countess Newhall. I would be happy to speak to the count about recovering my property, if you so wish."

Word of his mother's marriage had reached him while he was working in Paris. She was now the wife of an Austrian count, the same man she had run off to be with all those years ago.

She waved her delicately painted, evening fan in his face. "Oh, very well. I shall call upon you tomorrow and you may have your trinkets back. To be truthful, they are rather garish. The gold on the tiara your father gave me has tarnished somewhat, which I suppose is what comes from cheaply made goods."

Julian was quickly tiring of the encounter with his mother. It had been more than ten years since he had last seen her, and the enmity between them had not lessened with time.

"Speaking of cheap goods, I see you have not developed any taste when it comes to women," she said. Her gaze was now locked firmly on Caroline, who dug her fingers into his arm. "God forbid you would taint the English purity of the Palmer family blood with a half-French wife. Your father would turn over in his grave. Please tell me she is your mistress and nothing more."

Julian was about to summon up gallant words to defend Caroline's character and breeding, but he didn't need them.

"Having met you, I should hope never to simply be a man's mistress. From the way you are aging, I can see the years of living in sin have done nothing for your looks," remarked Caroline.

You could have cut the air with a knife. Julian wondered if his mother had ever been addressed in such an insulting and disrespectful manner before in her life. He doubted it.

The countess opened her mouth, and Julian steeled himself for a vile retort.

"Considering your reputation as a cock-tease, I don't expect you shall ever have to worry about any man bedding you, my dear," said the countess.

She had not failed him.

Caroline gasped.

Out of the corner of his eye, Julian saw the white-haired Francis Saunders come in from the garden. He waved him over in the vain hope of avoiding imminent bloodshed.

"Ah, Newhall. Thank you. I have been looking for Caroline for the past fifteen minutes. Well done in finding her," said Francis.

Caroline let go of Julian's arm and hastened to her brother's side. She gave Julian a brief nod in thanks, and Francis hurried his sister away.

The countess watched them go, then turned back to Julian. "Seriously, Newhall, why are you wasting your time with a harlot like that? Everyone knows she has a private group of young men who follow her everywhere. Of course, if you want a wife who will give you a brood of children all fathered by different men then be my guest. It would save you the trouble. I had heard you were not that bothered about women. If that is true, then the Saunders chit might be exactly what you are looking for."

Julian took a deep breath and forced down the automatic response to his mother's barbed insults. They were just the latest ones in a long series of taunts, all designed to cause him maximum pain and embarrassment.

They did however agree on one thing. Caroline Saunders would make a terrible choice for the next Countess Newhall.

"No, your highness. Rest assured, Caroline Saunders is the very last woman I would ever wish to make my wife. From my short acquaintance with her, I would say that she is as ruthless and cold as you. And after enduring the misery of my childhood, I would never inflict that same unhappiness upon my own children."

And with that, he gave the countess a curt bow and took his leave. What should have been a quiet and relaxing evening in good company had been turned into one of frustration and slow-burning rage.

As he climbed into his carriage, he pulled a hip flask from his coat. He quickly emptied the flask down his throat before stuffing it back into his pocket.

Beautiful, conceited women could go to the devil.

Chapter Six

"I cannot believe that woman has the gall to parade about town wearing the estate jewels. She has no right. Even if she had not remarried, your mother gave up all rights to them the day she walked out on your father," said Lady Margaret.

"Yes, well after today, that will no longer be an issue. She has sent word this morning that she will be arriving just before noon, and the jewels will be handed over. After that I don't expect to see her again," replied Julian.

Lady Margaret shifted uncomfortably in her chair. He saw that her hands were clenched into fists. "Would you like me to withdraw to my room for the duration of her visit? She still does not acknowledge me in public."

Julian shook his head. "No. As far as I am concerned, until I take a wife, you are the lady of the Newhall estate. The countess has no rights in this house. You should not have to hide from her."

Lady Margaret picked up her diary and smiled. She may not have been his mother, but after what she had done to heal his father's broken heart, Julian had become fiercely protective of her.

From her diary she pulled out a folded-up piece of paper and showed it to him. "I have finalized the list of suitable young ladies for your estate party. I thought you might like to go over it. The sooner I am able to extend invitations, the more likely the chance that we shall have a full house."

Julian held out his hand and took the piece of paper. He ran his gaze down the list of names. He barely knew any of the girls Lady Margaret had selected, so he would have to trust her judgement.

"If they meet with your approval, I am sure they will do fine," he said.

A footman entered the drawing room and bowed low. "Her Highness, the Countess of Lienz."

Margaret and Julian looked at one another as Julian handed back the invitation list.

His mother swept into the room with all the occasion that arriving at a grand ball would demand. She took one look at Lady Margaret and averted her gaze. She held out a gold case toward Julian, and let go of it. He made a hurried catch before it hit the floor.

"I have brought your cheap trinkets. My darling count says we cannot have you making noises about town that I have stolen from you. I forgot just how ugly some of the pieces were," she said.

Julian ignored her comments and placed the case on the nearby table. A gasp of dismay came from his mother as he opened the case and examined the pieces one by one.

"You don't trust your own mother? That is the height of bad manners, Newhall," she said.

He looked up from the box and fixed her with a steely glare. "Madam, the Crusader Ruby is missing. Did you think I wouldn't look for it?"

Lady Margaret rose from her seat. "I shall leave the two of you to sort out this matter."

The countess looked her slowly up and down. Her gaze settled on the list in Lady Margaret's hand. She quickly snatched it away, then stood reading it.

"So, what is this?" She laughed.

"It is none of your business," replied Julian.

The countess waved the piece of paper in his face and laughed once more. "I know what this is: it's a list of names of young, eligible ladies. Don't tell me you are finally going to select a wife, Newhall?"

"The necklace," replied Julian.

The countess looked from Julian, to the list, and back again. A wicked smile appeared on her lips. "I should have a say in my successor. How is this for a bargain? The Crusader Ruby, for the list."

"What?" he replied.

"I give you the necklace, you allow me to make the final list and send out the invitations. I will make sure that the next countess is from the right family. I have already spotted several girls on the guestlist from new money, so clearly Lady Margaret has no idea what she is doing. You cannot possibly allow your father's mistress to handle matters regarding your future marriage. As your mother, it should fall to me."

Julian looked at Lady Margaret. He gritted his teeth when he saw tears shining in her eyes. His mother had him at a disadvantage, and they all knew it. If he didn't agree to her terms, he may never see the most priceless piece in the Newhall collection ever again.

"Agreed. You get to make the final list and send out the invitations. But Lady Margaret is to be given a copy of the final names. As she is helping me to host the house party, she should know who will be coming," he replied.

The countess quickly folded the list and slipped it into her reticule.

For several minutes after the countess had left, Julian and Lady Margaret stood in silence in the drawing room. His mind was a whirl of half-thoughts and worries. What was his mother's game? Negotiating with the various European powers after the fall of Emperor Napoleon had been easier than dealing with her.

Locked firmly in his memories was the knowledge that the countess was a woman who always had a secret agenda. Nothing was ever straightforward with her. The one thing he could be certain of was that his mother could not be trusted.

Julian's mind had already made up a long list of possible outcomes from allowing his mother to help select the guests for his house party. Of the myriad of outcomes, very few were favorable for him.

He would need to tread carefully when it came to the party. Knowing his mother, she would do everything in her power to arrange a marriage for him that was entirely unsuitable.

A wife who would treat him in exactly the same fashion as she had his father—that would be her ultimate revenge for him having the temerity to be born. Nothing would make her happier than to see her only son miserable.

Even now, he could imagine her sitting in her fine carriage on her way back to her fine new husband, plotting how best she could hurt her son.

"Just remember, no matter whom she chooses to invite, you don't have to marry any of them," said Lady Margaret eventually.

"Yes. But what damage will she manage to do in the meantime? Will the mothers of the *ton* be told that I am some kind of monster, entirely unfit for marriage?"

Only after he returned to London following the end of the week-long party, would he know whether the price of recovering the Crusader Ruby had been set beyond his means.

Chapter Seven

Julian and Lady Margaret stood inside the entrance to the ballroom at yet another society ball. He had only finally agreed to accompany Lady Margaret in order to help calm her nerves over the impending house party. If he'd had his way, he would be sitting quietly at home enjoying a glass or two of fine French brandy.

"We won't have to stay till the end. I just wish to see some friends," said Lady Margaret. She leaned in close. "And to put my ear to the ground to pick up any rumors your mother might be spreading about." She pointed in the direction of a group of recent arrivals and gave Julian a cheerful wave goodbye. "I shall see you in a few hours. Now go and have some fun."

He dipped into a bow. "Be careful. The countess has a lifetime's experience in undertaking wicked deeds. You do not want to get caught up in any of her machinations."

After hunting down a glass of brandy, Julian began his usual circuit of the room. It was interesting to observe London society in its favorite habitat: the ballroom. For every young, finely dressed dandy there were a dozen overweight middle-aged men who barely fitted their clothes.

Then there were the matrons, with their strict pecking order. The wives of the senior titled men were always the center of attention in the various circles of women. Then came the wives of the lesser titles, their friends, and finally, at the edge of the circle stood the women from new money.

He huffed, frustrated. The fact that the women whose families had new money could buy the estates of the older titles several times over did not seem to count for anything. It was far more important that a relative in the dim and distant past had once been close to some long-dead king. Or had fought in some bloody battle. The *ton* and its rules.

Rounding a corner, he came upon the dance floor. It was a crush of couples. In typical high society fashion, too many guests were crowded into too small a space. The room was stiflingly hot. He downed the last of his brandy and handed the glass to a passing footman.

He was about to seek out the fresh air of the supper room and sample its delights, when he caught sight of her. "Bloody Caroline Saunders," he muttered under his breath.

True to form, she was standing with several admirers, all of whom were jostling to pay her their respects. He watched her for a time. She was a beauty; he could not deny that fact.

His body stirred to life as he took in her soft curves. Her hips were a perfect round shape. The fabric of her silver gown barely kissed them before falling gracefully to finish just above her matching silver slippers. His gaze lingered on the mound of her breasts which peaked out the top of the bodice of her gown. They were an enticing delight, which had his fingers itching to touch them. In her hair she wore several long ribbons. They trailed down her back and came to rest on the top of her womanly rump. Julian licked his lips. How delightful it would be to run his tongue down her naked back and place soft kisses on those hips.

He caught himself with a start. He had been indulging in a private fantasy about her, forgetting for a moment where he was, and who she was. He didn't need to look down to know that he was rock hard.

The object of his attention turned and caught his unsuspecting gaze. Without thinking, he smiled at her.

Blast.

The grin fell from his face as she began to march with great purpose toward him, her group of admirers scurrying behind her.

Damn and double blast.

"Lord Newhall," she said, stopping a few feet in front of him.

He forced himself to give her the bow which polite society demanded of him. After their last encounter, he would have much preferred to turn and show her his back as he walked away. But manners were deeply ingrained in men of his rank and as much as he wished it, he could not simply ignore her. "Miss Saunders, how are you this evening?"

She looked at the men who had followed her and sighed. At the back of the group stood the hapless fool who Julian had supposedly rescued her from at the ball earlier in the week. The gentleman in question had either not taken the hint, or as Julian suspected, not been allowed to leave Caroline Saunders's sphere of influence.

He wondered if her fair-maiden-in-distress act had been just that: a means to get the attention of yet another man and make her disciples jealous. The more he looked at Caroline, the more he disliked her.

"I should like to dance. You owe me that much," she said.

Her offer to dance with him did not go down well with her cluster of admirers. A hubbub of disapproval rippled through the members of the Ice Queen's entourage. Julian, the interloper, was being pulled up the ranks to the head of the line and her steadfast followers were not happy about it.

She had a spine made of steel, he would give her that. After the charming way she had dealt with both him and his mother, he was certain that it was she who owed him, but the look on her face told him he would get nowhere by protesting.

Caroline held out her hand and wriggled her fingers impatiently at him.

Julian would have dearly loved to slap those long, elegant fingers. "Are you certain one of these other gentlemen could not accompany you in a dance? I can assure you that any one of them is far more eager than I to spin you around the dance floor." He curled his toes up in his boots to stifle his delight at the anger which flashed across her face. When their gazes met, he slowly blinked. Fiery temptresses like her were easy prey to a man with a cool head.

Yet he hungered for her. Desire and dislike of Caroline now battled for his attention.

"No. I should like to dance with you," she replied.

Julian considered the options set before him. He could say no, and then be torn limb from limb by her flock of admirers for his insolence. Perhaps that was not such a good way to start the evening.

He could cry off with an existing injury, but that would be cowardice, and he would have to limp around for the rest of the evening. It would also mean admitting to himself that she had got to him. He would poke sticks in his eyes before he admitted to such a foolish notion.

Which left the remaining option. The least appealing of them all.

He would have to dance with her.

"Of course," he replied with a tight grin. He took hold of her hand, ignoring the low howls of protest from the others.

Julian led Caroline onto the dance floor as a waltz was beginning, and in one deftly timed move, pulled her roughly into his arms. He ignored her squeal of protest. As far as he was concerned, she had not made her stipulations about the dance clear enough.

"Lord Newhall, don't hold me so tightly," she said.

"Shut up and dance," he replied.

Her other muttered protests were fortunately drowned out by the orchestra. When a frustrated Caroline attempted to stomp on his foot, Julian nipped the side of her evening slipper with his boot. He felt a wicked sense of satisfaction as his boot connected with her delicate foot. "Mind your feet, Miss Saunders. You could do yourself some harm."

He spun her into a tight turn, and her arms flayed about as she struggled to hold onto him. Of course, he knew exactly what he was doing; his grip was sure. He was more than content to insult her on the dance floor, but he would not stoop to actually letting her fall.

At the next turn she managed to stay with him, while also avoiding getting her feet under Julian's large boots. He raised an eyebrow in acknowledgement. She was a skilled dancer. And a fighter.

Caroline refused to meet his gaze. Instead she smiled at all the other couples that they passed by. While she had a smile plastered firmly on her face, he was certain he heard her mutter "blackguard" as he swept her into another turn of the waltz.

When the music finally came to an end a short time later, Julian slowed through the final turn and set Caroline safely back on her feet. They applauded the orchestra. He then looked down at her and took in the expression of anger which was locked on her face. Her jaw was set hard and her lips tightly held together. She was furious.

Julian, silently enjoying his moment of triumph, simply smiled back at her.

As the other guests wandered from the dance floor, Caroline stood where she was. Julian waited for the customary curtsey from his lady partner, but her hands were locked tight in fists of rage. "You. You fool of a man," she stammered.

He cleared his throat. "Actually, I have several degrees from the University of Edinburgh, so I am no one's fool, least of all yours, Miss Saunders. You demanded that I dance with you, and that is exactly what I did. Nothing more and nothing less."

Her cheeks turned from a soft pale pink to bright red. He could hear her breathing heavily, the air sucking in through her nose and out through her mouth. "How dare you? You brute of a man. I shall never speak to you again."

In for a penny, in for a pound.

"One can only live in hope of such pleasure," he replied.

The gasp which came from her lips made Julian's night complete. He wished someone would hand him a glass of champagne and a medal for his efforts.

"You are the rudest man I have ever met. You flung me around the dance floor like a wet dishrag. I shall never ever speak to you again," she bit back.

"And yet, your lips are still moving. Really, Miss Saunders, you should make up your mind," he replied.

At this, his last and most satisfying retort, Julian stepped back and began to walk away. Hell would freeze over before he bowed to the Ice Queen again.

As he headed toward the supper room in search of a sweet cake, he turned one last time and watched with disgust as Caroline's group of admirers all rushed across the floor and gathered around her.

"Fools," he muttered.

But just as the last of her court stepped in close, and Caroline was lost from his sight, Julian could have sworn that she was still staring at him. And was that a soft grin he saw on her lips?

No. He must have imagined it.

Chapter Eight

C aroline dragged herself somewhat reluctantly out of bed the following morning. If she'd had any say in it, the bed covers would have remained over her face and she would have slept through to noon. But members of her family apparently had other ideas.

"Your father wishes to speak to you as a matter of urgency," said her maid.

With a large huff, she threw back the blankets. Swinging her legs over the side of the bed, she dropped to the floor. "Ow!"

She looked down and spotted the bruise on the outside of her right foot.

"Big-footed lump," she muttered.

She had little doubt in her mind that Lord Newhall had deliberately trodden on her foot. She had seen the sly smile which threatened at the corner of his mouth as his boot connected with her dance slipper.

A mouth that was blessed with full lips. They made her heart flutter when she looked at them. And those grey eyes. They promised all manner of wicked delights. Julian Palmer had featured strongly in her dreams that night.

He was most certainly an unusual man. He had openly challenged her status as queen of the ballroom. Few other men in the *ton* would have had the temerity to address her the way he did. It was clear that whatever magic she wielded over others had little effect on Earl Newhall.

He instilled in her a heady mix of frustration, annoyance, and simmering lust. She was innocent in the ways of love, but the thrill of heat which coursed through her body every time he was near told her all she needed to know. He could teach her a great deal about desire.

After dressing and hurriedly putting her hair up in a simple bun, she knocked on the door of her father's study.

"Ah, there you are," said Charles Saunders, stepping out from behind his desk.

Caroline closed the door behind her and took a seat in her usual spot on the couch nearest the fire. Her father's office, though small, was always cold.

He came and sat in the armchair opposite her. "I have had a visitor this morning."

The look on his face, coupled with those words made her heart sink. How many more times would they have this conversation?

"Who?" she asked.

Her father sighed. "The fact that you had to ask who could be visiting me to offer for your hand in marriage speaks volumes, Caroline. It was Timothy Walters. I hope the name at least rings a bell."

"I am sorry, Papa. He had not spoken to me, nor made me aware that he was coming to see you," she replied.

Charles sat back in his chair and brought his hands together. He looked at her over steepled fingers. "This cannot go on. Your mother is deeply concerned that you are getting a reputation as a . . . well—and we French do not use the word lightly—an *allumeuse*," he said.

Heat raced to Caroline's cheeks as she reeled from her father's words. Her parents thought she was a tease. "But I never encouraged him. In fact, only a matter of days ago I asked him to stay away from me," she pleaded.

"Yes. I know you don't think you encourage these young men, but clearly, they feel that you do. Now while neither your mother nor I are saying you are giving them mixed signals, we think it best that you stay away from social gatherings for a little while. Some time at home might do your reputation some good," he said.

Caroline rose from the couch. She felt nauseous. No unmarried young woman wanted her reputation held up to scrutiny. Society matrons were inclined to discourage their sons from offering marriage to young ladies with sullied reputations. Even those such as Caroline who came from one of the top *ton* families.

"Actually, Papa, I was thinking I might ask Uncle Ewan if I could go to Scotland and stay at Strathmore Castle. That will keep me out of social circulation for a little while," she replied.

Charles nodded. "That is an excellent idea. While you and Francis are off boating in Hyde Park this afternoon, I shall send word to Strathmore House. If his grace is agreeable, you could leave for Scotland soon."

Caroline hugged her father. "Thank you, Papa."

Her plan to escape London was now in motion.

Chapter Nine

How much effort would it take to pitch his mother into the Serpentine? Julian wasn't sure, but walking beside her as she rattled off a long list of his supposed failures in life, he was becoming more willing by the minute to take a chance.

It had not been an easy decision to accept her offer to spend the morning with her before she sailed back to Europe. He had been regretting it with every passing moment since their arrival. It would be the first and last time he played the role of dutiful son in public.

She was toying with him. The final guest list for the house party, along with the Crusader Ruby, was still in the countess's hands. The public outing was purely for the keeping up of appearances. The grown man made to be at his mother's beck and call.

"You could have taken up an ambassadorship. I hear the Americans are keen to repair some relations with England now that beastly Napoleon is gone. Washington would be a good start for you to rise up in the political ranks. Anywhere would be better than that drab castle in Derbyshire," she said.

"I have an estate to run in England, and besides that, Washington is supposed to be bitterly cold in winter," replied Julian.

They were walking alongside the shore of the elegant lake in

Hyde Park, heading toward the popular cake house for some cheese cake and coffee. The countess was in fine form, much to his disappointment.

"Look at that! Some people just don't know how to behave in public," she said.

Julian roused from his musings and looked to where his mother pointed. Across from them, in the middle of the lake, were a pair of boats side by side. Standing in the middle of each boat was a young man wielding an oar, making every effort to splash the inhabitants of the other vessel.

The male in the nearest boat to them stumbled and nearly tipped it over. The woman, who was seated in the middle of the boat, screamed.

"James, for heaven's sake, you will put us all at the bottom of the lake. Take me back to shore!"

Julian stopped at the sound of the familiar voice of reproach. As the boat slowly turned and began to make its way back to the shore, he caught sight of the offended young woman. It was Caroline Saunders. He would know that angry, disapproving face anywhere.

The countess harrumphed. "I told you the Saunders girl was common. No respectable young miss would go out on the Serpentine and make such a spectacle of herself. Pity the boat didn't turn over. I would have enjoyed seeing her fall into the water."

As the boat neared the shore, Caroline looked up, and she and Julian locked gazes. She glared at Julian. Her lips moved, and he quickly registered the word *fool* directed at him.

The second boat came racing into the shore. It hit the bank with some force and the occupants fell out of their seats. Francis Saunders struggled to get to his feet at the end of the boat. The young lady with him managed to get a foot over the side and was making a valiant attempt to find dry land. Ignoring his mother's protests, Julian hurried to the water's edge and assisted the young lady safely to shore.

"Thank you," she said.

The boat containing Caroline pulled up alongside him. The young man in charge of it leaped out and tried to grab the end. He missed, and the boat began to drift away from the shore.

"Sorry!" he yelled. He was laughing, but the look on Caroline's face was one of anything but amusement.

"James!" she cried.

As the dry land slipped away, she made an ill-timed leap from the boat.

Julian could have caught her if he had wanted. Instead, he took a step back and watched as she fell to her hands and knees in the wet mud at the edge of the lake.

"Ooof!" she cried.

The others raced down to the water's edge and helped her to her feet. Her skirts were covered in thick black mud. It caked her hands and her arms all the way to her elbow. She looked a terrible sight.

"James, please go and find our driver and carriage. We had better get Caroline home and changed into dry clothes before she catches her death," said Francis.

The woman Julian had helped out of the other boat a moment before, took off her coat and lay it over Caroline's shoulders all the while offering words of comfort. Caroline closed her eyes and began to sob.

Julian, ashamed at having let Caroline fall into the mud, quickly averted his gaze. He backed away from the side of the lake and rejoined his mother.

"Well done, Newhall. You gave that little bitch exactly what she deserved. I didn't think you had it in you, but you did," she said.

Julian followed the countess around to the old brick cake house situated by the lake side. The whole time, he silently cursed himself for his disgraceful act. The one and only time his mother had approved of something he had done, and instead of feeling good about it, he felt nothing but utter shame.

Chapter Ten

"Caroline, do join us."

Her mother had sent word for her to put aside her sewing and come to the formal drawing room. They had a special guest.

With her hair freshly brushed and pinned up into a soft bun, Caroline checked her gown for creases before making her way to her mother's elegant drawing room. Only the best guests were received by Adelaide in there.

The placid smile she had fixed to her face as she entered the room froze as she beheld the sight of the Countess of Lienz seated on one of her mother's deep green silk-covered sofas.

"Your highness, may I introduce my youngest daughter, Caroline," announced Adelaide.

Caroline's heart began to thump loudly in her chest. Had the countess come to complain about Caroline's behavior at the ball?

"Ah yes, I see the resemblance," replied the countess.

"Caroline, this is the Countess of Lienz, formerly Countess Newhall. She has come to share some wonderful news with us," said Adelaide.

Caroline dropped into a deep curtsey. "Your highness."

The countess held out a hand, and Caroline was left with no

choice but to accept it. The countess looked at her and smiled sweetly. "So, the rumors are true. You are a diamond of the first water. How can it be then that you are not yet married? Don't tell me you are holding out for a love match, my dear."

Adelaide softly chortled. "My husband and I have set the example of a happy marriage. Both my daughters believe in love."

The countess coughed, and Caroline sensed it was taking every ounce of self-control for her not to mock Adelaide for having created such expectations of marriage for her daughters.

"Well, love may come to you, but don't forget duty. You owe it to your parents to make a good match. Many marriages are based on friendship, or at least respect," replied the countess.

"Yes, your highness."

"Now go sit with your mother while we discuss the good news."

Caroline took a seat on the sofa next to her mother, and placed her hands in her lap.

The countess smiled once more. "I have come to invite you to a house party at Newhall Castle. My son has decided to invite a select group of young ladies and their chaperones to spend the week at the castle. Isn't that exciting?"

Adelaide turned to Caroline and took her by the hand.

"Lord Newhall feels terrible about your accident at the Serpentine, and wants to help make amends."

Caroline's gaze went from her mother to the countess.

The countess shook her head. "Julian was beside himself with remorse after we got home. While it was purely an accident, he blames himself for you having fallen into the mud on the lake shore. He feels he should have done more to save you. And while you of course would not hold him to fault, he is most keen for you to come to Derbyshire so that he can personally apologize."

The countess's words dripped with insincerity, but Caroline saw the beaming smile on Adelaide's face. There were few reasons why an unmarried nobleman invited a group of eligible young ladies to spend a week at his country estate, and all of them contained the word marriage.

She couldn't understand the countess's reasons for inviting her, but from her mother's reaction to the invitation, Caroline knew she had no choice.

"Thank you, your highness. I would love to attend the party," replied Caroline.

The countess rose, and picked up her gloves. "My only regret is that I will not be able to host the gathering. My husband and I sail for the Continent in the next few days and he is unable to change his schedule. Newhall will find someone to assist with any preparations that I have not finalized before my departure."

"How disappointing for you," replied Adelaide.

"Yes quite."

Caroline caught the edge of the countess's remark, and forced herself not to frown. Lord Newhall's mother seemed anything but displeased at not being able to attend the house party.

Once the countess had left, Adelaide and Caroline gathered once more in the drawing room.

"Do I really have to go? Could we cry off at the last minute?" said Caroline.

Her mother looked mortified. "No, absolutely not. Lord Newhall is one of the most eligible men in all of England. Of course, you must go."

"But . . ."

Caroline was on the verge of explaining to her about the several unpleasant encounters she'd had with Lord Newhall, but she thought better of it. It was bad enough that her parents thought her a tease; for her to turn down even the slightest opportunity to become Countess Newhall was unthinkable.

"But nothing. You wished to get out of London. And I know you wanted to go to Scotland, but look at this as a much better opportunity than just sitting up on the windswept ramparts of Strathmore Castle. Who knows, you may even get a husband out of the trip."

A resigned Caroline went back to the upstairs sitting room and picked up her sewing. As she pushed the needle back into the hem of the nightshirt she was making for Francis, she swore.

"A whole week with bloody Newhall—that is all I need."

Chapter Eleven

"A house party at this time of the year is a bit odd, don't you think? The weather up north will be getting rather chilly. There won't be a lot of opportunity for outdoor party games for a start. Could you imagine trying to play bowls and nine pins in the snow? I for one am glad I will not be attending."

Caroline glanced at her mother and Aunt Mary, who were seated on a nearby sofa in the Saunders's family sitting room, before answering her cousin. "You are not coming?"

"No. My friend Leah's wedding is in a few weeks, and she has asked that I spend time with her while she makes the last of her wedding preparations. A trip to Derbyshire is simply out of the question," replied Claire.

Caroline had spent the better part of the past day mulling over the Countess of Lienz's visit and invitation. Lord Newhall could invite all of the unwed young misses from London to his party, but she, for one, would be spending as much time as she could away from him.

His pathetic behavior in sending his mother to apologize for the incident at the Serpentine filled her with rage. He had stepped back and deliberately made sure she fell into the mud. Her one regret from the afternoon by the lake was that she had not got to her feet fast enough to lob a large lump of wet mud in his direction. The next time she encountered Lord Newhall, she would give him a piece of her mind. He could take his apology and give it to someone gullible enough to believe it.

Rude, pompous, horrible man.

"Mama says I have to go. Apparently, I have to do something about my own marital status, and she thinks Newhall presents a perfect opportunity. She and Papa are worried that I am getting a certain reputation. She says I need to make some new friends. She wants me to try and be nice to Newhall, can you believe it? After what he did to me at the lake, he would stand a better chance of making friends with the devil," she replied.

Claire leaned in close so their mothers could not overhear. "Could you possibly take James with you? That brother of mine has inexplicably fallen into a funk of late. He mopes about the house all day, and only grumbles at you if he speaks at all. The most animated he has been was when you fell out of the boat."

Caroline's ears pricked up. She and James were close. Her cousin shared many of her tastes in music, dance and theatre. A week spent with him in the country was appealing. Misery did love company, and if she was going to have to go to Newhall Castle under protest, having James alongside would make it closer to bearable.

"Yes, of course. I shall speak to Francis and get his agreement. The three of us shall make our own little band of travelers," she replied.

The addition of her favorite male cousin to the group would be a most welcome bonus. Caroline could then share the entertainments with Francis and James, while watching with amusement as the other young unmarried misses vied for the hand of the devilishly handsome, but thoroughly unsuitable, earl. They would make their own fun at the house party.

Word of the party had spread fast throughout the drawing rooms of London society. Unattached dukes and marquises were thin on the ground after the end of the official season, so the prospect of an earl actively searching for a wife was a sudden and welcome distraction to the matrons of the *ton*.

"Did the Countess of Lienz invite you? I hear she is a fearsome creature," said Claire.

Caroline snorted. The countess was a consummate actress when it suited her, but Caroline saw her as having all the charm of a snake. "Yes, though it is somewhat of a relief to know that the Countess of Lienz won't be attending the party. She is simply dictating who should go before she sails for home. All a bit odd, don't you think?"

Claire's eyebrows were raised. "Well, you have been spared the company of the countess at least. And you shall be doing all of my family a great favor by getting misery guts James out of the house for a week or so."

Caroline smiled. "Derbyshire it is then."

Chapter Twelve

C aroline heard the door of the breakfast room open and looked up to see her older brother William enter the room.

She leapt from her chair and greeted him with a hug. He had been back in England for a number of months, but the Saunders family members still greeted him the same way they had the first time he set foot back in the house after five years away in France.

"Lovely to see you. Did you bring Hattie with you?" she said.

"No. She was out late at the soup kitchen last night and is still sleeping. I thought I might come over and see you before you head off to Derbyshire," he replied. He held up a tiny pair of blue baby booties and smiled as he looked at them. "And Mama has presented me with yet another pair of knitted boots for the baby."

Will's recent marriage to charity worker, Harriet Wright, had been followed quickly with the news that they were expecting their first child. Adelaide Saunders had already finished a number of baby garments for her long-awaited first grandchild.

Her tall, dark-haired, brother took a seat at the breakfast table, and Caroline resumed her seat. "It was nice of you to come and see me," she said.

Knowing Will, there would be more to the purpose of his visit than just saying goodbye to his sister.

Caroline waited for Will to take his first sip of coffee before posing the obvious question. "Papa tells me you know Lord Newhall from your time in France after the peace. I am assuming you have come to tell me he is not a bad chap after all and that I should be nice to him. Would that be the sum of it?"

Will put down his cup. "Yes, that is exactly why I am here. I understand from Francis that you and Newhall have been at loggerheads for some time, and I have come to simply ask you to attempt a fresh start."

"Why?"

"Because Julian Palmer is a good man. He has done a great service to his country and even if you do not particularly like him, he deserves your respect," replied Will.

Will was not one for bandying about his words. He was more direct than other men. Life living as a secret agent during the reign of Napoleon had changed him. So too had the death of his first wife. Caroline knew she could not be as flippant with Will as she could be with Francis.

She wanted to tell him that few men deserved respect. That men were tiresome creatures at best. But she wasn't a fool. Will would give those sentiments short shrift.

"Alright. I will be polite and respectful to him while I am a guest in his home. It is not as if I am planning to marry him. In fact, I am hoping to remain a spinster for quite some time to come," she replied.

Will huffed in obvious frustration. "Don't act like a silly miss, Caroline. Marriage is a wonderful thing. I have loved and lost, and by God's grace I have found love again. Promise me you will go to Newhall Castle with at least an open mind, if not an open heart."

"I don't know about the open heart. Lord Newhall doesn't strike me as a man capable of much emotion," she replied, hurt by his words.

"And there you are very much mistaken. I was with Newhall in Paris when he received word of his father's death. Believe me, Caroline, he was utterly crushed. Don't judge others by your own cold indifference, you run the risk of one day falling in love with someone who only values you for your beauty. It would break my heart to see that happen. You deserve more," he said. Will downed the last of his coffee and rose from the table.

Caroline remained in her seat, staring at her rapidly cooling toast. Her parents worried that their daughter was a heartless tease. And the brother she had missed for all those years thought her cold and indifferent to love.

They stood in judgment of her, yet none of them had any understanding as to why she had become the Ice Queen.

None of them knew how desperately lonely she was.

Chapter Thirteen

The week was fast drawing to a close. And while the countess had finally sent the guest list to Lady Margaret, there was still no sign of the Crusader Ruby. With his family's honor at stake, Julian decided it was time to confront the countess and demand she hand it over.

He knocked several times on the front door of the Count of Lienz's townhouse before a servant finally opened it.

"Lord Newhall to see the Countess of Lienz," he said.

The footman nodded. "Please come inside. I have instructions to hand over an item to you."

Julian followed him inside and waited while the footman hurried off into a nearby room. He returned with an envelope, and nothing else. "Their royal highnesses departed London early yesterday morning. They left this for you my lord."

With a sinking feeling in the pit of his stomach, Julian took the letter and tore it open. He read the short note and then screwed it up into a tight ball and stuffed it into his coat pocket.

He waited until he had got back into his carriage before pulling the letter back out and reading it for a second time.

Newhall,

My darling husband wishes to sail tomorrow so we left London a little earlier than expected.

I am sure you would agree that the necklace suits me better than it would any future wife of yours, so I have decided to keep it. Consider it payment for having given birth to you.

Your dearest mama

"You fool, Newhall," he muttered.

He had trusted her, and yet again, she had betrayed him. She had never intended to hand over the necklace, using it as a means to once more get the better of him. She knew how much the Crusader Ruby meant to the Palmer family, and by keeping it she was exacting every drop of revenge she could.

He threw the letter across the carriage and huffed in frustration. If he never saw the necklace again it was his own stupid fault.

The Count of Lienz's yacht would have sailed with the evening tide and be well on its way to the port of Ostend in Belgium. His mother was out of his reach.

The only bright side he could find in discovering the countess's early departure from England was that she would not be making an unexpected appearance at Newhall Castle to disrupt the house party. Apart from having made the guest list, she would have no other input in the most important decision in his life—choosing a wife.

Chapter Fourteen

L ady Margaret folded the guest list and put it into her travelling desk. She closed it and placed it on the seat beside her.

Julian looked up from the estate papers he was reading. "All in order?"

Lady Margaret pursed her lips, then nodded. "Yes. Oddly so. Your mother has invited the most eligible young women in London. And most of them have accepted."

Knowing the sort of overbearing woman his mother was, Julian was not in the least surprised that few had dared to decline. "That still does not make up for having stolen the necklace."

As soon as the house party was over, he would follow the countess to Austria. If he did ask one of his lady guests to be his bride, it would be with the express understanding that their honeymoon would be spent trying to retrieve the Crusader Ruby. The countess may have thought she had got the better of him, but Julian was far from done with his mother.

"You sent word ahead of all the preparations that need to be in hand before our guests arrive on Saturday?" he asked, changing the subject.

Lady Margaret nodded. If anyone could arrange a successful house party it was her. He could trust all the arrangements to her, knowing that she would have Newhall Castle shining like a new pin before the first guest arrived. She cared that the castle should have a new mistress, one who would see it well-managed for the next generation.

He sat back in the travel coach and looked out the window. It was good to be going home. He had spent too little time at his estate since his father's death.

"Thank you."

"For what?" she replied.

"For being here. For all that you have done for me over the years. I know when you were with my father you looked after him out of love, but as for me, you have no obligation. You have always been the one person I can count on. I just wanted to acknowledge that. You are the mother I never had," he said.

He chuckled as Lady Margaret quickly wiped a tear from her eye. She reached over and gave him a soft slap on the knee. "You just did that to make me cry, you wicked boy."

When their travel coach made the final turn into the grounds of Newhall Castle, Julian sat up in his seat. He looked out the window, watching the deer, which freely roamed the castle grounds, scatter as the coach approached.

His joy at being home was tempered by the fact that his father would not be waiting for him on the steps of the castle. He would never get used to the emptiness he felt at not seeing the earl's smiling face.

He sighed and looked back to Lady Margaret. She was staring at him with a wistful look.

"He would be pleased to know that you are moving on with your life. That hopefully the halls of the castle will soon echo with the laughter of children. Running wild over the castle grounds with his siblings was always his favorite memory of his own childhood here.

It pained him to his death that you were never able to experience that same happiness," she said.

Julian shrugged off the lovely sentimental thought. Laughter had always been in short supply while his mother reigned over the estate. To this day, he still felt a sense of guilt over the one time she had made him happy. When he had stood out the front of the castle and watched her climb into the carriage that had taken her away. The very last time she had left Newhall Castle for good.

"Well, let us hope that one of the young ladies we have invited is agreeable and would make a suitable countess," he replied.

Having daily borne witness to the disaster that had been his parents' union, Julian was content to settle his matrimonial sights on a woman who could stand to be in the same room as him. A marriage of respect and kindness was the limit of his expectations.

He went back to looking out the coach window. Banks of snow sat on the verges either side of the driveway. Snow that was deep enough that it would not melt with the morning sun.

"I hope you have plenty of indoor activities planned for the week; it looks like the weather could turn foul earlier than it usually does. The last thing we want is to be trying to host outdoor events when the guests are in danger of freezing to death," he said.

"I had thought about that before we left, so I shall have the staff empty the main ballroom. We can set up archery contests in there if the weather closes in," Lady Margaret replied.

Julian put his face to the glass and looked up at the sky. The clouds were thick grey ones which sat low in the sky. There was not a patch of blue to be seen.

His hopes for the weather sunk further when his gaze followed Lady Margaret's hand as she pointed toward the west, the direction from which their weather normally came. More low, dark clouds followed those which already hung overhead.

"Oh dear. That does not look good. I shall send word to the village to bring over more supplies of wood and food. If we do get snowed in for a time, the least we can do is to make sure your guests are warm and well-fed," she said.

With the members of the house party expected two days hence, there was not time enough to send word to London to cancel the party. Whatever the weather, they would have to make do.

The coach slowed to a halt outside the front door of the castle. Julian helped Lady Margaret down and they accepted the welcome greetings from the Newhall estate steward.

"Here he comes," said Lady Margaret.

Through the castle door bounded a black cocker spaniel who made straight for Julian. He jumped up at his master, tail wagging.

"Hello Midas. You have missed me," he said.

His steward chuckled. "He began whimpering a few minutes ago, long before the coach came into view."

Julian bent down and scratched Midas's ears. His late father had given him the dog as a present just before Julian left to serve in the war against Napoleon. Midas was one of the few living reminders of his father that he had.

"You are happy to have us home. Well, we will have lots of people in the house this week, so I am sure you will be spoilt rotten by the end of the party," said Julian.

One of the tests he had set for his choice of wife was how well she handled the dog. His future countess would have to be comfortable in letting Midas have the roam of most of the house. Any young lady who asked for the dog to be kept to the stables would find her name quietly removed from Julian's list.

Chapter Fifteen

Caroline dug an elbow into James's ribs. Her cousin sprang awake and glared at her.

"You are snoring, and it is keeping me awake. You might want to use the extra blanket to prop you up into a better position. One which allows you to breathe better," she said.

James looked to Francis who was seated on the bench opposite. He shook his head. But there was no support to be found from his cousin.

"You snore like that large dog of yours when it falls asleep in the hallway. Or did you buy the dog to hide your own terrible secret?" said Francis.

Caroline chuckled. The Radley family dog's name was officially King, but to everyone he was known as Pound. As in the pound of flesh he normally gulped down in one go at every meal. Once fed, he would take to his favorite sleeping place, which was the middle of the hallway at the Bishop of London's family home at Fulham Palace.

"Very amusing. You should be on the stage," replied James.

Caroline applauded his clever response, and even Francis smiled. She moved along the bench and tried to make an inch more space to get comfortable. Their Uncle Ewan, the Duke of Strathmore, had graciously granted them use of his private travel coach for the long journey to Newhall Castle, but even in the well-appointed coach there was little room to find comfort.

While the journey to Derbyshire was much shorter than the one they made each year to the family estate in Scotland, it was still not something Caroline was particularly enjoying.

Instead of happily telling all her friends of her grand plans for the week or so away, she was leaving London under a cloud. If her own family thought poorly of her, what did others outside of her kin think?

She pulled up the thick woolen blanket which was on her lap and wrapped it about her shoulders. Autumn was fast turning into winter. From the pockets of snow, she had observed on the ground as they passed through Northamptonshire, she wondered just how cold it would be when they finally reached Newhall Castle.

As if reading her mind, James stomped his feet on the floor of the coach. He shrugged his shoulders before huffing loudly. "I should not have packed my heavy coat in with my luggage. At our next stop, I shall ask the coachman to retrieve it from the rooftop."

"Where did summer go? Oh yes, we did not get one," replied Francis.

Caroline sighed. Long coach journeys were always a trial, but usually entertainment could either be found in a good book or made from conversation. With neither her brother or James in a particularly happy frame of mind, the trip was taking its toll on her already stretched mind. She had to break the black mood before it took a deeper hold.

"Apparently Newhall Castle has some of the best hunting in all of England. The current earl's father stocked up on game birds and deer over the years he held the estate. You two should find plenty to do outside of the normal party games," she said.

"That could be fun; I am always up for some venison pie. We should try to get a spot of shooting practice in before we head to Scotland," replied Francis.

James nodded. He was an expert deer stalker, considered even better than his father, Hugh, who had been family champion for many years. "If Newhall will let us hunt outside of season, that would be splendid. I could do with a good stomp over some muddy fields."

"And me. I bagged a brace of grouse last time I went hunting on Strathmore Mountain. I think I have finally found my eye when it comes to shooting," she said. Caroline loved being rugged up in a heavy overcoat and boots and wandering off into the wilds of Scotland. The bracing chill of the air cleared the cobwebs from her mind.

"You are supposed to be a potential bride for the host. I am not so sure that you will be considered for the manlier entertainments of the week," replied Francis.

Caroline snorted in disgust. She was not going to be brushed aside that easily by her male relatives. Why should they have all the fun of gadding about the estate while she was left to keep company with other young ladies? While they were vying to win Lord Newhall's affections, she just wanted to keep clear of him altogether.

She and Lord Newhall were not close. They were not even remotely friends. She was in no doubt that her name would be stone last on his list of potential brides. "I was invited to make up the numbers. His mother arranged the guest list, so I expect she felt obliged to invite me rather than risk offending our family."

Francis growled at her. He clearly shared the same opinion about the trip that Will had. She was wasting an opportunity if she intended to keep her distance from their host and other guests.

"How about you and I make a bargain? I shall speak to Newhall about allowing you to join the hunting party, if you agree to make an attempt to be warm and amenable to him and the other guests," replied Francis.

The low whistle of shock from James echoed in Caroline's ears. She was being taken to task over her haughty demeanor.

The Caroline Saunders of only a few weeks earlier would have lashed out and given her brother a piece of her mind, but now she sat and quietly considered his words. Aside from her family members, she had few real friends. With her sister, Eve, living her own life, Caroline's social circle had reduced to her small court of admirers. None of whom she considered to be friends.

"Am I really that horrid?" she asked.

James reached over and took her gently by the hand. "We are not saying you are a horrible person, but you could do better by being more tolerant of others. You do have a harsh way about you at times."

She sniffed back the tears which threatened. It was difficult enough to think poorly of oneself, but having recently heard it from several members of her own family the realization that she was not a particularly nice person, cut to the bone. Somewhere she had lost herself, and finding her way back would not be easy.

While she had found herself becoming more reflective as of late, overcoming deeply ingrained habits would take a depth of character she feared she did not possess. So many times, she had promised herself to be kind to her court of suitors, but every time she had failed.

"Alright then. If you put in a good word for me with Lord Newhall, I shall make every endeavor to be pleasant and hospitable," she replied. She let James keep hold of her hand, smiling when he gave it a friendly squeeze. She understood that their comments came from a place of affection for her, and that they were not seeking to reprimand her.

"Good. Though from the look of the weather, I am not so sure we will get to have much hunting time. It's beginning to snow," said Francis.

Caroline looked out the window and her mood brightened. She smiled. Winter was her favorite time of the year.

James chuckled. "I can't wait to see the look on the faces of the other guests when they see you do your snow dance. The Ice Queen comes!"

Chapter Sixteen

They overnighted at Leicester. The following morning revealed a light snowfall in the streets, but within a mile or so of leaving the main city roads, they found themselves staring out at meadows covered in several inches of snow.

"How far is it to Newhall from here?" asked Caroline.

Francis looked up from his book and frowned. "Another twenty-odd-miles. Depending on the roads, it will be late before we arrive. The coachman told me this morning that there are several villages between here and Newhall Castle, so if we have to make an unplanned stop, we should be able to find suitable accommodation."

"Good. I would hate to be caught out in the dark in the middle of a snowstorm," replied Caroline. Her love for snow only went so far. No one wanted to find themselves on the road, in the dark, in the middle of a snow storm. They agreed to press on and try to make the castle before nightfall.

"So, who else is going to be at this party, do we know?" asked James.

Caroline began to wrack her brains, but couldn't come up with anyone she was certain to be at Newhall Castle. "To be honest, I am not sure. From what the countess said, I expect it will be almost every girl in the upper levels of the *haute ton* who did not secure a husband this season, but who is still considered eligible. That makes a good dozen or so young ladies, and of course, me." she replied.

Eligible meant being in possession of all of her teeth and a generous dowry. Men of title did not normally marry for foolish notions like love; they married women who could add to the estate coffers. Women who could be trusted to supply their husbands with an heir and turn a blind eye to any mistresses who may happen to pop up from time to time.

The thought stopped her for a moment. She had a good set of teeth, and due to her father's excellent business brain, both she and Eve had been bestowed with sizeable dowries. But the notion of marrying someone for anything other than love was not something she was prepared to consider.

Lord Newhall would no doubt find a nice amenable girl in the house party group to marry, and Caroline would never have to worry about dancing with him again.

"You are one of the selected young ladies that Newhall put on his list of potential brides, dear cousin. Hmm. Caroline Palmer, Countess Newhall. It has a certain ring to it, don't you think, Francis?" said James.

"I think Caro would make a fine countess. Pity she has been rude to poor Newhall on every occasion she has met him. A chap might find it hard to form a sense of affection for a girl who treats him poorly. The fact that he was prepared to let you fall into the Serpentine does not bode well for your chances of securing his heart," replied Francis.

Caroline caught her brother's grin, but decided not to take the bait. She had promised to be agreeable during the house party and she was going to start before they arrived. A deal was a deal.

"And what about you, James? Are you wishing to know who is coming so you can perhaps look the field over? See which of the starters might take your own fancy?" said Francis.

James huffed. "I am not the only one of our travelling party who is still unwed. Perhaps you should speak for yourself, Francis. Or if not, then holding your tongue might be the wiser option. I don't wish to hear anyone's opinion about my marital status thank you very much."

There was a distinct angry edge to his words that caught Caroline off guard. Francis looked at her, a puzzled expression on his face.

Caroline resisted the temptation to respond. She had her suspicions as to the reason for James's terse words. Something to do with his best friend Guy, getting married in a couple of weeks. It had not passed her notice that every time someone mentioned the forthcoming nuptials James would go quiet or suddenly leave the room. The week away at Newhall Castle would perhaps present her with the opportunity to speak with him and get to the bottom of his uncharacteristically dour mood of late.

Francis went back to his book, leaving Caroline and James to play another hand of Piquet. When Caroline won for the fourth time in succession, James handed her his cards and refused to play again.

It was late in the afternoon when they passed the road marker at Midway and made the turn off the main road to Burton-on-Trent. It began to snow, and as the temperature dropped, the snow turned into rain. The rain eventually became icy sleet.

Caroline looked out the window at the fading light, and silently prayed they would make it to Newhall Castle before the weather completely closed in. She retrieved a thick woolen scarf from her travel bag and wrapped it around her neck. The air soon turned chilly.

The icy rain drove hard against the coach. She spared a thought for the coachman and his mate up on top. They would be bearing the brunt of the weather. Fortunately, they had a short distance left to cover before they could find the comfort of a warm fire and a stiff drop of whisky to take the chill from their bones.

The road they now travelled was little more than a narrow track, full of ruts and large holes. The coach bounced through several of these, one of which had James out of his seat and scrambling for the leather holding-strap to save himself from harm.

There was little to be seen out of the coach window. The glass box on the side of the coach which contained a lit candle threw the barest of light. They were travelling in near total darkness.

The coach slowed. The horses barely made a brisk walk along the wet, muddy road.

"Lights ahead!" came the cry from the top of the coach.

A sigh of relief came from all the passengers. Soon they would be at their journey's end. Caroline packed away the cards and her small piece of needlework, and closed up her travel bag. She had just sat back in her seat when the coach dropped heavily and she heard the sickening sound of breaking wood.

The coach came to an immediate halt, then began to tilt to one side. She tumbled from her seat and crashed into James. Putting his arms around her, he managed to draw her safely back onto the bench. The coach remained tilted at a dangerous angle.

"Stay here. I will check on the driver and his assistant," said Francis.

He opened the coach door and jumped down. The wild wind seized the door and slammed it hard behind him as he disappeared into the darkness.

A few minutes later, he poked his head inside. He was soaked through. "We have broken a wheel. The horses are in distress and we shall have to unhitch them. James, you will need to help us," he shouted.

James grabbed his hat and shoved it over his ears. He climbed down from the coach and followed Francis. Above the howling wind, Caroline could hear the horses roaring in fear.

The door swung open once more. Francis appeared, holding a lantern. In the pale light, she could see the deep lines of worry on his face. "One of the horses has been injured. The others we are now struggling to free from the harness. We need to bring the coach upright, so you are going to have to come out. I'm sorry, but there is no other way."

Caroline didn't hesitate. Handling injured and frightened horses was a tough ask at the best of times. In the middle of a freezing storm, it would only take a slight slip for them to be dealing with a dead animal. Or worse.

She retrieved her heavy travel cloak from her bag and wrapped it around her, tying the laces tightly at her throat. Francis lifted her clear of the coach and stood her on her feet. He held the lantern up and Caroline got her first view of the situation they were in.

"Oh, dear lord," she muttered.

On the side of the road, James and the head coachman were trying to hold the reins of a panicked horse while the driver's mate attempted to cut through the reins which had become twisted about the horse's head. To add to the already dire situation, she could see that the driver's mate was badly injured. Blood poured from his nose and mouth.

Francis came quickly to their aid and pulled out his own knife, slashing at the tangled reins.

A second horse reared up on its hind legs. James only just ducked out of the way of the slashing hooves.

Caroline looked back down the hill to where she could see lights. Newhall Castle was a mere quarter mile away. In the maelstrom, it seemed a vast ocean.

"I will go for help," she said.

Francis frowned, but there was no other option. They needed help to get the animals under control and if they stayed out in the storm for much longer, they stood the real chance of catching their deaths. "Take the lantern. It will give you some light. Be careful. The road is already turning slippery under the mud and ice."

With the men left behind to try and settle the horses, Caroline started on the walk toward Newhall Castle and help.

Sleet lashed her face and stung her eyes. The hood of her cape billowing behind her did little to protect her as the wind continually tested the ties at her throat.

The road was wet and dangerous. Pockets of slippery ice made the going slow and treacherous. Every step held peril as she sought to find purchase in the dark. At one point, she put her foot down only to discover that there was a large rut in the road.

She crashed to her knees. The lantern flew out of her hand and into the black night. She heard it smash on the road, but it was lost from sight in the dark. Placing her hands out in front of her, she attempted to get to her feet.

Her boots slipped on the icy road, and she fell heavily once more. Pain shot through her left hand, leaving her gasping for air.

"Oh!" she cried as stars appeared before her eyes. She had found the broken glass from the lantern.

Pulling off her glove with her teeth, she tentatively touched her left hand. Another bolt of excruciating pain shot up her arm. The cut was deep.

"Come on, Caro, get up. You cannot stay here. People need help," she muttered.

Struggling to her feet, she stood for a moment, sucking in air. Her heart was pounding. She peered into the night, grateful that the lights from the castle held firm. With slow, unsure steps, she continued toward them.

It took longer than it should have to finally reach the hard, ground of the castle forecourt. It wasn't a typical castle with moat and drawbridge like her family's in Scotland. Newhall Castle was more elegant and homely, it dated from a time long after castles needed heavy defenses from armed invaders.

Reaching the front door, she took hold of the giant brass knocker in the shape of a rose and banged it loudly. She took a step back, not bothering to look for shelter. She was soaked to the bone; it was impossible for her to get any wetter. Her injured hand hurt like the devil. Pain throbbed through it constantly.

The door opened and the kindly face of a servant appeared. He took one look at the bedraggled stranger on the doorstep and held out his hand. "Dear, sweet girl, what are you doing out there on a night like tonight?"

She was ushered inside and the door closed against the elements. Relief flooded her mind. She had made it.

"Please, our coach has broken a wheel at the top of the drive. One horse and a groom have been injured. Our coachman and my brother and cousin are attempting to free the horses from their tangled reins. It is a driving icy rain out there; they need help urgently," she said.

The castle footman dashed over to one side of the door and picked up a bell. Holding it in both hands, he rang it loud and long. Within minutes, the front foyer of the castle was filled with servants.

Caroline quickly explained the rest of the story to the castle steward who organized a cart and a team of men to head to where the others were waiting. A maid brought her a towel.

Caroline attempted to untie the laces of her cloak, but her damaged left hand refused to work. Finally, she stood and waited while the maid worked to loosen the tight knots. With the ties finally open, the maid slipped the cloak from Caroline's shoulders.

Julian appeared at the top of the stairs. There was a hive of activity about the front door with servants hurrying to and fro. A stranger in a dark green gown stood in the midst of the action. He raced down.

"Go and find some dry clothes for this young lady," he ordered the maid.

The next words he was about to speak died on his lips when he saw the face of the woman who stood dripping water all over his floor.

It was Caroline Saunders.

"Lord Newhall. I am so sorry we have arrived in such a manner. We thought the weather would hold out on the last part of the journey. The storm came out of nowhere."

"Miss Saunders?" he stammered.

He had rarely been stuck for words in his life, but seeing Caroline standing in the front entrance of his home was not just unexpected, it was a hell of a shock. What was going on?

She looked down at her sodden gown, the hem of which was covered in thick, wet brown mire. Her skirts looked like she had fallen on her knees in the mud. Her boots had made an unsightly mess of the beautiful floor tiles of the front entrance. Spots of blood dripped from her fingertips.

When she looked back up at Julian, he saw tears shining in her eyes. "Do you have a physician or someone who is skilled in stitching skin?" she asked.

"Yes. Yes of course. Whatever injuries your servant has our castle steward should be able to attend to them. I myself am quite skilled at stitching wounds; I saw war service in Belgium, so I can also assist if needed," he replied.

"Oh good," she said, and held up her hand. The source of the dripping blood was now evident in the deep, ugly gash which crossed the palm of Caroline's left hand.

She studied the wound for a moment before a look of incredulity appeared on her face, then her eyes rolled back in her head and she dropped like a stone.

Julian bolted across the floor. He knelt beside her and lifted her head, cradling it in his lap. "Miss Saunders?"

Chapter Seventeen

"Oh!" cried Caroline, as pain ripped through her. She opened her eyes and attempted to sit, but found that her arms would not move. Through her blurred vision she could see that her right arm was bound to her body by a leather strap. Panicked, she looked to her left arm. It too was bound, but someone had hold of her left hand and was busy stitching it.

"It is alright, Caro, you are safe," said Francis. Her brother appeared beside the bed. He bent down and gave a tender kiss to her forehead.

"What happened?" she replied.

"You cut your hand badly out on the road. Something quite sharp, by the depth of the cut."

She turned to where the unfamiliar voice had spoken, and found herself staring up into a pair of pale grey eyes. They held a kindness which went straight to her heart.

Lord Newhall smiled back at her. "We had to bind your arms while you were unconscious, just in case you came to and struggled while I had the needle deep in your hand."

"I remember reaching the castle, and your servant opening the door. I'm not sure what happened after that," she replied.

"You fainted. It was fortunate you did not have to walk too much farther to find help. You could have easily bled to death outside in the dark," he said.

She looked at her hand, watching as he continued to stitch the skin together. Her stomach turned at the sight. Memories of the coach accident and her fall on the dark road flooded back into her mind. "What about Master Cook, the groomsman—is he alright? He looked to have a very nasty cut on his face," she said.

"The castle steward is looking after Master Cook. He did indeed take a nasty blow to the face and needed quite a few stitches. His nose is broken and several of his teeth are still out on the roadway, but he will survive. Help arrived just in time, thanks to you," said Francis.

Caroline lay back in the bed as her mind cleared. She flinched in pain as the needle went back into the soft flesh of her hand. A bottle of laudanum would have been most welcome. "I remember now. The road was deadly with ice and I fell. The lantern broke and I cut my hand on the glass when I tried to get back to my feet."

What a night. It was not how she had intended to arrive at the house party. With the host seated beside her bed, holding her hand while he tended to her wound, she had missed the opportunity to make the understated arrival which she had intended. No doubt the other guests would be sitting downstairs talking about her. Caroline Saunders had once again stolen the attention of the party.

"Did the other guests arrive unscathed?" she asked.

Lord Newhall reached over and picked up a pair of embroidery scissors. He tied off the silk thread in a knot then cut off the loose end. She noted that he avoided her question but put it down to his concentrating on the task at hand.

"I'm sorry, I am having to use silk rather than catgut as my steward used the last of it on the young lad from the coach. If you keep the wound bandaged and clean, the stitches should hold. I will send someone into Burton-on-Trent hopefully in the morning to secure some more catgut. I can re-stitch your hand if necessary," he said.

It took a little while longer to bandage her hand. It was only as

Lord Newhall began to pack up his small surgeon's field kit that Caroline was able to think about trying to get some sleep.

A footman brought up a large hot toddy, which she downed with relish. Anything to take the edge off the pain.

"I would offer you laudanum, but you did bang your head rather hard on the floor when you fell. A nip of whisky is enough for your brain to handle, rather than strong opiates," said Lord Newhall.

After Lord Newhall and Francis left, a maid helped Caroline into a clean nightgown and comfortably back into bed. As the strong whisky worked its magic on her, she drifted off into a deep sleep.

"Would you like to get settled into your rooms and then join me downstairs for a spot of supper?" asked Julian.

Francis and James both nodded.

"Excellent idea. I expect we might have already missed supper with the rest of the guests," replied James.

"Yes," said Julian.

When Julian left the room, he immediately went in search of Lady Margaret. She was waiting for him in the main drawing room. As soon as he opened the door, she got to her feet. She looked over his shoulder and, seeing he was alone, gave voice to the question that had been sitting at the forefront of Julian's mind for the past hour.

"We didn't invite them, did we?" she whispered.

"No. But my darling mama knows how little Caroline Saunders and I think of one another, so I expect this was another of her sweet little parting gifts. She probably thought it most amusing to send Caroline to the party and not tell us," he replied.

Lady Margaret picked up her diary and took out the piece of paper that the countess had given her. She ran her finger down the list of names, but none of the recent arrivals were on it.

"At least the Saunders party is a half day early. I still have time to add them to all the lists for the dinners, balls, and games. I suggest we say nothing to them over the issue of invitations. They obviously were invited by your mother, and it would be deeply embarrassing for all concerned if they discovered the truth," she said.

Julian stood and listened, but he was not paying full attention. The sudden arrival of Caroline Saunders and her kin on his doorstep should, by rights, have put him in a filthy temper. Once more his mother had tried to get the better of him. Yet, he found himself to be oddly calm about the whole situation.

He was genuinely surprised at Caroline's heroic effort to find help for her travelling party. The Caroline he thought he knew would have remained in the warmth and dry of the travel coach, refusing to step out into the storm. Yet the girl whose hand he had stitched together had bravely ventured alone into the dark and dangerous night. He admired her pluck.

"We will need to find some supper for Francis and James. I gave Caroline a country-sized hot toddy, so I do not expect to see her again until the morning. In the meantime, we shall simply tell them that they have arrived a day early, which is the truth. Hopefully by this time tomorrow, the house will be full of guests and we won't have to make mention that some of our guests were not actually expected," he replied.

Lady Margaret nodded, and tucked the guest list back into her diary.

"Caroline Saunders will soon be lost in the crowd, and I doubt you will have much more to do with her after tonight."

"Exactly."

Chapter Eighteen

By mid-morning the following day, Julian had begun to worry. The weather had improved somewhat during the night and the road had been cleared of the damaged Strathmore travel coach. Yet no other carriages or coaches had arrived at Newhall Castle.

He was headed back toward the castle proper when Francis Saunders came out from the stables.

He wore a pensive look on his face. "A word, if you wouldn't mind, Newhall? Something is a little out of sorts. It's a delicate matter, so I would appreciate a light touch, if you would indulge me?"

"Yes?" replied Julian.

Francis scratched his head, then looked back toward the stables. He was clearly ill at ease. "I spoke to the stable hands this morning and they couldn't find which stall had been reserved for our horses. I thought to check on them this morning and I pressed your head stableman for the list of where all the horses and carriages were to be housed."

Julian quietly formulated a polite response that would not have Francis Saunders take offence on behalf of his sister. "Ah yes, we seem to have had a slight mix-up with the invitations. Lady Margaret confessed to me last night that she and my mother had somehow managed to get the guest list out of kilter. A little embarrassing, but no harm done."

"I see. So, what you are telling me is that we were not expected. Do I have the right of it?" replied Francis.

Julian puffed out his cheeks. If he got his response wrong, the whole week-long party could end before it began. The other guests would surely hear about it. "As I said, my mother and Lady Margaret missed some names off the final list. You and the others are of course part of the house party. I am looking forward to your company over the duration of your stay."

Francis looked at the ground, managing to find a small stone to kick around. When he finally met Julian's gaze, he showed no emotion. "Thank you, Newhall, I appreciate your discretion. Let us agree that we say nothing of this to Caroline. Considering how the two of you have behaved toward one another, she was genuinely surprised to receive the invitation from your mother. My sister has been under some strain of late, and we undertook this trip in order to give her a respite. It would not help her in that regard if she was to discover that she was not on *your* list."

Julian nodded, relieved that Francis Saunders was an understanding man. For all Caroline's faults, she did not deserve to be shamed in public. It would not do for her to be leaving the estate as the other guests arrived.

"Good morning. I hope you managed to get some sleep last night."

Caroline had just reached the bottom of the main castle staircase and was pleased to see Lord Newhall as he stepped in the front door. She had had time in which to consider how she should approach him. A thank you was first on her list, followed by an apology.

She nodded. "Yes, a maid brought up a second large glass of whisky in the early hours and after that, I didn't know a thing until I woke a little while ago."

His gaze fell to her heavily bandaged hand.

She held it up. "You did a marvelous job in repairing it. Mind you, it still aches like the world, but the bleeding has stopped."

"Have you eaten?" he asked.

"I will go and seek some breakfast shortly, but I wanted to find you first. I must thank you for ministering to me last night. I made an awful mess of the tiles in the castle front entrance and then had the audacity to pass out on them. So please, accept my heartfelt gratitude for being such a generous host," she said. A small smile came to her lips as she saw Lord Newhall look away. It was comforting to see that he too felt ill at ease. These were the first kind words to one another they had ever exchanged.

"It was my pleasure. I hope that when the hand heals you regain full function of it. Unfortunately, I cannot guarantee that it will not scar. My stitches are, at best, that of a battle surgeon," he replied.

She sucked in a deep breath and readied herself to make a formal apology for the way she had treated him in the past.

James appeared, and Caroline took a step back. Her apology would have to wait until she could secure another private conversation with Lord Newhall.

"I say, Newhall, your cook is a godsend. I miss hearty country cooking so much. My father is always having to entertain dignitaries at Fulham Palace and so the fare at our table is very rich. With the amount of cream laden food, I eat, I expect to have gout, like my father, before I am forty. It might be called the king's disease, but bishops are not immune." He reached out and, taking Caroline gently by the arm, looked down at her heavily bandaged hand. "And how are you, dear cousin? Did you get some sleep? You gave that large hot toddy a swift taking so I hope it brought you rest. Not like the last time you found yourself tucking into the whisky, eh?"

Caroline softly chuckled and turned to Lord Newhall. "James, here, is being a little naughty. When I was ten, I found our uncle Ewan's whisky barrel in the Strathmore Castle kitchens. I helped myself to a number of glasses. Suffice to say, I was rather ill."

All these years later, she still felt nauseous at the memory of her mother holding her hair while she knelt in the snow and cast up the contents of her stomach. The resultant hangover was a lesson she did not ever wish to repeat. The previous night had been the first time she had touched whisky since that dreadful day.

"Oh dear, that must have been terrible for such a young girl. I hope everyone else has forgotten about it," replied Lord Newhall.

She softly laughed. "You clearly don't know my family. I give his grace a bottle of whisky every Christmas in penance for my crime. He and everyone else enjoy a hearty laugh at my expense when he offers me a glass, and I shudder as I decline."

Julian stood staring at Caroline, unsure of what to say next. Could it be that the famed Ice Queen actually had a sense of humor? A feather could have knocked him down at the notion.

"I'm sorry, Newhall; we tend to be a tad less formal around family members. For a moment, I forgot we were guests. We do promise to behave when everyone else arrives. Speaking of which, I have not seen any other carriages yet. When are you expecting everyone to be here?" said James.

"Sometime today," replied Julian.

It was odd no other guests had yet arrived. He consoled himself with the likely explanation that his other guests had stayed overnight at either Leicester or one of the other villages en route. Travelling at night was a dangerous occupation, let alone in a snow storm. Julian had instructed his steward to send riders out to check that no one else had been caught in the storm of the previous night.

"Well I shall go and have a quick word with Francis, and let him know you are up and about, Caroline. He went off earlier to check on the coach driver and Master Cook. I had better call in and give them my best regards as well," said James.

Caroline and Julian were left alone. The uneasy air settled between them once more.

Caroline cleared her throat. "I feel I owe you an apology."

For the second time in a matter of minutes, Julian found himself wrong footed by Caroline. First, she had thanked him, now she was offering an apology.

"Lord Newhall, I was rude to you the night we first met. I was angry, but you were trying to be a gentleman and resolve an argument. I was then rude to you a second time at the ball. You were right to treat me the way you did. I apologize for my behavior toward you," she said.

He knew he should have felt a sense of satisfaction over having managed to secure an apology from Caroline, but instead he felt regret. There was a spark about her which disappeared the instant she became formal with him. That spark had intrigued him.

"And I owe you two apologies. One for your foot, which I deliberately stepped on. And two, for my disgraceful behavior at the Serpentine. I could have and should have saved you from falling. To my utter disgust, I did not. I am deeply ashamed of myself and offer you my unreserved apology," he replied.

They stood in silence for a time, neither looking at the other. Finally, Julian mustered up the courage to offer a way forward. "If you are agreeable, then let us put our past behind us. I hope you and the others enjoy your stay here at Newhall Castle. We have many activities and entertainments planned; I am sure you will find something that appeals to you."

He was genuine in his wishes for Caroline to enjoy herself. She would not be someone he would ever consider as a candidate for his future bride, but still there was something about her he found appealing.

She was truly a beauty. Her blond hair verily shone in the morning light. His gaze settled briefly on the bodice of her deep-blue gown. She wore her clothes a little tighter than other women, which he secretly liked. His gaze was afforded an easy and appreciative show of the outline of her ample breasts and slender waist.

He swallowed as he fought the unexpected attraction to the woman he was supposed to thoroughly dislike.

"So, Lord Newhall, we shall attempt to be friends?" she replied.

He smiled. "Yes, but only if you call me, Julian."

The smile she gave him in return lit up her whole face. Her emerald-green eyes sparkled with warmth and humor. Julian was certain that in that instant his heart missed a beat.

"Very well. In the spirit of friendship, I would also ask that you call me Caroline. Friends are permitted those small indulgences," she replied.

Julian stood in the front entrance of the castle after Caroline left to follow James and enquire as to the health of the injured servant. That simple act, coupled with her apology, had him wondering what other surprises she would spring on him over the next week.

The Caroline who had arrived on his doorstep in the middle of a storm was not the same woman who had berated him at a ball a matter of days ago. And her family certainly did not treat her with anything other than familial warmth and concern. Francis and James had both dashed upstairs upon hearing that Caroline had been injured.

He shook his head, refusing the tempting thought that he had figured her all wrong. "Don't be a fool, Newhall. This is how these women get you to do their bidding. A soft batting of the eyelids, a simple smile, and then they have you," he muttered.

He would choose his countess from the other ladies present at the house party. Caroline Saunders would not figure in the decision of his future life partner. He would not make the same mistake his father had.

Chapter Nineteen

By mid-afternoon, Julian was seriously worried. The riders from the estate had gone out earlier and returned with news that the road leading back to Midway was empty of all traffic. While the roads were wet and muddy, they were still passable. Yet no other guests had arrived.

A welcome supper had been arranged for the first night. It was set out as an opportunity for the guests to mingle informally after their long journey from London. The castle kitchen had been as busy as a beehive since the early hours, baking small pies and cakes for the expected arrivals.

He puffed out his cheeks. His reluctance over hosting the house party had been replaced by a burning desire for it to be an outstanding success. Sourcing a bride from the guest list was part of his motivation for agreeing to have the party; the other was to establish new friendships.

He lacked real friends among the members of the *ton*, something he had felt keenly since returning to England. As an only child, without a mother to actively support the development of his social connections, he had grown up with few friends. Most people he knew were merely acquaintances.

He was about to host a week-long party with a house full of strangers which would normally have filled him with dread. Yet as the hours passed and no other guests arrived, he found himself privately fretting.

"The invitations were clear about the party kicking off today? Excuse my questioning but I just want to check my understanding," he said.

Julian was standing in the upstairs drawing room, a space he and Lady Margaret had reserved as off limits to their guests for the duration of the house party. It was somewhere for them to gather at the end of each day and decide how well things were going, and what, if any, changes were required for the following day's entertainments.

Lady Margaret held open her diary. The date was clearly marked as being the start of the house party. He knew she would not make such a simple mistake, but he could not help his rising anxiety.

"And you and the countess were clear on when the party was to take place?" he added.

She nodded. "Very clear. In fact, I was with her when she wrote the last of the invitations. Since I don't particularly trust your mother, I made a point of checking all her notes."

Julian strode over to the window and looked outside. Caroline, her brother, and cousin were walking the snow-covered grounds. He smiled as he saw James fashion a large snowball and toss it in the direction of Francis.

It hit Francis square in the back. He turned, and Julian caught the look of indignation on his face.

Francis took off his hat and handed it to Caroline. She pointed a finger at James. Julian couldn't hear what they were saying but it was clear the challenge had been accepted. A snowball fight was looming.

Lady Margaret came to his side and looked out the window. "Why don't you go outside and spend time with the guests who are here? I am sure the rest of them will start to arrive shortly."

Julian hurried downstairs and put on his long winter coat, a hat, and warm leather gloves. Midas followed him out of the house.

Outside, he stopped and paused for a moment. While he was

eager to join the frivolities, he wasn't sure how he should step into the game. He was an outsider in his own home.

Midas had no such reservations and bounded over to Caroline, barking loudly in welcome.

Stepping onto the snow-covered grass, Julian headed toward where Caroline stood, still holding Francis's hat. She was in neutral territory from what he could ascertain. Beside her, Midas was watching the fight with wide eyes.

"Ah, Julian. Welcome to the box seat for the next round in the never-ending snowball fight between Francis and James," she said.

"Never-ending?" he replied.

A large snowball landed in the middle of James's chest, and he staggered back as if he had been shot. Francis bellowed with laughter. Midas barked.

"Yes. This started in Scotland many years ago. Neither has ever called time on the battle. It's not quite the Hundred Years War, but I think they intend it to get close," she said.

"Oh!"

The sickening sound of Francis taking a snowball to the side of his face had them both wincing. Even James paused for a moment, but within seconds was back hurriedly scooping up snow in his hands and making the next of his deadly missiles.

"It must be nice to have such a close family," said Julian. He was about to add a further remark about how much fun they must have when his vision was suddenly blacked-out. A snowball had hit him square in the face. Midas growled, but stayed by Caroline's side.

"No! You can't attack our host!" cried Caroline.

The evil laughter that emanated from both Francis and James told Julian they thought otherwise.

"Righto. If the two of you wish to play that way, you shall reap what you sow," she said.

Julian had just finished wiping the snow from his face when, to his surprise and secret delight, he saw Caroline unceremoniously drop Francis's hat to the ground before bending down and scooping up a sizeable handful of snow. With her one good hand, she tossed it into the air several times, crushing it into a snowball as she caught it.

Francis took the first blow from his sister, and it nearly knocked him off his feet. Julian nodded his approval of Caroline's deadly throwing arm.

James and Francis moved to line up alongside one another. With Julian and Caroline facing them, the battle began in earnest.

For someone with a badly damaged hand, Caroline was more than able to hold her ground. She and Julian quickly settled into a well-oiled snowball-making and throwing machine. As fast as Julian could gather up the soft snow in his hands and form a decent-sized ball, Caroline was throwing it with her highly accurate aim. She never missed.

"Traitor!" cried Francis, as he took yet another snowball to the head.

Julian and Caroline exchanged feigned outrage, then laughed.

"How much do you love your brother?" asked Julian.

Caroline chuckled. "With all my heart. But then again, I do have William, and he is the older of them. I am sure my parents won't be too heartbroken if we injure this one."

"Good. Because at the rate he is taking blows to the head, you may actually kill him. I just thought I should mention it," replied Julian, with a grin.

A roar of protest went up from Francis as James dropped the last of his snowballs and held up his hands.

"I surrender!" cried James. He raced across the yard and dropped to his knees before Caroline. Julian laughed as James put his hands together and begged for mercy. Midas took the opportunity to bury his wet nose into the side of James's face.

Caroline turned to her ally. "I am not sure what our official war policy is here. I am all in favor of shooting prisoners, but as you are the diplomat, I shall leave it to you to decide this man's fate."

James hurriedly crawled over to kneel before Julian. Francis tossed the last of his snowballs at the back of his cousin's head, and strolled over.

"I would shoot the turncoat if it was me," said Francis. He held out his hand and helped James to his feet.

"Swine," James muttered.

"Julian and I are prepared to be merciful in this case," said Caroline.

She was smiling as she spoke, but Julian did not fail to see the odd look which passed between James and Francis. He took it as a good sign. They were protective of her.

Only a minute or so ago she had been trying to kill them, but Caroline's male relatives wasted no time in making sure Julian knew where he stood. While Francis took hold of Caroline's arm, James placed himself in the space between her and Julian.

"No one else has arrived?" asked James.

Julian frowned. "No, and the road is clear through to Midway at the moment. Though I am not so sure what the later hours will bring."

A collective gaze to the heavens had them all shaking their heads. The clear morning skies had been replaced with low, dark snow clouds. If the other guests did not make it through to Newhall Castle within the next few hours, they would not make it for supper.

"Well let's hope for more arrivals before nightfall. If not, James and I will ride out with you at first light to check the roads," said Francis.

When Caroline smiled up at her tall brother, Julian sensed she was thanking him for offering to help.

"Let's head inside and find some hot food. Our cook has been baking all morning, and I have been waiting to test the latest batch of her famous chicken pies," said Julian.

Caroline gave Midas a friendly pat. "And who are you, apart from a brave battle dog?"

"His name is Midas. My father gave him to me just before I went to war," replied Julian.

As they continued back toward the front door, Midas fell in beside Caroline. She happily chatted away to the dog, who in turn wagged his tail.

James and Francis wasted no time in taking the lead. As Julian followed, he quietly indulged in a gentleman's study of Caroline's curves. The soft swing of her hips was sweet enough to have him gritting his teeth.

The sensible Julian Palmer, who knew only too well the heartache that came from loving a beautiful woman, now found himself battling against a new opponent—the Julian who longed to hold Caroline in his arms.

Chapter Twenty

C aroline unwound the bandage that protected her stitches. She looked away as Julian gently held her hand and examined his handiwork.

"You are not going to faint again?" he asked.

"No. As long as I don't look at my hand, I shall be fine," she replied.

"How is it?" asked Francis.

Her brother stood close to the low couch where Caroline was seated next to Julian. Much as she had reassured Francis that she was capable of receiving medical attention from their host without there being any hint of impropriety, he had insisted on being present while her injury underwent inspection.

Julian ran the tip of his finger along her palm, carefully avoiding the stitches. Caroline shivered at his touch.

"That's a good sign. It means you haven't damaged the nerves," he said, as he raised his head and smiled at her.

"Shall I be able to play the pianoforte properly once this wound heals?" she asked.

Julian nodded. "Yes, I hope so."

"Excellent. So, something good will come from your injury Caroline. You shall finally be able to play the pianoforte. Who would have thought that all those years of suffering from your terrible playing could have been avoided by merely stabbing you in the hand," said Francis.

A tart response was almost on her lips, but the look of surprise on Julian's face at Francis's remark stopped her short.

"I'm sorry, Julian. You must forgive the way we tease one another. It is what we do. When my hand is fully recovered, I promise to play for you. Then you can be the judge of whether I am accomplished or not." Caroline cast an evil glare at Francis, who raised an eyebrow in return. She prayed he would soon grow bored of watching Julian tend to her wound and decide to take his leave. Had he never heard of three being a crowd? She most certainly did not need him to chaperone her in a sitting room in the middle of the day. His brotherly quips were fast becoming embarrassing.

"I shall change the bandage and wrap it again. If you could keep it dry, and try not to use the hand too much over the next few days, the stitches will allow the wound to begin to heal," said Julian.

Disappointment flared at his words. Her injured hand would restrict her from much of the dancing. Also, now in jeopardy would be the opportunity for her to join the hunting party. The more she thought about it, the more she realized that for the first time in her life, she would be relegated to the role of wallflower for much of the house party.

Caroline was not used to the idea of sitting in the wings. She was the star. Front and center stage, where everyone could see her. Her stay at Newhall Castle was throwing up a whole new set of unexpected challenges.

Julian unrolled a clean bandage and began to wrap it around her hand. He hummed softly to himself as he worked. Caroline watched him. The deep tone of his voice was a warm lullaby. She leaned closer. Their faces were mere inches apart.

When he glanced up at her, she felt her heart flutter. A flush of heat raced to her cheeks. She lowered her head, hoping that Francis had not seen.

She sent a silent prayer to the heavens as Francis made several steps toward the door. "I won't be long. I shall retrieve a book from my room and come back to join you both shortly," he said.

To her surprise, Julian softly chuckled as Francis left the room. "Is he always as protective of you as he has been since you got here? Because if not, a chap might get the impression that Francis did not trust him," he said. He finished wrapping the bandage and tied it off with a clever little knot which he then tucked back under the bandage. It was a neat job. Caroline was impressed.

"I have had a trying time of late. He is simply doing everything he can to make sure I enjoy myself while at the house party. Speaking of which, it looks more than likely that there shall only be our small gathering for supper," she replied. She was oddly conflicted over the lack of other guests. She was sad for Julian because his party was not starting off according to plan. A great deal of preparation had obviously gone into having Newhall Castle ready for some thirty-odd guests. Her heart went out to him as she sensed his growing unease.

On the other hand, a small spark of something she thought might possibly be joy lit in her heart. As he put the scissors and spare bandages back into the small leather bag, she watched him with an interested eye.

Julian picked up the bag and rose from the couch. "Yes, I believe you might be right. Anyone still on the road through from Leicester at this hour is likely to stop at Ashby-de-la-Zouch and stay at the Queen's Head. I will of course have the stable hands and grooms ready for any late arrivals. In the meantime, I had better go and speak with Lady Margaret and see what can be done with the mountain of pies that were baked this morning."

After Julian left, Caroline wandered over to the window. The light was fading fast.

Francis returned shortly after, carrying the book he had promised to retrieve. "Bit of an awkward situation with no one else arriving," he noted.

Caroline nodded. "Yes, well fortunately, Julian has a castle full of servants who no doubt will find a good use for all that extra food. I feel embarrassed for him. The first time he holds a house party and nothing seems to have gone right."

Her brother knitted his eyebrows. He came to Caroline's side. "Since when did Newhall become Julian?"

She knew he wasn't trying to tell her what to do, the Saunders males were not that foolish, but still, she resented his tone. The warm, but slightly patronizing one that he used when trying to win her over to his way of thinking.

"Since we all agreed in the coach on the way up from London that I would attempt to be more amenable and pleasant," she replied.

"Don't you think you are being a little too familiar with him?" asked Francis.

"So, you don't want me to call him by the name he has offered to me as part of our attempt to be friends. Why not?" she added.

"I am not saying you shouldn't be friends with Newhall; I am simply saying you may want to be careful about being overfamiliar with him. By using his first name, you will make others think you have already laid a claim to our host. Considering you have declared no interest in becoming his countess, I would suggest that it is not such a good idea."

She had come to Derbyshire to get away from London. To be free of the constant unwelcome attention from her devoted but delusional suitors. She had no business in muddying the waters of Julian Palmer's marriage pool.

"Alright, as soon as everyone else arrives tomorrow, I shall go back to calling him Newhall. If he asks me why, I shall explain it is to keep a level playing field for all the potential candidates. I am sure he will find that somewhat amusing," she replied.

Francis was right; she had no intention whatsoever in marrying Julian. They were friends, nothing more. She had to take a well-considered large step away from him.

Chapter Twenty-One

I t began to snow again in the early evening. By the time the small house party came down for supper, there were a good four inches on the ground outside.

Caroline stopped on the stairs and looked out the window. She clenched her right hand into a fist and punched the air with glee. Caroline loved snow. For all the inconvenience and mess, it brought, she liked nothing better than to stand out in the freezing air while snowflakes swirled around her.

She raced back to her room and grabbed her coat and gloves. She managed to get her right hand inside its glove, leaving her left hand only protected by the bandaging.

Heading back downstairs, she opened the front door and stepped out into a white winter wonderland. She checked the driveway to ensure no one was coming, then with arms held out wide, she began to slowly spin.

"She is doing it," muttered James.

Francis looked over to where his cousin was pointing and smiled.

For as long as anyone in the family could remember, every Christmas at Strathmore Castle, Caroline would stand outside in the snow and slowly spin. For hours she would silently worship the sky as it poured white heaven over her.

"What is she doing?" asked Julian, coming up the stairs.

"Caroline's snow dance. Few people outside the family have ever seen it. You should feel privileged," replied James.

"She loves the winter. Some unkind people have given her the name of the Ice Queen, but they don't realize just how close to the truth it is," added Francis.

At that moment, Caroline stopped spinning. She tilted her head back and opened her mouth. In the golden glow from the torches lighting the drive, Julian caught the incredible sight of a young woman in rapture. Snow fell on her face and at times into her open mouth, all the while Caroline stood with her eyes closed and arms held out.

"I have never seen anything like it in my entire life," murmured Julian, thoroughly entranced.

As he stepped away, he caught sight of a movement in the shadows near Caroline. Midas was keeping a close guard on their guest.

Caroline slipped off her snow-soaked coat and single glove and handed them to a footman.

He pointed in the direction of the downstairs sitting room. "Lord Newhall said to tell you that he and the other gentlemen are waiting for you."

"Don't tell me it has stopped snowing," teased James as she entered the room.

She laughed, full of the joy of winter. "No, but it was beginning to seep through my coat, and Midas made his protests known. Besides, I heard there would be hot food and you know me after I have been outside in the snow. I need pies."

Julian stepped forward and bowed low. The blush that unexpectedly raced to her cheeks brought some sense of feeling back to them.

"Then you shall have pies, as many as you can eat. I understand it is part of the tradition that when one has finished worshipping the snow god, one indulges in pies," he said.

She looked to Francis, who shrugged.

"We had to explain to Newhall why you were standing outside, spinning in the snow," he said.

Heat burned on her cheeks for a second time. What was it that being in Julian's presence did to her? She was used to men crowding around her, jostling to find her favor, yet there was something different when it came to him. He made her feel uncomfortable. No. He made her feel different. *Perhaps I am losing my touch.*

Caroline pushed the notion away. She had clearly been standing for too long outside in the freezing air, and her brain had simply become a little muddled.

"So, it will just be us again tonight? I am so sorry, Julian. I hope that tomorrow will bring a cavalcade of carriages and coaches to your front door," she said.

"Not to worry. I must say, you three are the sort of guests that are always welcome when it comes to a snow-bound estate," he replied.

The door of the sitting room opened and in stepped an older woman. Julian came to her side and taking her arm, walked her over to where Caroline and the others stood. "Lady Margaret, may I introduce our guests? This is Caroline and Francis Saunders, and their cousin, James Radley."

Caroline curtseyed sweetly and the others bowed. As she looked up, she caught the sight of Lady Margaret holding out her hands to her.

"My dear girl, welcome to Newhall Castle. I must apologize for not coming to see you when you arrived late last night. I understand you injured your hand," she said.

"Yes, but Julian did an excellent job of fixing me up with first-class battle stitches. I still have feeling in the hand, which at the moment is a mixed blessing, but hopefully I shall regain full use of it," she replied.

Lady Margaret winced as Caroline held up her heavily bandaged hand. She turned to the others. "And this is Francis? Oh and of course James, I know your father."

James had the pained smile on his face that he always adopted whenever his father was mentioned in company. Everyone in the *ton* knew the Bishop of London. James was forever being asked to give regards to his father from those that he met. Caroline's heart went out to him; she was not the only one who society had set expectations upon.

"My aunt has worked hard to get this house party ready. She worked with my mother to arrange all the invitations. The countess, unfortunately, could not join us this week," said Julian.

Caroline looked at her brother. An unspoken agreement passed between them. No one was going to mention the countess, and the lack of her presence at Newhall Castle.

"Yes, I expect there was a lot of work involved in planning everything. Did you have to bring much up from London?" she asked.

"Actually no, the local town of Burton-on-Trent has much of what we need. We have a day trip planned there on market day. If the weather clears, we shall journey up to the town next Thursday," replied Julian.

The gentlemen gathered at the nearby sideboard and began an earnest discussion of the merits of the various fine Scottish whiskies which had been set out for them. Lady Margaret took Caroline by the arm and they wandered over to the far wall where a number of paintings hung.

Caroline stood and closely studied the first piece of artwork. It was a sweeping landscape of rugged mountains and deep valleys. She appreciated the rustic reds and greys used by the artist. Portraits were well enough to look at, but paintings of nature and scenery were, to her mind's eye, far more appealing.

"Is that from around this area?" she asked.

Lady Margaret shook her head. "No, that is where my family comes from. It's farther north in the Peak District. Lord Newhall's father had it commissioned for me not long after I came to Newhall Castle."

Caroline bit down on her bottom lip, unsure of what to say next. If Lady Margaret was not Julian's aunt on his father's side, and she was not related to his mother, then how exactly was she his aunt?

Lady Margaret caught Caroline's eye. "I am not really his aunt. I did my best to raise him in the years after his mother left. I was left a widow at an early age, and Julian's father and I came to realize that being his mistress was a far better solution for me than having to go through the business of finding another husband. We did love one another, which was more than either of us had had in our respective marriages."

"I didn't mean to pry, but thank you for telling me. I promise not to mention it to anyone else," said Caroline.

"At the rate things are going, we may not have anyone else. I am pleased though to see that you and Julian are making efforts to be friends," replied Lady Margaret.

Caroline looked back to where Julian and the others were standing. They had been enemies until only a day ago. And she was still a little more than surprised at how warm and friendly he had been to her since her arrival.

"Lady Margaret, I must beg a favor of you, and ask that you be honest with me. I don't understand why the countess was at such pains to invite me. Our previous meeting had been most unpleasant. So, I am at a loss as to why she extended the invitation," she said.

The silence that followed added to her unease. Instead of immediately offering her reassurances that all was above board, Lady Margaret hesitated. "The countess made some last-minute changes to the guest list just before she left London," she explained.

Caroline forced a smile to her lips and did her best to blink away unbidden tears. She now understood the look of genuine surprise on Julian's face when he saw her standing inside the front door of the castle. Since he had not invited her to the house party, Caroline Saunders was probably the last person he had expected to find on his doorstep in the middle of the night.

Lady Margaret reached out and took hold of Caroline's good hand. "You and Julian are friends now. Please let any past misunderstandings between the two of you remain in the past." She glanced quickly at Julian, then turned back to Caroline. "You are welcome here at Newhall Castle, and are a guest the same as everyone else. I would ask that you not say anything to him; it would be deeply embarrassing to him if he discovered that you knew."

Caroline considered Lady Margaret's words. It was not something she was accustomed to doing, but she had made a promise to herself and her family to change her ways. She came to the uncomfortable decision that she would swallow her pride and say nothing to her host. "Of course. Besides, we are having a marvelous time. Julian and I defeated my brother and cousin on the snow-covered battlefield this afternoon. And he has offered for me to eat as many pies as I can this evening," she warmly replied.

When a soft sigh of relief escaped Lady Margaret's lips, Caroline wiped away another tear and made a silent vow. From this moment on, she would make every effort to deserve her place at the party.

After supper, Lady Margaret made her apologies and left them. The rest of the group lounged about on sofas and swore collectively to never eat another pie.

"So, Newhall, are we going to ride out tomorrow morning and see if we can greet some of the other guests?" asked Francis.

Caroline looked up from the book she had been reading by the fire. The expression on Julian's face said enough. He was becoming concerned that no one else was going to come to his party.

"That sounds like an excellent idea. It will be fun to see who is on the road. You could dress up as highwaymen and cry 'stand and deliver,'" she said.

James shot her a look of feigned horror. "Yes, and you can explain to my father why I am about to be hanged when someone does not see the funny side of the jest."

Francis took hold of his cousin's throat and pretended to throttle him. James, in turn, made an excellent impression of having his neck broken and crumpled to the floor.

The applause for his terrible acting was short.

"Perhaps you had better just rug up well against the cold and forget about playing Dick Turpin. I promise to be waiting here with hot coffee and more pies in readiness for your safe return," said Caroline.

Julian turned to her and dipped into an elegant bow. "Thank you. That would make the journey out tomorrow all the more worthwhile."

Caroline smiled back at him self-consciously. Her heart was beating an unfamiliar tattoo. Had the Ice Queen's heart began to thaw?

Chapter Twenty-Two

T he sun was up, but it was still freezing cold when Julian, James, and Francis assembled out the front of the castle. Grooms brought over three strong horses from the stables.

To Julian's surprise, Caroline was good to her word and was dressed to bid them a fond farewell on their journey.

"Hello, and good morning," she said, as Midas bounded up to greet her.

"He seems to have taken a particular fancy to you," replied Julian.

Caroline bent and gave Midas a friendly rub behind the ears. Midas wagged his tail, and Julian sensed the strong connection that had formed between them. He felt an odd pang in his heart as she spoke softly to the dog.

"Are you going to wait out here with me, boy? I expect you are glad to be blessed with a nice, thick, fur coat on a morning like this," she said.

Julian took the reins from the stable groom without paying attention to him. His gaze was fixed firmly on Caroline. It was only when she stood and James spoke to her that the spell, she held over him broke. He blinked in the bright early morning sun and tried to regain his focus. As Midas began to nuzzle against Caroline's leg, Julian felt a second pang in his chest.

I cannot be jealous of my dog. If I was, that would mean . . .

The notion of him forming any sort of attachment to Caroline was ridiculous. They were former enemies, temporary friends, stuck together due to circumstance. When they returned to London, he expected they would go back to being nothing more than cool acquaintances.

"How long do you think you will be gone?" she asked.

"Well, we shall head toward Midway first; that is only a short distance from here. If we do not encounter anyone on the road, then we may ride on toward Ashby de la Zouch," replied Julian.

It warmed his heart to think that she cared how long he would be gone, but when Francis jumped up onto his horse, Julian convinced himself she was more concerned about her family members than him.

"Well, good luck. I hope you encounter a stream of coaches all headed this way. I don't think any one of us want to have to eat another hundredweight of pies if they don't arrive," she said.

Julian put a foot into the stirrup of his saddle and in one smooth motion mounted his horse. In a world where all men rode, he was particularly skilled at handling horses. As he settled in his seat, he chanced a glance at Francis and James, stifling a smile at their obvious appreciation of his skills.

With a gentle tap of his boots on the side of his horse, he led the small group away from the front of the castle and out onto the long drive.

The morning was crisp, but since there was only a slight breeze, Julian was warm and comfortable in his woolen coat. They rode on in silence for a time. Rather than attempt to start a conversation, Julian was content to enjoy the pleasant peace of the Derbyshire country-side. It was good to be back in England.

When they reached the turn in the road which led to Midway, Julian pulled his horse up. "Perhaps it is a little early for anyone who made it to Ashby and stayed the night to have set out on the road."

Francis nodded. "We must find someone if we head on to the next village. The weather when we left London was not that bad. It was only after we left Leicester that we encountered any snow to speak of."

As they rode on toward Ashby de la Zouch, the worry that had sparked in Julian's mind late the previous evening began to grow. It was odd that only the Saunders party had arrived at Newhall Castle. Even more concerning was the fact that they were the only people he and Lady Margaret had not put on the initial guest list.

"She wouldn't," he muttered under his breath.

He and the countess did not see eye to eye on many things, but until this morning, he would not have thought her capable of actively seeking to do him or the Newhall title harm. She had stolen a prized necklace from the estate. Could her spite plumb to a deeper level? The closer they drew to Ashby, the more the fear within him grew.

They passed through the village of Packington, but still did not see any travel coaches. Julian licked his lips; his mouth was dry from sucking the cold morning air in through his teeth. An image of his mother sat in the forefront of his mind as he rode. He pictured her laughing long and loud over her foolish son and her cuckold of a late husband.

When a local gentleman passed them on the road, it took a great deal of effort for Julian to muster a nod of acknowledgement. If his mother had indeed managed to sabotage his house party, he would be the laughing stock of the *ton*. He didn't want to think how much damage his reputation would have suffered by the time he showed his face in London again.

Francis dug his heels into his horse and came to ride up alongside Julian. Julian then looked across at him, taking comfort from the fact that Francis looked as worried as he felt.

"I can go into the local taverns or inns to inquire if you like. You shouldn't have to do it yourself," offered Francis.

A bitter chuckle was Julian's response. "Ashby is not that big a place. The amount of people who were supposed to be coming should mean that the town would be full of coaches. If no one has arrived from London, we will soon know."

Julian found himself liking Francis Saunders. He was not your usual run-of-the-mill son of the *ton*. He, like his father, Charles, actually worked for a living. Francis's older brother, William, who had been with Julian in Paris, was cut from the same cloth. Will was a warm and friendly chap, who was as at home in the dingy taverns of Paris as he was in the glittering ballrooms of London.

As they reached the town, they turned into Market Street. The Bull's Head Inn was on the left. There were no coaches or carriages out the front. Francis took the lead and brought them around into the stable yard at the back.

As James and Francis dismounted from their horses, Julian remained in his saddle. He wanted to get down from his mount, but he knew the moment he did he would have all his worst fears confirmed. A young stable boy came over and took the reins of James's and Francis's horses.

Francis looked up at Julian, then patted Julian's horse on the rump before strolling off toward the door of the inn. "I will be back shortly," he said.

"You might want to get down off your horse, Newhall. The lad, no doubt, has other jobs to do," said James.

With a resigned sigh, Julian climbed off his mount.

As the stable boy led all three horses away for a well-earned drink of water, James stood, hands on hips, and surveyed the yard. "I've never stopped in this town before. I'm usually in too much of a hurry to get to Burton-on-Trent," he said.

"You know this area?" replied Julian.

James nodded. "Yes, I have some old school friends who regularly come up to Burton. I was hoping to try and squeeze a visit in to see them while we were staying at Newhall Castle. I thought that with all your guests taking up your attention, you wouldn't mind if I went missing for a day or so."

Julian's hopes for a full house were diminishing by the minute. Out of the corner of his eye, he saw Francis returning. The look on his face said it all.

"No coaches, no carriages. In fact, I am the first gentleman they have seen all week," said Francis.

Julian growled. "She couldn't leave it alone."

Francis and James exchanged a quizzical look. "Who?" replied James.

"My mother. She was adamant in having a hand in settling the house party guest list. I would not be the least bit surprised if she has done something to set my plans all to waste," he said.

"But she is your mother. Why would she do such a thing?" said Francis.

Julian felt a familiar pang of pain in his heart. How did one explain to other people that not all families were loving and caring?

"Gentlemen, I need a drink. No, make that several drinks. In fact, I would like to start drinking and when you think me unable to ride back to Newhall, I would ask that you buy another round," he said.

He didn't want to talk about the countess, or even think about her. He needed very badly to dull his brain. To imbibe as much alcohol as his body could stand, as long as it numbed the pain.

Francis nodded. "James and I shall take care of the drinks."

Chapter Twenty-Three

"Poor Julian," said Caroline

While the men had been out in search of guests, she had sat outside on a chair with Midas asleep on the ground beside her. Her gaze was fixed firmly on the road. As the hours slowly dragged on, she found herself willing hard for a fleet of travel coaches to appear.

Upon leaving London, she had only seen the party at Newhall Castle as a means to escape her own problems, but her view had changed. She wished very much for Julian to have a successful party. For him to find a lovely girl to marry. For him to be happy.

"Where on earth is everyone?" she whispered.

Midas stirred beside her and got to his feet. He shook his head, then his whole body, before letting out a soft woof.

Caroline reached out and gave him a friendly pat. "You are awake. What has stirred you?"

Midas leaped forward and raced toward the drive. At the top of the rise, three horses appeared. Their slow progress toward the castle, coupled with the lack of other movement on the road, did not portent well.

She rose from the chair and fixed her skirts. She wanted to appear calm. If the returning riders brought bad news with them, she wanted to show Julian that he had her full support.

Midas reached the horses and scampered around them in a big loop, barking with unrestrained joy. Caroline waved.

Francis managed a half wave in return. When she saw Julian, her heart sank. He was slumped, his head bowed in the saddle. A man crushed by disappointment.

"Oh no," she muttered.

When the horses finally made it to the front of the castle, Francis jumped down from his horse. James slowly dismounted. They both came to the side of Julian's horse.

"Come on, Newhall, let's have you," said Francis, holding out his hands.

Julian mumbled something incoherent in reply, then shooed Francis away. "I shall get down off my own bloody horse, Saunders, or I shall break my neck in the process. Either way, I couldn't care less."

A small *O* formed on Caroline's lips as she realized the truth of the situation. Julian was not crushed; he was completely foxed.

"What happened?" she asked.

Francis walked over to her, while James lingered close by Julian's horse. His gaze was fixed on their drunken host. "We rode all the way to Ashby de la Zouch and there were no other party guests to be seen. Newhall then declared that he required the support of a copious amount of alcohol," he explained.

Caroline winced as she watched Julian attempt to dismount. He finally wriggled his right foot out of the stirrups after several failed attempts. Leaning back on the horse, he dislodged his left foot from the other stirrup. He swayed in the saddle for a heart-stopping moment, but when James stepped forward, Julian glared at him.

"Stand your ground, Radley, you son of a bishop," he slurred.

In what could only be described as an inelegant move, Julian then swung his right leg over the saddle and slid down the side of the horse, landing on his knees.

"Ooof!" he cried.

To Caroline's relief, James took it upon himself to ignore Julian's protests, and putting his hands under their drunken host's arms, he lifted him to his feet. Julian attempted to push James away, but her cousin held on tight.

"Come on, Newhall, let's get you inside before we all die of exposure. The whisky in your system might be keeping you warm, but I'm freezing out here," James said.

Caroline and Francis followed James and Julian into the main hall. Midas trotted behind.

James managed to get Julian into a nearby sitting room where, with a little assistance from the others, and despite Julian's slurred protests, they got him settled on a low daybed. Caroline found a footman who quickly went in search of a warm blanket.

With Julian now tucked up and soon fast asleep and snoring loudly, the rest of the group left him in private. They gathered in the upstairs library and closed the door.

"Well that was a long and rather wasted journey," said James.

Caroline frowned. "So, what do you think has happened? Why has no one other than ourselves arrived?"

"He is not completely sure, but Newhall suspects that his mother has something to do with it. He made mention while we were out on the road that he had demanded the return of several pieces of Newhall estate jewelry that the countess had taken when she left his father. She apparently handed over some of them, but kept an ancient family heirloom. He thinks she has done something to scuttle his plans in order to exact revenge on him for having demanded the return of the jewels," explained Francis.

And knowing that she and Julian had had several public spats, it didn't take a great leap of the imagination for Caroline to wonder if the countess had decided to throw her attendance at the house party in as an added slight. To Caroline's mind, the countess had pressed a little too keenly for her to attend. And her apology over the incident with the boat on the Serpentine had lacked sincerity.

With Julian's event now looking a complete failure, the obvious question raised its head. What were she and the others to do?

"I expect we shall have to return to London," said Francis.

Caroline was not surprised at her brother's words. He had taken on handling a significant amount of the family import business over the past year and was fast making a name for himself as an astute businessman. Time spent away from the city was not something he did lightly.

"For myself, I would like to stay. I am not in a London frame of mind at present. Newhall and I have already discussed me making a short trip up to Burton-on-Trent to see some old school chums," said James.

Caroline could have hugged her cousin there and then, especially when she saw the look of annoyance on Francis's face.

Francis turned to her. "There is something you should know".

She nodded. "You mean that I was not on Julian or Lady Margaret's initial guest list? That it was his mother who made the decision to invite me? I think I have got some of the measure of the countess, and my presence here was her way of vexing Julian."

James huffed in obvious disgust at the revelation. "I can leave and go onto Burton by myself. If you take me through to the inn at Ashby, I can make my own way north from there."

Francis stood silently looking at Caroline. He was an odd creature. At times quite distant, but at others, like now, she sensed he could read her mind. He was waiting for her to make her declaration of intent.

"I want to stay," she said.

If pressed, she could have concocted a number of sensible reasons for wanting to remain at Newhall Castle. For a start, it would be rude to simply abandon Julian at this point. He needed his friends, however newly acquired, to stand by him.

Secondly, for herself, she did not wish to return to London. If she did leave Newhall Castle, then she too would head north, to the Strathmore family seat in Scotland.

The truth of her reason for wishing to stay was something less clear in her mind. For the first time in her life, it was her heart which was speaking loudly. She had been at Newhall Castle for only a matter of days, yet it had already gotten under her skin.

"I just think it would be terribly unkind of us to simply pack up and leave Julian alone at this time. I am also holding out hope that other guests do arrive, and if they do, they will feel more comfortable in knowing that we are already here," she added.

Francis raised an eyebrow, but nodded. "Alright, we stay. Let it not be said that the Saunders or Radleys ever abandon a friend in his hour of need."

Chapter Twenty-Four

A sheepish-looking Julian eventually emerged from the sitting room late that afternoon and sought out the others. They were quietly ensconced in the library. Caroline had found a book that noted the ancient Roman roads which ran through the local district.

"Good afternoon," he said, stepping into the library.

They all looked up from their books, and Francis got to his feet. "Hope you're feeling a little more rested, Newhall. We thought it best to throw a blanket over you and let nature take its course."

James chuckled. "To be honest, he was all for leaving you outside with the dog, but Caroline thought that would be disingenuous of us and pleaded your case."

Julian looked at her and a wan smile appeared on his lips. She smiled back, encouragingly. Would the earl ever learn to be comfortable around the easy banter of the Radley and Saunders cousins?

"Thank you, Caroline, for coming to my aid. And thank you, Francis and James, for getting me so drunk that I don't remember the journey home. It was exactly what I needed."

Francis cleared his throat and came to Julian's side. "We have had a bit of a chat while you were sleeping and would like to ask if we could stay on for the rest of the week. It's a long journey back to

London, and none of us is in any particular hurry to leave. That is, of course, if it suits your purposes. If not, we shall make our arrangements to depart as soon as possible."

Caroline's heart went out to Julian as Francis's words registered on his face.

His head dropped. "I am truly humbled by your kindness. Of course, I would be honored for you all to stay on at the castle. I must confess that I was not looking forward to the rest of the week here on my own. At times, I am not good company for myself."

True to nature, Francis read the mood right, and knew what to do. He slapped Julian hard on the back. "Well then, Newhall, if you insist, we shall stay. But just remember whose fault it is when James and I take all your best game birds and drink your house dry of whisky. Not to mention the damage Caroline will do to your expensive French wine collection."

Caroline laughed. A gentle ribbing was her brother's way of letting her know that while he had agreed to her demands, he was still in charge. Just as long as they stayed at Newhall Castle, she was content to let him keep hold of that piece of fiction in his mind.

Julian and Caroline's gazes met. He did look a little worse for wear. His bloodshot eyes were a window to the pain of his hangover. She would have dearly loved five minutes alone with the Countess of Lienz, so she could give her a piece of her mind.

"I have an excellent wine cellar if you care to take a look. I had a shipment of bottles brought over when I returned from Paris. In fact, your brother, William, helped me to select them," he replied.

She looked to Francis who was beaming with pride. William had spent years as a secret British government agent in France, working with the allies to overthrow Napoleon. His recent safe return to England had been to the bone-deep relief of his family.

"Will made mention of the fact that the two of you worked together after the war, but I hadn't realized that you were actually friends. He did say some kind words about you just before we left town," said Caroline.

"Will is a good egg. I missed his and Hattie's wedding, so I must have the two of them to stay at some point," replied Julian.

The door of the library opened, and Lady Margaret stepped into the room. She was smiling. "A carriage has been sighted at the top of the drive. Someone else is coming," she announced.

In an instant, all books were set aside, and the group of friends went racing down the main staircase. Caroline let out a huge sigh of relief. Their worries had all been for naught.

"Quick. Let us form an honor guard for the new arrivals. It will help to set a fun tone for the rest of the week," said James.

Caroline came to Julian, who having just dragged himself from a drunken stupor looked to be floundering with the news of the arrivals.

"Here, let me help you," she said.

He gave her a tired smile. She straightened his cravat and brushed the sleeves of his coat.

"Bend your head forward," she said, and ran her fingers through his hair, catching the tangles which a long afternoon's sleep had brought to his dark brown locks.

"Thank you. I dread to think what I look like," he replied.

"You look very handsome, especially when you smile."

He reached out and took hold of her hand. Their gazes met, and for a brief moment they stood silently looking at one another, stirring only when Francis called for them to hurry. Caroline gave a quick check of the rest of Julian's attire before giving him a nod of approval.

Outside the front door, they caught sight of the carriage as it reached the top of the rise and began to descend toward the castle. The four of them lined up side by side, Lady Margaret having gone to check with the housekeeper that the fires in the guest rooms had been lit. They waited for the carriage to arrive.

Julian looked down at Caroline, who was standing to his left, and mouthed *"thank you."* She beamed up at him, happy that he was finally going to receive more houseguests.

When she looked away, focusing on the carriage, her smile disappeared. What if the young lady in the carriage was the perfect woman for Julian? He may even fall in love with her at first sight. Then what?

She silently cursed herself. She had been too overeager to remain at Newhall Castle, and had not thought things through. A week of watching him fall in love with someone else would be a week from hell.

If there was a price to pay for having been cold and distant with all her admirers, perhaps it was that she would have to stand by and watch the one man who had stirred her blood have his heart captured by another woman.

Now, as she stood in silence, she heard her heart speak for the first time.

Julian Palmer was about to break her heart.

Chapter Twenty-Five

J ulian straightened his back and cleared his throat. His head throbbed from a deserved hangover, while his stomach made its own protests at having been so badly abused. But new guests were arriving, and he willed himself to rise above his physical discomforts.

As the carriage drew closer, he noted it was not a large one. Nor was it a formal travel coach. It would hold two to three people at best. But its arrival gave him hope. If one guest could make it up from London, then perhaps others were also coming not far behind.

The carriage stopped, and a footman stepped forward to open the door. Julian gave one final look at Caroline standing beside him, and after receiving an encouraging nod from her, he broke ranks and went to greet his guests.

A tall black hat appeared in the doorway, followed by a pair of long dark trousers. A hand came up and quickly removed the hat, revealing a dark brown head of hair. Julian held out his hand in welcome, but it was not accepted.

"Well this is all very formal, but welcoming. If I had known you were so eager for my arrival, I would have pressed on from Leicester last night and been here earlier."

Julian blinked. The man standing before him was from Caroline's court of admirers an odd chap who tended to stand at the back of proceedings and come to her rescue when needed. Harry Menzies.

"Harry, what on earth are you doing here?" Francis asked.

A smiling Harry stepped forward and greeted Francis with a friendly pat on the shoulder. "Coming to save you and my dearest Caroline." He looked at Julian and gave a brief, barely respectable nod. "Newhall."

Julian clenched his left hand and withdrew his offered right. He turned and looked back to where Caroline was standing. She had a deep-set frown on her face.

Harry brushed past him and went to her. "My precious Caroline, it has been almost a week since last I set my gaze on you. I hope your time here has not been too trying, all things considered. Never fear, I am here to help set things to right." He leaned forward and placed a kiss on Caroline's cheek. She stiffened noticeably at his touch.

Francis hurried to his sister's side, forcing Harry to take an awkward step back. "What do you mean you have come to save us?"

With a loud, inelegant sigh, Harry turned his gaze to Julian. "Newhall cancelled the house party, or didn't he bother to tell you? Damn rude thing to do after you had already set out for Derbyshire. After much discussion, I had finally convinced my sister to attend and was going to accompany her. Fortunately, we received word from the Countess of Lienz's household in time."

"That's not true," said Caroline, stirring to life.

Harry gave her a condescending smile. "You poor thing. I know this trip was supposed to be good for you, but this blackguard has lied to you all."

Julian gritted his teeth. If this was how Harry Menzies conducted himself, then he could get straight back into his carriage and leave.

It was James who stepped in as peacemaker. "Now then, Harry, I think you may not have the right of it. While there have been some misunderstandings with invitations, we are Newhall's invited guests and intend to stay on at the castle."

Julian nodded to James with gratitude. His words took the wind out of the sails of self-important Harry and he mumbled something, which Julian took to be a half-apology.

The castle footmen were gathered around the rear of the carriage, still waiting on instructions. Julian nodded in their direction. It was late, and no matter how he felt about Harry Menzies, he could not bring himself to send the man back out onto the road.

Harry was also the one person at Newhall Castle who had any idea as to what the countess had done in London. Julian was keen to know exactly the extent of the damage to his reputation.

"You had better come in. We shall have a room made up for you," he said.

Caroline followed the men inside, reluctantly taking Harry's offered arm. He was behaving very oddly. If she didn't know better, she would have said he'd had one too many sips of brandy on the road and his mind had become addled.

"If you take Harry up to the drawing room, I shall have a word with Caroline," said Francis quietly to James. Their cousin nodded and hurried to catch up with the new guest.

Francis steered Caroline into the downstairs sitting room and closed the door behind them. "Have you and Harry come to some private understanding? I know he has always carried a torch for you, but I didn't think you felt anything in that way toward him. I am wracking my brains to find any reason other than that for him having made the journey up from London. He did just call you precious and then kissed your cheek."

She met his worried gaze. "No. I have no idea why he is here. But he is acting most peculiar. I suggest you ask him to stay for a couple of days, just to be polite, but that you make it clear he should return to London as soon as possible," she replied.

"Agreed. Just promise me that you will let me handle Harry. I don't know what he is playing at, but until I can figure it out, just try and stay clear of him," he said.

The last thing she needed was for Harry to appoint himself as yet another knight in shining armor ready to defend her honor. She already had an overabundance of protective men in her life.

If she was ever to find love, she had to break free from those chains.

Chapter Twenty-Six

When Caroline and Francis finally joined the others in the drawing room, Julian was quietly planning how he could get rid of Harry Menzies without causing offence. The headache he'd thought was slowly moving to the back of his brain had returned with a vengeance. He would do anything to go downstairs and find more sleep on the not-so-comfortable daybed.

At the sight of Caroline, however, his thoughts of self-pity vanished. She moved to the back of the room, maintaining as much distance as she could from their recently arrived guest.

Harry stepped forward and met Francis. "I was just telling Newhall and Radley here that it is all about London how the house party was cancelled at the last minute. The Countess of Lienz has spread a few rumors that Newhall was going back to France. Something about him and some young diplomat that he decided would warm his bed better than a wife."

"Vicious rumors, by anyone's account," replied James.

Julian's hand remained tightly fisted. His mother was staying true to form in her efforts to tear him down, but he had other more pressing concerns.

Julian wanted to wipe the simpering smile from Menzies's face.

He was enjoying retelling the story of the ugly rumors far too much in Julian's opinion. His dislike of Menzies coalesced into hatred as Harry looked toward Caroline and he bowed his head.

"My apologies, dear, sweet Caroline. You should not have to hear those sorts of rumors. One can only hope that they are not true. Though it must be said that diplomacy is not the most manly of pursuits," said Harry.

⁂

Caroline feared for Harry's safety as he spoke. From where she stood on the other side of the room, she could see the veins on the side of Julian's neck bulge. If Harry did not cease with his mad rant, she was certain violence would soon follow.

"Speaking of manly pursuits, we were talking about a hunting party this week, were we not?" she said.

She had promised Francis to let him broach the subject of her being allowed to hunt with the men, but at this point she was prepared to say anything in order to break the tension in the room. Harry frowned at her and opened his mouth to speak, but Julian stepped in.

"That would be an excellent idea, Caroline. It has been some time since I got some shooting practice in. One cannot let one's war skills get rusty. What do you say, Menzies? Oh, my apologies. I forgot you have not picked up a rifle or sword to serve king and country," replied Julian.

Harry, who had not served in the military at any point, muttered something under his breath then fell silent. Julian and Caroline exchanged a look of shared relief.

Julian stepped forward and offered Caroline his arm. "May I accompany you down to the hunt room so you can select your rifle? I am sure I have something that would suit you perfectly."

"That's a capital idea, Newhall. If we all come down and choose our weapons, we will be able to get off to an early start tomorrow. Caroline is a superb shot, and will make a great contribution to the hunt," said Francis.

"It's been ages since we went hunting. I am looking forward to it," replied Caroline.

As she took Julian's arm, she heard a low huff of displeasure come from Harry. He was clearly not happy with her inclusion in the hunting party.

She ignored his protest. Whatever his reasons were for coming to Derbyshire, he had no right telling her how she should behave. The sooner Francis could get Harry to go home, the better.

Chapter Twenty-Seven

The ice-covered grass crunched under Julian's boots as he walked across the lower field. It was not long after dawn, so the sun, hidden by low clouds, had made little headway in melting the frozen night rain.

Beside him Caroline walked, humming a happy tune to herself. Midas, who was coming along to help with the hunt, kept close to her heels. Francis, James, and Harry walked on ahead of them. Every so often, Julian caught Harry looking back over his shoulder and stealing a look at Caroline.

If she knew Harry was trying to capture her attention, Caroline hid it. She carried her hunting rifle under her left arm, having politely refused all offers for one of the others to carry it. "I love the early morning. The air is so crisp," she said.

Julian pulled a hip flask out from his coat pocket, slipped off the lid, and handed it to her.

She smiled. "It's not whisky, is it?"

"No. Since I was made aware of your checkered history with it, I have made a solemn vow to only carry the finest French brandy in my hip flask," he replied.

She took a sip, then nodded her approval. "Thank you, that is very kind."

A flutter of warmth went through Julian's body as he watched Caroline take a second, longer drink. She licked her lips, then handed the flask back.

Julian downed a mouthful of the brandy, trying desperately not to think about how much he would love to taste those rose-red lips of hers.

At the end of the field, they crossed over into a narrow laneway. Midas trotted ahead, no doubt happier to walk on the dry patches of the lane rather than the wet grass of the field. But when Harry made an effort to drop back in the group, and try to talk to Caroline, Midas bared his teeth and growled. Harry quickly retreated.

"I don't think Midas likes Harry," noted Caroline.

That makes two of us.

Julian stifled a satisfied grin. With a rifle tucked under her arm, and a pair of thick walking boots on her feet, she seemed perfectly at home in the chilly Derbyshire countryside.

"Do you hunt often?" he asked.

"Only in Scotland. The whole extended Radley family are big on hunting and fishing when we are at Strathmore Castle. The only thing I am not allowed to hunt are the wild boars. 'Too risky for young ladies to go chasing after them in long skirts,' or something to that effect. Papa won't even let me be a beater," she replied.

There was a distinct note of disappointment in her voice, and Julian suspected that given half the chance, Caroline would take on a wild Scottish boar. He was relieved that the most dangerous animals that could be hunted in the grounds of Newhall Castle were the local deer. From the easy way she carried her rifle, he sensed Caroline would be more than up to that challenge.

They rounded a bend, and Julian pursed his lips and whistled. The others ahead of them stopped and waited. He pointed toward a nearby thicket. It was the prime place on the Newhall estate for grouse to hide.

He bent down and spoke to Midas. "Softly now, boy. Walk ahead and find us some supper."

The dog trotted off and headed into the trees. Julian took the lead, with Caroline following closely. Francis, James, and Harry brought up the rear.

At the bottom of a tree in the center of the thicket, they found Midas standing as still as a stone. At the sound of a rifle being cocked, Julian turned and caught sight of Harry readying to take aim. He pointed at Harry's rifle and then to the ground.

With a roll of his eyes, Harry lowered his weapon. Julian nodded to Caroline, who quietly readied her rifle. With her heavily bandaged left hand sitting loosely on the side of the rifle she aimed for the top of the tree, then stopped and lowered it.

"I can't hold it properly. It is not safe," she said.

Julian cocked his own rifle. The insufferable Harry Menzies could wait his turn. "Can you see the birds?"

He leaned in close to her, and allowed Caroline to point out the grouse. He could see them quite clearly, roosting on the low branches of the tree, but the temptation to tell a little white lie in order to get closer to her was too much to resist.

He caught a hint of her perfume as he took a deep breath. For a moment he wished all the world away. "Ah yes, I see them," he said.

"Good. Swing ahead, and shoot a yard to the left of them once Midas has stirred them from cover," she said.

"Come on, Newhall. We don't have all day," said Harry.

Julian indulged in one last deep breath of Caroline's scent before reluctantly stepping away. He turned to Midas and gave a short whistle.

At Julian's signal, Midas leapt into the bushes. A rustle of leaves followed as the grouse stirred from their hiding place in the tree. Julian lifted his rifle and shot at the exact spot that Caroline had pointed out. He hit the first bird and brought it down cleanly.

Francis, James, and Harry all then took turns to bring down a bird. With a decent haul of four birds, they called the morning hunt a success and decided to head back to the castle.

While Julian gathered up the birds and dropped them into a carry sack, Harry wasted no time in vying for Caroline's attention. "Did you see my shot? I swear I could have taken all those birds by myself.

Pity that your damaged hand could not permit you to shoot. If we hunt again during our stay, I would be more than happy to help you make the shot."

"Thank you, Harry, that is very kind of you. Perhaps another time," she replied.

Francis patted his friend on the back and gave him a gentle nudge forward. James dropped in beside him, and the three of them started toward the lane. Caroline and Midas followed behind, with Julian bringing up the rear.

As they reached the wide grassy meadows, he caught up with her. "You did well on the hunt this morning. You have a keen eye. Promise me that when your hand is recovered, you will return to Newhall Castle and show me how you can handle a rifle."

"Thank you, I shall do just that," she replied.

As the others walking ahead put more distance between them, Julian savored his time alone with Caroline.

"Can I apologize once more?" he asked.

She looked at him quizzically. "What for?"

"The lake. I know I have already said I was sorry, but every time I think about it, I am filled with shame. I am not sure if I shall ever get it right in my mind. So, if you would indulge me, I shall keep apologizing for a little while longer," he replied.

Caroline stopped. When she looked up at Julian and smiled, it was like the sun was shining just for him. A wicked glint sparkled in her eyes. "I have forgiven you. But I never said I wasn't planning my revenge. Don't be surprised if you wake up one morning and find that your bed is floating in the castle lake."

Julian's deep, hearty laugh rang through the trees. The others turned and looked back at them. Caroline raised an eyebrow and continued on her way.

Julian no longer felt the touch of his boots on the ground. His ears rang with the heavy thump of his heart.

Cupid's arrow had found its mark.

Chapter Twenty-Eight

J ulian walked as slowly as he could back to the castle, wanting to spend every precious second with Caroline.

As soon as they stepped inside the front door, he caught the scent of hot food and freshly baked bread wafting from the breakfast room. "Breakfast is ready, everyone," he said.

"Food! I am famished," cried Harry. He and James wasted no time in racing for it. Francis ambled after them.

As the rest of his guests disappeared, Julian seized the opportunity to steal a private moment with Caroline. "Would you like to come with me while I take these birds down to the kitchens? Cook will have them baked up for supper with bacon and a red wine sauce."

"Of course, I love the kitchens. Our cook at home is always making secret meals for Francis and I. Mama thinks I am being suitably ladylike at supper, but the truth is it's because I am already stuffed," she replied.

The trip to the kitchens took only a few minutes. Julian introduced her to the head cook, who appeared to be at pains to thank Caroline enough for coming to visit. She politely pressed Caroline into promising she would return before her stay was over.

Once back upstairs from the kitchens, Caroline started for the breakfast room. Julian, to her surprise, had other ideas.

"Would you care for a pre-breakfast stroll? I am sure the others will be too busy with bacon and coffee to be bothered much about our absence," he said.

She considered his offer for a moment, then nodded. The walk back from the woods had ended too soon for her liking.

They made for the lower part of the castle grounds. The elegant gardens slowly gave way to what, she assumed in summer, would be lush green grassy slopes. At the bottom of the small rise on which the castle stood was a lake. The pale mid-morning sun glistened off its flat surface.

Julien pointed toward the lake. "I checked this morning and there is a thin layer of ice across most of it. A few more weeks and the ice will be thick enough to skate upon. Your evil plan to drop me into the water will have to wait until the spring."

Caroline turned to him and smiled. "Do you skate? I love to skate."

If there was one thing above all that she loved about winter, it was being able to ice-skate. Every year, she and her family skated on the River Thames when it was frozen. Twirling around on the ice gave her a freedom of activity rarely afforded to a young woman of London society.

"Yes, I do. I skated a lot while I was at university in Scotland. The winters up there are magnificent for racing on the ice," he replied.

"I would love to see you skate. Perhaps when you are next in London, we might put together a small group and head down to the Thames. It is a pity that they don't hold the ice festival anymore, but still, it could be fun," she said.

Julian caught her gaze, and Caroline could have sworn that his eyes sparkled as he smiled back at her. "Come. I have something to show you," he said.

He led her up a small rise which ran to the west of the castle grounds. At the top, he pointed toward what appeared to be a round stone stage. When they reached it, she was surprised to discover it was a small man-made pond. She guessed that it was probably somewhere in the range of twenty-five feet from edge to edge.

The stones ran all the way around the pond. At the end, a small gap had been left, which allowed the two of them to walk to the edge of the water. Caroline looked down. The water was frozen solid.

"What is it?" she asked.

Julian dipped into a low bow. "Your skating pond, your royal highness,' he announced. He cursed under his breath. "I am sorry. I should not have called you that. I know you don't like it."

Caroline waved his apology away. "No. I was a tyrant and rightly deserved the name of the Ice Queen. I was cold and at times, cruel. But I promise I am trying to find myself again." She pointed to the skating pond, and Julian took his cue.

"My father had it built for my mother when I was small. In those days, he was still trying to find favor with her. I think she may have skated on it once, and then abandoned it, like all his other gifts," he said.

Caroline had tried not to judge Julian's mother for how she had treated her late husband. She did not know the countess's life story well enough to have an appreciation of what her marriage had been like. Instead, she reserved her anger for the way she treated her son. There was a distinct sadness in Julian's voice every time he made mention of his mother.

He put the toe of his boot onto the ice, then lifted his foot and brought it down hard. The ice gave a deep moan, but remained perfectly intact.

Caroline looked out toward the middle of the pond. The water was a satisfying deep-blue. "It's frozen. Perfect."

Julian stepped out onto the ice and walked confidently across to the center of the pond. He held out his hand to her. "Care to join me?"

She sucked in a deep breath, unsure as to whether it was from the trepidation of stepping onto the ice, or the fact that she was well away from the castle and quite alone with him. She hesitated for a moment. Her heart told her that this was more than a simple step forward.

"It's quite safe. It was designed so that the water would settle at different depths and so the middle actually freezes first. My father was a personal friend of Humphry Repton, the landscape designer. He is responsible for most of the castle gardens and the land which runs down to the lake. He built the pond as a special favor to my father."

Caroline stepped out onto the ice and, taking tentative steps, walked to Julian. She shyly took his offered hand. They stood silently in the middle of the pond for a time, listening to the odd sounds that the ice made as it shifted deep under them.

"This is marvelous. I would spend every day in winter out here if I lived at Newhall Castle," she said. She looked away, down toward the lake. The air was still chilly, but heat prickled on her cheeks.

Julian drew close. "I have ice skates which you could use. I would love to see you spinning on the pond. I watched you dance in the snow the other day, and I thought it was magical."

He was so close now that she could feel the heat of his breath on the back of her neck. Caroline shivered. "That would be nice."

Her heart raced. Never before had a man had this sort of effect on her. Her sense of control was slipping away. When he brushed his fingers softly on her cheek, she let the air slowly leave her lips before taking in a shuddering breath.

He drew back. She dared not look at him. What was she to say? That while men paid constant attention to her, she was afraid to open her heart to any of them?

From all the many men in her life, she knew Julian was different. His open honesty told her that he was not one for playing games when it came to love. He was the first man who'd made her feel as if she could lower her guard and he would keep her safe. The champion of her heart.

She walked toward the edge of the pond, only turning to face him when she had put some distance between them. He was still standing in the middle of the frozen pond, his eyes cast downward. There was a vulnerability about him she had never noticed before. When he finally looked up and began to walk toward her, his posture was stiff. "As I said, you could come and skate here if you like. I shall ask the castle housekeeper to find a pair of ice skates for you."

She nodded, allowing him to change the mood between them back to one of host and guest. "Thank you. I would like that very much. I suppose we had better head back to the others."

For the first time in her life, Caroline found herself afraid of what else she might say. Her mind usually dictated her words, but now it was her heart which cried out to be heard. She knew enough to know that once she had declared her love for him, there would be no going back.

Doubt filled her mind. What if she was not reading the signs from Julian right? Could she take the risk, knowing that if she had it all wrong, the bitter taste of rejection would soon follow?

Chapter Twenty-Nine

They were met partway back to the castle by an angry Harry. Francis and James were nowhere to be seen.

"Where in the devil have the two of you been? You didn't come to breakfast. Frightfully indecent of you, Newhall, to spirit Caroline away from her chaperones without their notice," he said.

Julian ignored the underlying accusation in Harry's words. "We took the birds down to the kitchens and then decided to go for a short stroll before coming in to join the rest of you for breakfast. I was merely showing Caroline around the grounds; there is nothing indecent in taking a walk."

Harry huffed in disgust, then turned his attention to Caroline. "You know you should not go anywhere without one of us accompanying you. What would your mother say?"

"My mother would say, 'One should avoid pompous asses by whatever means necessary.' Harry, you are not my chaperone, and I do not answer to you," she snapped.

It took a great deal of self-control for Julian not to applaud Caroline's entirely suitable response to being chastised like a child. She stepped past Harry and headed toward the front door. Julian gave Harry a curt nod as he followed Caroline.

"Stay away from her," said Harry in a low, angry tone.

Julian didn't immediately respond to the threat, and was still considering his options when Francis and James appeared.

"Ah, there you are. We were looking everywhere for you," said Francis.

Julian chuckled and gave Harry a friendly pat on the shoulder. "Yes, I was just telling Menzies here that Midas needed a few more minutes outside before we came in for breakfast. All the excitement of the hunt had him stirred up. No harm done. I hope you left us some bacon."

The look on Harry's face was a study in perfect frustration. Julian gave him a second pat just to confirm their unspoken understanding. He silently dared Harry to make mention of the fact that Midas was nowhere in sight. Neither man would want an escalation in hostilities to take place in front of Caroline.

"It's always hard to keep Caroline inside during the winter. She is the first to offer a ramble through the woods on Strathmore mountain. Give her a pair of solid boots and my sister will wander the hills for days," said Francis. If he had noticed any tension between Julian and Harry, he was keeping it to himself.

Harry, in turn, mumbled something about it not being ladylike, but only Julian seemed to catch the disapproving comment.

After following his guests back inside, Julian excused himself. If Menzies thought his words would keep the earl from spending more time with Caroline, he was gravely mistaken.

Julian found the butler and instructed him to go through the cupboards and locate some ice skates. Only two pairs would be needed. One for him, and one for Caroline.

Later that afternoon, Francis, Harry, and James headed into the local village to have a drink at the tavern. With Caroline and Lady Margaret settling in for a ladies-only embroidery afternoon, Julian found himself with welcome time alone.

Outmaneuvering Harry Menzies had taken much of the humor

out of him over the past day. Added to that was the undisputable fact that not only were he and Caroline Saunders no longer enemies, but he was falling for her.

He had been so close to her when they were at the ice pond that the heady scent of her perfume still lingered in his mind. His interest in her had turned to simmering desire.

Leaving the castle, he sought refuge at the small stone cottage which sat at the edge of the frozen lake. A grove of trees had been planted at the back of the cottage and over the years they had grown and now created a green frame around three of its sides. The cottage was hidden from view from the main part of the castle grounds, and Julian liked it that way.

It was a place of solitude and comfort. His father had come here often in the final years of his ill-fated marriage. It had been somewhere for him to hide away from the blistering rows he and Julian's mother regularly conducted.

With his father now gone, Julian had kept the standing order for a fire to be kept burning in the fireplace of the old cottage whenever he was in residence. It was a place to retreat and think on his life and the choices which now stood before him.

The welcoming crackle of logs burning on the fire greeted him as he stepped inside the small stone cottage. He closed the door behind him and immediately felt the comforting warmth.

He peeled off his gloves and threw his hat onto the nearby bed. Without thinking, he picked up a brandy bottle from the table, and poured himself a generous glass.

"What a week it's been," he muttered.

He made a beeline for his favorite chair by the fire and slumped down into it, swearing as he splashed brandy on his waistcoat. With one smooth motion, he downed his drink. He looked over to the table where the brandy bottle sat, but decided it was not a wise move to indulge in a second glass.

He leaned back in the chair and closed his eyes.

Large bright circles danced before his closed eyes. From a young age, he had been plagued by stress headaches, usually brought on by one of his parents' legendary rows.

Today's headache had a different name. *Harry Menzies*. He slowly clenched and unclenched his fists, wishing he could squeeze Francis's interfering friend by the throat. He had gotten under Julian's skin like a weeping rash.

He hated him. Not just because Harry thought himself Caroline's self-appointed protector. It came down to pure inelegant jealousy. He knew the look that Harry wore whenever he was close to Caroline; it was the very same one he knew sat on his own countenance when in her presence.

He considered the ludicrous situation he found himself dealing with. Instead of a castle full of young ladies all vying for his attention, he was now locked in a battle for the affections of the only woman he had not invited to his house party.

He picked up his hat and gloves, and after downing another half glass of brandy, he headed for the door. Closing it behind him, he stepped back out into the freezing air.

Shoving his hat down hard on his head, he began to march purposefully back toward the castle. He was at one with the previous fighting lords of Newhall. But instead of taking to the bloody field of battle to win against a skillful opponent, this lord of Newhall was set to go into battle against a foe he knew he could beat. When the war was over, he would be the one who had won Caroline's heart.

Chapter Thirty

After supper, the group gathered in one of the main drawing rooms upstairs. Caroline and Lady Margaret retreated to a spot near the fire and quietly played cards.

Julian was content to nurse a glass of shiraz, while James, Harry, and Francis gave the castle brandy stocks a good nudge.

When James and Francis began to regale the group with tales of their younger years at Strathmore Castle, Julian sat and listened. Harry, meanwhile, slumped in a chair and scowled.

"We climbed to the top of the castle keep and hid there for hours. Good old Caro, here, hitched up her skirts and scaled one of the outer walls to smuggle us some food. Uncle Ewan and my father were furious when they finally found us," said Francis.

Caroline laughed. She had only climbed a small wall with her skirts barely lifted, but the story, over the years, had gotten legs and become family legend.

"It was a long time before they finally discovered I was the inside agent. Papa was still angry, but since I was nearly an adult, he decided it was all too late to punish me for my youthful transgressions," she replied.

Harry downed the rest of his brandy and thumped his glass down on the table. Everyone turned and looked at him. "If you were my daughter, I would still have meted out a suitable punishment. Damn foolish to have risked your neck," he snapped.

He rose from his chair and stood, shaking his head. When a stunned Francis tried to calm him, he pushed him away. "I can see I am in poor company. I am going to bed. Good night." With a perfunctory bow to the women, Harry turned and marched out the door. It closed loudly behind him.

"I am terribly sorry, Newhall. I do not know what has got into him; he is not the Harry I have known since school. I shall have a word with him in the morning. I think, perhaps, it is time I gave him a firmer nudge about going back to London," said Francis.

Relief dropped lightly into Caroline's mind. She too longed to see the back of Harry.

Francis and James settled into their chairs and made an agreement to kick on and continue drinking. Julian rang the bell and when a footman appeared, he ordered another bottle of brandy be brought up for his guests.

Across the room, Julian met Caroline's gaze. When she smiled at him, he raised his glass and silently toasted her.

The following morning saw only Caroline, Julian, and Lady Margaret in the breakfast room. The castle butler informed them that Mister Radley and Mister Saunders had indeed made good on their promise and seen it through to dawn. They had only taken to their beds a little more than an hour prior to the rest of the household rising.

"Well that will make for a quiet day around here," noted Lady Margaret.

Caroline picked up her coffee and took a sip. Now, if only Harry would sleep through the morning, she would be able to enjoy some free time.

"We managed to find the ice skates late yesterday. So, when you feel ready to take to the ice, I shall have them brought to you," said Julian.

Caroline touched the bandage of her injured hand. While she was an excellent ice-skater, she was still hesitant to put herself at risk. If she fell on the ice, the stitches would likely burst.

"Thank you. But I may wait a few days more and then see how my hand feels. I do hope to be able to set foot on the pond before I leave," she replied.

Lady Margaret looked up from her plate of baked salmon and mashed potatoes. "Are you going to skate on the ice pond? Julian's father always wanted me to try it, but I must confess to being terrible on the ice. The last time I tried to skate was on the Newhall village pond. I crashed into the local vicar and he was most put out," she said with a wry smile.

At the end of the table, Julian's body shook with suppressed mirth. He looked up at Lady Margaret with tears in his eyes. "Of course, the fact that you also knocked down his wife, his sister, and a distant cousin had nothing to do with him being so terribly upset."

Lady Margaret raised an eyebrow, as the sound of Julian's laugh rang through the room. Caught up in the moment, Caroline found herself laughing along.

"Well yes, there was that, now that you mention it," replied Lady Margaret.

Caroline liked Lady Margaret immensely, and it was clear she and Julian were close. There was a warmth between them that was non-existent between him and the countess.

"I promise, if you do decide to venture out onto the ice pond, I shall keep Lady Margaret at a safe distance. In the meantime, since the rest of our small house party are not looking like they will be making breakfast anytime soon, could I tempt you with a post-breakfast walk around the grounds?" he said.

There had been a light rainfall overnight, and Caroline was eager to get out and walk. The sound of frozen grass crunching under her boots was another of her favorite winter delights.

"I shall get my things," she said.

What she really meant was if she got her cape and scarf, she and Julian could be away from the castle before anyone else found their way to the breakfast room. She rose from her chair and quickly headed upstairs.

She met Julian outside a short time later. Taking her by the arm, he led her swiftly away from the castle via a small copse of trees.

Once out of sight of the front door, he stopped. "Sorry about the rude hurry, but I wanted us to get away. While you were upstairs, a footman came down and mentioned that Menzies was up and about. I wasn't particularly keen on inviting him to join us. Lady Margaret has kindly offered to keep him company for breakfast."

Caroline made a mental note to keep scarce about the castle for the rest of the morning. Harry was the last person she wished to spend time with, especially after his boorish behavior of the previous evening.

"Lady Margaret is a treasure. She certainly has a soft spot for you," she said.

"She is one of the most important people in my life. After my mother abandoned us, Lady Margaret was the one who took up the reins of running the castle. I was more than happy when she and my father fell in love. She gifted him with a calm mind and a sense of joy," he said.

As he spoke about his late father's mistress, Caroline could see the look of happiness on Julian's face. He genuinely cared for her.

The wind had picked up from the previous day and it now bit through her cloak. She shivered. Winter was fast approaching and she feared it would be as harsh as the previous year.

"You look cold. Perhaps we should seek out somewhere warm. I have just the place," he said.

"That would be nice, thank you."

He led her toward the lake, and as they drew near, Caroline caught sight of a small stone cottage nestled within the trees close to the lake. From the top of the grounds, the cottage had been well hidden from view.

Julian opened the door, and stood back to allow Caroline to go first. As she stepped across the threshold, she was greeted with the welcome warmth of a well-tended fire. The room held a few items of furniture. A pair of chairs sat either side of the small but effective fireplace. There was a table, which had four mismatched chairs, and a bed in the corner. To the right of the fireplace hung a single frame, its painting turned to face the wall.

"This was my father's retreat for many years, especially when I was young and he and my mother were at war. He used to sleep down here, hence the bed. I like the privacy it affords me, so I have the staff keep the fire going and the liquor supply maintained," he said.

"It is a lovely spot. I can see why you would want to come here," she replied.

He poured them both a glass of brandy and handed one to Caroline. "A little early in the morning, but it does take the chill off. Please, sit," he said.

After taking a seat by the fire, her gaze returned to the painting on the wall. Why would anyone hang a painting and then have it turned so it could not be seen?

Julian crossed to the painting and took it down. He handed it to Caroline before taking the seat opposite her. "I cannot abide the sight of it, but have not yet mustered the courage to throw it on the fire."

The painting was a likeness of Julian's mother. She was reclining on a long daybed, clad in a black shoulder less gown. Around her neck was a magnificent necklace. The length of it was studded with rubies and diamonds. The largest ruby had been fashioned into the center of a diamond-encrusted crucifix and hung as a pendant.

"That is a stunning necklace," said Caroline.

"It is the Crusader Ruby. The most important heirloom of the Newhall estate—a priceless jewel handed down through the generations," replied Julian.

There were many magnificent pieces of jewelry in the Duke of Strathmore's collection, but Caroline could not see any of them holding a candle to the Crusader Ruby. "Why is it called the Crusader Ruby?"

"One of my forebears brought the main ruby back from the holy land during the crusades. He had it fashioned into the necklace, intending to give it to the King of France, but his wife took a fancy to it and so he kept it," he replied.

"I had no idea that the Newhall line went back that far," she said.

"Yes, its one of the oldest titles in England."

He stood and took the painting from her, placing it back face-forward to the wall.

"I would love to see the real Crusader Ruby sometime," said Caroline.

Julian huffed. "So, would I. The countess took it with her when she left my father. He used to come down here and stare at the painting for hours. I am not sure what he craved most: her or the necklace. After he died, I turned it so it faced the wall. I don't want to look at her arrogant smile even if it is just a likeness."

Caroline now understood the bitterness in Julian's voice. Not only had his mother abandoned him, but she had taken an ancient relic with her that rightly belonged to him.

She sipped at her brandy, then set the glass down on the floor. Julian had only spoken in snatches about his mother. And, having had the misfortune to meet the countess, Caroline could fill in many of the gaps of his childhood. His father, however, was still a mystery.

"Tell me about your father. Were you close?" she asked.

He paused for a moment. She sensed he was choosing his words carefully before he spoke. "It was an odd relationship. When I was young, I blamed him for my mother hating me. She always said it was his fault that our home was such an unhappy place. And I believed her. If I had not been born, my mother would not have hated me. I dare you to find sense with that piece of childish logic. It was only after she finally left my father that he and I discovered we actually liked one another."

There was an underlying pain in his words. She had been raised by two loving parents, who had a strong marriage, never once having to question the bonds of paternal affection.

"So, you had your father's love?"

He screwed up his face "I was nine years' old when my mother left, and I barely knew my father. It took a long time for us to build the trust that should have been there all along. It was only after Lady Margaret came to Newhall Castle that he began to show me his love. I have her to thank for helping to mend his broken heart."

Caroline blinked back tears as she pictured a young Julian in her mind. A lonely boy waiting for one of his parents to show him that they cared.

"It was not his fault. He came from a long line of stoic men. Emotions such as love do not run deep in my family."

"But your father loved your mother; it's just that she didn't return his affections. And you most certainly are not an uncaring man," replied Caroline.

Their gazes met. Caroline silently prayed for Julian to open his heart, just a little, to her. She was disappointed when he simply replied, "Thank you. That is a kind thing to say."

Caroline picked up her brandy glass and took another sip. Her impression of the Earl of Newhall was a long way from that of when they had first met. While the current moment was a little awkward, she took heart. If he didn't care anything for her, they would not be having this conversation.

She would forever feel a sense of shame and regret over the way she had treated him. Fate must have finally decided to smile upon her and had granted her with the opportunity of a second chance with the man who sat opposite her.

They had made small but positive steps towards being firm friends. After the moment at the ice pond, when they had stood so close that Julian was able to briefly touch her cheek, she knew her heart was beating to a different rhythm. She wanted more than friendship. She longed to run her fingers through his hair once more and place a soft kiss on his lips.

"Enough about me. What about you? What are you going to do once you return to London; will you go back to your court of admirers?" he asked.

She sat in her chair and considered his question. "The Ice Queen will have to abdicate. I cannot continue to live my life the way I have in recent times. I have become someone that not many people like. I intend to go to Scotland and spend an extended period of time away from London. I need to withdraw somewhere and find myself."

"Please don't do that. I would be disappointed if you went away," he said.

His response took her by surprise.

He reached out and took hold of her hand. "I am pleased that you and I have managed to reshape our relationship, that we have become friends. I simply ask that you reconsider your plans. Of course, if I cannot change your mind, then, as a friend, I will respect your decision."

She looked down at her hand, and felt her breath catch at the warmth of Julian's gentle grasp. Her usual ingrained response to a gentleman attempting to take her hand was to pull away and offer a harsh rebuke. Yet not with this man. His touch held such comfort that she felt it to her bones.

His earnest entreaty captured her mind. He was asking, not demanding, nor pleading. She raised her head and looked into his smoky-gray eyes.

She no longer saw him as merely a friend. Her gaze drifted down to settle on his full lips. She would give anything for him to take her into his arms and kiss her.

When Julian withdrew his hand, Caroline blinked back tears.

"We had better return to the castle. I would not want to incur the wrath of either your brother or your cousin," said Julian.

"Yes, of course."

She had allowed herself to think Julian felt something more than mere friendship toward her. She silently chastised herself for being such a fool. Cupid's arrow had missed after all.

Julian placed a couple more logs on the fire before he and Caroline left the cottage. Depending on how things went during the day, he planned to come back later and lie on the bed. Perhaps enjoy the afternoon sun as it filtered in through the window.

He scowled at the sky as they slowly climbed the rise which led to the castle. The softly falling snowflakes indicated he would have little chance of seeing the sun for the rest of the day.

Caroline walked silently beside him. She appeared lost in her thoughts, deep in her own world. When she stopped and turned to look back at the lake, Julian halted.

"Thank you," she said.

"What for?" he replied, searching his mind for what he had done to earn her gratitude.

"For asking me to stay. I know this sounds a little odd, but few men outside of my immediate family ever ask for my permission. You talk about my court of admirers as if I had gathered them to me, yet not one of them has ever asked if I wished for their company," she replied.

Her words took him by surprise. He'd been operating under the assumption that Caroline had handpicked her group of gentlemen friends. It had never occurred to him that the Ice Queen had been put on the throne without her consent.

"Isn't that one of the benefits of being beautiful?" he said.

She came to his side. "Not necessarily. I am not saying I would prefer to be plain, but having a fine face does come with its own price."

The Newhall Castle steward appeared through the stone arch of the nearby walled garden, and approached them. "My lord."

"Good morning. Though from the weather that is settling in, I cannot say it will be a fine day," replied Julian.

His steward nodded. "Yes, and we have had a spot of bother with the straw that was laid over the gardens just after your arrival. It would appear that it is not deep enough and some of the plants have been burnt by the rain as it froze. I shall have to send the wagon over to Ashby to buy some more," he said.

Julian would have preferred to stay with Caroline, but he had been an absent lord for too long. His steward had done a fine job in managing the castle and grounds while Julian was in France, but the task was ultimately his to undertake.

"Would you please excuse me, Caroline? I should go and examine the garden. It was my decision not to lay the straw too deep; it would appear, I was wrong. I shan't be long."

"Of course," she replied.

Caroline found it encouraging to know that Julian was comfortable in owning up to his mistakes, because she still found it hard to admit when she was at fault. Her stubborn streak ran deep, and it would take a determined man to help her overcome it.

She could only pray that he was strong enough for the both of them.

Chapter Thirty-One

After Julian and his steward disappeared behind the high walls of the garden, Caroline was content to slowly wander on toward the castle. She stopped every so often to look back at the lake and take in the winter wonderland that was unfolding as the snow continued to fall.

She secretly hoped that by dragging her feet, Julian might catch up with her before she reached the castle, and they could spend a little more time talking privately. Thoughts of the earl were becoming near constant in her mind. He treated her differently than other men did. Dare she hope that Julian saw beyond her looks?

She had turned from one last gaze at the snow-covered grounds when Harry unexpectedly appeared from the front door of the castle. Standing in the open, she was easy to spot. He made an immediate beeline for her. There was no escape.

"Don't be rude. Just be firm and polite," she muttered as he approached.

As he drew close, she saw he was red-faced and flustered. Grim determination sat on his lips. She sighed. His mood, it would appear, had not improved from last night.

"You really should not be out here alone," he said.

Caroline pursed her lips, forcing her temper down. "I wasn't. Julian and I took an early morning walk. He has just gone off with his steward to deal with an estate matter," she replied.

A flash of rage crossed Harry's face. As he huffed, a great cloud of vapor appeared from his mouth in the cold air. "That is even worse. Do you not have any regard for your reputation, or the feelings of others?"

Caroline made to step past him, but Harry seized her by the left arm. He held it tight.

"Let go, Harry. You are hurting me," she demanded.

He shook his head violently. His grip on her arm tightened. Caroline feared he was about to have a fit.

"No! It won't do. I have done my time. Now it is up to you to yield," he said.

A rising sense of panic took hold of her. She punched Harry hard on the arm, repeatedly, and he finally released his grip.

"What the devil has got into you? What do mean yield? Yield to what?" she replied.

His breath was coming hard and fast, and he angrily wagged his finger at her. "I have done my time waiting for you to finish with all those other fools. But I am no longer prepared to indulge your girly whims. You will accept my proposal of marriage and then we will be done with it."

She stared hard at him while rubbing her bruised arm. The notion, wherever it had come from, was insane. There was not a chance on earth that she would ever consider marrying Harry Menzies. She tolerated his incessant need to be near her purely for the sake of Francis. This time, however, he had gone too far.

"No, Harry. You cannot make those sorts of demands of me. This is utterly ridiculous. Now go away!" she snapped.

The Harry she thought knew would have done as she asked. The man who stood before her was suddenly a stranger. "You will marry me and that is the end of it!"

She gritted her teeth. He had run mad. "Harry, you are my brother's best friend and because of that I have been tolerant of your idiosyncrasies over the years. But hear me now. I don't love you. I won't marry you. Now leave me alone!"

"But you have to marry me," he replied.

"Why?" she asked, throwing up her hands in exasperation.

He stepped forward and stood over her. When she looked up and saw the sly smile which appeared on his lips, Caroline felt an icy chill of premonition.

"Because the day before I left London, I posted an engagement announcement in *The Times*," he replied.

A punch of shock hit Caroline with such force that she staggered back. It took a moment or two for her to breathe again.

This had to be a cruel jest. No one in their right mind would try and force her to marry them. She would make his life a misery.

He put an arm around her waist and pulled her roughly to him. Caroline squirmed but Harry held her tight. "I know it was a little bold of me, but there you have it. As the Duke of Wellington put it, *virtutis fortuna comes*. And now I have made my claim upon you to the world."

Betrothals were not entered into lightly, especially by women of her social standing. In the eyes of many of the matrons of the *ton*, she would already be considered Harry's wife. If she tried to back out of the arrangement, her reputation would be in tatters.

"How . . . how could you do such a thing?"

"You forced my hand. After your sister married, I had assumed you would come to me and we would settle on our future. But instead of rewarding my long-suffering patience, you cruelly decided to come here and throw your hat in the ring to become Newhall's countess," he said.

He lowered his head and forced his lips against hers. She struggled, but he was too strong. Too determined to have his way. He placed hot, wet kisses on her cheeks and then ran his tongue down the side of her neck. "So beautiful. Oh, Caroline, you are so beautiful. I cannot wait to have you naked beneath me," he growled.

Hot, burning anger welled up inside. She lifted her right boot, and brought it down as hard as she could on his foot.

"Oh, you bitch!" he cried, releasing her from his harsh embrace.

Caroline rounded on him. "Yes, and a bitch you won't be marrying!"

Harry snorted. "We shall see about that. If you defy me now, Caroline, I will show you who is the master once we are married. I promise, you will yield."

He raised a fisted hand and swung at her face. Caroline stepped to one side and avoided the blow. From his angry roar, she knew she would not be so lucky a second time.

Behind Harry, Julian reappeared from the walled garden. At the sight of him, Caroline sucked in a shuddering breath and screamed, "Julian!"

He broke into a fast run. "What on earth is going on?"

Caroline quickly moved to stand close to the safety of him. She looked back at Harry. He had not moved; his fist was still sickeningly clenched.

"Harry posted a betrothal notice in *The Times*. Oh Julian, all of London thinks I have agreed to marry him. When I told him no, he attacked me," she said. The words burned in her mouth as she spoke. The pain was made worse by the look of shock and anger which appeared on Julian's face.

"Is this true?" he said.

Harry looked from Julian to Caroline and snorted. "I didn't attack her. I simply kissed her. In time she will learn to accept my advances, willing or not."

Julian's posture stiffened. Caroline sensed he was about to launch himself at Harry and do him a grave injury. When Harry made a bold step toward them, Julian held up his hand.

"Menzies, I would not take another step, because if you do, I shall put you down like a wild beast." A deadly look glittered in Julian's eyes. "And I will show you no mercy."

Chapter Thirty-Two

J ulian genuinely surprised himself. He managed to get both Caroline and Harry back to the castle without murdering Harry in the process. He was sorely tempted to do him great harm, but it quickly became apparent that Caroline was in need of his support. He would have to wait to exact revenge on the man who had laid his hands on her.

Francis was not so gracious.

As Caroline went to sit with Lady Margaret, the men gathered in the drawing room, Harry on one side, faced down by the others.

"Harry, for the love of our friendship, tell me this is something of a foolish and badly timed jest. Tell me what Caroline has accused you of doing is all some terrible misunderstanding," said Francis.

"I assure you that I am completely earnest in my resolve to marry your sister. You should be congratulating me, not taking me to task. Her reputation will be salvaged by her becoming my wife," replied Harry.

"But not her health from the way you assaulted her," snapped Julian.

The memory of the fear he had seen in Caroline's eyes burned bright in his mind. Harry shook his head, but his gaze remained fixed on Francis. Caroline's brother was the one man in the room who had any real power over her future.

"Now, Francis, if I could just talk to Caroline alone, I am certain we could get the matter of our betrothal settled. She just needs to learn to do as she is told," Harry implored.

Julian puffed out his cheeks. He knew it was his imagination, but he was certain that somewhere he could hear a small voice telling him that Harry was in desperate need of a solid punch to the head.

Make that two.

Francis raked his fingers through his hair. Julian felt sorry for him. No matter what was resolved from the current crisis, the long-standing friendship was likely beyond repair. With his sister's reputation at risk, Francis was now in the unenviable situation of having to take sides.

"What Caroline needs is for her family to support and protect her, which is exactly what I am going to do. You attacked my sister and now have the gall to try and force her into marrying you. Have you run mad?" he said.

A determined Harry held his ground. "I am not mad. In fact, I am seeing more clearly now than I have ever done. I made certain to set things in motion. So, whether you like it or not, Caroline now has to marry me."

All six-foot-four of Francis stepped forward and towered over Harry. Julian and James exchanged a concerned look. This moment could very well end in bloodshed.

"You will not speak to Caroline. You will go to your room and pack your things. You and I shall leave for London before the day is out," said Francis.

"What?" replied Harry.

Julian had heard enough. He was not going to stand idly by while Harry questioned the whys and wherefores of what was to happen. Especially not after what he had done to Caroline.

"Menzies, this is my home. I shall be the judge of what happens under my roof. As of this moment, you are no longer welcome as a guest at Newhall Castle. Until you leave later today, you will remain in your room. I shall have a footman bring you food and drink," he said.

"But—"

"But nothing," replied Julian.

"Don't think for one minute that this is over and done with, Newhall. That betrothal notice will carry a great deal of weight in forcing Caroline to accept my suit," sneered Harry.

Julian held back on his reply, and opened the door. He slammed it shut with great force after Francis and James had led Harry away. They accompanied Harry to his room, returning a short time later.

Francis handed Julian a key. "He continued to demand to see Caroline, so I thought it best to lock him in. Mostly for the sake of his own safety."

Julian nodded his agreement. It was a wise course of action. He had retrieved his pistol from his room upon returning to the castle. It was now loaded and sitting in his jacket pocket. It may have been overkill on his part, but after having seen how shaken Caroline was after her encounter with Harry Menzies, he was not willing to take any chances.

The Caroline of old would have taken her brother to task for not having dealt with the Harry situation earlier. But she now held her tongue as Francis closed the sitting room door behind him. No one could have foreseen the events that had transpired earlier that morning, least of all Francis.

"Thank you for sitting with my sister," said Francis, as Lady Margaret gathered up her shawl and left the room.

His face was drawn and held an expression of dark resolve. Caroline knew he was doing his utmost to keep his temper in check. Francis was one of those people who could tolerate a thousand insults, but once he received one too many, pity help the man on the receiving end of his wild Viking temper.

Caroline rose from her seat and they met in the middle of the room. He held out his arms. "I am so sorry, Caro. I had no idea. Thank god Newhall arrived when he did," he said.

It was with a great sense of relief that she stepped into Francis's embrace. Long arms wrapped around her and pulled her close to him. She hugged him as best as she could, taking care not to disturb her injured left hand. Her tall, white-haired warrior from the north would do all he could to keep her safe.

"What is to happen?" she asked.

He looked down at her. "Harry is locked in his room and won't be allowed out until we leave for London. That should be in a couple of hours. Newhall's stablemaster is getting the carriage and horses ready for the road."

Caroline pulled out of her brother's hug. "Then I had better hurry and pack."

Francis stepped in her way as she headed for the door. "Only Harry and I are travelling today. Would you please sit?"

As he took a seat beside her on a nearby sofa, Francis cleared his throat. "Now I know you want to come back to London with me to get this all sorted, and if it were anyone else, I would be inclined to agree. But this is Harry. And we go back a long way. What I am asking you to do is to go to Scotland with James. And once the situation in London has been resolved, I shall send word," he said.

Caroline sat and considered his words. Knowing her brother, he was thinking of both the immediate situation and beyond. When she finally nodded her agreement, it was with the unspoken understanding that matters needed to be handled delicately.

Harry had a younger sister who was out in society, but as yet, unmarried. If it got about town that her brother was a hothead, it could seriously damage her prospects. By not racing back to London to denounce Harry, she would afford her family the opportunity to find a way to quietly resolve matters with the least amount of damage. There were others to consider besides herself.

Francis did not need to show their parents the slow-forming bruises on Caroline's arm for them to gain an understanding of the gravity of what had happened in Derbyshire. By sending Caroline to

Scotland, she would be away from the ugly business of dealing with Harry Menzies, and she would be safe.

"As long as James is prepared to travel to Scotland, then I shall go with him. In a few more days, my hand should be healed enough for me to travel. We could be on the road north by the start of next week," she replied.

There was a low sigh of relief from Francis at her words. She felt sorry for him. No one could envy him the long journey home with Harry.

Francis leaned over and placed a soft kiss on Caroline's cheek. "Thank you. You know if I could stay here and comfort you I would, but things have to be sorted in London as soon as possible. If we leave by early afternoon, we should be able to make it through to Markfield before nightfall, and then press on tomorrow."

She followed him to the door of the sitting room. "What are you going to do once you get home?"

It was all well and good her agreeing to go to Scotland, but she was not prepared to be left in the dark as to what was to be done about her own future.

"I shall speak to Father, but my first inclination would be to have a word through private channels with *The Times* and ask that they print a retraction and an apology. While the blame lies clearly at Harry's feet, they should know not to have printed the notice without it having been signed by both parties," he replied.

Caroline let her brother go. She dreaded what he and their father would have to go through in order to sort out the unholy mess that Harry had put them all in. The *ton* thrived on rumors, and a false betrothal would be perfect fodder for the midafternoon gossip sessions, which regularly took place over tea and cake, in the finest homes of London.

Chapter Thirty-Three

❧❦❧

A little more than an hour later, the residing party stood outside as Francis and Harry climbed aboard Harry's carriage. Francis was true to his word in being eager to set out as early as possible.

Harry went quietly, and from the determined looks on the faces of Francis, James, and especially Julian, there was nothing he could say that would change anyone's mind.

When Caroline's gaze dropped to Julian's hands, she noted that while one was tightly fisted, the other was held in his jacket pocket. She saw the unmistakable handle of a pistol.

She gave Francis a farewell kiss and accepted his promise that he would find a solution to her predicament. Harry kept his head down and would not meet her gaze before climbing into the carriage and slamming the door loudly behind him.

The carriage made its way down the drive before finally disappearing over the small rise. James came to Caroline's side and put his arm around her. "He will find a way. Between Francis and your father, they will make certain that your reputation remains intact. I'm not so sure about Menzies, but then again, he has brought this on himself."

Julian turned to the rest of them. He was still as grim as he had been the moment she had cried out in panicked desperation and he had raced to her side. "And now we are down to four."

"James and I will also be leaving soon," replied Caroline.

He frowned. "What do you mean?"

"Francis asked that James and I travel to Scotland and remain at Strathmore Castle until matters have been resolved in London. With your permission, we shall stay on for a few more days so that my hand has time to heal. After that, we will take our leave. You have endured enough of us, I would say."

The look on his face at her words changed from hard resolve to one of disappointment. Her heart lifted at the thought that Julian would be saddened by their departure.

"I would rather that you stayed here. James, I thought you wanted to travel over to Burton-on-Trent and see your friends? If you remain here at Newhall then you can still visit them," said Julian.

Lady Margaret chimed in. "Please reconsider your travel plans. Burton is a lovely town, and I am sure Julian would be happy to take you both to see it. They have a market every Thursday and the town gets very busy with lots of people from throughout the district."

James looked to Caroline. "Well, it won't actually make any difference if we do stay on here for a bit longer. We can still travel to Scotland in a while if it suits."

Her heart went out to her cousin. Poor James. In all this mess she had quite forgotten that he too had sought refuge in the countryside for his own unspoken troubles. By venturing over to Burton, he could at least see his friends. She owed him that much.

She nodded, pleased that they would stay. With Francis headed back to London, she keenly felt the need to be close to Julian.

"But only as long as you are happy to have us as house guests. The moment we become a burden, then you must tell us how lovely Scotland is at this time of the year and we shall take the hint and make ourselves scarce," she replied.

The warm, broad smile which appeared on Julian's face nearly made her cry. He was not simply being polite; he genuinely wanted them to stay. She found herself looking away, suddenly awkward in his presence.

James shook Julian's hand. "Excellent, Newhall. I shall send word to my friends in Burton and let them know that we will be making the trip over on Thursday."

❧

Julian sought Lady Margaret out a short time later. An enormous weight had been lifted from his shoulders with the departure of Harry Menzies, but now he was at a loss as to what to do about his remaining house guests. Especially Caroline.

"Do you have a moment?" he asked.

Lady Margaret held out her hand. "Of course. I always have a moment for you, dear boy. What can I do?"

He took her hand and kissed it, then with measured steps, he wandered over to the fireplace. He needed her counsel. "It's good that Caroline and James have agreed to stay on for a time. I am most keen to show them Burton. I think Caroline would enjoy the town market."

Lady Margaret raised her eyebrows. "Yes, I expect Caroline has never seen apples, vegetables, or livestock before."

Julian caught the impish grin which Lady Margaret could no longer hide, and decided it was no good trying to stand to attention next to the fire. He took a seat in the well-padded armchair opposite her and folded his hands in his lap.

Lady Margaret leaned over and gave him a gentle reassuring pat on the knee. "It's a funny thing, life. You make all these plans and grand statements about what you are going to do with your future, yet fate often pushes you in an entirely different direction. One that you may never have considered before. I know I never thought I would end up here at Newhall Castle, and especially not as your father's mistress."

Lady Margaret's words served to reinforce his own surprise at the recent turn of events in his life. Apart from the infatuations of his youth, Julian had never actually been in love. Having seen his parents' marriage splinter into a thousand pieces, he had actively avoided it.

His travels throughout Europe as a diplomat had, until now, given him the perfect excuse to keep his heart under lock and key. Discreet liaisons and uncomplicated relationships had kept his heart safe. He hadn't held out any serious hope of finding love during the house party, but he now knew his heart had settled on Caroline.

"I do not know what to do," he said.

A matter of days ago he would have laughed at the notion of him ever falling in love with Caroline Saunders. They had been sworn enemies. She was the last person he would ever have considered marrying.

Yet from the moment he saw her drop to the floor in the downstairs foyer, she had slowly but inexorably found her way into his soul. The enemy at the gate was now a wounded friend living under his protection.

"Nonsense, your heart knows exactly what you need to do. Why else would you have made the offer for Caroline and James to stay on? You closed that particular loophole in quick time. I must say, I was impressed," she replied.

"Of course, I could be making a fool of myself. Who is to say that I will not just be another one in a long line of suitors who have failed to win her heart?" he said. Harry Menzies, damn him, had certainly muddied the waters. Before his arrival and shock revelation, Julian had been privately entertaining thoughts of spending time during the day with Caroline. She already owned his nightly lust filled dreams.

"I don't believe you are the same as the others, and especially nothing like Mister Menzies. From the time he arrived, she was doing everything she could to avoid him. If he was dull enough not to see that she was not interested, then I am afraid he has been the maker of his own misfortune."

With Harry and Francis both gone from Newhall Castle, Julian was left in a delicate situation. He had offered protection to Caroline from unwelcome suitors. It did not then behoove a gentleman of his status to try to claim the playing field for himself. He would need to tread very carefully if he was to stand any chance of finding her favor. Julian frowned. And what if Caroline did only see him as a friend?

"Can I offer you a word of advice?" asked Lady Margaret.

"Please. This is unchartered territory for me," he replied.

"Take it slowly. Look and listen for the signals. Men can be a little blind to what women are really feeling. You might be busy pondering the battle, but at the same time fail to notice that your army is not behind you. Though most men, in my experience, are not as dim as that Menzies chap. Little wonder he felt the need to make such a grand gesture," she said.

Julian took Lady Margaret's sage words to heart, vowing not to make the same mistakes that other men before him had. If there was one thing, he did know about her, it was that Caroling yearned to have her voice heard.

Trying to force love on her was the last thing that would win her favor. A slow, steady wooing of Caroline Saunders would be the only way to her heart. He would need to do all he could to convince her to remain at Newhall Castle.

Chapter Thirty-Four

A flock of winter birds took off from the far side of the lake and soared into the gray sky. The hood of her cape fell back as she looked up, and the chilly wind kissed her face. For a moment, she was one with the birds and the wind.

"I have never understood your love of winter. How can you bear to be out here?"

Caroline turned and saw James approaching. His hands were stuffed into his coat pockets and a scarf was wrapped around his neck. From the unhappy look on his face, it was clear he did not share her passion for winter.

"Because I feel free when the icy wind hits my skin, and who could not love that vista?" she replied.

James came and stood by her side, facing the lake. "Alright, I will grant you that the view of the frozen lake is rather picturesque from up here."

He cleared his throat. "How are you feeling now? I haven't had the chance to speak to you since the unpleasantness of this morning. Before he left, Francis told me he was very worried about you. To be honest, so am I."

"I am still a little numb with shock, and my arms will have

bruises showing before the day is out. It is a relief not to be travelling home today. I don't think my nerves could cope with being in a confined space with Harry. I still cannot believe what he did," she replied.

James put an arm around her and gently pulled her to him. "I must say, it was very kind of Newhall to offer for us to stay on. Not everyone is so accommodating when it comes to the sniff of a possible scandal. Mind you, he does seem to have a bit of a protective streak when it comes to you."

Caroline began to pick at the edge of the bandage on her left hand. She slowly pulled at a thread. "At least my hand is feeling better today. It aches less," she said, changing the subject.

Julian had taken on the role of her protector, slipping into it with uncommon ease. Every time her thoughts turned to the man with those deep-gray eyes, she found herself unable to construct a clear thought.

She looked down at her hand. He had got under her skin with more than just a needle.

"That is good news. It was a devil of a mess when I first saw it. We were fortunate that Newhall has some battlefield surgeon skills. The stitches he made were worthy of a seamstress," he replied.

She motioned toward the path which ran down to the lake. James was right, it was bitterly cold, but she needed to walk. Her mind was an uncertain whirl of questions about Harry, and Francis, but most of all, about Julian. "Could we please walk?"

The simple motion of putting one foot in front of the other soon created a sense of calm for her tortured mind. The frown on her face, however, still remained.

"Are you alright?" asked James.

She looked at him and nodded. "Yes, though at one point earlier today I thought I might go mad. The odd thing is that now that Harry has finally shown his hand, I am somewhat relieved."

"Relieved?"

"Yes. Harry haunted my steps all summer. I never mentioned it to anyone because I thought he was just being protective of me. He withdrew when I had to spend time with Eve after she and Freddie had their falling out, and I thought matters had returned to normal," she replied.

"Oh, I hadn't realized things had become that difficult."

"No, no one had. I thought keeping it to myself was the most suitable way to deal with it. Clearly, I was wrong," she said.

James sighed. "I suppose Harry has been such a fixture around the Saunders house over the years that I never really took much notice of him. Most of the younger family members guessed he had a tendre for you, but I expect we all assumed that in time it would pass. Though, I have always found him a little odd," said James.

"I lost count of the times I politely refused to dance with him, only to have Francis unwittingly play matchmaker. At least when things did finally come to a head, we were well away from London society. That is why I have hope for a sensible outcome. The idea of having to marry Harry is unthinkable," she said.

She bent and picked up a broken stick from the ground, playfully poking James in his side with it. "Speaking of being odd, what is it with you and Guy Dannon's wedding next month? I thought you would be happy to see him settled with your sister's best friend. Leah is a lovely girl. I didn't think you had an issue with her."

When James gave a half-hearted shrug, Caroline saw it as a clear signal for her to leave matters alone. Something was not right about her cousin and the impending nuptials of his best friend. But with a world of her own problems to deal with, she decided it might be wiser to wait until they were away from Newhall Castle before she tried to press him again.

"Oh, what's that?" James pointed in the direction of the stone cottage.

"I expect it's a cottage for one of the castle ground staff, or a tenant. It must take a lot to keep an estate this size in shipshape," she replied.

She did not wish to share the news with James that not only did she know the truth about the cottage, but that she had been there alone with Julian. As long as James remained in the dark, Caroline reasoned she stood at least a small chance of being able to repeat a private meeting with Julian.

Harry's act of lunacy had achieved one unexpected outcome—Caroline was no longer afraid of what she felt for Julian. Her love was strong enough for her to take her chances and declare herself to him.

She had to find a way to be alone with him.

And to confess her love.

Chapter Thirty-Five

For the first time since their arrival at Newhall, James was up bright and early. Julian was surprised to discover his house guest had beaten him to the breakfast room and was full of cheery humor. He even had what looked like the beginning of a smile on his face.

The change in his mood helped to lift the spirits of those in the carriage as they made their way to the Thursday market at Burton-on-Trent.

"So, these friends of yours, do they live in Burton?" asked Julian. He was seated in the carriage across from Caroline and Lady Margaret, next to James.

"No. They are undertaking a commission to create a series of paintings of the local area. They have a patron who is moving overseas and who wishes to take some memories of their home county with them. Knowing their habits from our university days, and also their correspondence over the summer, I am confident that I shall find both of my friends in the Union Inn on market day," he replied.

An oddly somber Caroline nodded toward her cousin. "James is a skilled painter in his own right. I am certain that if he was not destined to follow my uncle into the senior ranks of the Church of England, he too would have trodden the path of the artist."

Her words surprised Julian. James Radley did not seem, to be the sort of man who would suit a life in the church. He could, however, imagine him as an artist. He had a free spirit about him. But, as with many others of their social standing, James's life had been set out for him since birth.

"My friends are far more skilled with a paintbrush than I will ever be; they have a small but dedicated number of patrons. I was hoping to convince Francis to buy a couple of their works and get them in front of the Prince of Wales, but he was oddly not keen on the idea," James said.

"I expect Francis has his reasons. He may not appreciate all your friends the same way you do. Just because they are your chums does not mean that they are naturally his, or mine, for that matter," replied Caroline.

After her cryptic response, Caroline opened her reticule and began to rummage about. She and Lady Margaret shared a few quiet words, after which she fell silent. Julian knew enough of her by now to know when to leave her alone with her thoughts.

"I promise I shall find my friends and give them my regards, then come back and join the rest of you as soon as I can. Does that suit you, Caroline?" said James.

With Francis now on his way back to London, it fell to James to act as Caroline's official chaperone. Julian was pleased to see that he did not appear to be taking the role too seriously.

With a little more wriggle room than he'd had under Francis's watchful gaze, Julian intended to press home the advantage and spend more time in private with Caroline. He wanted to get a deeper understanding of the real Caroline Saunders, to convince his heart that it was not mistaken in having settled on her.

"Yes, go and spend time with your friends. I am sure I will be perfectly safe with Lord Newhall and Lady Margaret as my chaperones. You can meet with us when you are done," replied Caroline. She chanced a look in Julian's direction. Their gazes met for a split-second before she looked away.

"Splendid," replied James.

As soon as they turned into the main street of Burton, their carriage came to a halt. Julian leaned across and opened the door. Ahead of them was a jumble of wagons, carts, and people.

"We may have to walk from here. I cannot see a way through the crowd," he said.

He instructed the driver to pull the carriage over to the side of the road. Within a few minutes, the four of them were making their way into the main town square.

The square was filled with rows of various market stalls, all selling local produce. Market day was a big enough event that some stalls were selling finished goods from larger towns such as Derby.

"I didn't realize it would be this big." James glanced in the direction of Caroline, but she barely noted his words.

The farther that they walked on, the more distracted she appeared to become. Julian and Lady Margaret shared a concerned look. Neither of them had encountered this kind of behavior from their guest until now.

"There is the Union Inn, are you still alright for me to go and see my friends?" said Julian, pointing toward the small double-story public house which stood on the corner of the square.

For the first time since their arrival at the town, Caroline looked up and paid attention to the goings-on around her. She focused her gaze on the whitewashed building and straightened her shoulders. She muttered something under her breath which Julian failed to catch.

"Thank you. I shan't be long," said James. He gave a hasty bow to the women and darted off in search of his friends.

"And there is the tea shop, right next door," added Lady Margaret. She touched Caroline on the arm. "Would you like to come with me?"

"No, thank you. I am happy to wander the stalls. I might see if I can find a pair of mittens that will fit my hands. That is, if Julian will accompany me?"

Lady Margaret nodded her agreement. "As we are in Derbyshire,

I expect we can relax the rules on a gentleman escorting a young lady without a chaperone."

Caroline looked at her sadly. "I doubt that wandering the market stalls will do anything to change what people already think of me."

Julian's heart sank at her words. He had foolishly allowed himself to think she was dealing well with the Harry situation, but her words now told him otherwise. Caroline was suffering. "I shall be glad to accompany you."

He wished desperately to put his arms around Caroline and offer her comfort. To tell her that everything would be alright, and if it wasn't, he would personally take care of Harry Menzies. It was heartbreaking to see such a spirited young woman now caught up in the darkness of self-doubt.

With both James and Lady Margaret gone, Julian found himself in the unexpected but welcome position of being alone with Caroline. He quietly followed her as she wandered over to a local merchant stall, praying that his presence would help bring her comfort.

"Oh, red-skinned Pippin apples. I haven't had any of these in ages!" she exclaimed.

It was the first time since they had arrived that Caroline had shown any spark of her usual self. She pulled a handful of coins from her reticule and, with a smile, handed them to the stallholder. "Six of your finest Pippins, please."

The man handed a small cloth bag of apples over to her which, despite Caroline's protests, Julian insisted on carrying.

"You are my guest," he said.

When she rewarded him with a smile, Julian saw an opening. He plucked up his courage. "I know it might be a little forward, but would you care to sit and have a hot drink somewhere? There are a number of places around the market that are in the open where we could sit. I get the impression you could do with a cup of tea."

"Thank you, that would be nice. I could also do with some food. I didn't have any breakfast before we left," she replied.

They found a nearby stall that was selling hot pies. Julian chuckled at the sound of Caroline's stomach rumbling when they got close. His own stomach added to the chorus as he took in the appetizing smell of the roast beef pies.

He caught the attention of the pie man. "Two beef pies, please."

They stood to one side of the stall, near to a high brick wall, and tucked into the pies. The pastry was crispy on the top, but once he bit down, his tongue tasted the rich gravy and beef treasure inside.

"Oh, this is good. Thank you," said Caroline.

Her smile was all the thanks Julian needed. If she was happy, then so was he. She nodded in the direction of the tea shop, and he waved as Lady Margaret made her way over to them.

"Derbyshire pies. Is there anything better?" said Lady Margaret.

Julian took the packets of tea that she had bought and put them into the bag with the apples. He was enjoying a day out at the local town market far more than a man of his social status should. And he was no fool in recognizing that it was due to the presence of the young woman standing beside him.

A young woman who had a healthy appetite when it came to locally baked pies. He swallowed deep as he watched her lick the sauce from her fingertips.

"Well I have some other errands to attend to while we are here. If the two of you are content to continue to wander the market, I can meet you in a little while. Then we can partake of luncheon somewhere," said Lady Margaret.

Julian held his breath. He was grateful that Lady Margaret had read the mood between himself and Caroline. Further steps had been taken in progressing their friendship, and he was keen to hold the ground he had made.

"I passed by a stall selling woolen goods on my way here. With any luck, you might be able to find the mittens you were seeking," added Lady Margaret.

When they finished the rest of their midmorning snack, Julian and Caroline headed over to the edge of the town square in search of the woolen goods stall. It was close by the Union Inn. Caroline, oddly, did not make any mention of her long-delayed cousin. Instead, she put her head down and began to examine the selection of mittens that were on display.

"I think these might do the trick," she said, picking up a pair of green mittens and showing them to Julian.

"I didn't realize your hands were getting that cold," he replied.

She carefully slipped her damaged hand inside one of the mittens and held it up. "Perfect. Now I may be able to ice-skate. That is, if the offer to use your ice pond is still open."

Julian hurriedly nodded. "Absolutely. I will have the grounds staff check it as soon as we return to the castle. If your snow dancing is anything to go by, I know you will be an amazing sight on the ice."

She reached into her reticule and withdrew her purse, she took out a handful of coins and handed them over.

While Caroline was busy settling her purchase with the stall-holder, James appeared from the tavern, leading two other gentlemen.

Julian waved at James, who hurried toward them. "Your cousin appears to have found his friends."

Caroline stilled at his words, only stirring once again when the stallholder shook the coins in his hand and she finally took her change.

"Newhall, good to see you. May I introduce my friends. This is Timothy Walters and Timothy Smith, otherwise known as 'the two Tims,'" said James.

Julian took one look at James's friends and the blood in his veins turned to ice. While one of the Timothys was a complete stranger, the other was someone Julian had encountered before. Timothy Walters. Timothy of the dance card argument, and lurker on the fringe of Caroline's court of admirers. Another rival for her affections.

Good manners meant he had no choice other than to shake hands with both men. Caroline, meanwhile, kept her back turned to the group.

"And of course, you both know my cousin, Miss Caroline Saunders," added James.

As James introduced her, Caroline finally turned to face them. She gave a small nod. "Gentlemen."

Julian took a hurried step back as Timothy Walters rushed

forward and attempted to seize Caroline by the hand. She shied away. Walters gasped at the sight of the bandage.

"Miss Saunders had a small accident and injured her hand. I rendered assistance and managed to stitch the wound," explained Julian.

"Oh, my dearest Caroline, you poor thing," gushed Timothy.

Out of the corner of his eye, Julian caught Timothy Smith fix Caroline with a thinly-veiled look of disgust. There was clearly some bad blood between them.

Timothy Smith bowed low to Caroline, but did not offer her his hand or any words of greeting. Julian gritted his teeth as he forced down the burning desire to teach Mister Smith a lesson in manners.

"How are you enjoying your stay in Derbyshire? Radley here tells me you have a commission for a series of paintings," said Julian.

"Yes," replied Walters, his gaze not moving from Caroline.

"They are headed up to the Marchington Woodlands tomorrow to do some initial drawings. I was thinking I might go with them. I would only be gone for a few days and could find my own way back to Newhall Castle. Do you think Lady Margaret could act as chaperone for Caroline while I am gone?" said James.

Walters took another step closer to Caroline. "You would be welcome to accompany us, if you wished. Fair Caroline, I would so love to show you the wild countryside of Derbyshire."

The hairs on the back of Julian's neck raised as he heard the longing in Walters's voice. The prick of jealousy he had felt on first seeing Walters now flared bright in his heart. "I have been showing Miss Saunders much of the countryside around Newhall Castle. She does appreciate the greener parts of England."

He turned to James, keeping his voice steady. "I am certain my aunt would be more than happy to look after Miss Saunders while you are gone, Radley. They are already such good friends. That is, of course, if Miss Saunders finds it agreeable for her to continue to stay at Newhall Castle."

He added emphasis to the last Miss Saunders. He hated the familiar way Walters spoke to Caroline. In his world, only he had the right to address her by her Christian name.

Walters looked at him and a silent battle of wills began. Julian comfortably held the other man's gaze. Walters may well have considered himself to be talented enough to lure a young lady with his artwork, but he had not counted on Julian Palmer. *Try it, lad. I have a title and a bloody great big castle. Not to mention a very possessive dog. What could you possibly offer her? Caroline is not the sort of girl who would enjoy living in a freezing attic while you pursue your next poorly paid commission. Step away.*

"Yes, it is lovely around Newhall and I have become quite settled during our stay. Thank you for your kind offer, Mister Walters, but I shall remain as Lord Newhall's guest for a little while longer," said Caroline.

When she offered Julian a welcome smile, he knew he had won the battle. While the gushing Walters had tried to force Caroline into doing his bidding, Julian had played a smarter hand and actually asked her what she wanted.

That's what comes from making an effort to get to know a woman. Consider yourself vanquished Walters. She. Is. Mine.

"Well then, we must be going. James, since you are coming with us, you might wish to purchase some personal supplies from the local shops for the trip. Miss Saunders, Lord Newhall, it has been a pleasure to make your acquaintance," said Timothy Smith.

James and Caroline made hurried goodbyes, with James promising to return as soon as he was able. When Caroline insisted that her cousin take as long as he wished with his friends, and not to be in any great hurry to return to Newhall, Julian serenely nodded in Timothy Walters' direction.

As James and his friends walked away, Caroline let out a sigh of relief.

"Thank you. I had hoped to avoid that encounter. I don't know what I would have done if you had not been there to save me from Mister Walters and Mister Smith," she said.

He was about to ask her why she needed saving, from Mr. Smith in particular, but she looked at him and simply said, "Let us talk once we get home."

Home.

The word rolled easily off her tongue.

As they continued to walk the town square, and finally met up with Lady Margaret, Julian was deep in thought as to how he could make Caroline's word become a reality. How he could make her see that her home was at Newhall Castle.

That her future lay with him.

Chapter Thirty-Six

"I owe you an explanation."

Julian looked up from the newspaper he had purchased during their visit to Burton and saw Caroline standing in the doorway of his study. He rose and offered her a seat. She sat on the edge of the chair, hands clasped. Her posture was stiff and unsure, the same as it had been since the moment James and his friends had met them at the market.

"You may have guessed that I was not happy to see Mister Walters today. As I said, I had hoped to avoid him, but poor James was excited for you to meet his friends," she said.

Julian had done his best to absorb the news in the three-day-old London newspaper, but he had found it impossible to focus. The hungry look which had sat on Walters' face, coupled with Smith's outright rudeness when they met Caroline, concentrated much of his mind.

"I took it, from your reaction, that you hold the same opinion of him as you did the first night we met. You are not his lady. He, however, does not appear to have got that message," he replied. His words, while calmly spoken, belied the green edge of jealousy he still felt over the gentleman in question.

Caroline nodded. "I would like for you and I to be honest with one another. We have done much to reframe our relationship, and I wish very much to continue in that vein. I think it only fair then that I tell you that Mister Walters asked my father for my hand in marriage a matter of weeks ago. Papa told him no."

One of the myriads of questions which had been rolling around Julian's head all afternoon was the exact nature of the relationship between Caroline and Walters. Her words did little to calm his mind.

"While it explains your comments in the carriage, about not everyone being friends with Radley's chums, it doesn't excuse your cousin's behavior. It was thoughtless and cruel of him to bring Walters and Smith to meet with you," replied Julian. He would be having stern words with James Radley once he returned to Newhall. Fancy exposing her to a jilted suitor in the middle of a public square. The man was a dolt.

"James is unaware of the situation with Mister Walters. Turning down a marriage proposal is not exactly something that one makes public," she said.

"But from the way his friend looked at you, I would suggest Mister Smith was well aware of the nature of your connection?" replied Julian.

The half-hearted smile she gave him in return confirmed his suspicions.

"I did nothing to encourage Mister Walters affections. I offered him some kindness over a private matter, after which he convinced himself that he was in love with me. And yes, I expect Mister Smith does not hold me in any favorable regard, having caused his friend such pain," she added.

"To be honest, I saw several expressions on Mister Walters' face which I also witnessed on Harry Menzies's countenance when he was here. If there is one thing you can claim as your own, Caroline, it is that you have an effect on men. Whether you or they like it or not," he replied.

As soon as he spoke the words, Julian regretted them. He had been trying to offer her his support and tell her that it was not her fault. Instead, all he had managed to do was mangle his words and insult her.

Caroline slowly rose from the chair, and walked toward the door. As she reached for the handle, she stopped and turned to him. Julian's heart sank as he saw the tears shining in her eyes.

"So, like everyone else, you think I am a tease? Thank you for at least clearing up that misconception for me. I had thought that since you were my friend, you might try to understand. Perhaps it would have been better if I had gone with James. At least I know where I stand with the likes of Mister Walters. Excuse me, Lord Newhall."

Caroline closed the door softly behind her, but the click of the latch echoed loudly in Julian's brain.

He got to his feet, intending to follow her, but as his fingers touched the doorknob, he stopped. He should run after her and offer up pleas of apology, but she had been right. He didn't like the effect she had on other men.

There were too many males in Caroline's life for Julian's liking. He faced a painful decision. Could he offer himself up to a life of forever being jealous?

&

Caroline avoided all company for the rest of the afternoon and took her supper in her room. She wrote a long letter to William and another one to her mother. With Francis now en route to London, they would know the situation regarding Harry by the time they received her letters.

To Adelaide, she restated her promise to change her ways. The members of her cluster of admirers would be encouraged to find other young ladies to focus their attentions upon. Flowers, gifts, and unannounced visits to her family home would no longer be welcome. If she wanted society to treat her differently, it would have to begin with her own behavior.

To Will, she confirmed his words about Julian Palmer. He was not the brute she had claimed him to be. In fact, he was quite a pleasant man. Her brother would be pleased to know that she and Lord Newhall had become friends.

She put the pen back into the inkwell. It was odd to read the words, let alone write them. Julian was no longer her enemy, but after their earlier conversation, she was not sure if he was, indeed, her friend either. A friend would not think, let alone say, such a thing.

Yet he was right. She had acted the tease with men, especially those she felt she could safely manage. Slowly at first, but then, over time, she had become cold and calculating in her dealings with her cluster of suitors. Eventually becoming someone, she no longer recognized.

It hurt to look into her own heart and know she was an unlikeable person. Her beauty, at times, was only skin-deep.

"I don't even like me," she muttered.

How then could she expect Julian to like her? She should not care; there were many more men who would take his place if he didn't want her. But she did care what he thought of her, and it was deeper than a simple desire for him to like her. Because if Julian Palmer could not see that there was more to her than just her looks, how could he ever love her?

"Come now, Caroline. You have to find a way."

Both of her married siblings had fought back from loss to find love and happiness, so she knew it was possible. Will had found love again after the death of his first wife, while her sister, Eve, had succeeded in securing love after suffering a cruel heartbreak.

Her brother had of course been right; you never did know when love would find you. Or what you would do when it did.

She picked up the pen and set it back onto her letter to Will. Tomorrow was a new day, and with it came the hope that she could find her way into Julian's heart.

To make him see that she was someone worthy of his love.

Chapter Thirty-Seven

B reakfast the following morning was a mostly silent affair, with only the clink of cutlery on china to be heard.

Lady Margaret spent her time reading a book which she had purchased at the town market, while Julian sat with coffee cup in hand, deep in thought. He hadn't slept well.

Every time the door to the breakfast room opened, he sat up in his chair, ready to greet Caroline with the well-rehearsed speech of apology that he had spent half the night preparing. But each time, it was another footman or maid who appeared, rather than his house guest.

Finally, Lady Margaret looked up from her book and sighed. "Why don't you go and find her, because if I have to listen to you muttering under your breath any longer, I shall throw this book at your head."

He raised an eyebrow and shot a dirty look in her direction. "Remind me to move you to the dowager house when I finally marry. The roof has plenty of holes and I hear there is quite a selection of spiders. You should be right at home."

"I dare you. This place will fall apart the second I move out. You men have no idea when it comes to running an estate. Nor, would it appear, in securing the hand of a suitable countess." She met his gaze. Mischief sparkled in her eyes.

Julian set his cup down and rose from the table. Lady Margaret, for all her gentle teasing, was right. If Caroline was not going to come to him, he would have to seek her out.

"Excuse me," he said.

"About time," came the reply.

He found a maid in the upstairs hallway just leaving Caroline's room. He asked her to go back inside and enquire as to whether she was coming down for breakfast.

The maid looked a little surprised. "I am sorry, my lord, but Miss Saunders is not in her room. She went out an hour or so ago. She had her cloak with her, so she may have gone for a walk."

Julian hurried downstairs and retrieved his heavy winter coat. He searched the grounds, first going to the ice pond, but Caroline was not there. He then went down to the cottage by the lake. Again, no luck.

Over the next hour, he scoured the castle grounds. Finally, after climbing back up from the lower fields and getting his boots and trousers wet from the deep early morning snow, he stood at the top of the rise and tried to catch his breath.

"Where the devil are you, woman?" he said.

She was not inside, and not at any of the usual places he would have expected to find her. It was as if she had disappeared into the earth.

Julian looked toward the ridge which sat at the back of the castle. On top of it stood a grand stone temple. The temple housed the Palmer family crypt where all the previous generations of the Earls of Newhall were buried, including his father.

He trudged up the hill, holding tightly onto hope. If she was not there, then it would be time to gather a search party.

As soon as he reached the top of the hill, he was greeted by Midas who bounded down to him, tail wagging with delight.

"I might have known you would be with our elusive guest," said Julian. He quietly chided himself for not having had the nous to call the dog in the first place. Midas had taken to Caroline from the start and was never far from her side. He followed Midas down to the opening of the family crypt.

Inside, he found Caroline sitting on the cold stone paving in front of his father's grave, a fresh bouquet of wild flowers clutched in her hand. She looked at him as he approached and softly smiled. Midas hurried over to sit beside her.

"Good morning."

"The morning is nearly gone, and I have spent much of it in search of you. I was beginning to get worried," he replied.

"Oh, I'm sorry. I went for a walk and eventually found myself here. When I saw your father's grave, I decided to go into the woods and pick some wild flowers for him. There wasn't much of a selection, with it being so cold, but I found some winter cherries. The pink flowers are lovely. Do you think he would like them?"

Julian nodded. He came and sat beside her on the stone floor. His father's grave bore a simple inscription.

Arthur Julian Sloane Palmer
30th Earl of Newhall.
One who loved not wisely but too well

He wiped a bitter tear away. How many arguments had he and his father had over that simple sentence? Yet the late earl had been adamant that it be written on his tombstone. His final message to the world.

"Didn't you say you were nine years of age when she left?" asked Caroline. She was an intelligent young woman, no doubt familiar with the tragic love story of *Othello*, from where the quote came.

Julian closed his eyes and swallowed back the lump in his throat. When he opened them again, he saw Caroline's right hand resting gently on the glove of his left hand. "Yes, I had just celebrated my ninth birthday when she finally packed up and left for the last time. I expect she thought that a suitable gift for me."

She nodded toward his father's grave. "An odd inscription for a final epitaph. What does Lady Margaret think of it?"

Julian paused for a moment, unsure of what to say. His father had long ago thought to marry Lady Margaret, but had unwisely allowed himself to be blinded by the beauty of Julian's mother. An arranged marriage, and all the heartache that came with it, had quickly followed.

The 'unwise' part of the quote had been for the former countess, but the 'too well' had been reserved for the woman who had eventually healed his heart. The woman he should have made his countess.

"She is fine with it. She was the one who finally convinced me to go ahead and have it made. 'If a son cannot honor the last wishes of his father, then what sort of son is he,' or words to that effect," he replied.

"Yes, it is hard enough to have a say over one's life. But in death, we must trust to our family to honor our wishes," said Caroline.

She reached into her pocket and pulled out one of the apples she had bought on their visit to the market. She handed it to Julian. "You must be hungry after all that searching for me."

He took the apple, and with a quick hard twist, broke it in half. He handed Caroline a piece.

"So why were you looking for me?" she asked.

"To apologize." He felt terrible over what he had said to her the previous day, knowing it was why she had hidden in her bedroom and not come down for supper.

Her brow furrowed. "You have nothing to apologize for. You should not be punished for having spoken the truth. You were right, I do have an effect on men, and I am well aware of it. It just hurts to hear people you care about say it to your face. And I am trying to rectify the faults in my character, but it is not easy to change ingrained habits."

When Midas whimpered and nudged her, Caroline bit off another piece of the apple and set it down on the floor. The dog snatched it up in his mouth and set to the juicy fruit with gusto.

"I would have bought a dozen if I had known he loved them so much," she said.

Julian smiled at Midas, who quickly finished his piece of the apple. Then, spying Julian's half, Midas made a great show of nuzzling against his master and whimpering softly.

"You are playing both sides now, are you? You were no help when

I could not find this young lady, but now you want my food," he said.

Midas barked softly and Julian knew he was not going to be allowed to finish his apple in peace. He bit off a piece and lay it in the palm of his hand. A hot, slobbery tongue brushed his fingertips as Midas took the apple.

"I hope I was not intruding on the family privacy by coming here. It's a tradition within my mother's side of the family to sit with our ancestors up on the side of Strathmore Mountain. I would spend hours in front of my grandfather's grave when I was younger," said Caroline.

"You are welcome to come and sit with my family. I am sure my father would appreciate the company. I have not spent enough time up here with him. I was in France when he died," he replied.

"Will mentioned that he was with you in Paris when you got the news. That must have been hard, being so far away," she said.

"Your brother is a good man," he replied.

Caroline smiled at him. "He says the very same thing about you."

She shifted on the hard, stone floor and pushed back her shoulders. Julian stood and held out his hand. She accepted his offer and he helped her to her feet. It was then that he noticed the pair of ice skates on the floor which had been hidden by her cloak.

She looked down at them. "I thought I might go for a skate on the ice pond this morning. Of course, once I got down there, I realized that I could not tie the boots properly with only one good hand. So, I went for a walk instead and ended up here."

He reached down and picked up the skates. "I can help tie your boots and catch you if you fall."

She snorted. "I never fall."

Julian sighed. "How am I to rescue you if you refuse to pay the helpless female?"

A blush of heat raced to her cheeks at his words. She wanted nothing more than to be rescued by him. Julian was the only man who could save her from herself.

Chapter Thirty-Eight

At the ice pond, Julian found a rope and tied Midas to a nearby tree, much to the dog's growls of protest. Once Midas realized Caroline was not going to come and untie him, he plopped down on a piece of stone path that was being warmed by the sun and simply watched.

Julian made short work of Caroline's ice skates. When the boots were secure, he offered her his hand and helped her to stand on the ice.

"Now I know you say you never fall, but I just want to be close enough to catch you if you do. Trust me, Caroline, I shall always be there to catch you," he said.

Caroline did not protest. She would normally have boasted about her many times on the ice, and the fact that she was an accomplished skater, but something held her back. She was in no hurry to let go of Julian's hand. She was enjoying the soft fluttering in her stomach which came from touching him.

She pushed out, still holding on, and began to skate around him. Julian turned on the spot as she glided around in a large circle. A soft laugh came to her lips. The freedom of the ice, and being able to move on it, sparked joy in her heart.

"I could go a little faster if you like?" she said.

He screwed up his face. "I don't know if I will be able to stay on my feet if you do."

Caroline slowed. When she stopped, she was standing closer than she knew she should. It was a bold move, testing his reaction. He towered over her.

She rose up on her skates and looked him in the eye. "Let go. I promise to come back."

As she skated away from him, Julian held onto Caroline's hands until only their fingertips touched. She heard his soft sigh when the connection finally broke.

Free from his hold, she skated to the far side of the pond, did a half twirl, and then stopped. She looked over her shoulder at him. He was smiling, but she could tell he was not comfortable with having her so far away from him.

With a hard push off, she raced across the ice. Just before she reached him, Caroline darted to the right and made a half loop behind Julian.

He applauded her skillful move. "Very clever, Miss Saunders. But don't get carried away."

With a whoop, she raced over to the far side of the pond. This time, when she turned and came back to Julian, it was at even greater speed. The smile disappeared from his face as she bore down on him. Once more, she circled behind him and came out the other side.

Midas barked loudly from the side of the pond, protesting this strange sight. But Caroline still had one trick or two she intended to show his master.

In the middle of the pond, she stopped briefly to check the distance from the center to the side. It was enough; she would risk it.

Skating to the edge of the ice, she skirted the outside for a few yards before leaping toward the middle and throwing herself into a tight spin. Round and round she went, faster and faster. Holding her back straight and her head up, she crossed her arms as she spun on one foot.

At the end of the fast spin, she threw her arms out to the side and brought herself slowly to a standstill.

On the other side of the pond, Julian held out his hand. "Magnificent! In my entire life, I have never seen anyone so accomplished on the ice as you, Caroline," he said with a smile.

She looked at him, and all the bravado that had filled her moments before suddenly fled. With her head lowered, she slid across the ice to him.

She shyly took his offered hand. As she looked into his eyes, Caroline was struck by an overwhelming sense of need. To hold his hand and never let go.

"Are you alright? Did you spin too fast in that last one?" he asked.

"No. I . . . Never mind."

He took a step forward, closing the distance between them. "Tell me," he murmured.

She lifted a hand to his cheek, tenderly brushing her fingers on his chilled skin. Julian closed his eyes and took a deep breath. "You are not like other men. Well, not the way other men are with me. I feel that you actually see me, if that makes sense."

His hand slipped around her waist and drew her close to him, after which he stilled. She could read him. He was waiting. Seeking her permission to move the moment forward.

As he bent his head, she whispered, "Yes."

Warm, soft lips touched hers, then drew back. She smiled. He was going to tease every moment out of their first kiss.

She reached up and wrapped her fingers around the bottom of his cravat. A murmur of a chuckle came from deep in his throat as she pulled him back to her.

When their lips touched for a second time, the shyness between them evaporated. Taking Caroline's face in his hands, Julian placed ever-deepening kisses on her lips. She groaned with pleasure. This was the tender, loving kiss she had so longed for from a man. A kiss that sought to discover all the secrets of her heart.

She exalted when he finally threw all caution to the wind and took her mouth fully. His tongue swept past her lips and into her mouth where she tasted the spice of the apple they had shared.

Their tongues danced together as gracefully as she had danced on the ice. A natural ebb and flow existed between them. The give and take of destined lovers.

When they finally, reluctantly, broke the kiss, she looked up and saw the glaze of passion in his eyes. He was as fully invested in the moment as she had been. The kiss sealed the promise of their hearts being given up to one another.

"So beautiful, oh, Caroline," he whispered.

As Julian spoke the words, Caroline froze. The image of Harry Menzies, as he spoke the very same words to her, appeared before her eyes. Of how he had held her in his cruel grip and tried to claim her as his prize. Of his hard, cold lips on her skin.

Julian reached out to hold her once more, but she slid back onto the ice out of his reach. He stood on the edge of the pond, concern etched in the worry lines on his brow.

"Did I overstep the mark? Forgive me if I read the moment wrong," he said.

She saw the pained look of confusion on his face. How could she explain her reaction to his words? That for the first time in her life, she hated being told she was beautiful.

They walked back to the castle, neither saying a word. Julian watched Caroline out of the corner of his eye. She seemed lost, deep in thought. He prayed she was not having regrets about the kiss. He tried to console himself by recalling that she had said yes, but it did little to calm his worried mind.

He hadn't sought her out with the intention of kissing her. He had simply wanted to offer her an apology for his behavior the previous night. But when she stood close to him and looked into his eyes, his heart took control of the moment.

Walking alongside her, he still couldn't believe that he had just kissed Caroline Saunders. This was the woman who, only a matter of days ago, had been the last woman on earth he would ever have wanted to kiss. The woman he had made certain not to invite to Newhall Castle.

Midas raced ahead of them, tail wagging. It was obvious he thought he had done his job and brought the two of them together. But one kiss did not make a spring. She had let her guard down just enough to give him hope, but Julian sensed he was still a long way from the finish line.

Her reaction to being told she was beautiful had taken him by surprise. It was as if the words had caused her pain. The moment after he had spoken, a chill wind had blown across the pond. And for the second time in a matter of days Caroline had turn to ice before his eyes.

He cursed himself for his bold move. He had offered to protect her by allowing her to stay at Newhall Castle. But he was now left wondering if instead of being her protector, he had turned hunter. If so, then he was no better than Harry Menzies or Timothy Walters.

You fool. You pushed too far. Now you will have to work to gain her trust all over again.

Lost in thought, he tripped over a fallen branch, only managing to save himself from sprawling onto his face by taking several large ungainly steps and stumbling into a half-run. Caroline, head cast down, did not look up. Even Midas kept hurrying toward the castle front door.

As Julian settled back into his normal stride, he cursed the sky. The gods, it would appear, had spoken their disfavor of him.

Every step he took from this moment on would have to be well-thought-out and calculated.

The kiss that he and Caroline had shared was enough to finally seal the deal on his heart. He was in love with her, and now he desired the greatest prize of all.

But he would take all the lessons from those who had tried and failed before him and use them to his advantage. Because no matter what it took, he was not going to become yet another fallen soldier in the battle for Caroline's heart.

He was going to succeed in winning the love of the Ice Queen.

Chapter Thirty-Nine

Julian excused himself as soon as they reached the front entrance to the castle, and as he walked away, Caroline softly sighed.

Her first real kiss had been everything she had hoped for. She put a fingertip to her lips. Memories of the scent of his cologne flooded her mind. The heady mix of sandalwood, jasmine and cedar had been intoxicating.

Midas bumped hard against her leg, demanding her attention. She bent down and gave him a rub behind the ears. The dog buried its head in her lap. She sensed his worry.

"It's alright, boy, your master and I are still trying to find our feet. These things take time with us humans," she said.

She was annoyed with herself, angry that she had reacted in such a way when Julian had told her she was beautiful.

The notion of love had now taken seed in her heart. Emotions that were both foreign and surprising only a day or two ago were well settled and familiar within her soul. The odd feeling that she experienced every time she saw Julian, she now understood and embraced.

Will, as per usual, had been right. Love was something that you didn't seek. Love was that unusual guest who slipped quietly into a room and waited patiently for you to notice them. And once you did notice, then your life was forever changed.

She placed her hand over her heart, feeling it beating strongly in her chest. Her destiny was now calling to her. It was time to decide whether she was strong enough to reach out and claim it.

"I must try."

❧

Julian sat silently through supper, pondering the countless permutations of actions he could undertake to win Caroline's heart.

"You were saying that your sister is travelling to Paris with her new husband. Is that wise?" asked Lady Margaret.

Julian knew she was throwing a line for him to pick up on, but he was in no mood to explain to Lady Margaret that Paris was perfectly safe for English tourists. France was slowly returning to the fold of being a friendly nation with the rest of its European neighbors.

"Yes. Several members of the family have visited France since the end of the hostilities. In fact, I understand it is quite the fashionable place for members of the *ton* to visit," replied Caroline.

"Your father is French, is he not?" asked Lady Margaret.

Caroline nodded. "Yes, though I don't know if he has any plans to ever return to France. My grandmother fled to England after my grandfather was killed during the uprising in the Vendée. Papa still feels conflicted over the whole thing," replied Caroline.

Julian silently chided himself. He was being taciturn and rude by focusing on his own concerns.

"Your brother Will visited the family's hometown with me when we were in France. He found it quite emotional to stand outside the house where your father was born," he said.

Caroline met his gaze and softly smiled. "I would like to visit Fontenay-le-Comte someday. I know a lot of the town was burned during the bloody uprising against Robespierre and his reign of insanity, but it would be nice to walk the streets where my French forebears once trod."

Lady Margaret sipped the last of her wine and set her glass down. As she rose from the table, Julian stood.

"Well perhaps when you marry, you can ask your husband to take you to France. Any man who succeeds in winning your heart would know what joy it would bring you." She looked straight at Julian as she spoke the words, leaving him in no doubt as to where her opinion of Caroline now stood. "I shall bid you both a fond good night. I have a number of letters to write."

"Good night," said Caroline.

With Lady Margaret now gone, an awkward silence settled in the room. As Caroline finished a hearty serving of hot baked apple, Julian studied his brandy glass.

After the misstep of the morning at the ice pond, he was unsure as to what to say, but forced himself rather than risk having her follow Lady Margaret out of the room. "I was planning to take a walk down to the cottage by the lake shortly. I am not sure if you wish my company, but you are welcome to join me."

To his surprise, Caroline immediately rose from her chair. "I shall get my cloak and things. I won't be long."

A few minutes later, they left the castle behind them and made their way toward the lake. The full moon lit the garden, and on the frozen surface of the lake, it left a silver ribbon of light.

Taking the key from his coat pocket, Julian slipped it into the lock of the cottage door. Standing back, he waved Caroline inside.

The cottage was warm, and the glow from the fireplace bathed the room in a golden light. He quickly added a few more logs to the fire, expecting to spend a lonely night in the cottage if Caroline told him she did not want him. He was treading new ground, unsure of himself. If she did say no, he would have to rethink everything.

"Wine?" he asked.

"Yes please. I must say, you have a wonderful wine collection here. Francis was impressed when you showed him the castle cellars. James declared his intention of sleeping in them, if he got the chance," she replied.

"Didn't your brother threaten to raid my wine cellar?"

She chortled softly. "I am also partial to a glass of good wine, so I would have been right behind him."

While Julian poured them both a welcome glass, Caroline took a seat on the well-padded leather couch. She pointed to the nearby low table, and taking his cue, Julian set both glasses down. With his heart racing, he sat on the couch next to her.

Caroline sat with her shoulders pulled back and her spine straight. "I was fifteen the first time a man came to our house and asked for my father's permission to marry me. Papa, of course, threw him out and told him never to come back. Over the intervening years, there have been a number of other gentlemen who have come, unbidden, to his study door with the intention of asking for my hand. I am grateful to say that my father has turned every single one of them away."

A flash of heated jealousy flared inside him. He hated every one of those men and their audacity at thinking they could have Caroline. "So, you are saying that none of them ever asked you for your permission before speaking to your father?"

Caroline frowned. "Yes, as ridiculous as that sounds. Though from having seen how Harry Menzies and Timothy Walters behaved, it should not be too great a leap for you to understand that others may have done the same."

"Men, from what I understand, see you as something precious and beautiful that they want to possess. Timothy Walters would have fallen at your feet if you had asked him that day in the market. I have never seen such rapture on a person's face outside of a religious shrine. Harry Menzies, of course, tried a different tact by attempting to circumvent your father and placing that notice in the paper," he replied.

He waited for her to continue, sensing she had put a deal of thought in to what she was about to tell him.

"I am sorry I panicked today when you told me I was beautiful. I was enjoying the encounter right up to that moment."

His fingers and hers touched on the seat of the couch, but neither made any move to hold hands.

"I am immensely relieved to hear that you don't regret our kiss.

Though I am still a little perplexed as to why you reacted the way you did when I told you I thought you were beautiful," he replied.

She looked at him and he met her gaze. "It's odd to think that beauty can be a curse. My looks are just one part of me. But I want people to see the rest of me, and to be valued for that as well."

With their fingers now entwined, Julian lifted their hands and placed a tender kiss on Caroline's fingertips. "And that is why you froze when I told you that were beautiful? I did come to that conclusion on my own. I said you were beautiful because, for me, it is not just a word, it is part of how I feel about you. Julian pulled in a shaky breath. He felt as if he were standing on the edge of a high cliff, and the only way down was to take a leap of faith.

"I love you."

He released her hand from his and let it settle on his knee. When she did not move it away, he took it as her unspoken agreement for him to make his next move.

Cupping her face, he set his lips to hers. Relief flooded his mind when, instead of pulling away, Caroline kissed him back. He deepened the embrace. She yielded her lips and mouth to his, inviting him to linger and play.

Slipping a hand inside his jacket, she pulled him closer. His fear over her never wishing him to hold her again vanished, replaced with the knowledge that Caroline wanted him.

When he finally pulled back from the kiss, he saw the glaze of passion in her eyes. Someday, he would watch as he brought her to completion. That day could not come soon enough.

"Touch me," she whispered.

He hesitated. Caroline was, as far as he knew, sexually inexperienced. His idea of touching a woman and what she was asking for were likely miles apart. He would take everything from this moment forward slowly. Very slowly.

He lifted her hair to one side and placed a trail of soft butterfly kisses down the side of her neck. Caroline slipped her hand from his waist and began to loosen the ties at the front of her gown.

Julian took a gentle hold of her hand. "I don't think we are quite ready for that yet."

She looked deep into his eyes. "Don't you want me?"

Using every ounce of his self-control, Julian pulled back and let her go. A line had to be drawn here and now if he was going to achieve his final goal.

"If I loosen the top of your gown and set my hands and lips to your breasts, we will have no choice but to stand in front of the Bishop of London and say our vows. It's more of a question of you wanting to say yes when the time comes, rather than me wishing to stop."

"But you do want me, don't you?" she asked. There was an uncertainty in her words that revealed a side of her he had never seen before.

"Yes, I do, but I want us be sure of our future before I have the inevitable conversation with your father. I want to be the man your father says 'yes' to when I call upon him. There will still be residual rumors from what Harry Menzies did. We need to lay them to rest completely before we marry. We have a lifetime ahead of us, so we owe it to ourselves to take our time. And of course, there is the matter of my pride."

"Your pride?"

He nodded. "I intend to enjoy the deep satisfaction of showing all the others exactly where they went wrong in their pursuit of Miss Caroline Saunders. Ergo, I am going to woo you in public so they can see."

The look of surprise on Caroline's face would have been amusing had Julian not been in complete earnest about his motives. Their budding romance had, until now, been conducted in private and was still secret to all but Lady Margaret, whom he suspected had put two and two together and made a wedding.

She sat quietly for a moment. Julian watched her. He had made a throw of the dice and now held his breath, waiting for the pieces to land.

"I must confess, I quite like the sound of you wooing me in front of the matrons of the *ton*," she replied. She rose from the couch, ignoring his outstretched hand, and walked over to the window. She leaned forward and her face touched the glass. She then turned and looked at him. "You want to know if I love you. Because the last thing you would ever want would be to repeat the story of your parents' marriage."

He came to her, pulling her into his arms. He bent down and tenderly kissed her lips. "All I ask is that you are honest with me. If you do not love me, or ever think you possibly could, then tell me now and I shall withdraw from your life."

She looked deep into his eyes and spoke the words he had never thought he might hear. "I love you, Julian. I want us to spend the rest of our lives together."

Chapter Forty

The look of pure joy which appeared on Julian's face brought tears to Caroline's eyes. The kiss he gifted her with in reply to her declaration of love set her heart racing.

"Good. Because I love you too, and after a formal courtship, I will make you my countess," he replied.

She lay her hand over his heart. They had declared themselves. A combined future now lay before them. Dare she take the first step in claiming it?

"I want this cottage to become our special place, a private place where we can seek refuge from the world. Make me your woman here tonight," she said.

He raised an eyebrow. "As long as you make sure that your father will say yes when I come to see him."

Caroline's fingers traced the edges of Julian's cravat. She tugged gently on the first of the topknots. Then, with slow precise moves, she unwound the length of linen. Julian sighed as she pulled it from his neck and draped it over a nearby chair.

"Your turn," she whispered.

He threw off his jacket, then set to the laces on the front of her gown. When they were loose enough, he pulled the front panels apart and pushed it down.

Caroline eased the gown over her hips and let it fall to the floor. Only her thin shift now separated her skin from his sight and the cool night air.

"The shirt?" he asked.

She tugged at the sides of his shirt and freed it from his trousers. Julian made short work of lifting it over his head and tossing it aside.

He shivered in the cold air, then chuckled. "Can we hurry up with this? I don't wish to freeze before we get to the important part."

His jest helped to calm Caroline's nerves. She had come to the cottage with the full intention of seducing Julian, but only now realized that she had little idea how to go about it.

"Boots next, I would suggest, otherwise we won't be able to deal with your trousers," she replied.

With the matter of outer clothes and pesky boots out of the way, the only remaining garments were Caroline's shift and Julian's trousers. He pulled her to him and kissed her once more.

She took the opportunity to bring her right hand to the buttons on the placket of his trousers, and with her nimble fingers soon had them undone. With a shuddering breath, she bravely slipped her hand inside. Julian closed his eyes and she heard his appreciative groan as she took hold of his manhood. Her sister, Eve, had given her a rough guide as to what a woman should do in the situation, and Caroline was busy trying to recall every step of those instructions.

Julian cupped Caroline's breast in his hand and rolled his thumb back and forth over her nipple. It hardened under his skillful touch. He lowered his head and slowly traced soft kisses down her neck and across the top of her shoulder.

"You smell so good," he murmured.

She continued to stroke him, feeling him getting larger and harder in her hand.

Strong hands grasped the sides of her shift and pulled it up. Caroline released Julian from her attentions for a moment, while he lifted her shift free over her head.

She was fully naked before him. He kissed her.

"From this moment on, you and I belong to each other," he said.

With those words, he lowered his head and took her nipple into his mouth. He suckled strongly and Caroline felt heat pool in her loins. Desire she had never known before flared.

He guided her over to the bed and lay her down. Pulling her to the edge, he knelt before her on the floor and arranged her legs to rest on his shoulders.

She gasped as his tongue touched the soft hair at her entrance. Using his thumb and forefinger, he opened her to him and began to lick and suck at her clitoris. Caroline sobbed with need.

When his tongue speared into her wet heat, she cried out, "Oh my god, Julian!"

With repeated strokes of his tongue across her sensitive nib, and his thumb pressed deep into her, Caroline rode the heights of pleasure. On and on he teased her, demanding her submission to his sexual onslaught.

She had touched herself enough times to know when the peak was coming. She began to frantically push him away, determined that when she did come it would be with him inside her.

He read the signals. Getting to his feet, he stripped off his trousers and freed his erection. She licked her lips, forcing all fears away.

She drew back farther on the bed as Julian climbed on. He hovered over her and their gazes met. The moment of truth had finally arrived.

"This may sting a little the first time," he said.

She nodded. Eve's recounting of her first night with Freddie had set Caroline's mind at ease when it came to losing her virginity. In her sister's opinion, the stories of young women being deflowered that they had overheard in the ladies' withdrawing rooms at parties had been vastly overdramatized.

"Take me. Make me yours," she pleaded.

He guided his erection to the wet folds of her entrance and slowly pressed inside. Caroline arched her back and closed her eyes. When she opened them again, she looked up at him and saw the joy of love in his eyes.

"Now you are mine," he whispered.

With long strokes, he began to ride her. Caroline moaned as her body succumbed to the ecstasy of their love making. She pulled her legs up and took him deeper.

"Yes, harder please, Julian," she begged.

Higher and higher he took her. His manhood ground hard against her sensitive nib, sending waves of sexual pleasure through her body.

As she neared the crest, he took her nipple into his mouth and nipped it with his teeth. Shards of hot pleasure shot through Caroline and she crashed into a blinding orgasm.

Julian didn't wait for her to come down. He lifted the intensity of his strokes to a frenzy of deep and hard thrusts.

"I wanted you from the first time I saw you," he said.

No sooner had he said the words, then he stilled, before thrusting in one last time. He shuddered with fulfilment before collapsing into her arms.

Julian rolled off her and grabbed the blanket, quickly wrapping it around them. He kissed her tenderly on the lips, saying, "Let's use the heat of our lovemaking to keep us warm."

A little while later, he stole from their bed and piled more logs onto the fire. He handed Caroline her glass of wine and they sat under the blankets and watched the flames.

He kissed her on the forehead and wrapped his arms around her. "You did well for your first time, my love. You are a fast learner. Which means I had better hurry up and make that appointment with your father. The sooner I can court you in public, the sooner we can continue your sexual education in private."

In the early hour, just before dawn, Julian took Caroline a second time. With her arranged before him on the bed, he knelt behind her and gently guided his erection into her heated core. With his hands wrapped around her waist and his thumb stroking her delicate nib, she came on a soft, sobbing cry. He followed her quickly into completion.

Chapter Forty-One

Julian woke later that morning and reached for Caroline. His fingers touched empty sheets. With a start, he sat up in the bed. Caroline was nowhere to be seen. Wiping the early morning condensation from the window, he peered out.

He quickly dressed and stuffed his sockless feet into his boots. Opening the door of the cottage, he stepped out into the cold morning air. Julian was still doing up the last of his coat buttons when he came to her side.

She was standing not far from the cottage, looking out over the ice-covered lawn and beyond to the lake. She turned to him and smiled.

Julian pulled her into his arms and kissed her tenderly on the lips. "I can see we are going to have to establish some rules about you leaving the bed while your master is still in it."

She returned his kiss. "Good morning, my lord and master. You were snoring like James's dog, so I thought it best to leave you be."

He huffed. He didn't snore. Did he?

As Caroline turned back to look at the lake, he held her. They stood silently watching the water birds skimming over the frozen water.

"Wait until spring. The lake is full of all manner of birdlife returning from the warmth of the southern climes. We shall have to have your parents up here so that I can take your father fishing for mirror carp," he said.

"Speaking of my parents, are we still in agreement about arrangements for London? I mean, that you will ask permission to court me before an official betrothal announcement is made?" she replied.

After the proceedings of the previous night, it seemed a little silly to still go ahead with a formal courtship, but Julian wanted to show the rest of London society that he and Caroline had conducted themselves in a manner above reproach. Their marriage would not be stained in the way that his parents' union had been. "Yes."

They returned to the cottage and picked up the remainder of their belongings. Julian stuffed his socks into his pocket. He would change once they got back to the castle. Closing the door of the cottage behind them, he and Caroline walked hand in hand back up the hill.

As they reached the top, a carriage appeared over the rise in the drive.

"I love you," she said, slipping her hand from his grasp.

The carriage slowed and came to a halt close to the front entrance of the castle. The carriage door opened and James jumped down. Catching sight of them, he gave a friendly wave.

"Fantastic morning, is it not? Hope I am not too late to catch a spot of breakfast," he said.

"Welcome back, Radley. We were just coming in for breakfast ourselves," replied Julian. He pretended not to see the sly smile which appeared on James's face when Caroline passed him by. Julian resisted the urge to run his fingers through her tussled hair. She looked as if she had just tumbled out of bed. *His bed.*

§

Inside the breakfast room, James grabbed a plate and piled it high with food. Julian followed suit.

The night of love-making with Julian had left Caroline famished.

She set aside all pretense of ladylike dining and filled her own plate with hearty serves of roast potatoes, bacon and baked salmon.

"So, tell me, what could be so pressing as to have you travel from Burton at the crack of dawn?" she said.

James finished his mouthful of food, then set down his knife and fork. "While I was in the wilds of Devonshire, I had an epiphany. As soon as we returned to town, I had the chaps arrange a carriage to bring me back here this morning. Pack your things, Caro. We are leaving for London today."

Caroline kept her emotions in check, not daring to look at Julian. The journey home to London, while inevitable, was not something she had been expecting for at least a few more days. She silently cursed James and his sudden impetuous decision. She ached to be back at the cottage with Julian, lying naked and sated in his arms.

"Are you sure you have to leave in such a hurry?" replied Julian.

"Yes, well you did a sterling job of helping Caroline during this most unfortunate situation, but we should not impose on your good self any longer. Besides, I need to get home and speak to my father," said James.

Caroline knew that tone from James only too well. When his mind was made up, there was little point in arguing with him. James would surely have a well-presented case for the urgency of their departure. Nothing she, nor Julian, could say would make any difference.

"I shall make enquiries with the stable master and your coachman after breakfast. They will want to have plenty of time to make ready for your departure," said Julian.

Once he had finished, Julian excused himself.

As soon as he was gone, Caroline rounded on James. "That was more than a little rude on your part. Julian has been nothing but the most gracious of hosts and you simply arrive on his doorstep this morning and tell him you have had enough and we are leaving. You could have at least consulted with me before you made your grand announcement." she said.

James looked at her and huffed. "Having seen that which I did through the window of the carriage, I would say we have overstayed our welcome. That is, unless you and Newhall plan to make an announcement this morning," he replied.

He'd caught her on the spot. She glared at him.

"I thought so. Don't try and tell me you and Newhall were compelled by some sudden urge to go for a lakeside stroll in the early hours of the morning. From the state of your attire, I would say you have only recently tumbled out of bed and not had the services of your maid. I won't be so crass as to ask whose bed it was," he added.

Caroline knew when she was bested. If she pushed James, he would, as her male relative, be quite within his rights to press Julian for an explanation of the events of the previous night. Julian, being an honorable man, would have made an immediate offer of marriage to Caroline.

They owed it to their combined future to undertake a proper courtship. For all of London society to see that the union of the Earl of Newhall and Miss Caroline Saunders was indeed a love match.

She consoled herself that by returning home today, she could see what had transpired with the Harry situation before Julian made his first visit to see her father.

"Alright, we leave today, but if you say one word of having seen Julian and I together this morning, I shall tell your father that you abandoned your duty to me in order to go off into the wilderness and paint with your friends," she replied.

James rose from his chair and came to Caroline's side. He bent down and brushed a hand gently on her cheek. His manner was still and solemn. "I had no idea that Timothy Walters had proposed to you. Smith mentioned it because Walters would not shut up about making the journey over here to see you. I now understand why you behaved so oddly with him when the two of you met at the market," he said.

Caroline shrugged. "I didn't want to tell you because, like Francis with Harry, Timothy Walters is your friend. I did tell Mister Walters that I was not for him, but he ignored both my words and wishes and spoke to my father."

"Yes, well, I made it very clear that he was to stay away from Newhall Castle while you were a guest here. Though from the look of it, that might need to become a permanent ban. Have you and Newhall reached an understanding?"

"No and yes. No, we are not engaged, but yes, we are going to see where a period of courting takes us. Julian will speak with Papa once he can make arrangements to come to London. After that, we shall see."

James resumed his seat. "Good. While I would hate to stand in the way of true love, Caro, I need to hurry back to London. Time away has given me some perspective about my future, and I need to speak to my father as a matter of urgency. If you go and pack your things now, I shall make sure I give Newhall a proper farewell over a glass or two of his best French brandy."

Caroline admitted defeat and headed upstairs. As she climbed the long staircase, she wondered how soon it would be before she stood once more within the ancient walls of Newhall Castle—when she would finally be its mistress.

Chapter Forty-Two

The Duke of Strathmore's travel coach was ready and waiting a little more than three hours later.

Julian and Lady Margaret stood out the front of the castle and watched as the last of the travel trunks were lifted and loaded onto the roof of the coach. The injured driver's mate was making a strong recovery and was fit enough to journey home.

James appeared from the castle foyer. He was well rugged up for the journey with a heavy woolen overcoat, thick leather gloves, and a long scarf wrapped several times around his neck. "Do you know where Caroline has got to? She disappeared not long after breakfast and I have not seen her since."

Julian pointed toward the end of the main driveway. Caroline was running around with Midas chasing her heels and barking loudly.

James stood beside Julian and watched them for a moment or so. "That dog of yours has taken a shine to Caroline. Let us hope that the friendship is able to continue."

Julian took heart at his words. James Radley was a decent chap, and if he supported the relationship between Caroline and himself, that was encouraging news.

"I had better go and get her, otherwise it will be mid-afternoon before we get started. I don't know if anyone has ever made mention of it, but my dear cousin is not the most punctual of people. The poor chap who does marry her will be in for a lot of waiting."

Julian put two fingers to his lips and whistled. Midas stopped in his tracks, and Caroline looked up and waved.

She called the dog to heel and they walked over to join the others. "Time to leave?" she asked. Bending down, she gave Midas one last hug and scratch behind the ear. "I shall see you again soon. Now you be a good boy for your master."

She came to Lady Margaret and they embraced. When they pulled apart, Julian saw tears in Caroline's eyes.

Lady Margaret took a handkerchief from out of her skirts and wiped her own tears away. "Thank you so much for coming to Newhall Castle. No matter that it was only a small gathering, I am declaring the house party a resounding success. You and your family are welcome to return any time."

"Hear, hear. The Radley and Saunders cousins took an unfortunate situation and turned it into a fun week for us all. Thank you, Caroline. I could not have survived this past week without you," said Julian.

She looked away shyly from him. Julian meanwhile, was fighting against all his urges to reach out and pull her into his arms. He ached to kiss her one last time before she left. London should give them the future they sought, but the idea of Caroline climbing on board the coach and leaving Newhall Castle made his heart ache.

She lifted her head and met his gaze. He saw love shining back at him and for an instant, Julian thought his heart had stopped.

"It was a house party I shall never forget. I hope this will not be the last time I walk the snow-covered lawns of Newhall Castle, nor the last time I skate on your ice pond," she said.

They had made their private agreement and the reasons for keeping it were sound. Yet as Caroline held out a hand to bid him farewell, he wanted nothing more than to go down on bended-knee and offer for her. Anything to stop her leaving.

Instead he mustered every ounce of self-control at his disposal and politely shook her hand. "Promise me that you will get your family physician to check your wound each day once you are back home. The stiches look like they are healing nicely."

Not that her injured hand would make an ounce of difference to how magnificently beautiful she was, nor to how deep he knew her beauty ran. The real Caroline was a delicate blooming flower.

He had changed her bandage for the last time earlier that morning, after breakfast, watched over by an interested James. If her cousin had suddenly decided he had better take his role of chaperone more seriously, it was all too late.

"Come now, Caro, let us take our leave. Thank you, Lady Margaret. And thank you, Newhall. It has been an interesting trip; let us hope for a quiet and boring journey home. I, for one, could do with some sleep," said James.

With final goodbyes now complete, Julian stood back and let James help Caroline into the coach. Midas tried to follow her, and an embarrassed Julian was finally forced to retrieve his whimpering dog.

The door of the coach closed. A spark of silly joy lit in his heart when Caroline's face appeared at the window. She held her good hand up to the window, fingers spread.

He took his cue and placed his hand on the outer side of the glass. They looked at one another. When she mouthed the words *"I love you,"* he finally understood what all the foolish poems and ballads had been trying to tell him all along.

The driver of the coach flicked his whip over the horses and the coach pulled away. Midas fussed terribly as it cleared the drive and started on the long road out of the castle grounds.

Julian bent down and tried to comfort him. "I promise you, I will do everything I can to bring her back here. You are not the only one who wishes to see Caroline walking the grounds each day."

Lady Margaret came over to him. "Now what? I am assuming since you let her go you have some plan in place to win her over. If not, then you are a fool."

Julian snorted. He looked her up and down, then a sly smile crept to his lips. "That gown must be several seasons old. I am surprised you are still wearing it."

Lady Margaret's eyes lit up. "Cheeky blighter. I shall have you know that this is the latest fashion in London."

He shrugged. "Pity. Because if it was an old gown, then you would have been compelled to come to London with me when I leave tomorrow, and I could have bought you some new ones. As it is, I will now be left with no one to accompany me when I make my social visits to Caroline's home."

Lady Margaret chortled. "Well in that case, this is a terrible color on me and it won't do your marriage prospects any good for you to be paying social visits without the requisite female relative. I shall be ready to leave at first light. Once we are in London, I shall make sure to visit my modiste and have several new expensive gowns made up. I need to look my best while you set about the task of securing your future countess."

Julian chanced one last look to watch the coach as it cleared the rise.

The coach suddenly stopped. The door flung open and Caroline jumped down. She began to walk back down the drive toward the castle. Julian and Lady Margaret looked at one another.

"Oh, for heaven's sake, run after her," said Lady Margaret.

She took hold of Midas's collar while Julian broke into a fast run to meet Caroline. When they finally met, she held out her hands to him. Tears shone in her eyes.

"I couldn't leave without telling you one more time that I love you. My life without you will be utter torture. Promise me you will come to London as soon as possible," she said.

He pulled her into his arms and, ignoring anyone who could see them, placed a long warm kiss on her lips. "You are demanding and willful," he said with a smile.

"Yes, and as I recall, it is you who is infuriating," she replied.

They shared a silly, private grin. How things had changed since that horrid encounter between them at the ball.

James poked his head out of the coach. "Come on, Caroline. I want to make Leicester before it is dark. Newhall, unless you are coming with us to see my uncle, I suggest you unhand my cousin and let her leave!"

Julian helped her back into the coach. He stole a kiss right in front of James, who rolled his eyes and looked away. "I shall see you in London. In the meantime, don't forget that I love you."

As the Strathmore coach disappeared over the rise, Julian headed back to the castle, a happy whistle on his lips.

Chapter Forty-Three

"Well, that was an interesting visit on all accounts," said James. Caroline nodded. She had been fighting back tears all the way to the village of Newhall. Several times, she had been tempted to rap on the roof of the coach and ask the driver to turn around. But each time, she had sat back in her seat and counselled herself that she and Julian had agreed on a way forward and she should stick to the plan.

"Do you think the two of you could make a go of it?" asked James.

"I think so. Julian had a terrible childhood as a result of his parents' disaster of a marriage, which means it will take time for him to become comfortable with the notion of a happy family. By undertaking a formal courtship, it will give us the opportunity for him to get to know the rest of our extended clan," she replied.

"Yes, I had heard that the countess was an unpleasant woman. When she visited at Fulham Palace and tried to press my mother into forcing Claire to attend this week, she was quite forthcoming in her opinions. My mother is not used to being told what to do. Newhall's mother did not take kindly to being given a firm 'no.'"

Caroline was more than a little relieved to know that the countess had sailed back to the Continent. Austria was a long way from England, and for that, she was grateful.

"And what about you? I could tell from the lovestruck look on Newhall's face that you have stolen his heart. Then again, I have seen that look on the faces of many men over the years. I hope your reasons for becoming the next Countess Newhall are sound. I must say, it does have a nice ring to it," he added.

Countess Newhall did sit well with her. Not that the title in particular would sway her when it came to choosing a husband. Her mother was the daughter of a duke, and there were a few other noble titles floating around the family.

She wanted to marry for the very same reason that had made her sister elope with Viscount Rosemount's second son. She wanted to love a man with all her heart and for him to love her in return.

"I love him. I just want the rest of London society to know that, and understand we are serious about our marriage and future."

The journey back to London was as boring as James had said he hoped it would be. Without Francis taking up space, Caroline and he were able to spread themselves out on the benches of the coach and sleep most of the day.

A pleasant evening at an inn in Leicester, followed by an overnight stay with friends at Northampton saw them back in London in less than three days. James escorted Caroline inside the front door of the Saunders's house in Dover Street, before making his hurried exit.

"I have to speak with my father before he meets with the Archbishop of Canterbury on Monday. I shall try to catch up with you before the week is out. Oh, and do send word on the Harry situation."

With that, he was gone, leaving Caroline standing alone with her luggage, until a pair of burly footmen came and retrieved her things.

She eventually found a friendly face in her father's study. The door was open, and she knocked on the wooden doorframe as she stepped into the room.

Charles Saunders was seated at his desk. At the sight of his youngest daughter, he leapt from his chair and came to her, pulling her into a fatherly embrace. "Caroline. *Ma douce enfant*, it is so good to see you. Welcome home. I have missed your sweet face."

The weight on her shoulders fell away as she lay her head against her father's chest. Charles was a modern father, not one who kept a distance from his children. Having lost many members of his family during the French Revolution, he was especially close to his offspring.

He leaned back and looked at Caroline a concerned expression on his face. "You have had an interesting time away from London, by all accounts. Have you seen Francis since you arrived home?"

"No, Cousin James literally dumped me and my luggage in the front hallway and then left. I have been in the house for mere minutes," she replied.

Her father frowned but Caroline decided to leave the question of James alone for the moment.

"Well then, I shall call for tea and inform you of the developments since Francis returned home," her father said.

Caroline took a seat on a nearby low couch and her father went to his desk. He returned momentarily, with several pieces of paper in his hand, including a copy of *The Times*. He set them on the low table, which was at the end of the couch, and took a seat next to Caroline.

He handed her the newspaper and pointed to a small square bordered notice.

Apology. The Times wishes to acknowledge an editorial error with regard to the false announcement of a betrothal, and hereby issues a full and unreserved apology to the following persons: Mister Harold Menzies of Mount Street, London. Miss Caroline Saunders of Dover Street, London. The error was made by a junior editor whose services have been subsequently terminated.

Caroline put the newspaper down and looked at her father. She dreaded to think how much money had changed hands to get the paper to print the apology. And a young man had lost his employment due to Harry's pigheadedness.

Charles nodded. "*The Times* were very good about it, though it took Francis quite some effort to get Harry to go with him to Printing House Square. He still had it in his head that you might come to see sense and agree to marry him. It finally took both Harry's father and myself to get it through his thick skull that you would not be changing your mind."

"I don't think it is fair that someone has lost their livelihood over this," she replied.

Charles handed her a second piece of paper. It was an employment contract for a shipping clerk with the Saunders family business. Caroline read the front and then reached over and placed a tender kiss on her father's cheek. "I take it this is for the young man who made up the betrothal notice for Harry at *The Times?* Thank you, Papa. I shall rest easy knowing we have set matters fairly to right."

A footman knocked on the door and carried in a tray with a pot of tea and several cups. Adelaide Saunders followed.

Caroline rose from the couch and went to greet her mother. Adelaide took one look at Caroline's bandaged hand and sighed. "Oh, my poor girl, you have been in the wars."

"I am fine. The wound is healing well. Julian has a good hand with a needle and thread," replied Caroline.

Adelaide raised her eyebrows. Caroline knew her mother would not have failed to notice the familiar use of the Earl of Newhall's name rather than his title. Caroline simply smiled.

"Well now you are home. And, just as importantly, not engaged," said Adelaide.

Caroline looked down, unable to meet her mother's gaze. If luck would have it, her status would be changing very soon. She yawned, tired from the long days of travel in the cramped confines of the coach. "Yes, and I would like to take to my bed for a few hours if that is alright? I did not sleep well the night before we left and have been trying to catch up ever since."

Her parents did not press her for further news of her stay at

Newhall Castle, but she knew that in time, the questions would come.

Adelaide accompanied her upstairs and to Caroline's bedroom. "Get some rest today; we can talk later at supper. I will have your things unpacked and hung in the wardrobe. You will need your formal gowns for the day after tomorrow."

Caroline stopped unbuttoning her coat. "What do you mean I will need my gowns so soon?"

Adelaide took hold of Caroline's right hand and met her gaze. "The whole mistaken betrothal issue is far from over. While *The Times* printed an apology, I can assure you that there are plenty of people within the *ton* who think that there is more to it than a simple error made by a newspaper clerk. There is a charity ball at Collins House, at which you need to make an appearance. The sooner you are back out in society, the sooner we can take the heat out of the rumors."

Caroline sat on her bed after Adelaide had left. Her mother was the pragmatic one in her parents' marriage. As the daughter of a duke, Adelaide Saunders had intricate knowledge of the workings of London high society. If Adelaide said Caroline had to be back in circulation, she said it with good reason.

Caroline lay down on the bed and stared up at the ceiling. She wished she was in Derbyshire. Newhall Castle was a simpler place. There were snow-covered grounds to ramble over, with Midas following behind. The little cottage by the frozen lake was a haven of tranquility.

Rolling onto her side, she dragged part of the bedclothes over her. As she drifted off to sleep, a soft smile sat on her lips. An image of Julian looking back at her from outside the cottage formed in her mind. He held out a hand and beckoned for her to join him.

"Soon. Come soon," she whispered.

Chapter Forty-Four

"Come on in out of the rain, you foolish creature." Midas gave Julian what he took to be a dog's version of a dirty look. He had been playing in the rear garden of Newhall House and had found himself a muddy puddle. A puddle which, with the now constant London rain, had turned into a mud bath. Midas was having a whale of a time.

Midas slowly made his way in out of the wet and Julian closed the door behind them. "Thank you. What would Caroline say to the mess you have made of your coat?"

At the sound of Caroline's name, Midas pricked up his ears. His head moved quickly from side to side, as if searching for her.

"No. She is not here, but if you want her to be, then you have to stay clean. I must venture out into polite society tonight and I cannot do that if you are going to make me stand and call you, as I have done for the past five minutes," said Julian. He playfully frowned as Midas lowered his head. "Oh, come now. I wasn't that hard on you."

A footman appeared from upstairs and took Midas away for a bath, leaving Julian free to seek out Lady Margaret. She was in the main ground floor sitting room.

"How did you go with finding out the lay of the land?" he asked.

Lady Margaret smiled. "Very well. An apology for Mister Menzies's foolish act was published in *The Times*. I managed to speak to a mutual friend of Caroline's mother, and they are setting about putting her back into society. There is a charity ball at Collins House tonight and she will be in attendance."

Julian nodded. "Excellent. Now to secure some tickets so we can also be among the guests."

Lady Margaret reached into her reticule and pulled out a single ticket. She handed it to Julian. "I have an early appointment with my modiste tomorrow to spend lots of your money, so you go on ahead without me. I expect you and Caroline have plans for a secret rendezvous. Three makes for a crowded room."

He gave her a hug. "Make sure you select the finest fabrics."

After arriving at Collins House, Julian made himself scarce. He took the glass of brandy offered by a footman and then retreated to a quiet, dark corner of the main ballroom. If Caroline was true to form, sooner or later, she would make her way to the dance floor.

He didn't have to wait long. Caroline and Francis appeared in the doorway of the room. A group of young gentlemen hurried over to her side, followed almost immediately by Francis bowing to his sister and leaving the room.

Wishing to avoid having to speak to anyone of his acquaintance, he retreated further into the shadows. His gaze was now fixed firmly on Caroline. Much had changed between them during her time at Newhall Castle, but here in London, he suddenly felt the need for confirmation that the woman he had lost his heart to was the woman he wanted to share his future with. That Caroline would remain true to her word.

Caroline's usual court took it in turn to declare how much they had all missed her. Julian was mighty pleased to see that neither the troublesome Mister Menzies or Mister Walters was present.

He took a sip of his brandy and continued to watch. His vantage point was out of sight, but still within earshot. If Caroline reverted to her old ways, he would soon know. A hubbub quickly rose in the group, and Julian pricked up his ears.

"Where is your dance card, Miss Saunders?" exclaimed one of her admirers.

"I have no need of a dance card this evening. I am here to see friends and help raise some badly needed funds for our returned injured soldiers."

One of the other young gentlemen then stepped forward and dipped into a low bow. He held a dance card in his hand. He turned to his fellow courtiers and smiled sweetly. With Harry Menzies now out of the picture, there was an opening for the role of Caroline's closest protector. He held the card out to her.

Julian held his breath. Waiting.

Caroline looked down at the card, but did not take it. "Thank you, no. As I said, I have no need for it tonight. Gentlemen, I think it is time that you all found other young ladies with which to spend your evening. I am sure there are plenty of pretty girls who would love to dance."

Julian clenched his fist. If it would not have caused others to look at him, he would have raised his arms and punched the air. She was not dancing, and he was the reason why.

"Well then, could I interest you in a glass of champagne?" offered another admirer.

Julian paused his quiet celebration. Caroline did not tolerate fools who did not listen.

To her credit, she simply shook her head. "No, thank you. Gentlemen, it is time we put an end to this group. Recent events have compelled me to look long and hard at my character, and I realize I have been more than a little cruel to you all. I apologize for my behavior. It was wrong of me to lead you on. I also want to wish every one of you the very best of health and happiness for the future. Good evening to you all."

Silence fell on the small group. Then one young man stepped forward and bowed low to Caroline, and departed. Followed by another. One by one, the members of her court dismissed themselves.

Caroline was left standing alone in the middle of the room. The temptation to step out from his seclusion was strong, but Julian remained hidden. He had not yet spoken to her father. *Well done, my love. I am proud of you.*

He would take the place of her court of admirers, but in good time. The gossip of the *ton* would only be silenced if the next time her name was mentioned in social circles was when she appeared on his arm in public.

Julian drained the last of his brandy and made for the nearest exit.

Chapter Forty-Five

A knock at Caroline's bedroom door roused her from a deep sleep. She had been dreaming of a tall man pulling her along at high speed on the frozen Thames. Every time she tried to skate faster and catch up to him, he drew away and she was left struggling to remain upright.

She rolled over and faced the door as Adelaide came into the room bearing a large box. She set it down on Caroline's dressing table and then stood, waiting.

"What is it?" asked Caroline.

Her mother hurried over to the chair where Caroline's dressing gown hung, picked it up, and handed it to her.

"I have no idea, but I had hoped that your efforts in dissuading young gentlemen from making rash displays of devotion would have had an immediate effect. Clearly, I was wrong. Whatever it is, you had better open it and then send it back," said Adelaide.

A reluctant Caroline put on her dressing gown and padded barefoot to where the box sat. She looked at it for a moment, examining the outside.

It was an elegant pale blue box, with silver ribbon wrapped around it which finished in an enormous bow. Someone had spent some serious blunt on a gift, if the box was any indication of what was inside.

Caroline pulled on the ribbon and loosened the bow. Adelaide leaned closer. Then, with a great flourish, Caroline whipped the lid off.

"Oh."

Inside the box was a pair of ice skates.

Adelaide screwed up her face. "That is an odd gift. Who would send such a thing?"

Tears pricked Caroline's eyes as she picked up the small note which lay on top of the skates. Her bottom lip trembled as she read it.

Midas misses you terribly, as do I. We shall be in Hyde Park at 5pm this afternoon. I have an appointment with your father at 3pm.

She closed her eyes and put a hand to her mouth. Julian knew exactly how to touch her heart.

Adelaide slipped a hand around Caroline's waist. "May I ask who has sent you this?"

Smiling through her tears, Caroline handed her mother the note. "Lord Newhall, Julian. Midas is his dog."

Julian had waited only a day before setting out to follow her. Knowing that he was impatient to see her again brought a welcome sense of relief.

"Do you love him?" said Adelaide.

Caroline nodded. The past days being separated from Julian had been torture. Almost every waking moment was spent thinking about him, and wondering where he was and what he was doing.

She looked at the note once more. He would be in Hyde Park at 5pm today. It would only be a matter of hours before she saw him again.

"He is going to speak to Papa this afternoon and ask for permission to court me. I had better go and tell Papa that he can finally say 'yes' to a young gentleman. After that, will you come with me to Hyde Park? I would very much like for you to meet him," replied Caroline.

"Of course. I am pleased to hear that his intentions are serious. Now hurry and get dressed. I need to hear more about what happened at Newhall Castle, and why an earl would be sending you a pair of ice skates.," said Adelaide.

Caroline pulled one of the ice skates out of the box and held it up. The blade glistened in the morning light. "Rest assured Mama, both of us are serious in our intentions."

Adelaide smiled. "Countess Newhall. I think you would do the title a great service."

Chapter Forty-Six

J ulian and Lady Margaret walked the short distance from James
Street to Hyde Park later that afternoon. It took them longer
than it should have due to Midas feeling the need to stop and
sniff every tree, bush, and post he came across. Fortunately, he
ignored all the other people headed for the park.

"You would think he had never seen a tree before," observed
Lady Margaret.

They stopped as Midas found yet another pile of interesting
leaves to snuffle about.

"Well I am glad that we left with plenty of time to spare. Hopefully Midas will be tired by the time we reach Hyde Park and will
allow me time to spend with Caroline," replied Julian.

He was quietly pleased with himself over the gift he had sent her
that morning. Anyone could send flowers, but it was the thoughtful
gift which he knew would capture her attention. He beamed,
knowing that he already held her heart.

The interview with Charles Saunders had gone far better than
even he could have hoped. By the time he managed to make his
goodbyes and leave the house in Dover Street, Charles had pressed
him into downing three large glasses of brandy, followed by gifting

him a smooth Cuban cigar, which had arrived on a ship that morning fresh from the West Indies.

He had barely got the words out to ask for permission to court Caroline before Charles had leapt from his chair and held his hand out in congratulations.

Hyde Park was a crush of people by the time they finally arrived through the gates. The season was over and it was a chilly day, but still the elite of London society had turned out in their droves.

The plan to meet Caroline and her mother in the park suddenly seemed not such a good idea. He was having serious second thoughts about it when without warning Midas yanked hard on his lead and Julian lost his grip.

The dog dashed ahead of them, barking loudly.

"Midas!" bellowed Julian.

He raced after the dog. Midas disappeared between two parked carriages, leaving Julian with no other option but to go the long way around. With Midas out of sight, he feared he had lost his dog for good. "Bloody dog," he muttered.

The crowds made it near impossible to chase after Midas, but he finally managed to make it onto a large section of the lawn. There he spied his prey. And Caroline.

She waved to him. Midas, meanwhile, was barking and chasing his tail, clearly beside himself with delight at having found her. Caroline crouched down and allowed Midas to jump into her lap. The woman standing beside her looked down, and a soft smile came to her lips.

He saw the older well-dressed woman next to Caroline and his eyes lit up. He had abandoned Lady Margaret!

He raced back to find her. "Sorry about that, but I did manage to find Midas, along with Caroline and her mother."

She checked his cravat before taking his arm. "All is forgiven. Anyone would think you were nervous over meeting your future mother-in-law," she replied.

Julian straightened his back and made a great effort to appear as unflustered as possible as he accompanied Lady Margaret to the lawn area.

When they reached Caroline and her mother, Julian bowed. "Lord Newhall, at your service," he said formally.

Adelaide held out her hand. "Adelaide Saunders. A pleasure to meet you, Lord Newhall. My son William speaks most highly of you, and Caroline here has been telling me all about her stay in Derbyshire. It appears you are quite the skilled surgeon when it comes to stitching up wounds. Our family physician was most impressed with your handywork," she replied.

"Thank you, Lady Adelaide. I had some experience in Europe during the last campaign at Waterloo," he said.

He studied Adelaide's face. Apart from the shape of her mouth, Caroline did not bear a strong resemblance to her mother. But he could see where both Francis and Will got their eyes from.

"Please, just call me Adelaide. I only use my family title when there are good opera seats at risk."

Julian ushered Lady Margaret forward. "May I introduce my aunt, Lady Margaret. She was the hostess of the house party."

Adelaide held out her hand to Lady Margaret and Julian smiled. It was well known in the *ton* that Lady Margaret had been his father's mistress, and many society matrons would not have spoken to her in a social setting. Adelaide Saunders was fortunately a sensible and fair woman.

"Thank you for taking such good care of Caroline. It was a great comfort to know that she was in the hands of people who cared for her. Francis said he had no hesitation in recommending that she stayed on at Newhall Castle while he came back to London to deal with business," said Adelaide.

Caroline finally finished with Midas and stood. She smiled at Julian. Midas lay his head against the side of her hip and Caroline continued to gently pat him. A spark of green jealousy lit in Julian's brain. He longed for the day when it would be, he who was so close to her.

He blinked away the sexually-charged thought and took a deep breath. The middle of a crowded park was not the place to be having private daydreams about Caroline and what he would like to do to her.

"Lord Newhall," said Caroline.

Julian bowed, unable to hide the schoolboy grin which seeing her again brought to his lips.

"Miss Saunders."

When she softly chuckled, his heart soared.

"Oh, and thank you for the wonderful gift. It is perfect. I hope when winter becomes deep, I shall have the chance to use them," said Caroline.

Julian beamed. He had that much up on Midas.

Adelaide turned to Lady Margaret. "Would you like to walk? I am sure that Midas could do with the exercise. Lord Newhall has spoken to my husband and has received his permission to court Caroline."

Lady Margaret took up Midas's lead and offered Adelaide her arm. The two ladies set off across the lawn, leaving Julian alone with Caroline.

Julian stepped in close, resisting against all his urges to plant a hurried kiss on her lips. Hyde Park was a sea of people all on the lookout for the next piece of gossip. He would not risk putting Caroline's name back on the list of scandalous chatter again.

"When did you arrive in London?" she asked, taking his arm.

Julian hesitated with his reply. "The last day or so."

She looked at him sideways and smiled.

"And how has your time at home been?" he asked.

"Better than expected. Papa and Francis managed to sort out the Harry problem. Well, as best as they could. Francis is still not speaking to him, and I am afraid that the friendship has been permanently damaged."

Julian struggled to muster any sympathy for Harry Menzies. In his opinion, Harry had acted selfishly and was now reaping the rewards. Lady Margaret had kept her ear to the ground and reported that while the matter had been officially put to rest, there were plenty of people who thought Caroline a jilt.

"I have a small confession to make," he said.

Caroline stopped. Ahead of them, Adelaide and Lady Margaret continued to walk, and soon were well out of earshot. She turned to Julian. "Yes?"

"I watched you from the shadows, at the ball last night. You are no longer the ruler of a small nation of admirers. I am proud of you, but a little ashamed at my deception," he said.

She looked up at him, and he held his breath. It had been a foolish thing not to show himself to her, and in the cold light of the afternoon sun he realized she may not take his deception kindly.

"I know. I saw you being all mysterious and hiding in the back of the room. It left me all a fluster and when I got home, I lay on my bed. I touched myself while thinking wicked thoughts of you," she replied.

Julian swallowed deep. When she licked her lips in a deliberate and provocative manner, he felt himself go hard.

"Wicked, naughty girl," he murmured.

"Don't forget willful and demanding. I expect you shall have to use a firm hand with me once we are married," she teased.

As other people walking in the park passed them by, Julian forced himself to look away from the tight folds of the bodice of Caroline's gown. His fingers itched to cup one of her soft, supple breasts and roll his thumb over her perfect rosy nipple.

When Caroline began to fidget with the bandage of her injured hand, Julian reached out and took a hold of her fingertips. His thumb traced gentle patterns over her skin. "I could take a look at your hand, if you would like. You should be able to take the bandage off soon."

He wanted to see the bandage gone so he could place a betrothal ring on her hand instead.

Chapter Forty-Seven

C harles Saunders greeted his wife and daughter as they stepped inside their house in Dover Street a short while later.

"Caroline, you have a visitor. I told him I would ask if you were prepared to see him, but I gave no undertakings that you would. After what happened in Derbyshire, he says he will understand if you say no," he said.

She had been expecting a visit from this particular person from the day she returned home. "Where is he?"

"The lower sitting room. I thought it best that he should not venture too far into the house, in case Francis suddenly came home. Your brother is in no mood to forgive him."

Harry Menzies stepped away from the window as Caroline entered the room. He held his hat and gloves tightly in his hands. At the sight of her, he dropped his head. "Thank you for seeing me. I promise not to take up too much of your time."

The last time she had seen Harry, Caroline had been ready to throttle him. But seeing him now made her hesitate. She had never known him to be so ill at ease.

"I came to say I am sorry. Sorry for all that I did to you and for the utter mess I made of things. As a result, your reputation has been held up to scrutiny that was entirely undeserved," he said.

Caroline silently studied Harry's face. There was nothing to show that he was anything but the kindhearted Harry she had always known. But she now knew the other side of him. The dark, dangerous Harry, who would use violence against a defenseless woman. The sooner this meeting was over, the better.

Caroline held out a hand to him. She had Julian's love and Harry was no longer a part of her life; let them shake hands and part ways.

He refused to take it. "I don't deserve your good graces. I behaved like the worst of scoundrels. My parents have barely spoken to me since they discovered the betrothal notice in *The Times*. It doesn't matter that they do not know what else I did to you. Newhall was right in threatening to put me down. I am deeply ashamed of myself."

It was a relief to know that Harry had finally accepted the gravity of the terrible things he had done to her. But the damage was done. They would never again be friends. The trust she had once had in him was gone.

"So, what now?" she asked.

Harry retrieved his gloves from inside his hat. "My father is sending me to work at our Manchester office. He says I need to be away from London until I can find myself. It pains me greatly to know that I have lost your trust and friendship. But it is entirely my fault and the punishment does fit the crime."

Caroline nodded. Harry's father was a sensible man, and getting his son out of London, for a time, was a prudent move. It would give space for the *ton* to move onto the next rumor or scandal. By the time he returned, people would have forgotten about the matter of his non-engagement to Caroline Saunders. But she would never forget that morning at Newhall Castle, and the certain knowledge that if Julian had not come to her rescue, Harry would have taken to her with his fists.

The door to the sitting room opened and Adelaide's head appeared around the door. "Are you alright?" she asked.

"Yes. We are fine," replied Caroline.

"Please give my regards to your mother," Adelaide said.

"Thank you, Lady Adelaide. I shall do that," he replied.

As he headed for the door, Caroline reached out and touched Harry on the arm. For all the hurt he had caused her, he didn't deserve to find out in public about Julian and herself. "Lord Newhall has asked my father for permission to court me. We had begun to build a tentative connection before you arrived at Newhall Castle, so please don't think that Julian took the opportunity to capitalize on your grave error of judgement," she said.

His posture stiffened at her words, and surprise and disappointment appeared on his face. "Thank you. I appreciate you telling me this in private; it is more than I deserve."

After she had escorted Harry to the front door, Caroline went in search of her father. Charles was busy stacking papers on a table in his study when she knocked on the door.

"How did you go with young Menzies?" he asked.

"As well as could be expected," she replied.

He put down the papers. "Did you tell him about Newhall and yourself?"

Caroline nodded, after which her father produced a small card out of his jacket pocket, and showed it to her. Caroline recognized the Newhall coat of arms on the top of it. "Lord Newhall is a fine chap. Will likes him immensely, so that will be a good start for the two of you. Your mother likes him as well. It was nice to finally be able to say 'yes' to a young gentleman appearing at my door. Though I must admit, I was not expecting a formal courtship."

Caroline's mood lifted. It was nice for her and her father to finally have this conversation. At last count, her father had turned away well over a dozen young men who had come to him and offered for her hand. All of them had failed. Not one of them had thought to ask Caroline for her permission. Julian had been the one who had broken the mold.

Everything about her relationship with Julian was a first. He had been the first man to openly challenge her. He had not fallen at her feet like all the others. He had treated her as an equal and demanded the same in return.

Most importantly of all, he had been the first man to stop and look beyond her beauty. To call upon the real Caroline to step out into the light. The Caroline whose blood heated at his slightest touch. The woman whose soul he owned, possessed.

"I love Julian and I want to spend the rest of my life with him. We have agreed that a formal courtship is necessary. Both of us have things in our past we wish to smooth over. Thank you, Papa, for saying yes," she replied.

Her father pulled her into a warm hug. "As far as our family is concerned, you have nothing to answer for. Though, when the time comes, I would ask something of you."

"Yes?"

"You are not allowed to run off to Scotland like your sister did. Your mother deserves to have one of her daughters married in the proper fashion. If you do marry Lord Newhall, it will have to be a full wedding service at St. Paul's, with your Uncle Hugh officiating."

Her father's stipulation would be easy to meet. Julian was far from the rash and impetuous Freddie Rosemount, who her sister had recently married. There was little chance of him suddenly spiriting her away to Gretna Green.

"Yes of course. I know how much a society wedding and ball means to Mama. I promise not to disappoint her," she replied.

"Excellent. So, when Lord Newhall next comes to pay a house call with Lady Margaret, I shall wait until you ladies are busy discussing the latest *on dit* before arriving to rescue him. A shipment of wine arrived from France this morning, and I have a few cases of Cabernet Sauvignon from Chateau Mouton-d'Armailhac. Will and Francis may just happen to fortuitously drop by and share a bottle or two with us."

She kissed her father on the cheek, grateful for such a wonderful parent. An afternoon of bonding between Julian and the Saunders men was the seal of approval for which she had hoped.

The man she loved was being drawn into the embrace of her wonderful, big, family, and her heart felt fit to burst.

Chapter Forty-Eight

Caroline stared at her gowns lying on the bed and huffed. Not one of them suited her mood, or in fact, the occasion.

She and Julian had spent several pleasant afternoons taking Midas for a walk in Hyde Park. There were benefits in having formal permission to court, one being that she was able to venture out with only a footman and maid in tow. A coin had been slipped into the hand of each of the Saunders family servants to encourage them to lag behind and out of earshot.

A week from now was a formal society ball. She and Julian were to make their social debut as a courting couple. They would dance together with more than just friendship between them. Everything she did that night would be publicly and privately scrutinized by London society.

No doubt tongues would wag, but the matrons of the *ton* would get the message loud and clear—she intended to marry Julian Palmer and become the next Countess Newhall.

The gowns, however, were not suitable. A pale blue one, a pretty pink gown with white embroidered flowers, and an elegant silver one all failed to pass muster.

Adelaide knocked on the bedroom door and came to stand next to

Caroline. She looked at the gowns. "They are rather beautiful. Do none of them appeal to you?"

Caroline pursed her lips. She needed her mother's counsel at this critical time. In order to get it, she would have to make a personal revelation. "They are the gowns of an innocent, young woman. After my stay at Newhall Castle, I am no longer that."

She stilled, waiting for her mother's response. Adelaide reached over and placed a kiss on her daughter's cheek. Caroline gave a sigh of relief, grateful for having a supportive mother.

"Well then, if that is the case, we need to find you something with more color. Something that a young woman on the cusp of marriage would wear. One which makes a clear statement," said Adelaide.

"I tried Eve's room, but all her best gowns are gone," replied Caroline. She had searched her sister's wardrobe earlier, hoping to find something which she could use. Eve had always been one for wearing stronger colors and gowns which skirted the edge of propriety. But she had taken all the most elegant gowns with her when she eloped.

"The ball is still a week away. We shall make an early morning visit to the modiste and see what she has that can be readily made up for you. We should also commission a gown for your engagement ball, since it is now merely a matter of time before an announcement is made," said Adelaide.

The following morning, Adelaide and Caroline were on the doorstep of the modiste an hour before she was due to open. Adelaide had sent word as soon as she and Caroline had spoken the previous day, and being one of the modiste's best customers, she had been granted a special appointment.

"Being out of season, my seamstresses have been able to catch up on making stock. I have a selection of gowns that you might find suitable," said the modiste.

Caroline and Adelaide stepped into the showing room of the salon. Before them were five gowns, draped over low sofas. Caroline's eye was immediately drawn to a crimson gown. She looked to her mother and Adelaide nodded. The deep, rich red was the color of a fiery summer sunset. It held the promise of passion and love.

Taking the gown and draping it over her arm, she knew it was the perfect one to wear at the ball. A night when she would finally show the world that Julian had captured her heart, and she was ready to take her place by his side.

She was counting down the days until they appeared together as a couple at a formal event.

"It's perfect," she whispered.

"Try it on," replied Adelaide.

In the fitting room, the modiste and her team of seamstresses pinned the gown to hug Caroline's figure. While they worked, she stood and watched herself in the mirror. In her face she saw someone she did not recognize. Gone were the hard edges of her lonely existence. In their place were the beginnings of the warmth that came from newfound happiness.

"You have the look of a woman in love. I am so proud of you for having opened your heart," said Adelaide.

"Ow, you, foolish girl!"

Adelaide and Caroline looked at one another as they heard the outburst from the adjourning fitting room. The modiste made her hurried apologies and left the room.

"It is not good enough. If you cannot afford to employ skilled seamstresses, you should not expect my custom."

"I am sure it was an accident, your highness. All my girls have been highly trained. But I shall make sure a discount is added to your bill," replied the modiste.

"Some women do not know how to behave. I am sure the seamstress did not mean to prick her," said Adelaide in a hushed tone.

Caroline and her sister had been taught from an early age to remain still while their gowns were being pinned. The occasional accidental prick from a dressmaker's pin was a minor inconvenience in the creation of a new gown.

"Whoever she is, I would not want to cross her," replied Caroline.

When she returned, the modiste was red-faced and wiping away tears.

"Who was that?" asked Adelaide.

The woman composed herself. "The Countess of Lienz. She arrived unannounced just after you and demanded a fitting. Most of her luggage is apparently still on board her husband's yacht and she needs clothes. I could not refuse."

Caroline frowned at herself in the mirror. She should have recognized the voice, but Julian's mother had sailed for the Continent weeks ago; so, what was she doing back in London?

As quickly as good manners would permit, she and Adelaide finished with their appointment. Once they were seated in the privacy of the Saunders family town carriage, Caroline confided the truth of the house party to her mother.

"That could have been very embarrassing if Lady Margaret had not been so quick to smooth things over. And Lord Newhall does not know the countess is in town?" said Adelaide.

"No. I am certain he would have made mention of it to me if he did. The countess has a priceless piece of estate jewelry with her, and Julian is most keen to retrieve it. If he knew she was in town, he would be knocking on her door and demanding the return of his property," replied Caroline.

"Well then, you shall have to speak with Lord Newhall when next you see him," said Adelaide.

As soon as they returned home, Caroline retrieved Eve's favorite black cloak from her wardrobe. She had no intention of wasting any time to see Julian.

The cloak had been used many times when Eve and Francis had slipped out of the house and gone to secret parties without their parents' knowledge. But Caroline knew her mission for later this evening was more important than attending an illicit gathering of the younger members of the *ton*.

She had to warn Julian that his mother was back in town.

Chapter Forty-Nine

Caroline waited until after supper that evening, then cried off spending time with her parents and headed up to her room.

When her maid came to help her ready for bed, a fully dressed Caroline slipped a coin into her hand and sent her away.

The rear garden at Dover Street had a break in the fence which was hidden by a bush. The younger Saunders siblings had an understanding with the family gardener not to have the hole repaired.

Stepping out into the dark garden, Caroline made her way to the fence and climbed through. Once she was in the laneway, she pulled the hood of the cloak over her head. If she passed anyone on the street, she would be incognito.

When she turned into James Street, a distance away, she spied Newhall House. She hurried across the road and made her way to the front steps of Julian's townhouse.

When the butler opened the door, he took one look at Caroline and started to close the door. "I am sorry, madam. You must have the wrong house."

"No, I must speak to Lord Newhall. It is a matter of urgency," she pleaded.

She was about to pull back her hood and reveal her identity when, to her relief, Julian appeared in the foyer. "What is going on?"

The butler pointed to the still-hooded Caroline. "I am sorry, my lord. I was trying to explain to this person that she has the wrong house, that we don't accept female visitors late at night."

Caroline lifted her now unbandaged, left hand and held it up to Julian's view.

Julian patted his butler on the shoulder. "Ah yes. I was expecting a visitor; it had completely slipped my mind."

The butler's brow furrowed but he said nothing. Julian dismissed him, then ushered Caroline into a nearby room and closed the door behind them.

"This is a pleasant surprise, but I don't recall us agreeing on late-night trysts as being part of the courtship," he said.

She flipped back the hood of the cape. Her heart leapt at the sight of him standing so close. "I had to see you. The countess is back in London."

The look of surprise on his face told her he had been in the dark regarding his mother's movements. "Are you sure? I mean, she sailed before I left London."

Caroline nodded. "Yes. I heard her voice from another room at the modiste this morning. I asked Francis to make enquiries, and apparently the count's yacht got into difficulties not long after they sailed. She has been in Brighton for the past few weeks making a nuisance of herself at the expense of the Prince of Wales."

"No doubt hiding from me after what she did to scupper the house party. I shall track down her highness and have a not-so-quiet word with her regarding the necklace," replied Julian.

"Francis says she is staying at the Austrian embassy. I don't suppose she wanted to make her presence too widely known until she discovered where you were. If she has any sense, she will be doing everything she can to avoid having to explain herself to you," said Caroline.

He smiled at her. "Thank you. I am grateful for your loyalty."

Caroline rose up on her toes and offered her lips to him. Mere thanks were not what she had in mind when visiting Julian in the middle of the night. Their lips met in a soft, tentative kiss.

"Who is waiting for you outside?" he asked.

She chuckled knowingly. "No one. I walked here."

The low primal growl he gave in response to her words set her blood on fire. Let him be angry with her. She was ready to take any punishment he decided to mete out, just as long as it ended with her in his bed.

"That was a dangerous and foolhardy thing to do. Promise me you will never do that again," he said.

Caroline worked up her best coy look, but when Julian took her by the arm, she sensed she had read him wrong. He was angry. Not just a little annoyed.

"Alright. I won't do that again, I promise. But I had to see you. And if I had come with Francis, then I wouldn't have been able to stay," she replied.

He held her gaze. His look was one of implacability, but she knew he was fighting a battle between social dictates and desire. By all accounts, he should be calling for his town carriage and taking her home. But when he slipped a hand around her waist, she knew desire had won.

"Just for a short while, after which I will take you home," he said.

Caroline pulled on the ties of her cape and it fell to the floor. A satisfying intake of breath from Julian told her she had chosen the perfect gown to wear.

At the front of the gown, where the laces should have been tied together, she had left them open. With the cape now gone, Julian was granted a full view of the mounds of Caroline's breasts. He needed no invitation.

He roughly pulled the gown's bodice fully open and she exalted as the cool night air kissed her nipples.

"Oh Caroline, you wicked girl," he murmured.

His mouth came down on one of her breasts. He took her nipple between his teeth and gently nipped. Heat pooled between her legs.

Julian lifted Caroline's skirts and his fingers soon found her heat. She groaned as he began to stroke deeply. Her hands clutched the side of his jacket, desperate to find purchase as her knees weakened.

He lifted her and lay her down on a nearby sofa. A lightning-quick fumble with the placket of his trousers soon had his erection free.

She took hold of his rapidly hardening manhood and stroked. He lay his fingers over hers and guided her in how hard she should hold him.

Emboldened by his reaction to her strokes, Caroline decided it was time that she took the next step.

She pushed Julian's hand away and sat up. Then, taking hold of him once more, she guided his erection to her lips. She heard the sound of his breath shuddering softly as she took him into her mouth. He gripped a handful of her hair while she ministered to him.

Tension built as she licked and suckled him. She listened as his breath became more ragged.

"Enough," he finally gasped, and stepped back.

Pulling her to her feet, he sat down on the sofa. Julian lifted her skirts and drew her to him. It took only a moment for Caroline to understand what she needed to do. Straddling Julian, she sunk down and took the length of him deep inside her.

If she had thought their initial encounter at the cottage had been intimate, she quickly discovered this new position took her breath away.

"Ride me," he commanded. With his hands on her hips, Julian instructed Caroline in how she should move. Gripping the top of the sofa behind his shoulders, she was able to establish a strong rhythm. She cried his name when she crashed through into her climax.

His lips sought hers as he pulled her hard down on him. Holding her firmly by the hips he thrust deeper and harder into her. Caroline willed her body to soften and accept his fierce lovemaking. She wanted to be all for this man, to exist purely for his pleasure.

He came with one last hard thrust and then stilled. She cradled his head against her breasts and waited for him to return to earth.

She longed for more of these evenings. Moments where they could share their love and then spend the night wrapped in each other's arms before drifting off to sleep in their own home.

She longed for when she would finally belong completely to Julian.

Chapter Fifty

Julian couldn't stay angry with her for more than a minute and in his heart, he knew it would always be that way. She may have given her love to him, but Caroline held his soul.

It was bloody dangerous for her to have walked the streets of London at that time of night. He was determined that she would never do it again. The thought of something happening to her or, God forbid, losing her filled him with bone-deep dread.

Taking Caroline by the hand, he led her upstairs. He would take her home, but first things first.

Inside his bedroom, he opened the top drawer of his dresser and took out a small blue box. He had made love to Caroline on three separate occasions; the time for playing at courting her was now over.

He placed the ring in his pocket. Taking hold of her hand, he went down on bended knee, an expectant smile on his face. "Caroline Saunders, you are the love of my life. I place my future happiness in your hands. Will you do me the greatest honor and agree to be my wife?"

"Yes." She dissolved into tears as he got to his feet.

Taking her injured hand in his, he gently placed the diamond and ruby ring on her finger. "I decided that, since ours is a true love match, it was time for the Newhall estate to have a special piece of jewelry commissioned. One that no other previous countess has ever owned."

The diamond-set ring, with a circle of rubies, had whispered her name as soon as he'd set eyes on it at Stedman and Vardon in New Bond Street. His father had been a stickler for shopping at Rundell and Bridge but, in the spirit of change, Julian had decided that the ring for his future wife should come from somewhere else.

Caroline held the ring up to the light from the bedroom fireplace. The flames, reflected in the diamonds, set the rubies to an even darker red.

"Will you speak with my father before the ball next week?" she asked.

"Yes, of course. Though it may not be tomorrow. I have a few urgent matters to attend to in the morning." A meeting with his mother, being the first order of the day.

They sealed their betrothal with an almost chaste kiss. Caroline's mewl of disappointment had Julian laughing before pulling her into his embrace. He then proceeded to kiss her thoroughly.

The following morning saw Julian in a more somber and determined mood. His mother was not going to best him. She had spent years trying to ruin his life and had done what she could to wreck his house party not to mention his reputation.

The matter of the Crusader Ruby now lay in the forefront of his mind. He had thought to travel to Austria at some point and confront her. But since she was back in London, he was steadfast in his resolve to regain the priceless piece. She would not outwit him again.

His first task for the morning was not a meeting with Charles Saunders, but rather, with Francis. Caroline's brother was a close confidante of the Prince of Wales. Julian was leaving nothing to chance. If he had to use every ounce of leverage to force the countess's hand, he would.

"Newhall, I was not expecting to see you here. I don't suppose you get down to the docks very often. If you want more of the wine, we drank the other afternoon, just let me know and I shall send around a case. By the way, did Caroline manage to send word to you regarding the countess?" said Francis.

"Yes, which is why I am here," replied Julian.

He had made discreet enquiries and confirmed that his mother was indeed staying at the Austrian embassy. She was cunning. She knew he could not simply march up to the front door and demand entrance. The Austrian embassy was considered Austrian sovereign soil, and, being married to the Count of Lienz, she would be protected there.

"I need to retrieve a certain article from my mother. While I am not beyond having her arrested, I thought that with your connections to the Prince of Wales, you might be able to help find a diplomatic way to resolve the situation," he said.

Francis stopped midway through pouring a glass of whisky. Julian could understand the position he was putting him in. One did not call on the friendship of the future king without making a considered reflection of what it may cost.

"You do know that this may not be an easy thing to accomplish?"

Francis finished pouring the drink and handed a glass to Julian. "But since you and I are to shortly be related, I feel a brotherly sense of obligation to help you. What can I do?"

"I intend to make an appointment to speak to Prince Esterhazy tomorrow and ask for him to intercede on my behalf. He knows the work I did in Paris after the fall of Napoleon. The Austrians owe me," replied Julian.

"I shall make some private approaches through various channels and see what can be done. I trust a letter from the Prince of Wales' private secretary would go a long way to help your cause," said Francis.

Julian took a long slow sip of his drink. A letter from the future king could be invaluable. "That would be most welcome. I am not sure how much longer the Count and Countess of Lienz will be in London, so time may be critical."

Francis chuckled. "You will find out that my family has a lot of connections. Just say the word and I am sure Will could make certain that the count's yacht was unable to leave port. Funny thing, boats— one minute you think you have them seaworthy, the next, you discover a new problem."

Julian already had agents watching the Austrian embassy around the clock. So that, combined with Francis's words of comfort, gave him the first real hope that he may actually succeed in regaining his family's heirloom.

Now he could concentrate on the next task at hand: getting Charles Saunders' official approval to marry Caroline.

Chapter Fifty-One

"I cannot begin to tell you how pleasant it is for me to be able to say 'yes' to a young man asking for my daughter's hand in marriage. Congratulations, Newhall. I think you and Caroline will make a fine match." Charles held out his hand, and Julian accepted his warm handshake.

"Thank you, sir. I am proud and honored to be the one who finally succeeded," said Julian.

Despite Caroline already having accepted his proposal, Julian still found himself nervous asking her father for his permission. He had not been able to see Charles the previous day, having received an unexpected summons from the palace to collect the letter that Francis had mentioned. A future brother-in-law with that amount of clout with the Prince Regent, was a boon any man would be happy to have.

"So, have you discussed wedding arrangements as yet?" asked Charles.

"Caroline has informed me that Lady Adelaide will be in charge of all the organizing. I expect it will be a smooth operation," he replied.

Weddings, and the commotion that came with them, were purely for females. His sole input, if he had his way, would be to arrive at the church on time and say 'yes' when asked.

Charles snorted. "You have been warned. My own nuptials had more planning involved in it than Hannibal going over the Alps. Though we did draw the line at elephants."

He loved Caroline; and his future countess was going to get the wedding she deserved. He shrugged and readied himself for the onslaught of frippery and fabric samples. If that was what it took to launch himself into wedded bliss, he was ready.

"Unfortunately, my wife and daughter are not at home. So, the champagne shall have to wait. In the meantime, I still have some bottles of that Chateau Mouton-d'Armailhac Cabernet Sauvignon left. I am sure one of those would suffice," said Charles.

"This is a serious matter, Lord Newhall. While I understand that there are difficulties between the countess and yourself, I would caution you against raising the issue of the necklace to a criminal matter. Accusing your own mother of theft is not something one does lightly."

Julian studied his fingernails for a moment, giving time for the ambassador to think that he was taking his words to heart. "I understand the situation fully, Your Highness, which is why I was careful in using my connections to obtain that letter."

Prince Esterhazy held the letter from the Prince of Wales' private secretary in his hand. He raised his eyebrows before setting it down on his desk. "So how would you like to proceed?"

As far as Julian was concerned, it should be a simple matter. The prince would speak to his house guest and explain the situation to the countess, and she would hand over the ruby necklace. But he knew his mother better than that. She would not go quietly. "I don't wish to make this a diplomatic issue, hence why I have not raised matters to the legal authorities in England. Nor have I made mention of it to those in London society who would be able to use this disagreement to their advantage. I just want what is rightfully mine."

The hard stare he got from the prince told him that his less than thinly veiled threat had got through. The prince picked up the bell on his desk and rang it. Within seconds, a footman appeared.

"Ask the Countess of Lienz to come to my study, would you? I did see her in the gardens not long ago, so I know she is somewhere about the embassy."

The prince rose from his desk and crossed over to a cabinet. He pulled out a bottle of brandy and showed it to Julian. "A spot of something to fortify your spirit?"

Julian shook his head. The bottle and a half of Cabernet Sauvignon which Charles Saunders had pressed him to drink was still taking the edge off his senses.

The prince poured himself a large glass. "If I may be frank, your mother is not the easiest of women to deal with at any time. Her husband is known to seek solace in the drink on occasion. When they sent word that they would be staying here, I immediately sent out for more brandy."

His mother would drive any man to drink, but Julian could not bring himself to feel pity for the count. He had knowingly stolen another man's wife. What he had sowed, he was welcome to reap.

The countess arrived a short while later. Upon seeing Julian, she marched up to the ambassador and then pointed at her son. "What is he doing here?"

Prince Esterhazy glanced at the brandy bottle, and his empty glass. "Lord Newhall has come about an item of his property, which he tells me you have in your possession. He has asked for it to be returned."

The countess huffed. "Lies. All lies. I have nothing to which I am not entitled."

She was, in many ways, predictable. Her usual mode of dealing with anyone who dared to challenge her was to play the outraged victim, then brand everything that they said to be a lie. Finally, she would cast aspersions on their character. "You don't know my son. He has been incapable of telling the truth since the day he uttered his first words, much like his father. The Newhall men are not of good character."

Julian ticked off the third point on his list, and rose from his chair. "Madam, you have a ruby necklace which belongs to the Newhall estate. I would like it returned, please."

A slow smile appeared on her face. "Exactly. The Crusader Ruby belongs to the Newhall estate. It was gifted to me as the Countess Newhall. A title which I am still permitted to use, though one would have to add the word Dowager if we were to be socially correct."

Julian clenched his hands into tight fists. It was never going to be easy with her. "But you have remarried, so you are no longer the countess," he ground out.

The prince held up his hand. "I will not have family squabbles in my embassy. Your Highness, please go and retrieve the necklace from your room."

The countess nodded. "Very well, if you insist."

While he and Prince Esterhazy waited for the countess to return, Julian pondered the possible reasons for his mother's easy acquiesce to the prince's instructions. There had to be an explanation that he had not considered.

When she returned a short while later, she strode into the room wearing the necklace. Prince Esterhazy gasped at the sight of the Crusader Ruby.

The length of its long silver chain was encrusted with diamonds. The pendant at the end had been formed into a large diamond shape with an enormous stunning ruby set in the middle. At four other points on the pendant, smaller rubies had been placed.

For an instant, Julian's mind was filled with the memory of the last time he had seen his mother wearing it. It had been at a ball held at Newhall House. She had paired the jewel with a dark silver gown which showed off the rubies and diamonds to stunning effect. She had been breathtakingly beautiful, a queen fit to rule over all her guests.

The painting his father had commissioned did little justice to the real thing.

Even now, the years had been kind. The hint of crow's feet at her eyes barely made a mark against her beauty. It was only the cruel lines of her smile at the corners of her mouth which revealed any sign of her age.

Julian's heart was racing. Could he actually walk out of the embassy with the Crusader Ruby in his hand? His palms itched as he fought the temptation to reach out and take the necklace from her.

She remained where she was as he took a step toward her, her back ramrod straight.

"Madam, I would ask you to remove the necklace and hand it over. If you do, I shall forget about any of the other pieces of jewelry you have kept. You and I shall never have to deal with one another again," said Julian.

The countess slowly shook her head. The smile which now appeared on her face grew wide. From out of her skirts, she produced a piece of folded paper. She waved it at him. "Read it, boy," she commanded.

With a sinking feeling in the pit of his stomach, Julian took the paper and opened it. He recognized the handwriting immediately as being that of his father. As his gaze drifted over the words, the countess remained silent.

The silence continued as Julian handed the letter to the prince. It was only when the ambassador shook his head that the countess let out a soft sigh of satisfaction.

"I think that makes my position clear. Until my son marries, I am well within my rights to retain the necklace," she said.

The prince looked sadly at Julian. There was nothing he could do. Even with the letter from the royal court, his hands were tied. The note from Julian's father was clear. Until Julian married, the necklace rightfully belonged to his mother.

"I hear your house party was a disaster, so there won't be any need in the foreseeable future for me to relinquish ownership of the jewel. Now if you don't mind, I have things to attend to this afternoon," she said.

As she closed the door behind her, Julian turned to the prince. "I will have that brandy now, Your Highness."

Chapter Fifty-Two

"Congratulations to you both. This is wonderful news." Julian accepted the good wishes of the Saunders family members, but Caroline could tell he was out of sorts. The happiness she felt coursing through her veins was not shared in full by her fiancé.

It took a little while, but she was eventually able to speak to him alone.

"What is wrong? You do not look like a man who is overjoyed at our betrothal," she asked.

He looked down at his half-finished glass of champagne. "After I spoke with your father this morning, I went to see Prince Esterhazy at the Austrian embassy to raise the issue of the necklace. I also met with my mother. Things did not go well. She will not return it."

The reason for his dark mood was now clear. The countess would put anyone in a poor temper. "But I though Francis was going to get things sorted through his royal connections. She cannot refuse the future king, can she?"

"She has a letter from my father, which he apparently wrote in a desperate attempt to get her to stay with him. It states that for the time being, she is fully within her rights to keep the Crusader Ruby," he replied.

From the way he seemed to carefully choose his words, Caroline suspected Julian was not telling her the whole story. But here and now, he needed her support. She would leave it to another time to press him further for details.

"I am sorry. I have been a poor fiancé tonight. We should be celebrating our engagement, not worrying about my mother and her evil machinations."

"What can I do?"

He leaned forward and stole a kiss. "Nothing. Let's enjoy tonight and worry about other things tomorrow."

§

"St Paul's is now booked. Your Uncle Hugh says you can have the first wedding on Saturday, four weeks from now. That should give us plenty of time to organize your gown, and the guest list."

Caroline spied the open notebook in her mother's hands. She had been carrying it around nonstop from the second Julian and Caroline's engagement had been announced.

Four weeks seemed an eternity. But from the long list of preparations that her mother had made and was constantly adding to, she knew they would need every minute of that time.

"Now, about the wedding ball. I know you are marrying into the Palmer family, but Lady Margaret and I have agreed that Newhall House is far too small to host it. I am going to speak to my brother and see about the summer ballroom at Strathmore House," added Adelaide.

The Duke of Strathmore's summer ballroom was the largest of its kind in all of London. It could easily hold more than a thousand guests. The wedding celebrations of both of her cousins, Alex and David Radley, earlier in the year, had been extravagant affairs attended by the upper echelon of London society.

The issue of who to invite had raised the issue of Julian's lack of family. While Caroline was certain they could rustle up a few friends and some foreign dignitaries for his side of the church, it did seem unfair to have such a lopsided guest list. He would know few people at their own wedding ball.

"How about we look to use the winter ballroom? It is smaller and more intimate. The wedding ball does not need to be that lavish an affair," she replied.

Julian's somber mood from the night of their engagement still sat in the forefront of her mind. He had attributed it to the argument with his mother, but Caroline wondered if there was more to it. Had she pushed him when he was not ready to take the plunge?

Adelaide huffed and snapped the notebook shut. "Really, Caroline, you are a daughter of the House of Strathmore. Your wedding should reflect your heritage and birthright. After Eve and Frederick made the decision to elope, I deserve to be allowed to send off my remaining daughter in the manner appropriate to her station."

Caroline knew her mother well enough to remain silent. This wedding was as important to Adelaide as it was to the bride and groom. London society would expect that no expense be spared. Earlier that morning, she had heard her mother giving her father a stern lecture after he had somewhat foolishly asked her to show some restraint on the cost of the wedding gown.

"I have a meeting with the shoemaker in an hour. Your father will need new shoes. Now you should head upstairs and have an afternoon nap. The betrothal ball will no doubt go late into the night, and you don't want to find yourself flagging before the end."

Her mother had moved with lightning speed and made arrangements for Caroline and Julian to celebrate their betrothal with a ball that evening at Strathmore House. She dared not think how many servants and merchants had been pressed into service in order to meet such a short deadline.

Adelaide left Caroline sitting on the floor of the drawing room, surrounded by fabric samples. She looked at the piles of pale-blue satins and silks and sighed. Her childhood dreams of a large wedding with matching attendants had never included all the planning that came with it.

"Ah. There you are. Having fun?"

She looked up to see Francis standing in the doorway. "Not particularly. Mama is doing her best impression of a dragon this morning. I don't know how I will survive tonight, let alone another month of this, if she keeps it up."

He dropped down on the floor next to her, pushing some of the fabric out of the way. "Oh, come now, you must be looking forward to tonight. You and Newhall will get to dance together as a betrothed couple. Being an engaged woman must be one of your dreams come true."

He frowned when she shrugged. "Hello. What's the matter?"

"I don't know. I am worried about Julian. He was not very cheerful when we celebrated our engagement announcement. His mother has to be the most malicious woman I have ever had the misfortune of encountering," she replied.

Francis awkwardly patted her on the back. Will would have put his arm around her and given her a consoling hug, but not Francis. Her brother always struggled with offering emotion and comfort.

"I tell you what, I am meeting Will for luncheon shortly. How about we hunt down Newhall and spend some time with him at our club? As his future brothers, we should welcome him with a few drinks before the ball tonight," he said.

Caroline's hopes lifted. What Francis lacked in emotional depth, he more than made up for with his pragmatism. Offering to spend time with Julian before the ball was the perfect answer. "Thank you, I would really appreciate it. If you could succeed in getting him into a happier frame of mind, I will be very grateful."

Francis got to his feet. "Done. I shall see you later."

Chapter Fifty-Three

"Her Highness, the Countess of Lienz."

Julian looked up from his papers to see his mother standing in the doorway. He slowly put the pen back into the inkwell, taking the time to compose himself. Anger still seethed in his veins over their encounter at the Austrian embassy.

He rose from his chair. "Madam."

There was no point in attempting any form of warm welcome when it came to his mother, and he would be damned if he was going to address her as 'your highness'.

She stood in the doorway of his study. Her gaze drifted to the nearby chair, then back to Julian. He ignored her pointed hint at hospitality. He was beyond offering her anything.

"I saw your notice in the newspaper this morning and came to congratulate you," she said, stepping into the room.

"Thank you," he replied.

The countess shook her head. "Congratulations on having not only fallen for my jest with the Saunders girl, but for following your father and marrying someone entirely unsuited to you. I do not know what it is with you Palmer men, but you seem determined to be miserable when it comes to marriage. Perhaps that is why you failed to mention your recent betrothal when we met at the embassy."

He knew he should have expected her to come and gloat over the necklace, but the spiteful manner in which she spoke of Caroline took him by surprise. Even now, his own mother could not offer him her best wishes for happiness. "You do not know Caroline, nor do I intend that you shall. So, if that is your sole purpose in your last visit to Newhall House, then I shall bid you a good day."

The countess feigned a look of hurt. "Well, just remember I did warn you. I expect that by the time you arrive to visit me in Austria, you will have come to that conclusion yourself. I am assuming you intend to collect your beloved property at some future date. You will need to bring evidence of your marriage and, of course, your bride."

Taking the countess firmly by the arm, Julian guided her to the front door and out into the street. He closed the door behind him, ignoring her muffled last words.

He could just picture the look of victory on his mother's face when he and Caroline arrived at the Count of Lienz's estate, cap in hand, to ask for the Crusader Ruby. She would milk the moment for all it was worth.

It was late morning, not close enough to midday to consider a long lunch, but the need to imbibe was suddenly strong. Grabbing his coat and hat, Julian called for his carriage. If he headed to his club now, he still had time to drink himself into a numb state before he had to face Caroline and the rest of their guests at this evening's engagement ball.

"Just the chap we have been looking for."

Julian put down his glass as Francis and Will Saunders claimed the chairs opposite him. "Gentlemen."

He was most of the way through his third glass of brandy, intending to push on and see if he could make it to five before he called time. A quiet nook in the corner of Brooks, with high-backed chairs facing toward the fireplace, had given him what he thought was the right amount of privacy.

Caroline's brother Will, however, was a man capable of finding the proverbial needle in a haystack. His years as an undercover agent for the British crown in Paris had honed his skills of espionage to a fine point.

"To what do I owe this honor?" said Julian.

Francis summoned a nearby waiter, and ordered two bottles of wine and a platter of food. It was clear that both he and Will intended to stay.

"We wanted to have a chat about our sister," said Francis.

"And the lack of enthusiasm that she has noted on your part since the announcement of your engagement. We just want to make sure that everything is right between the two of you, especially before tonight," added Will.

Julian picked up his brandy glass and downed the last of its contents in one long gulp. He sat for a moment, rueing the fact that his drink was yet to dull his senses to the desired level. Will's words did have an effect.

Caroline was worried that he had got cold feet.

Fool.

Once more, he had let his mother get to him and blind him to what really mattered. The necklace was worth a small fortune, but Caroline's heart was priceless.

"Is there anything we can do?" offered Francis.

Julian sighed. "No. Not unless you are offering to strangle my lovely mother."

Francis and Will collectively groaned.

"I take it that her highness has been her usual pleasant self," replied Will.

"Let us just say that the conversation with her at the Austrian embassy did not go well. My father, God rest his soul, signed over the necklace to her, on the condition that she only has to return it when a new countess comes into the title. So, until I marry, I cannot claim it back. And yes, she was her usual charming self about it, thank you for asking," he replied.

He did not want to make mention of the unkind words the countess had said about Caroline. He had seen them for what they were: a means to bait him into anger.

"So why not marry now, and claim the necklace before she leaves England?" replied Francis.

Julian had promised Caroline the wedding of her dreams. A full service at St Paul's, married by her uncle the Bishop of London. A glittering ball at Strathmore House would follow, attended by all of London's social elite. His mother would not steal that from his bride.

He was determined that their marriage celebration would be a triumph for Caroline. One that put all rumors by Harry Menzies to rest. She was Julian's chosen bride and his countess. "I understand what you are saying, and if it were anyone else, I might consider it, but this is Caroline. I would not do that to her. Not after what she has been through. She deserves a full society wedding, reflective of her status, and I am determined that she will have it."

Will and Francis exchanged a knowing look.

Two servants arrived at that moment, one carrying two bottles of French burgundy, the other, a platter of cold meats and pickles.

Will reached over and picked up a piece of cold pickled pork and looked at it. Just before he put it in his mouth, he met Julian's gaze. "How about the three of us have a glass or two of this fine wine and discuss the options before us?"

Chapter Fifty-Four

C aroline dismissed her maid as soon as the final button on her gown had been secured. She needed time alone in which to compose herself.

The red gown was perfect; it fitted like a glove to her body. The silver tiara, loaned to her by her mother, matched her silver and pearl earrings. She looked like a princess. Tonight, would be her moment of triumph.

Love had finally conquered the Ice Queen.

She would stand beside Julian and show the world that they were united in their decision to forge a future together. A glamorous prelude to the formal occasion of their wedding.

But a lingering doubt still sat in her mind. What if Julian had changed his mind about their love? He had been distracted at best since the moment he'd asked her to be his wife. While he had explained it away as being due to his ongoing conflict with the countess, but she was still worried. What if, after all that had happened, he felt only a moral obligation to offer her marriage?

It would be the most bitter of ironies. She, who had treated the love of others with such scant regard, left to flounder in a loveless union.

She looked at the diamond and ruby ring on her hand and forced a smile to her lips. She was just being nervous and foolish. The man she had shared that night with at the cottage was still the man she was about to marry.

"Don't be silly, Caroline. He loves you; he is just in unchartered territory. Have faith."

Following a quick knock on Caroline's bedroom door, Adelaide swept into the room. She had on her long woolen cloak with the fox fur trim. She sighed when Caroline turned to face her. "Absolutely magnificent. That color truly becomes you. I just wish your sister was here to see it."

Caroline smiled. Eve would be in for a surprise when she discovered that her sister was engaged. She could only hope that the letter her father had sent earlier that morning would reach Eve and Freddie in time for them to make it back to England for her wedding.

"The tiara is exactly what the gown needed," replied Caroline.

The jewel was from the Strathmore family collection, left to Adelaide by her father.

She scowled at the sight of her mother's cloak. "Aren't you ready to leave a little early?"

The ball was not due to commence for another two hours, and as much as she wanted to be on time, leaving now was too early for her not yet settled nerves.

"Your father and I are going soon. I want to check with your Aunt Caroline and Uncle Ewan to make sure everything is ready before the first of the guests arrive. Francis has offered to accompany you to the ball. He should be here any minute," replied Adelaide.

Her mother gave her a kiss on the cheek, careful not to disturb the tiara and Caroline's swept up hair style. "You look stunning, my darling," she whispered.

As soon as Adelaide was gone, Caroline went back to worrying. By the time Francis finally did knock on her door, nearly an hour later, she had convinced herself that she would be living alone in Newhall Castle while Julian lived in seclusion down at the lakeside cottage.

"That is a gown which makes a large statement. I wonder if you are prepared to make one of your own tonight," he said.

"Of course; I am ready for the ball and all it entails," she said. Walking into the room on Julian's arm and welcoming their guests would send a clear message to all of the *ton*. She straightened her back.

"That's not quite what I meant. There is someone you need to speak to before you decide where you go tonight," he replied.

"What do you mean? We are headed to Strathmore House within the hour," she said.

He stepped out of the room, and to her surprise Julian appeared. He nodded to Francis, who closed the door behind him. She bit down on her lip and tried to prepare herself for bad news.

"Julian? Why are you here and not at the ball?"

Tears welled in Caroline's eyes at the sight of the man she loved. He crossed the floor and, taking her face in his hands, placed a long, comforting kiss on her lips. He brushed the tears from her cheeks and kissed her again.

"I'm sorry. I have been a complete ass—I can only beg your forgiveness. I love you. Don't cry," he said.

She struggled to keep the tears from falling, but the sense of relief which coursed through her body at his words meant she failed. He put his arms around her and held her tight.

"I have been a fool. I didn't tell you everything that has happened between myself and my mother. I met with her at the Austrian embassy a few days ago, hoping to get her to relinquish the Crusader Ruby. She showed me a letter signed by my father, which gives her ownership of the necklace until either her death or my taking of a wife."

Caroline sighed. Their wedding was four weeks away. Julian's mother would be long gone by then. The countess was going to extract every last ounce of revenge that she could on the Palmer family. "And you and I will have to travel halfway across Europe to retrieve the necklace from her?"

"Yes. I am sorry to say that my mother has no sense of family honor whatsoever," he replied.

"No, she doesn't. Is she still here in London?"

The look on his face was grim. "Unfortunately, not. I have had her watched ever since you discovered she was in town. My sources inform me that she left for Brighton early this afternoon. With their yacht now repaired, I expect she and the count will sail for home as soon as possible."

Caroline crossed to her dressing table and began to pull out the hairpins which held the tiara in place. "We will need a special licence. The Archbishop of Canterbury is one of our guests tonight. If we hurry, we could beg him to issue us one before the ball. We can be on the road to Brighton as soon as we have it."

Julian reached into his coat and, with a wry smile on his lips, pulled out a piece of folded paper. A relieved Caroline nodded. He had been one step ahead of her.

"Your brothers convinced me that we might be in need of one. We could be married at the engagement ball tonight, and then leave," replied Julian.

She considered his suggestion for a moment. It would not be the full church service which her mother had set her heart on, but it would be in front of many of London's elite. By getting married tonight, they could put the rumors and gossip mongering to rest once and for all.

"No. Much as it would solve one of our problems, it would take too long. There are hundreds of people coming to the ball tonight; it would be hours before we could make our excuses and leave. We need to be on the road to Brighton as soon as possible," said Caroline.

She hurried to her wardrobe and took out a small travel bag. Within a matter of minutes, she had stuffed it with a spare gown, some personal effects, and the tiara. Hurried wedding or not, she was still going to wear it. "How soon could you have your travel coach ready?"

"It's ready and waiting in the mews outside, along with your cousin James and your uncle," replied Julian.

Caroline stopped folding the shawl she had in her hands and looked at him, perplexed. "Which uncle?"

"The one who knows how to rouse the Archbishop of Canterbury when he is having his afternoon nap. I thought Will was a persuasive chap, but your Uncle Hugh is a master of the art," he said.

Caroline chuckled. "Uncle Hugh has always had a golden tongue. We should all be grateful that he has used it in the service of the church."

Julian came to her side and took the shawl from her hands. Lifting her left hand to his lips, he kissed the scar. "Are you certain?"

Caroline rose up on her toes and placed a tender kiss of confirmation on his lips. "If eloping was good enough for my sister, it is good enough for me. Besides, if I see one more fabric sample in my life, it will be too soon."

She closed the clasp on her travel bag, and Julian picked it up. With her heavy woolen cloak wrapped about her, Caroline followed him out of the bedroom. She glanced back one last time at the room she had slept in nearly all her life and bid a silent farewell.

Will was waiting downstairs. At the sight of her luggage in Julian's hand, he hurried over to his sister and hugged her. "I have just arrived from Strathmore House. I explained the situation to our parents and the choice before you. Mama, of course, became a watering pot of tears, but said she would trust your judgement. She said to let your heart decide."

"Thank you, Will. I know that must have been a difficult conversation," she replied.

Will then handed Julian a small box. "Our grandmother only managed to bring a few personal items with her when she fled France during the revolution. This is the second of her two rings she left to the family when she died. Eve already has hers. My father has asked that, as a personal favor to him, you place this on Caroline's hand as you speak your vows."

Julian took the box. "I am truly honored. Thank your parents from the both of us for their support. It means a great deal to Caroline and I knowing that we have their blessing."

Francis appeared at the top of the stairs which led down to the family wine cellar, carrying a box. "Weddings require champagne and wine. I would be remiss in my duty if I didn't make sure we had enough."

Will chuckled. "You had better have left Papa some of the '94, or there will be trouble."

Francis beat a hasty exit toward the door, leading out to the mews. Will followed him, but stopped before he reached the door. He turned to Caroline.

"Good luck. I hope you make it to Brighton in time."

"You are not coming?" asked Caroline.

"No. We have six hundred and thirty-four guests waiting at Strathmore House. All of whom will be wanting to know why the newly engaged couple are on the road to Brighton, rather than taking the first dance of the evening. I must be with our parents and Hattie tonight. We will stand alongside Lady Margaret and deal with all the guests," replied Will.

He disappeared outside, leaving Caroline to wipe tears from her eyes.

Julian came to her side. "Ready for our grand adventure?"

She nodded. "Tonight, is just the beginning of our adventure together. I can't wait to spend the rest of my life with you."

"Let's go."

Outside in the rear mews, they found the Earl of Newhall's travel coach waiting. As she climbed inside, Caroline was greeted with the smiling faces of Francis, James, and the Bishop of London. Julian climbed in after her and closed the door.

"Well done, Caroline. I knew you would make the right choice," said James.

Her Uncle Hugh reached over and took her by the hand. "I hope you don't mind me coming along for the journey. I promised your mother that, after the disappointment of not performing the marriage rites for your sister, I would make sure I did them for you," he said.

Caroline was still surprised that her mother had given in so easily and let her go.

"I feel sorry for Mama; she has waited so long for this day. And now she has to go and tell all those guests that the betrothed couple are not attending their own engagement party because they are eloping to Brighton," she said.

Francis snorted. "Don't worry about Mama. I expect that at this very minute she is already beginning to add to her plans for your post-wedding ball. Father will be delighted because now Newhall will be footing the bill."

Julian smiled at her. "And it will be the best post-wedding ball all of London has ever seen."

Caroline sat back and looked out into the night as the coach pulled away from her family home. The next time she set foot inside the house at Dover Street, she would be the Countess Newhall. All she could do now was pray that they were able to make it to Brighton before the Count and Countess of Lienz sailed.

Her mother's sacrifice for the love of her daughter was not something she was going to waste.

Chapter Fifty-Five

Julian woke with a start. He had been having a vivid dream of seeing Caroline fall through the ice of the frozen lake. Every time he had got close to reaching her outstretched hand, she had sunk beneath the water and been lost from sight.

To his relief, the real Caroline was laying with her head against his shoulder, staring out the window. A sense of immense pride in her welled up inside him. She had chosen loyalty to him over her long-held dream of a society wedding. He vowed to make it up to her with a wedding ball fit for a queen.

The sun was beginning to peek above the horizon as the coach made its way into Brighton. Among their little band, James was still asleep. Francis stared out the window, the same as his sister, while the bishop was hard at work writing what Julian eventually recognized as a wedding sermon.

"I suppose the first thing we need to do is make sure that the Count and Countess of Lienz are still in port," said Julian. His greatest fear was that they would be sailing with the early morning tide.

"So, a visit to the port authority should be our first call. If I ask them to withhold permission for the Count of Lienz's yacht to leave, that should buy us some time to get the wedding sorted," replied Francis.

"I suggest you let Caroline and I out at St Nicholas's church. I will liaise with the local vicar to make the wedding service arrangements. You need to go and find your darling mother," said Hugh Radley.

Julian frowned. He needed his mother after the wedding, not before. The bishop was suggesting something which Julian found more than a little displeasing. "I am not having that woman at our wedding. She will make a mockery of the whole thing."

Given the slightest opportunity to make merry hell at his nuptials, she would do it. No. The countess had bested him for the last time.

"Think on it, Newhall. If she has no choice but to come to your wedding and play nice, who then is the victor?" said Francis.

"If the countess comes to your wedding, I shall make certain she behaves. I don't think even your mother would chance insulting a senior member of the Church of England," added Hugh.

Caroline shifted in her seat and sat up straight. She looked at Julian, then to his surprise, she leaned forward and placed a chaste kiss on his cheek. "What an excellent idea. We should invite both the Count and Countess of Lienz to our wedding. By being in attendance, your mother can never make any claim that we are not properly married."

&a.

As soon as Caroline and her uncle were let out at the ancient mother church of St Nicholas, the travel coach made its way to the marina. Fortunately, there were few boats in the harbor, and Julian quickly caught sight of the yacht belonging to the Count of Lienz.

The harbormaster took a little bit of convincing, and a small fee, before he agreed to have extra ropes tied to the yacht ensuring that it could not leave. It was only after Francis made pointed mention of his friendship with the Prince of Wales that the deal was finally sealed.

"Mind you, I can only guarantee that my men will stand guard until the evening tide. Without any legal reason for keeping the boat in harbor, I am already stretching the limits of my authority," said the harbormaster.

With that particular task sorted, Julian's attention now turned to that of convincing his mother that it was in her best interest to put an end to the matter of the Crusader Ruby.

They followed the harbormaster and his men to the docks. As soon as the dockhands began to lash extra ropes over the yacht and lock them in place, an almighty row broke out.

The captain of the yacht was none too pleased to be told he would not be sailing with the late morning tide, and went off in search of his master. The count soon returned, followed by his wife.

"What the devil is going on?" shouted the count.

The countess's eyes grew wide as she and Julian locked gazes. She clenched her fists and shook her hand in his direction. "You have no right to stop us!" she bellowed.

Her husband tried to take his wife by the arm, but she batted his hand away. The countess stood with her hands on her hips and glared at her son.

Julian smiled back. "Mother dearest, you have it all wrong. I am not here to stop you leaving; I am here to invite you to my wedding, which is taking place here this morning."

She huffed angrily. "Don't be ridiculous, Newhall. Nobles do not get married in Brighton! And even if you do, I won't be coming."

Julian pointed toward the harbormaster and the crew. Despite the protests of the yacht's captain, the extra ropes were being locked in place.

"You will if you wish to sail today. The Bishop of London and his niece are waiting for us at St Nicholas's church," he replied.

Francis sidestepped the furious Countess of Lienz and walked directly up to the count. He bowed low and introduced himself. "My name is Francis Saunders. I have travelled through the night with my family and friends in the cause of love. Love that has seen my sister Caroline give up her long-held dream of a wedding at St Paul's cathedral in order to support the man she loves. Your highness, I ask that you intercede on behalf of both that love, and the sense of justice that I know a man such as yourself would understand."

The count looked to his wife, who vehemently shook her head.

"Wait here," said the count.

When he turned and headed back to the boat, the countess scuttled after him, huffing loudly.

Until that moment, Julian had never fully appreciated Francis Saunders's negotiating skills, but his opinion was forever sealed when the count returned a few minutes later, holding a box in his hands.

Julian held his breath and hoped.

"It is time to end this disgraceful row. My wife and I would be honored to attend your wedding," said the count. He handed the box to Julian, who took it with trembling hands.

Julian unlocked the box and peeked inside. He closed it again and held it tight. "Thank you."

Chapter Fifty-Six

"Not exactly the place I expect you ever thought you would find yourself getting married in." Hugh Radley had spoken with the minister of St Nicholas's, and arrangements for the wedding were moving ahead with speed. It was not every day that the Bishop of London arrived on the doorstep, special licence from the Archbishop of Canterbury in hand, and asked to perform an impromptu wedding service.

The minister's wife had offered her services and helped Caroline pin her mother's tiara back into place. She had also kindly cut some red roses from her nearby garden and fashioned them into a small posy. Caroline tied the flowers off with a cream ribbon she had brought with her in her travel bag.

With everything at the church now all in readiness, she sat quietly in a pew and contemplated the fact that very soon she would be Julian's wife. "I wonder how Julian and the others have got on. I, for one, cannot see the countess coming quietly."

"But she is, and I have the necklace," replied Julian.

She turned to see him, along with Francis and James, march into the church. In Julian's hands was a box. Trailing behind them were the Count and Countess of Lienz. The countess had a face like thunder.

Caroline turned away and indulged in a private grin. Julian had succeeded against his mother.

With everyone now in attendance, the bishop called them all to gather at the front of the altar.

"Now this will not be a conventional wedding service. The groom has asked that I keep it simple so that their royal highnesses may sail with the next tide."

Francis took hold of Caroline's hand, assuming his father's place in giving away the bride. "Well done, Caro. Julian is a lucky man. I know you will make both an excellent countess and wife."

She could have sworn that she saw a tear in his eye as he placed her hand in Julian's and stepped back to stand alongside James. Caroline looked across at Julian. He grinned at her and her heart soared. Knowing he was happy made the sacrifice of not having her parents in attendance and a full cathedral wedding worth it.

Partway through the short service, her uncle stopped and looked up from the common book of prayer.

"I don't suppose anyone thought to bring a wedding ring, did they?" he asked.

The Countess of Lienz huffed. "That is what happens when you don't do these things properly."

Caroline bit down on her lip as Julian pulled the box containing her grandmother's ring from his coat pocket.

He handed it to the bishop. "Our families are in full support of this union, so of course we have a ring. A Saunders family heirloom, which will sit perfectly next to the betrothal ring I chose for my wife."

The countess said nothing at the obvious insult directed at her. Julian did not consider his mother to be part of his family.

The bishop blessed the ring and handed it back to Julian. When Caroline held out her hand, he turned it over and lifted it to his lips kissing the scar. It would always serve as a reminder of how their love had first begun.

Caroline watched through tears as Julian placed the ring on her finger and offered his vow. "With this ring, I thee wed. With my body, I thee worship, and with all my worldly goods, I thee endow.

In the Name of the Father, and of the Son, and of the Holy Ghost. Amen."

"I now pronounce you, man and wife."

Before anyone could step forward to offer their congratulations, Julian held up his hand. He retrieved the jewel box from a nearby pew then, turning to his mother, he offered it to her.

With a loud, indignant huff, she stepped forward. Julian opened the box, and after a moment's hesitation, the countess took out the diamond- and ruby-encrusted necklace.

As she caught sight of the Crusader Ruby, Caroline finally understood why her new husband had been so insistent upon securing its return. The version of it she had seen in the painting paled into insignificance against the magnificence of the real jewel.

The sunlight which streamed in through the upper windows of the church caught the rubies, and it was as if they had been set alight. Red fire glowed deep within them. A hum echoed in the church as the small gathering took in the sheer splendor of the ancient piece.

The countess lifted the Crusader Ruby and, as Julian stepped back, she placed it around Caroline's neck, securing the double clasp.

As the heavy weight settled on her chest, Caroline touched the main ruby with her finger. "I have never seen anything like it," she murmured.

"It is yours to keep and protect for our family," said Julian.

The necklace had returned to its rightful place in the hands of the Earl and Countess of Newhall. A priceless gift to his new wife.

"I expect you consider this a victory over me, but you will never do the rubies justice the way I did whenever I wore the necklace. You will always be a poor imitation of me," said the countess. As always, she had her thoughts centered on herself.

But Caroline's heart lay elsewhere. "You have it so wrong. None of this was ever about you. Everything that I have done today was for Julian. For my husband, and our future children."

The countess scowled, then turned her attention to her son.

Chapter Fifty-Seven

J ulian waited. His mother would no doubt be determined to have the last word. She lifted a gloved hand to his face and rubbed her thumb on his cheek. He steeled himself for a motherly kiss, one purely for public consumption.

"You look so much like your father that I cannot abide it," she said. Her hand dropped and she turned to her husband. "Now can we leave? And if those ropes are not gone from the yacht by the time we return, I shall take a knife to them myself."

The Count of Lienz gave a perfunctory nod toward the newly married couple, then took hold of his wife's arm. They walked from the church in silence. But as soon as they were outside, everyone heard the countess as she began to tear strips off her husband for having handed over her most valued prize.

"Safe journey," Julian muttered, as a huge weight lifted off his shoulders. If his mother had thought to disappoint him one last time, she had failed.

The countess was gone, and with her went the memories of that small boy who had never known his mother's love. The grown man that boy had now become had an adoring and devoted wife by his side. Someone who would give her love to him unconditionally.

Together they would fill Newhall Castle with children, and its walls would echo with their laughter. Lady Margaret would be his children's paternal grandmother. And his home would finally be filled with happiness.

"Righto. So now all that is done and dusted, can we please go and have some breakfast?" asked James.

Francis chuckled. "And some champagne. In fact, Papa's best French champagne awaits us. He always said he was saving it for our weddings. It is not my fault that he won't get to partake in any of it this morning. Come on Caroline."

Julian held out his hand, offering it to Francis with a mischievous smile. "You should address my wife as Lady Newhall from now on."

Caroline kept a straight face for all of two seconds as Francis bowed low before his sister. "The one and only time, Lady Newhall," he said.

Hugh Radley ushered everyone out of the church, leaving Caroline and Julian to a moment of privacy.

Julian ran his fingers over the precious jewels of the Crusader Ruby. "It suits you. Especially with the color of your hair."

"It is heavy. Could you please take it off?" she replied.

He reluctantly took the necklace from his wife's neck and placed it back in the box. "Only if you wear it to bed tonight," he growled.

From the moment he had set eyes on it, Julian had been making plans to strip Caroline naked on their wedding night, leaving her wearing only the necklace. The thought of watching the firelight reflect in the diamonds and rubies as he brought his new bride to completion had him licking his lips in anticipation.

She wickedly smiled back at him. "We are in church, my dear husband. Behave yourself."

Chapter Fifty-Eight

J ulian bent and placed the half empty bottle of champagne on the sand, twisting it so that it sat upright and none of the precious bubbles were lost.

Caroline stood on the water's edge, staring out to sea. He placed his arms around her and kissed the back of her neck. She lay against him and they stood for a time, silently watching the boats out in the harbor.

The Count of Lienz's yacht had already been far out to sea by the time the newlyweds made their way down to the beach. When it finally disappeared from view, Caroline gave a soft sigh of relief. Lienz was a long way from London, and she would count that blessing every day.

"So now what are we to do?" she asked.

Julian nipped the top of her ear with his teeth and murmured, "Well, my beautiful bride, we do have a hotel room at our disposal. And I am sure the others can find something to amuse themselves with while you and I discuss the matter of your role as Countess Newhall."

She turned and placed a soft, inviting kiss on her husband's lips. "Well then, husband of mine, let us take our champagne and adjourn to the hotel. Though I promise that once I have you all to myself, there will only be one topic of discussion."

Julian pulled Caroline into his arms and kissed her deeply. Her body was warmed by the morning sun, and she luxuriated in his embrace. His love had given her the strength to leave her cold and lonely existence.

She was the Ice Queen no more.

Epilogue

J ames held the bottle to his lips and took a long appreciative
drink. His uncle Charles certainly knew his champagne. After
he had finished, he offered the bottle to Julian who politely
declined.

"Caroline and I are going to head over to the hotel and get
settled in."

He looked at his new wife and smiled. James averted his gaze for
a moment. It was wonderful that the newly weds had succeeded in
their plans, but he felt his dark mood descending once more.

"The best of luck to the two of you. Will we see you later for
supper?" he asked.

Caroline stepped forward and after placing a soft kiss on her
cousin's cheek, she whispered in his ear. "Yes, but not before then,
and it will be a very late supper."

As Julian and Caroline made their way from the beach toward the
hotel, James lifted the champagne bottle and saluted them.

"Congratulations Lord and Lady Newhall, may you have many
long and happy years together."

He turned and went back to staring out to sea. The empty beach
was the perfect place for him. Away from people he could find solace

in the waves as they washed back and forth to the shore. The odd small boat bobbed up and down just off shore.

His father and Francis had decided a second visit to the port authority office was in order after the assistance they had received earlier that morning in dealing with the Count and Countess of Lienz. James did not accompany them, being more than content to remain on the beach and drink champagne.

He pulled a cheroot out of his coat pocket and lit it. With a smoke in one hand and a bottle of the finest French champagne in the other, any man would feel on top of the world. But not James Radley.

While he was happy for Caroline in having secured the future of her choice, he admitted to himself that he was more than a little envious of his cousin.

"At least someone has found happiness," he muttered.

At the sight of his father and Francis returning to the beach, he quickly stubbed out the cheroot and stuck the remains of it in his pocket. His father did not hold with such vices.

"Hey ho! Did the love birds abandon you on the beach?" said Francis.

James mustered a smile and offered Francis the bottle of champagne. "They left only a few minutes ago. Promised they would see us at a late supper. How did things go with the port master?" he asked.

Francis took a swig of the champagne. "Very good. He was most understanding. Especially when he discovered who the gentleman was that had accompanied me."

Hugh Radley chortled. "People are suddenly on their best behavior when they are introduced to me. All the nannies in the land must tell their small charges stories of the frightful Bishop of London, and the terrible things I will do to them if they misbehave. It's either that, or no one has ever thought to tell me that I look like a ferocious highland boar."

James smiled at his father. Behind his professional façade there was a warm and loving man.

"So, what are our plans? Caroline and Julian look likely to stay on in Brighton for a few days, but I doubt if they would want our company," said James.

"Back to London first thing tomorrow," replied Hugh and Francis in unison.

James nodded, it was to be expected. And much as he wished it, he couldn't hide out in Brighton forever. Four days from now he was to host a bachelor dinner for Guy Dannon on the eve of his wedding. Five days from now he would be standing in the church to support his best friend as he prepared to marry Leah Shepherd.

Leah Shepherd the odd girl who James had struggled to accept was the right woman for Guy. From the first time he had met her, she had done everything to gain his friendship. Yet no matter what she did, it tore him to see her and Guy together.

Something inexplicable had always made James wish she was someone else. That Leah Shepherd had not been the woman Guy had chosen for his bride. When the truth of his discomfort finally surfaced, he was faced with an impossible situation.

A bright light had sparked within him and now lived deep within his soul, warming him to his core. He knew it intimately. He even knew its name. That one heartbreaking little word.

Love.

While Francis emptied the last of the champagne, James made a silent vow to drink himself to the bottom of many bottles over the next few days. Anything that would dull the pain of having to stand up in church and watch his best friend marry the woman he loved.

Thank you so much for reading this story and I hope you loved it as much as I did when I wrote it.

Sasha xxx

Newsletter

Join my mailing list to receive news of new releases, special give-aways, free books and other exciting news at https://www.sashacottman.com/newsletter/

Bookbub
You can also follow me on Bookbub
https://www.bookbub.com/authors/sasha-cottman

Other places I hang out.

Facebook https://www.facebook.com/SashaCottmanAuthor
Goodreads https://www.goodreads.com/author/show/7136108.
Sasha_Cottman

For a full list of books by Sasha Cottman
https://www.sashacottman.com/books/

The Duke of Strathmore Series
Letter from a Rake (Free)
Alex Radley, Marquis of Brooke rules the *ton* like a god, but even gods make mistakes. It will take everything in his power to unravel the unholy mess he has made in his attempts to woo Miss Millie Ashton. Millie of course is having none of it.
https://books2read.com/u/3L9gQM
An Unsuitable Match
David Radley, the illegitimate son of the Duke of Strathmore will have to face down the rest of the *ton* to secure the hand of Lady Clarice Langham. But will her shocking secret keep them apart forever, and leave her at the mercy of a cruel villain?
https://books2read.com/u/38gM57
The Duke's Daughter
With the arrival of the mysterious war hero Avery Fox, Lady Lucy Radley's chances of finding love take a sudden turn for the better. But

after a scandalous encounter, the couple are forced to marry. They must face the truth of Avery's past before they can accept their love and forge a future together.

https://books2read.com/u/bwWdEP

A Scottish Duke for Christmas (novella)

A snow bound castle at Christmas. A secret baby. Some meddling relatives. A second chance at love for the Duke of Strathmore and Lady Caroline Hastings.

https://books2read.com/u/3Ro6NG

My Gentleman Spy

Former spy Will Saunders rescues Hattie Wright from the sea off the coast of Spain, only to have her disappear from his life, taking his heart with her. A sexy cat and mouse game then begins.

https://books2read.com/u/bzaVxD

Lord of Mischief

When Freddie Rosemount and Eve Saunders play a risqué game of dare, they don't realize that it is more than their hearts they are putting at risk. A dangerous and powerful organization will seek to tear them apart and destroy them both.

https://books2read.com/u/3nOk0P

The Ice Queen

Caroline Saunders and Julian Palmer (Earl Newhall) face down one another in a spirited battle of wills that leads to simmering desire. Could Lord Newhall finally be the man to thaw the Ice Queen's heart, or will he fail like all the others before him?

https://books2read.com/u/bWzYz1

London Lords Series

An Italian Count for Christmas.

A poor, beautiful widow, Isabelle Collins invites an Italian count to stay at her London home over Christmas. Unlucky in love Count Nico de Luca falls for her, but when he discovers the shocking truth of how her husband died, he realizes that he will have to risk everything he has to win Isabelle's heart and finally break his love curse.

https://books2read.com/u/mYgwlM

. . .

Did you know that every review for a book is like gold to the author?

If you enjoy any author's book please consider leaving a short review on the book retailer site from where you purchased the book. It takes many hours to write a book and authors rely on book sales to earn a living.

My fellow authors and I thank you so much for all your wonderful support.

xxx

Sasha

Author's Notes

The town of Burton-on-Trent (Burton-upon-Trent) still holds a town market on a Thursday, having been granted it charter by King John in 1200.

The cake-house, at the Serpentine was housed in the keeper's lodge. It traded from the early seventeenth century, finally closing in 1826. It was famous for its cheese cakes.

Read on for the first chapter of My Gentleman Spy, out now.

My Gentleman Spy

CHAPTER ONE

Gibraltar 1817

Hattie Wright sucked in a deep breath before slowly letting the air back out. The long drop over the side of the ship to the water below was a heart-rending distance.

What had seemed a plausible idea only a minute or two before; now revealed itself to be nothing short of madness.

She wondered how hard the water would be when she finally hit it. Had she overestimated her strength as a swimmer and was she fated to drown before she could make it back to shore?

Worst of all, were there sharks lurking in the murky depths below?

She lifted her gaze from the deep green of the bay and looked at the small town of Gibraltar a quarter mile across the water. Soon it would be out of sight and the *Blade of Orion* would be on her way to Africa.

Earlier that morning, with her fiancé holding her firmly by the hand Hattie had made the short journey up the gangplank and onto the ship. All the while her heart had been beating a loud tattoo within her chest.

No. no. no.

Gibraltar was the last stop before they embarked on the long journey down the West coast of Africa to their destination of Sierra Leone. When her parents first announced their mission to Africa, she had tried to convince herself that this was her destiny. Her parents were resolved in their mission to bring the word of God to the people of Freetown and she as their dutiful daughter was to accompany them. Reverend Peter Brown, her recently acquired fiancé, was just another part of the grand plan. One which had been laid out for her.

She rubbed her finger across the deep scowl line which sat just above her nose. She was by nature a person who worried about all manner of things. The impending journey to Africa had her lying awake every night.

Long before the ship had left London Dock a nagging doubt had sparked and grown within her mind. Was this what she truly wanted for her life? Once she was wed to the dour Peter, all choice would be gone. Her life would be set in stone.

And what of the friends she was being forced to leave behind. How would they survive without her?

She looked back at the ship's deck. Apart from the crew there were no other passengers up on deck. Her mother would no doubt, be busy rearranging their tiny cabin for the second time that morning. Hattie knew her mother well. A place for everything and everything in its place.

Her father and Peter would be locked in one of their never-ending conversations about how they were to set up the ministry on the edge of the African jungle. Every day on the journey thus far they had spent hours poring over paperwork and the building plans for a new church. A church in which she and Peter would be married.

Everyone was busy with their own priorities. No one would come looking for her until it was too late. By the time they did she would be long gone.

She looked down once more at the water lapping against the side of the ship. Soon the *Blade of Orion* would be far from port and the opportunity to change her life would be lost. She either accepted her future as the wife of a missionary or she jumped.

The chill wind ruffled her light gold hair. Her pounding heart reminding her in its heavy beat that she was still very much alive. But would she be so when her body hit the water far below and she sunk deep beneath the waves?

The ship's leading hand bellowed out orders to set out the sails. Sailors on the deck quickly scrambled up into the ropes. As the hive of activity swirled around the deck, she was grateful no one appeared to have noticed her presence.

Her conscience which had until this morning vacillated between acceptance and rebellion finally made up its mind. The truth was, she counselled herself if she were to die shortly, it would be the better death. Quickly drowning in the Bay of Gibraltar would be preferable to a long living death as Peter's wife in the dark heart of the African continent.

In the short period they had been engaged, Peter had revealed to her the kind of husband he would make. There would be little laughter or happiness in their marriage. Duty would be the only constant.

A tiny voice in the back of her brain whispered, urging her on.

"You have to move."

For every second that she delayed, the opportunity to determine her own future slipped further from her reach. Even now the swim to shore would test her endurance to its limits.

She slowly began to make her way along the deck to where the gangplank, having been raised, was now stored. The end of the plank still jutted a good eight feet out over the side of the ship. Not much, but it at least afforded her the semblance of a chance that if she went into the water from here, she could be clear of the ship and its dangerous wake.

Hoisting her skirts, she climbed up onto the long wooden bridge. Dropping to her knees, she crawled out past the edge of the ship and over the water. At the end of the gangplank she sat down and swung her feet over the side.

In the middle distance, Gibraltar was slowly, but certainly slipping away.

It was now or never.

"Lord if you grant me this boon I shall remain your devoted servant always," she vowed.

After a final glance back over her shoulder at the deck of the ship, Hattie took a deep breath and dropped over the side.

My Gentleman Spy

Former spy Will Saunders rescues Hattie Wright from the sea off the coast of Spain, only to have her disappear from his life, taking his heart with her. A sexy cat and mouse game then begins.

https://books2read.com/u/bzaVxD

Made in the USA
Middletown, DE
26 April 2023

29494216R00165